JAMES L. STEFFENSEN, JR. took his M.A. in the Final Honours School of English at Oxford. While there he directed and produced plays for the Experimental Theater Club and wrote sketches and lyrics for reviews at the Edinburgh Festival. He is a former William Morris Fellow in Playwrighting and David Sarnoff Fellow in Dramatic Arts at the Yale Drama School. GREAT SCENES FROM THE WORLD THEATER is one result of his work in workshop groups for young actors and playwrights.

*Other Avon Books by*
**James L. Steffensen Jr.**

GREAT SCENES FROM THE WORLD
THEATER VOLUME II

# GREAT SCENES FROM THE WORLD THEATER

## VOLUME I

Edited by
James L. Steffensen, Jr.

**Wesleyan University**

AVON BOOKS ◆ NEW YORK

For
Virginia Princehouse Allen
and
in grateful memory of
Gladys Simpson Shafer and
Dr. Benjamin D. Scott
who enlightened the actors
who gave life to the plays.

AVON BOOKS
A division of
The Hearst Corporation
1350 Avenue of the Americas
New York, New York 10019

Copyright © 1965 by Avon Books, a division of The Hearst Corporation
Published by arrangement with the author
ISBN: 0-380-00793-2

First Avon Books Printing: February 1965

AVON TRADEMARK REG. U.S. PAT. OFF. AND IN OTHER COUNTRIES, MARCA REGISTRADA, HECHO EN CANADA

Printed in Canada

UNV   30   29   28   27

# ACKNOWLEDGMENTS

From a STREETCAR NAMED DESIRE by Tennessee Williams. Copyright 1947 by Tennessee Williams. Used by permission of New Directions. All Rights Reserved, including the right of reproduction in whole or in any part in any form. Reprinted by permission of New Directions.

From ANGEL STREET by Patrick Hamilton. Copyright, 1939, by Patrick Hamilton, under the title, GAS LIGHT. Copyright, 1942 (Acting Edition), by Patrick Hamilton. Reprinted by permission of A. M. Heath & Company Ltd.

From BELL, BOOK AND CANDLE by John van Druten. Copyright 1948 as an unpublished work by John van Druten. Copyright 1949, 1951 by John van Druten. Reprinted by permission of Carter Lodge, executor, estate of John van Druten.
CAUTION: BELL, BOOK AND CANDLE is the sole property of the estate of John van Druten and is fully protected by copyright. It may not be acted by professionals or amateurs without formal permission and the payment of a royalty. All rights, including professional, amateur, stock, radio and television broadcasting, motion picture, recitation, lecturing, public reading, and the rights of translation in foreign languages are reserved. All inquiries should be addressed to Carter Lodge, executor, the estate of John van Druten, Valensi and Rose, 8665 Wilshire Blvd., Beverly Hills, Calif.

From BERNARDINE by Mary Chase.
Copyright, 1951, as an unpublished dramatic composition by Mary Coyle Chase.
Copyright, 1953, by Mary Coyle Chase. Reprinted by permission of Oxford University Press, Inc.

From BILLY BUDD by Louis O. Coxe and Robert Chapman. Copyright 1947 by Louis O. Coxe and Robert Chapman, as an unpublished play under the title, UNIFORM OF FLESH. Copyright 1949 by Louis O. Coxe and Robert Chapman, a revised version under the title, BILLY BUDD, as an unpublished play. Copyright © 1951 by Louis O. Coxe and Robert Chapman. Reprinted by permission of Hill and Wang, Inc.
CAUTION: BILLY BUDD is the sole property of the authors and is fully protected by copyright. It may not be acted by professionals or amateurs without formal permission and the payment of a royalty. All rights, including professional, amateur, stock, radio and television broadcasting, motion picture, recitation, lecturing, public reading, and the rights of translation in foreign languages are reserved. All professional inquiries in the United States and Canada should be addressed to Harold Freedman, Brandt & Brandt Dramatic Department, Inc., 101 Park Avenue, New York 17, New York.
Amateur rights in the United States and Canada are controlled solely

From AH, WILDERNESS!, by Eugene O'Neill. Copyright 1933 and renewed 1960 by Carlotta Monterey O'Neill. Reprinted by permission of Random House, Inc.

From ANASTASIA, by Marcelle Maurette, adapted by Guy Bolton. Copyright © 1955 by Guy Bolton and Marcelle Maurette. Reprinted by permission of Random House, Inc.

From BIOGRAPHY, by S. N. Behrman. Copyright 1933 and renewed 1960 by S. N. Behrman. Reprinted by permission of Random House, Inc.

From BLUE DENIM, by James Leo Herlihy and William Noble. © Copyright 1958 by James Leo Herlihy and William Noble. Reprinted by permission of Random House, Inc.

From PICNIC, by William Inge. Copyright 1953 by William Inge. Reprinted by permission of Random House, Inc.

From "PLAYBOY OF THE WESTERN WORLD," by John M. Synge. Copyright 1907 and renewed 1934 by the Executors of the Estate of John M. Synge. Reprinted from THE COMPLETE WORKS OF JOHN M. SYNGE by permission of Random House, Inc.

From SEPARATE TABLES, by Terence Rattigan. © Copyright 1955 by Terence Rattigan. Reprinted by permission of Random House, Inc.

From SUNRISE AT CAMPOBELLO, by Dore Schary. © Copyright 1948 by Dore Schary. Reprinted by permission of Random House, Inc.

From THE CORN IS GREEN, by Emlyn Williams. Copyright 1941 by Emlyn Williams. Reprinted by permission of Random House, Inc.

From THE DARK AT THE TOP OF THE STAIRS, by William Inge. © Copyright 1958 by William Inge. Reprinted by permission of Random House, Inc.

From THE DEEP BLUE SEA, by Terence Rattigan. Copyright 1953 by Terence Rattigan. Reprinted by permission of Random House, Inc.

From THE ENCHANTED by Jean Giraudoux, adapted by Maurice Valency. Copyright 1950 by Maurice Valency. Reprinted by permission of Random House, Inc.

From THE GLASS MENAGERIE, by Tennessee Williams. Copyright 1945 by Tennessee Williams and Edwina D. Williams. Reprinted by permission of Random House, Inc.

From THE RAINMAKER, by N. Richard Nash. © Copyright 1955 by N. Richard Nash. Reprinted by permission of Random House, Inc.

From TOYS IN THE ATTIC, by Lillian Hellman. © Copyright 1960 by Lillian Hellman. Reprinted by permission of Random House, Inc.

From AN ACTOR PREPARES by Constantin Stanislavski, translated by Elizabeth Reynolds Hapgood. Copyright 1936 by Theatre Arts, Inc. Copyright 1948 by Elizabeth R. Hapgood. All rights reserved.

# PREFACE

"The most we can hope is that she will not,
like Duse, be visible from only one angle,
having only one angle to be visible from."
                                Max Beerbohm, 1901

*Great Scenes from the World Theater* is a book *for* acting, not *about* acting. It professes no method and makes no
promises to reveal the secrets of the actor's technique, art,
or magic (choose the word that best suits you). The
hundred or so scenes reprinted here have proved useful exercises for actors studying the basic techniques of their
craft. They include excerpts from the works of playwrights
new and not so new, from dramas well-known or half-
forgotten, and have been chosen not only for their useful-
ness as classroom or studio projects but in the hope of introducing young actors to a wide range of writers and plays.
Though the book is intended primarily for acting classes,
actors working privately or preparing scenes for auditions
should also find it useful.

This, then, is a workbook, a compendium—a carefully
selective grab bag, if you like—of projects for students and
instructors who will certainly follow many different lines in
the practice and teaching of acting, but will, I trust, agree
that actors learn by doing—doing scenes. The scenes are
here; their interpretation and the ways in which they can
be employed to meet the needs of individual actors are
matters to be decided by students and their coaches. I hope
that nothing here is "visible from only one angle."

"In acting," Herbert Beerbohm Tree wrote, "there is an
infinity to learn." He should have added that any actor
worth his salt wants to comprehend that infinity immediately and completely for the actor is acutely aware that

the simplest scenes are complex enough to demand the sophisticated skills of a seasoned professional. In practice, however, the actor learns by mastering one objective, one aspect of his craft, at a time, and, in organizing this collection of actors' projects, I have grouped the scenes into chapters which roughly parallel the series of linked objectives that often forms the curriculum pattern for university and studio training in the fundamentals of acting. Thus, Chapters I and II—"Play It for Truth" and "Acting Means Believing"—are made up of scenes in which young actors should find characters and situations closely related to their own experiences and observations, scenes in which they should be able to avoid the embarrassments suffered by the aging leading lady whom Max Beerbohm saw attempt a youthful role in which she was, he reports, "unevenly matched in the duel with nature." In Chapter II, the selection of scenes emphasizes memory, imagination, and playing "as if it were real." There are scenes of recollection, scenes in which actors are called upon to use their emotional memories, and, at the end of the chapter, scenes in which they must put their imaginations to work to lend reality to situations of fantasy.

Chapter III relates to the core of acting as we know it: concentration, communication between actors, communication between characters in conflict, and the development of character through those progressions of feeling, thought, act, and word often called "beats" or "units and objectives." The scenes included here might have been grouped into several neatly labeled subsections, but such an arrangement would have been arbitrary at best, more limiting than helpful: these elements of acting overlap, and a scene set out as an exercise in conflict or communication is almost certain to serve as well as an exercise in "units and objectives." Therefore, I have divided the selections only into monologues and scenes (scenes markedly similar or contrasting in character or situation have, however, been set side by side—a sop for the editor's predilection for putting things in order or at least in piles). My own suggestions, thoroughly arbitrary, for using the scenes for particular purposes will be found among the scene-lists at the back of the book.

Chapter IV contains groups of two or three excerpts from the same play, selected to give actors experience in developing a character in more than one situation. The scenes in Chapter V—"Advanced Scenes"—are not necessarily more complex than those appearing in earlier chapters, but they do call upon performers to make full use of all their resources.

*Great Scenes from the World Theater* might also have included a selection of scenes from classical and contemporary plays in which language—and speaking it well—is of particular importance. But clear speech, like well-coordinated movement, is fundamental to acting, a tool which the would-be performer must possess before he can truly begin to study how to act. Even training in the intelligent speaking of verse or other highly studied language is, to my mind, a basic, preliminary matter which, if it does not precede the study of acting (as I believe it should), must come at least before any attempts at preparing a role or a selection from a verse-play. Thus, although every scene in this book is an exercise in diction and voice projection, there is no chapter of scenes for speech practice, for it would have been as out of place (or nearly so) as a chapter for fencing practice.

Having revealed the pattern of scenes set into chapters related to specific objectives or techniques, I must be quick to say that this division should not be followed rigidly. One scene may serve many purposes, depending on the individual performer and his immediate needs. Those who wish to choose for themselves should turn to the back of the book, where the scenes are listed according to the number of male and female characters involved, and broadly categorized (i.e., as comedy, drama, melodrama, and the like).

Actors in search of scenes for specific assignments or purposes may be helped by the introduction which precedes each of the excerpts. From these comments they will learn something of the story of the play, the nature of the characters, the setting, and the background of the scene itself. One word of warning, however: the introductions are not intended as a substitute for reading the plays. This is a book of "sides," not synopses. Once an actor has chosen a scene to rehearse and perform, he should read the entire play from which it has been excerpted, for in no other way can he hope to understand the characters or situations in his scene. If he also wishes to read other works by the same playwright, he will find the major plays listed on page 571.

In scanning the list of scenes that I have included in the book, I am conscious of more than a few sins of omission.

Excerpts from Thornton Wilder's *Our Town* and *The Matchmaker* would certainly be here had they been available for reprinting. The plays of Arthur Miller (in particular, *The Crucible*) and of Lillian Hellman are rich with scenes I might have chosen; the plays of Robert Anderson, Robert E. Sherwood, Arnold Wesker, John Osborne, and Sidney Howard would also have yielded many fine scenes and they should be at the top of an actor's reading list.

To the playwrights, publishers, and agents who have been generous in allowing me to borrow many fine moments from their plays, my thanks are here recorded. I am grateful, also, for the actors, directors, and teachers who have been generous with their time and suggestions; for Jerry Douglas, whose theatrical memory and library of plays I ransacked; for George de Kay, whose office I heaped with playbooks and manuscripts; and for Douglas L. Tweedy, in whose reading of those manuscripts displaced commas were marshaled and wandering stage directions given a proper local habitation.

It is for the actors, however, to give the book a reason to be. I mean to judge the success of *Great Scenes from the World Theater* by the extent to which the copies become dog-eared, their texts underlined, and their margins scribbled with actors' notes and stage directions. The harder they are used, the better—after all, that is what they are for.

James L. Steffensen, Jr.
New York City,
June, 1964

# CONTENTS

# CHAPTER I

## PLAY IT FOR TRUTH

You may play well or you may play badly;
the important thing is that you should play
truly.

Constantin Stanislavski, *An Actor Prepares*

# A Note to the Actors

It is never wise to cut or change a scene. However, in preparing scenes for class, it occasionally is useful or necessary to make minor adaptations, such as omitting the entrance of a maid or other character who appears for a line or two in a scene otherwise played by only two or three people. There are also times when students may wish to play without interruption two or three brief speeches or scenes which, together, form a monologue or scene of sufficient length for a classroom project. Such adaptations should never, of course, be performed publically without the specific permission of the playwright or his authorized agent, and, even for classroom presentations, editing must be done with the greatest care not to destroy the author's meaning or the natural, dramatic flow of his scene.

With a very few exceptions (always noted in the text), the selections in *Great Scenes from the World Theater* have been reprinted uncut, unedited, exactly as they were written and approved for publication by the playwrights. Where it seems that adaptations might be necessary or helpful in classroom work, the editor has marked these adaptations as follows:

§—§: lines which might be omitted to avoid the entrance of an extra character, or to allow two or three speeches to be spoken as a monologue.

[—]: a connecting or explanatory phrase necessary to bridge an omitted line or entrance, or to link two scenes.

Deletions in the printed texts are marked by three asterisks—***.

from
BERNARDINE
by Mary Chase

Act II, scene 1
ENID, WORMY

"I embarked," Mary Chase wrote, "on an impossible journey . . . into a world where I did not belong—a study of the viewpoint of a crowd of teen-age boys." The result of that trip was *Bernardine*, a boy-filled comedy that, like the teen-agers Mrs. Chase studied, is "irreverent, . . . happy, and wise." The leading man is Wormy, known to his parents as Buford. The plot involves a challenge as important to Wormy's gang of friends as any sacred quest was to the Knights of the Round Table—the winning of Bernardine. Bernardine is a dream, the boys' name for the most beautiful and desirable of women. She becomes a reality when Wormy sees Enid Lacey in a hotel lobby. "A real Bernardine," his friends agree, and Wormy brashly asks her for a date. Enid *is* beautiful; she is blond and sophisticated. She is not taken in by Wormy's story that he is an orphan about to be shipped off to South America, but she is touched by his eager, awkward charm and amused by his brashness. She agrees to a date and invites him to come up to her apartment. For him, it is a moment of triumph; for her, a time for nostalgia. Wormy is about eighteen; Enid is older.

The setting is Enid's apartment. The time, early evening.

*The room is empty. There is a light from the street outside filtering through the curtains at the window.*

*This room is exquisite, like the inside of a jewel box. The crystal chandelier hanging from the ceiling glitters in the dim light and we see the outlines of a small sofa center stage, coffee table, end tables, and occasional chairs with*

21

*slender carved legs. The carpeting is thick and all over.
The draperies are voluminous, hanging to the floor.*

*There is the sound of a key turning in the lock. The door
at backstage opens and Enid enters. She turns on a light
switch. The colors in this room are pink and ivory. She
comes in and removes her white ermine coat, throwing it
casually over the back of a chair.*

*Wormy enters slowly, looking everywhere curiously. Enid
turns and walks toward the door.*

**Wormy.**

Hey—I mean—wait. (*She stops.*) Where are you going?

**Enid.**

(*In low tone.*) I thought I'd just lock the outside door.

**Wormy.**

(*With what he assumes to be a man-of-the-world shrug.*)
Oh—sure—sure—why naturally. (*She smiles at him and
goes out.*) (*He straightens his tie, walks to the window,
peers out, walks to the other side of the room, tries a
door there, stops and draws a hand across his brow. He
takes out a cigarette, lights it, drops the match on the
floor, then guiltily picks it up and puts it in his coat
pocket. Enid walks back in, goes behind a mirrored screen
upstage.*) Well—ah—well—whose place is this?

**Enid.**

(*She comes from behind the screen carrying a silver tray
with a decanter of wine and two tall-stemmed glasses.*)
Mine.

**Wormy.**

That so—it's nice.

**Enid.**

Thank you.

**Wormy.**

(*He is smoking furiously.*) Live here—alone?

**Enid.**

(*She takes the tray to the coffee table in front of the little
sofa and sets it down.*) Yes.

**Wormy.**

I thought there might be some people—some other people
living back there or in there or up there. (*He indicates
each direction with a tilt of his head.*)

**Enid.**

(*She sits on the sofa.*) No one. Please relax.

**Wormy.**

Oh, I'm relaxed all right. I'm plenty relaxed. (*He sits
stiffly at the other end of the sofa.*)

**Enid.**

(*Handing him a glass.*) Wine? (*He takes it. She lifts hers high, looks at him, and smiles.*) Bon voyage!

**Wormy.**

Beg your pardon!

**Enid.**

(*There is a twinkle in her eye.*) Your trip—good sailing.

**Wormy.**

(*He must not forget the line he gave her.*) Oh—that— thank you—same to you. (*He downs the wine in one gulp. She takes a slight sip of hers and turns to set the glass down on the table. As she turns sideways to do this, away from him, he gives her that close, narrow-eyed scrutiny he gives all women, intense, absorbed, detailed. He is like a cat ready to spring, watchful, hair-trigger tension, but he must choose the right moment. He half rises—should he spring now? She turns and looks at him and he sits back down on the sofa.*)

**Enid.**

Can I get you something—a cigarette? (*She offers him a silver box.*)

**Wormy.**

(*As he reaches for one.*) Say—ah—

**Enid.**

Yes.

**Wormy.**

I was going to say, you seem a lot taller in here than you did down there and this afternoon too. You seemed like a little bit of a woman then, Bernardine.

**Enid.**

Bernardine—you've called me that twice tonight. My name is Enid. Who is Bernardine? (*She lights his cigarette.*) Your girl?

**Wormy.**

Oh no. Not that.

**Enid.**

But who is Bernardine?

**Wormy.**

Oh, that's a kind of a name the fellows in my crowd have for a kind of a daydream. This fellow named Beaumont—ever run into him?

**Enid.**

No, I don't think so.

**Wormy.**

He made it up. Bernardine Crud, he always says.

**Enid.**

(*Laughing.*) Bernardine Crud! Oh, how ridiculous!

**Wormy.**

(*Very seriously.*) He's quite a character, Beaumont. He's a smooth operator. So is Griner—Tub Griner—ever happen to run into him?

**Enid.**

No, I don't think so.

**Wormy.**

They're my best friends and they're plenty big wheels, those boys.

**Enid.**

Big wheels?

**Wormy.**

Make time with women, know how to hold their liquor, and something else too—a kind of know-how—savvy, sharp, hep.

**Enid.**

Are you a big wheel too, Ralph?

**Wormy.**

(*Why does she call him Ralph—oh yes—he told her his name was Ralph Bidnut. He must remember this.*) Well, a guy doesn't like to say a thing like that about himself. If he ever should, you can be sure he's not a big wheel— keep that in mind.

**Enid.**

I will. Tell me. (*She moves closer to him.*) How did you happen to come up to me this afternoon? Oh, I know you're going away and you're a stranger here, but how did you happen to decide to speak to me, especially?

**Wormy.**

(*Amazed at this question.*) Why did I walk up to you? Oh Bernardine! (*He moves closer to her.*) Don't you know what you do to a guy? Don't you realize? Is it possible you don't know? I think that would be pretty obvious. You send him.

**Enid.**

Send him? Where?

**Wormy.**

Now, don't con me, you know where. Away off there, out there in the clouds. You're like a song floating by. You're dreamy. You make him want to trail behind you, follow you wherever you're going, and never, never, never come back to where he is.

**Enid.**

(*After a pause.*) Don't you have a girl, Ralph? A girl your own age? You must know some.

**Wormy.**

(*Evasively.*) Oh sure. I know plenty all right—but—

**Enid.**

Don't you take them out—go dancing? You must do a lot of that—

**Wormy.**

(*His head is down now. He clenches and unclenches his fists.*) Oh sure—I take them out. One at a time. First one —and uh—well, the other. But you get tired of the same old faces. These girls I know, I've known them so long. You know how these things are!

**Enid.**

(*Nodding.*) Of course. You're bored with them.

**Wormy.**

(*With feeling.*) Oh boy—am I bored with them!

**Enid.**

When I was your age I wasn't bored with anything.

**Wormy.**

No. I don't suppose so. I guess you could interest just about anybody you wanted to—anybody in the world— any time.

**Enid.**

I wasn't bored—because I was miserable. I was so boy crazy.

**Wormy.**

You—boy crazy? You should have run into me then, sugar—what a collision.

**Enid.**

(*Still reminiscing.*)—so awkward—so over-anxious—the boys all ran away from me—but I kept running after them. (*She turns now to flick the ash from her cigarette into an ashtray on the end table by her side of the sofa. Wormy again half rises to make a lunge at her but again he sits down as she turns back. She smiles a sweet smile at him.*)

**Wormy.**

I wish you wouldn't smile at me like that!

**Enid.**

Why not? Do you want me to frown at you?

**Wormy.**

It would sure make it a lot easier. I'm more used to it.

**Enid.**

(*Moving closer to him.*) But I don't want to frown at you.

I want to smile at you. You make me want to smile more than anybody I've met in a long, long time.

**Wormy.**

A big joke, eh?

**Enid.**

Not at all. It's not that kind of a smile. Ralph, with these girls who bore you so—isn't there one of them you like?

**Wormy.**

(*He leans back against the sofa.*) Oh, well, I—

**Enid.**

There must be.

**Wormy.**

(*Dropping his head and studying the floor.*) Not any more. There used to be one I could never stop thinking about. Saw her this afternoon, too. But she turned out to be an awful jerk. I was surprised too. Thought there was more to her than that.

**Enid.**

I gather she didn't bore you.

**Wormy.**

Well, for a long time she didn't. Then she got so she did. It's all in the past now. I'm through with her. I wouldn't pick her up off a dust heap. You see—she would keep jumping to conclusions; the dumb little drip. She wouldn't sit still and all I ever wanted to say to her—was —well, I'd take her out, understand?

**Enid.**

Yes.

**Wormy.**

And, of course, on the way home, I'd park. And then I'd put my arm around her, like this. (*Puts his arm around Enid.*) There was something I wanted to say to her. But she'd go—(*Here he pushes Enid violently over to the other side of the sofa. His face is fierce with memory.*) And then I'd get so darned burned up with her, I'd go— (*Makes another lunge, grabs Enid with even more violence over to him.*) And she'd go— (*Flings her back again—like a rag doll.*)

**Enid.**

(*Alarmed—cries out.*) Oooooooh!

**Wormy.**

(*Nods with approval at this shriek.*) That's it. She'd let out a yak—just like that—same thing. (*Enid, now frightened of him, is about to slide off the other end of the sofa to escape from a madman. She stops as he continues*

*in the same tone, not looking at her at all. He is staring
into space.*) We'd be sitting in the car on a dark street
with the light from the street lamp falling on her face.
It made her skin look like wintertime and her hair blacker
than soot. (*His voice becomes tender.*) Oh, baby, do you
know how nice you are? You're not the little snoot-face
you pretend to be. You're sweet and I know just how
sweet. Nobody knows you like I do. I'll always know you
and even when you act jerky you can't fool me. You put
on an act because you're afraid somebody will suspect
what a sweet little jerk you are. Why do you do that,
baby? Why do you do it with me? (*There is a pause. He
knocks one clenched fist into the open palm of his other
hand. The look on Enid's face as she listens to him has
changed from fear to softness and sympathy. Wormy now
looks at her, brought back to the present. He is shame-
faced.*) Nertz—I must have been talking to myself!

**Enid.**

(*Slowly.*) Yes, you were talking to yourself. And in more
ways than one, I think.

**Wormy.**

(*Thoughtfully.*) There's an awful lot of hatred in this
sex stuff, isn't there? (*She nods.*) Is it always that way?

**Enid.**

(*Leaning back against the sofa.*) You go along believing
it's always that way until one day you look up and you
see somebody standing before you. Then suddenly, oh,
very suddenly, you feel like you've never felt before. You
feel refreshed. The weariness of years drops away from
you and you want to tell him everything you've learned,
teach him everything you know, forgetting yourself, even
your own name. (*She looks pointedly at Wormy now.*)

**Wormy.**

(*He doesn't understand that the "somebody" is himself.*)
So, if after a while you get to the place where a thing like
that happens to you—what's in it for you?

**Enid.**

Everything—nothing—

**Wormy.**

I don't know. I don't believe I could go for that. Sounds
—well—kind of one-sided—kind of softheaded.

from
# THE SUMMER WITH ELAINA
by Richard Leslie

Act II
JUDY, TYRELL

The play is an airy comedy which occasionally comes to
earth for a scene in which real characters and situations,
warm and true-to-life, shine through the gossamer. The
hero, Tyrell Lithespoone, is seventeen and English. Between June, when he finished school, and October, when
he will go to Oxford, he is living in Paris, visiting his
mother's friend Elaina. Tyrell's mother meant the trip to
be broadening—she felt that a summer in France with
Elaina as his guide might well give her son a necessary
familiarity with certain aspects of life which almost certainly were not a part of the curriculum planned by his
English schoolmasters. Elaina, the vivacious blond widow
of a French banker (she might have been a Gabor), un-
dertakes her duties as educator enthusiastically. Her
course of instruction for Tyrell includes visiting people
and places (as her escort), speaking French (with her),
listening intently to French music (mostly impressionist,
which she plays on the piano), and reciting French poetry
(yes, to her). Tyrell's outlook does indeed broaden. One
afternoon, while he is reciting in the garden, he breaks off
in the middle of a verse and proposes to Elaina. This was
not a part of the study-plan, nor is his violent reaction to
Elaina's sympathetic but firm refusal. She calls for rein-
forcements—Judy, the daughter of another English friend.
Elaina hopes that she can interest Tyrell in Judy who is,
after all, his own age, charming, and going to Oxford in
the fall. But the plan is blatantly obvious and Tyrell refuses to co-operate, for reasons which he attempts to explain to Judy in the scene below.

The setting is a bridge over the River Seine. Judy and
Tyrell have been to see a play in the Shakespeare Garden
in the Bois de Boulogne—an Elizabethan respite from

28

their all-in-French summer. Tyrell has enjoyed himself, which rather bothers him. Now, walking home to Elaina's, they have lost their way and stop on the bridge to try to spot a familiar landmark. It is night, the air is balmy, and the lights along the river glitter like a picture in a travel folder—a thoroughly romantic situation, if only Tyrell were in the mood.

**Judy.**

Are you absolutely certain you know where we are?

**Tyrell.**

(*fast—too fast*) Yes, absolutely! . . . almost . . .

**Judy.**

(*looking ahead*) Which bank of the river is that?

**Tyrell.**

Right bank. See that tall building? . . . with the squared-off things at the corners? I'm almost positive that's on the *right* bank.

**Judy.**

*Almost* positive?

**Tyrell.**

Yes . . . Don't you remember, it's near that picture shop.

**Judy.**

I thought the picture shop was on the *left* bank.

**Tyrell.**

Is it!? I'm almost certain . . . P'rhaps you're right.

**Judy.**

We could ask someone.

**Tyrell.**

Where?

**Judy.**

Oh . . . in a café.

**Tyrell.**

It'd seem a bit silly.

**Judy.**

Not any sillier than wandering around lost.

**Tyrell.**

(*embarrassed*) I suppose not . . . I'm rather enjoying it.

**Judy.**

So am I! . . . It's very late!

**Tyrell.**

(*authoritatively*) It's never late in Paris!

**Judy.**

I was forgetting. (*She goes to the railing of the bridge and looks over.*) It's lovely!

**Tyrell.**

I think Paris at night is more exciting than at any other time!

**Judy.**

Yes! But it would be lovely here any time.

**Tyrell.**

Perhaps. But it wasn't . . . (*ominously*) the other night.

**Judy.**

(*She turns to look at him.*) Oh?

**Tyrell.**

(*a little melodramatically*) I almost . . . jumped over . . . into the river . . . right here!

**Judy.**

Tyrell!

**Tyrell.**

This very spot . . . I think it was this very spot . . . this bridge, in any case.

**Judy.**

You're not sure about a thing like that?

**Tyrell.**

I was rather . . . upset at the time.

**Judy.**

You really meant to do it?

**Tyrell.**

Oh, absolutely!

**Judy.**

(*staring at him*) Whatever for?

**Tyrell.**

(*carefully looking away from her, glaring dramatically out across the water*) I had a . . . great disappointment, and I wasn't certain . . . I could bear it.

**Judy.**

What was it?! (*He doesn't reply.*) Oh, I'm sorry; you don't have to say, if you'd prefer not to . . .

**Tyrell.**

I don't mind . . .

**Judy.**

Really. I shouldn't have asked.

**Tyrell.**

No. You ought to know. I mean, well, these past few days —since you came to . . . Elaina's, I may have seemed a little strange.

**Judy.**

No!

**Tyrell.**

You don't have to pretend. And, you know, if we're all to be around each other the rest of the holidays, you may notice more . . . my acting . . . peculiarly.

**Judy.**

Peculiarly?

**Tyrell.**

(*quickly*) Perhaps that's not the right word. I'm not mental, or anything.

**Judy.**

I didn't think so!

**Tyrell.**

But you see . . . well, you noticed it yourself. That I'm very fond, you said, of Elaina.

**Judy.**

Yes. So am I.

**Tyrell.**

Not in the same way. . . . I mean, before you came here, Elaina and I were left . . . rather to ourselves. And she seemed to take an especial interest in me. And I grew to be very fond of her. And, well, you see I fell in love with her.

**Judy.**

So did I, immediately.

**Tyrell.**

That's what I meant—not the same way. I was—I *am*—really, genuinely in love with her. . . . You know, romantically. . . .

**Judy.**

I see . . . !

**Tyrell.**

Yes. And I assumed—thought, she was, too, with me, you know. I was certain. Only she isn't—wasn't. Anyway, I made a fool of myself, and offered to marry her!

**Judy.**

(*quietly*) Oh, Tyrell.

**Tyrell.**

I begged her, really. I see that now. It makes it all rather worse, you know. And I think she was amused, at first. And that would have been all right, only then she was all sorry and she called me her poor boy! As though I were a child, and didn't know what I was saying. But, of course, I did! Know what I was saying.

**Judy.**

Of course.

**Tyrell.**

You don't think it's amusing.

**Judy.**

Oh, no!

**Tyrell.**

Or childish . . .

**Judy.**

Of course not . . .

**Tyrell.**

(*wholeheartedly*) It was awful! So I just simply left. I didn't want to see her again—though, of course, I suppose all I wanted was to see her always. So after a while I got out here somehow—I don't remember where I went—and I decided . . . to do away with myself.

**Judy.**

I'm glad you didn't!

**Tyrell.**

Oh, so am I, I suppose. I was all *ready* to jump!

**Judy.**

But you didn't.

**Tyrell.**

No, I didn't.

**Judy.**

It's a dreadful feeling. I remember, a year ago I fell in love with our Latin master. And I was certain he noticed me, too. One day he asked me to remain after the other girls left class. I simply knew he was going to tell me. But all he wanted to say was that if I didn't bring more attention to class he would report me inadequate at the end of the term. I wanted to die.

**Tyrell.**

I don't think we—

**Judy.**

But I found out after a while I didn't want to die at all! So did you!

**Tyrell.**

Oh, no!

**Judy.**

But you didn't jump.

**Tyrell.**

No. I, well, I began to think that perhaps if I did jump, I might, well, after I'd got to the water, I might start to swim—automatically, you know from habit!

Judy.

I'm sure you would have.

Tyrell.

I don't know. And then (*sheepishly*) I got sick.

Judy.

(*quietly and with sympathy*) Oh.

Tyrell.

Right there. Into the river.

Judy.

How terrible for you.

Tyrell.

I thought you might laugh at it!

Judy.

Why?!

Tyrell.

Well, I think, now, that it all might be thought of as funny—you know, ironical. Everything about it! I even thought so at the time . . . myself.

Judy.

I don't think so. (*She shivers.*)

Tyrell.

Look here, you are cold, aren't you?

Judy.

I'm fine.

Tyrell.

I saw you shiver.

Judy.

I shivered because I was thinking of you jumping off the bridge because it was *ironical!*

Tyrell.

(*He starts to take off his coat.*) Now you *must* take my coat.

Judy.

(*laughing*) No, I mustn't. I'll be fine if we start walking again.

Tyrell.

You don't want to catch cold.

Judy.

(*moving to him, starting to button up his coat*) I shan't catch cold. . . . Thank you, for telling me.

Tyrell.

I thought you ought to know. I mean, you . . . well, you're not an unattractive person, and in ordinary circumstances, given the propinquity of our situation . . .

Judy.

(*Now she's amused.*) Yes?

**Tyrell.**
Well, you would have every right to expect me—someone in my position—to grow, you know, rather fond of you.

**Judy.**
I didn't have "every right" at all! Goodness, how dreadful if I did!

**Tyrell.**
I thought you ought to . . . understand . . . my feelings for Elaina.

**Judy.**
Quite.

**Tyrell.**
And now you know it's . . . nothing about you!

**Judy.**
Thanks, awfully! And I shan't be the least bit disturbed if you don't say "Boo!" to me.

**Tyrell.**
Oh, I won't be—

**Judy.**
(*giving his now buttoned coat a pat*) We shan't either one be anything. Right?

**Tyrell.**
Right.

**Judy.**
(*not moving away from him*) And it was very good of you to tell me.

**Tyrell.**
(*He is staring right into her eyes.*) Thanks.

**Judy.**
Now we should probably ask someone how we get home! (*Suddenly she pulls at his lapels, stands on tiptoe and kisses his forehead. Immediately she turns him around and starts to march him off the bridge.*) Spared death by drowning, it would be a shame for you to go off with pneumonia.

**Tyrell.**
Why did you do that?! (*He stops walking.*)

**Judy.**
To show you that I think of you as a very uncle-ish brother!

**Tyrell.**
Oh.

**Judy.**
And home, I think, is that way!

**Tyrell.**
You've known all along?

**Judy.**

Of course not! I just recognized the name on the café at the end of the bridge!

**Tyrell.**

Yes, I see it! Clever of you!

**Judy.**

(*as they walk off into the dark*) Hmm, wasn't it?!

from
AH, WILDERNESS!
by Eugene O'Neill

Act IV, scene 2
MURIEL, RICHARD

O'Neill's most gentle and warmhearted play is a lovingly
painted portrait of family life at the turn of the century.
Nat Miller, his wife and children meet their ordinary problems with ordinary annoyance and common sense, and
take their ordinary pleasures with ordinary enjoyment, and
it is all good. *Ah, Wilderness!* provides an extraordinary
contrast—an opposite side of the coin—to *Long Day's
Journey into Night,* the playwright's tortured study of a
family which seems to exist solely to destroy itself and
its members. One play presents, perhaps, O'Neill's dream
of the ideal family he did not know himself; the other, of
course, is a recollection of the family in which he grew
up. In each of the plays, a central figure is a young man
possessed by a poet's eagerness to discover and savor the
world. In *Ah, Wilderness!,* Richard Miller's experiments
with "life" provide the mainspring of the plot; and his
coming to manhood, with the understanding of his family
and the enthusiastic, if dewy-eyed, awakening of Richard
himself, brings about the happy resolution.

The scene reprinted here occurs near the end of the play.
The time is evening in the summer of 1906. The place is a
beach where Richard, going on seventeen and headed for
Yale at the end of the vacation, waits for his girl, Muriel
McComber. Richard knows about life from his books of
poetry—strong stuff to his family and to Muriel's father.
Indeed, the quotations he sent her in a love letter so outraged Mr. McComber that he forbade Muriel to see
Richard again. Stung by this injustice, Richard rushed to
drown his sorrows at the Pleasant Beach House, an estab-
lishment frequented by daring college men, traveling salesmen, and ladies whose reputations are questionable at
best. That was last night. This is the night for repentance—

36

and for explaining things to Muriel who has promised to slip away from home and meet Richard at the beach. As he sees her approach, Richard jumps up from the overturned rowboat on which he has been sitting. He strolls around with exaggerated carelessness and he whistles. Almost overwhelmed by anxiety and love, he is determined not to seem too pleased to see Muriel. "Let her suffer," he says, "for a change."

Muriel comes to the foot of the path, waits for Richard to notice her, then calls to him.

**Muriel.**

Oh, Dick.

**Richard.**

(*turns around with an elaborate simulation of being disturbed in the midst of profound meditation*) Oh, hello. Is it nine already? Gosh, time passes—when you're thinking.

**Muriel.**

(*coming toward him as far as the edge of the shadow—disappointedly*) I thought you'd be waiting right here at the end of the path. I'll bet you'd forgotten I was even coming.

**Richard.**

(*strolling a little toward her but not too far—carelessly*) No, I hadn't forgotten, honest. But I got to thinking about life.

**Muriel.**

You might think of me for a change, after all the risk I've run to see you! (*Hesitating timidly on the edge of the shadow*) Dick! You come here to me. I'm afraid to go out in that bright moonlight where anyone might see me.

**Richard.**

(*coming toward her—scornfully*) Ah, there you go again —always scared of life!

**Muriel.**

(*indignantly*) Dick Miller, I do think you've got an awful nerve to say that after all the risks I've run making this date and then sneaking out! You didn't take the trouble to sneak any letter to me, I notice!

**Richard.**

No, because after your first letter, I thought everything
was dead and past between us.

**Muriel.**

And I'll bet you didn't care one little bit! (*On the verge
of humiliated tears*) Oh, I was a fool ever to come here!
I've got a good notion to go right home and never speak
to you again! (*She half turns back toward the path.*)

**Richard.**

(*frightened—immediately becomes terribly sincere—
grabbing her hand*) Ah, don't go, Muriel! Please! I
didn't mean anything like that, honest, I didn't! Gee, if
you knew how broken-hearted I was by that first letter,
and how darned happy your second letter made me—!

**Muriel.**

(*happily relieved—but appreciates she has the upper hand
now and doesn't relent at once*) I don't believe you.

**Richard.**

You ask Mid how happy I was. She can prove it.

**Muriel.**

She'd say anything you told her to. I don't care anything about what she'd say. It's you. You've got to swear
to me—

**Richard.**

I swear!

**Muriel.**

(*demurely*) Well then, all right, I'll believe you.

**Richard.**

(*his eyes on her face lovingly—genuine adoration in his
voice*) Gosh, you're pretty tonight, Muriel! It seems ages
since we've been together! If you knew how I've suffered—!

**Muriel.**

I did, too.

**Richard.**

(*unable to resist falling into his tragic literary pose for a
moment*) The despair in my soul— (*He recites dramatically*) "Something was dead in each of us, And what
was dead was Hope!" That was me! My hope of happiness was dead! (*Then with sincere boyish fervor*) Gosh,
Muriel, it sure is wonderful to be with you again! (*He
puts a timid arm around her awkwardly.*)

**Muriel.**

(*shyly*) I'm glad—it makes you happy. I'm happy, too.

**Richard.**

Can't I—won't you let me kiss you—now? Please! (*He bends his face toward hers.*)

**Muriel.**

(*ducking her head away—timidly*) No. You mustn't. Don't—

**Richard.**

Ah, why can't I?

**Muriel.**

Because—I'm afraid.

**Richard.**

(*discomfited—taking his arm from around her—a bit sulky and impatient with her*) Aw, that's what you always say! You're always so afraid! Aren't you ever going to let me?

**Muriel.**

I will—sometime.

**Richard.**

When?

**Muriel.**

Soon, maybe.

**Richard.**

Tonight, will you?

**Muriel.**

(*coyly*) I'll see.

**Richard.**

Promise?

**Muriel.**

I promise—maybe.

**Richard.**

All right. You remember you've promised. (*Then coaxingly*) Aw, don't let's stand here. Come on out and we can sit down in the boat.

**Muriel.**

(*hesitantly*) It's so bright out there.

**Richard.**

No one'll see. You know there's never anyone around here at night.

**Muriel.**

(*illogically*) I know there isn't. That's why I thought it would be the best place. But there might be someone.

**Richard.**

(*taking her hand and tugging at it gently*) There isn't a soul. (*Muriel steps out a little and looks up and down fearfully. Richard goes on insistently*) Aw, what's the use of a moon if you can't see it!

**Muriel.**

But it's only a new moon. That's not much to look at.

**Richard.**

But I want to see you. I can't here in the shadow. I want to—drink in—all your beauty.

**Muriel.**

(*can't resist this*) Well, all right—only I can't stay only a few minutes. (*She lets him lead her toward the stern of the boat.*)

**Richard.**

(*pleadingly*) Aw, you can stay a little while, can't you? Please! (*He helps her in and she settles herself in the stern seat of the boat, facing diagonally left front.*)

**Muriel.**

A little while. (*He sits beside her*) But I've got to be home in bed again pretending to be asleep by ten o'clock. That's the time Pa and Ma come up to bed, as regular as clock work, and Ma always looks into my room.

**Richard.**

But you'll have oodles of time to do that.

**Muriel.**

(*excitedly*) Dick, you have no idea what I went through to get here tonight! My, but it was exciting! You know Pa's punishing me by sending me to bed at eight sharp, and I had to get all undressed and into bed 'cause at half-past he sends Ma up to make sure I've obeyed, and she came up, and I pretended to be asleep, and she went down again, and I got up and dressed in such a hurry— I must look a sight, don't I?

**Richard.**

You do not! You look wonderful!

**Muriel.**

And then I sneaked down the back stairs. And the pesky old stairs squeaked, and my heart was in my mouth, I was so scared, and then I sneaked out through the back yard, keeping in the dark under the trees, and— My, but it was exciting! Dick, you don't realize how I've been punished for your sake. Pa's been so mean and nasty, I've almost hated him!

**Richard.**

And you don't realize what I've been through for you— and what I'm in for—for sneaking out— (*Then darkly*) And for what I did last night—what your letter made me do!

**Muriel.**

(*made terribly curious by his ominous tone*) What did my letter make you do?

**Richard.**

(*beginning to glory in this*) It's too long a story—and let the dead past bury its dead. (*Then with real feeling*) Only it isn't past, I can tell you! What I'll catch when Pa gets hold of me!

**Muriel.**

Tell me, Dick! Begin at the beginning and tell me!

**Richard.**

(*tragically*) Well, after your old—your father left our place I caught holy hell from Pa.

**Muriel.**

Dick! You mustn't swear!

**Richard.**

(*somberly*) Hell is the only word that can describe it. And on top of that, to torture me more, he gave me your letter. After I'd read that I didn't want to live any more. Life seemed like a tragic farce.

**Muriel.**

I'm so awful sorry, Dick—honest I am! But you might have known I'd never write that unless—

**Richard.**

I thought your love for me was dead. I thought you'd never loved me, that you'd only been cruelly mocking me —to torture me!

**Muriel.**

Dick! I'd never! You know I'd never!

**Richard.**

I wanted to die. I sat and brooded about death. Finally I made up my mind I'd kill myself.

**Muriel.**

(*excitedly*) Dick! You didn't!

**Richard.**

I did, too! If there'd been one of Hedda Gabler's pistols around, you'd have seen if I wouldn't have done it beautifully! I thought, when I'm dead, she'll be sorry she ruined my life!

**Muriel.**

(*cuddling up a little to him*) If you ever had! I'd have died, too! Honest, I would!

**Richard.**

But suicide is the act of a coward. That's what stopped me. (*Then with a bitter change of tone*) And anyway, I thought to myself, she isn't worth it.

**Muriel.**

(*huffily*) That's a nice thing to say!

**Richard.**

Well, if you meant what was in the letter, you wouldn't have been worth it, would you?

**Muriel.**

But I've told you Pa—

**Richard.**

So I said to myself, I'm through with women; they're all alike!

**Muriel.**

I'm not.

**Richard.**

And I thought, what difference does it make what I do now? I might as well forget her and lead the pace that kills, and drown my sorrows! You know I had eleven dollars saved up to buy you something for your birthday, but I thought, she's dead to me now and why shouldn't I throw it away? (*Then hastily*) I've still got almost five left, Muriel, and I can get you something nice with that.

**Muriel.**

(*excitedly*) What do I care about your old presents? You tell me what you did!

**Richard.**

(*darkly again*) After it was dark, I sneaked out and went to a low dive I know about.

**Muriel.**

Dick Miller, I don't believe you ever!

**Richard.**

You ask them at the Pleasant Beach House if I didn't! They won't forget me in a hurry!

**Muriel.**

(*impressed and horrified*) You went there? Why, that's a terrible place! Pa says it ought to be closed by the police!

**Richard.**

(*darkly*) I said it was a dive, didn't I? It's a "secret house of shame." And they let me into a secret room behind the barroom. There wasn't anyone there but a Princeton Senior I know—he belongs to Tiger Inn and he's fullback on the football team—and he had two chorus girls from New York with him, and they were all drinking champagne.

**Muriel.**

(*disturbed by the entrance of the chorus girls*) Dick Miller! I hope you didn't notice—

**Richard.**

(*carelessly*) I had a highball by myself and then I noticed one of the girls—the one that wasn't with the fullback—looking at me. She had strange-looking eyes. And then she asked me if I wouldn't drink champagne with them and come and sit with her.

**Muriel.**

She must have been a nice thing! (*Then a bit falteringly*) And did—you?

**Richard.**

(*with tragic bitterness*) Why shouldn't I, when you'd told me in that letter you'd never see me again?

**Muriel.**

(*almost tearfully*) But you ought to have known Pa made me—

**Richard.**

I didn't know that then. (*Then rubbing it in*) Her name was Belle. She had yellow hair—the kind that burns and stings you!

**Muriel.**

I'll bet it was dyed!

**Richard.**

She kept smoking one cigarette after another—but that's nothing for a chorus girl.

**Muriel.**

(*indignantly*) She was low and bad, that's what she was or she couldn't be a chorus girl, and her smoking cigarettes proves it! (*Then falteringly again*) And then what happened?

**Richard.**

(*carelessly*) Oh, we just kept drinking champagne—I bought a round—and then I had a fight with the barkeep and knocked him down because he'd insulted her. He was a great big thug but—

**Muriel.**

(*huffily*) I don't see how he could—insult that kind! And why did you fight for her? Why didn't the Princeton fullback who'd brought them there? He must have been bigger than you.

**Richard.**

(*stopped for a moment—then quickly*) He was too drunk by that time.

**Muriel.**

And were you drunk?

**Richard.**

Only a little then. I was worse later. (*Proudly*) You ought to have seen me when I got home! I was on the verge of delirium tremens!

**Muriel.**

I'm glad I didn't see you. You must have been awful. I hate people who get drunk. I'd have hated you!

**Richard.**

Well, it was all your fault, wasn't it? If you hadn't written that letter—

**Muriel.**

But I've told you I didn't mean— (*Then faltering but fascinated*) But what happened with that Belle—after—before you went home?

**Richard.**

Oh, we kept drinking champagne and she said she'd fallen in love with me at first sight and she came and sat on my lap and kissed me.

**Muriel.**

(*stiffening*) Oh!

**Richard.**

(*quickly, afraid he has gone too far*) But it was only all in fun, and then we just kept on drinking champagne, and finally I said good night and came home.

**Muriel.**

And did you kiss her?

**Richard.**

No, I didn't.

**Muriel.**

(*distractedly*) You did, too! You're lying and you know it. You did, too! (*Then tearfully*) And there I was right at that time lying in bed not able to sleep, wondering how I was ever going to see you again and crying my eyes out, while you—! (*She suddenly jumps to her feet in a tearful fury*) I hate you! I wish you were dead! I'm going home this minute! I never want to lay eyes on you again! And this time I mean it! (*She tries to jump out of the boat but he holds her back. All the pose has dropped from him now and he is in a frightened state of contrition.*)

**Richard.**

(*imploringly*) Muriel! Wait! Listen!

**Muriel.**

I don't want to listen! Let me go! If you don't I'll bite your hand!

**Richard.**

I won't let you go! You've got to let me explain! I never —! Ouch! (*For Muriel has bitten his hand and it hurts, and, stung by the pain, he lets go instinctively, and she jumps quickly out of the boat and starts running toward the path. Richard calls after her with bitter despair and hurt*) All right! Go if you want to—if you haven't the decency to let me explain! I hate you, too! I'll go and see Belle!

**Muriel.**

(*seeing he isn't following her, stops at the foot of the path—defiantly*) Well, go and see her—if that's the kind of girl you like! What do I care? (*Then as he only stares before him broodingly, sitting dejectedly in the stern of the boat, a pathetic figure of injured grief*) You can't explain! What can you explain? You owned up you kissed her!

**Richard.**

I did not. I said she kissed me.

**Muriel.**

(*scornfully, but drifting back a step in his direction*) And I suppose you just sat and let yourself be kissed! Tell that to the Marines!

**Richard.**

(*injuredly*) All right! If you're going to call me a liar every word I say—

**Muriel.**

(*drifting back another step*) I didn't call you a liar. I only meant—it sounds fishy. Don't you know it does?

**Richard.**

I don't know anything. I only know I wish I was dead!

**Muriel.**

(*gently reproving*) You oughtn't to say that. It's wicked. (*Then after a pause*) And I suppose you'll tell me you didn't fall in love with her?

**Richard.**

(*scornfully*) I should say not! Fall in love with that kind of girl! What do you take me for?

**Muriel.**

(*practically*) How do you know what you did if you drank so much champagne?

**Richard.**
I kept my head—with her. I'm not a sucker, no matter what you think!

**Muriel.**
(*drifting nearer*) Then you didn't—love her?

**Richard.**
I hated her! She wasn't even pretty! And I had a fight with her before I left, she got so fresh. I told her I loved you and never could love anyone else, and for her to leave me alone.

**Muriel.**
But you said just now you were going to see her—

**Richard.**
That was only bluff. I wouldn't—unless you left me. Then I wouldn't care what I did—any more than I did last night. (*Then suddenly defiant*) And what if I did kiss her once or twice? I only did it to get back at you!

**Muriel.**
Dick!

**Richard.**
You're a fine one to blame me—when it was all your fault! Why can't you be fair? Didn't I think you were out of my life forever? Hadn't you written me you were? Answer me that!

**Muriel.**
But I've told you a million times that Pa—

**Richard.**
Why didn't you have more sense than to let him make you write it? Was it my fault you didn't?

**Muriel.**
It was your fault for being so stupid! You ought to have known he stood right over me and told me each word to write. If I'd refused, it would only have made everything worse. I had to pretend, so I'd get a chance to see you. Don't you see, Silly? And I had sand enough to sneak out to meet you tonight, didn't I? (*He doesn't answer. She moves nearer*) Still I can see how you felt the way you did—and maybe I am to blame for that. So I'll forgive and forget, Dick—if you'll swear to me you didn't even think of loving that—

**Richard.**
(*eagerly*) I didn't! I swear, Muriel. I couldn't. I love you!

**Muriel.**
Well, then—I still love you.

**Richard.**

Then come back here, why don't you?

**Muriel.**

(*coyly*) It's getting late.

**Richard.**

It's not near half-past yet.

**Muriel.**

(*comes back and sits down by him shyly*) All right—only I'll have to go soon, Dick. (*He puts his arm around her. She cuddles up close to him*) I'm sorry—I hurt your hand.

**Richard.**

That was nothing. It felt wonderful—even to have you bite!

**Muriel.**

(*impulsively takes his hand and kisses it*) There! That'll cure it. (*She is overcome by confusion at her boldness.*)

**Richard.**

You shouldn't—waste that—on my hand. (*Then trem-blingly*) You said—you'd let me—

**Muriel.**

I said, maybe.

**Richard.**

Please, Muriel. You know—I want it so!

**Muriel.**

Will it wash off—her kisses—make you forget you ever —for always?

**Richard.**

I should say so! I'd never remember—anything but it— never want anything but it—ever again.

**Muriel.**

(*shyly lifting her lips*) Then—all right—Dick. (*He kisses her tremblingly and for a moment their lips remain to-gether. Then she lets her head sink on his shoulder and sighs softly*) The moon is beautiful, isn't it?

**Richard.**

(*kissing her hair*) Not as beautiful as you! Nothing is! (*Then after a pause*) Won't it be wonderful when we're married?

**Muriel.**

Yes—but it's so long to wait.

**Richard.**

Perhaps I needn't go to Yale. Perhaps Pa will give me a job. Then I'd soon be making enough to—

**Muriel.**

You better do what your pa thinks best—and I'd like you

to be at Yale. (*Then patting his face*) Poor you! Do you think he'll punish you awful?

**Richard.**

(*intensely*) I don't know and I don't care! Nothing would have kept me from seeing you tonight—not if I'd had to crawl over red-hot coals! (*Then falling back on Swinburne—but with passionate sincerity*) You have my being between the hands of you! You are "my love, mine own soul's heart, more dear than mine own soul, more beautiful than God!"

**Muriel.**

(*shocked and delighted*) Ssshh! It's wrong to say that.

**Richard.**

(*adoringly*) Gosh, but I love you! Gosh, I love you—Darling!

**Muriel.**

I love you, too—Sweetheart! (*They kiss. Then she lets her head sink on his shoulder again and they both sit in a rapt trance, staring at the moon. After a pause—dreamily*) Where'll we go on our honeymoon, Dick? To Niagara Falls?

**Richard.**

(*scornfully*) That dump where all the silly fools go? I should say not! (*With passionate romanticism*) No, we'll go to some far-off wonderful place! (*He calls on Kipling to help him*) Somewhere out on the Long Trail—the trail that is always new—on the road to Mandalay! We'll watch the dawn come up like thunder out of China!

**Muriel.**

(*hazily but happily*) That'll be wonderful, won't it?

from
TWO ON AN ISLAND
by Elmer Rice

Act III, scene 9
JOHN, MARY

Two hopeful youngsters come to New York—separately—
seeking careers in the theater, she as an actress, he as a
writer. As their taxis pull away from the railroad station
they take their looks at the buildings and bustle of the
city. As weeks pass, then months, they make the rounds of
the producers' offices, are encouraged and let down. They
face the problems of compromise with careers and sex.
They learn what it is to be down and out in New York.
Their paths cross many times before they finally meet.
When they have met, grown to know each other, and
decided to marry, the successes for which they hoped
seem about to happen. And that is the play.

The setting for this scene is the top of the Statue of
Liberty, viewed from the outside. "We see the eyes, brow,
coiffure, and radiating spikes of the crown. In the brow are
the windows which frame the hemispherical observation
gallery. These windows diminish in size as they curve
away from center. The two middle ones are just wide
enough to accommodate two persons each, others give
room only for one. . . . At the back, on the right, a spiral
staircase, invisible to the audience, affords means of ascent.
A similar staircase at the left is reserved for descent." A
group of tourists has just started down as Mary comes up
the stairway, right, and takes a place at one of the windows. John already stands at another window. After a
moment, Mary catches his eye. She averts her head and
looks at the view. John hesitates a moment, then strolls
over beside her. They have not met before.

**John.**

Pretty impressive, isn't it?

**Mary.**

(*giving him a quick look*) Yes, isn't it.

**John.**

Your first visit?

**Mary.**

Yes, it is.

**John.**

I've been up here three or four times. So if there's anything I can point out to you—

**Mary.**

Well, I was just sort of letting myself be overwhelmed by the whole picture. But it *would* be nice to know what some of the places are.

**John.**

Well, the big island there with the hills is Staten Island.

**Mary.**

It somehow doesn't look like New York.

**John.**

No, it doesn't when you get there either. They say there are people living there who have never been to Manhattan.

**Mary.**

Well, look at me. I've been living in Manhattan for over two years and I never even knew where Staten Island is.

**John.**

Well, you haven't missed much. But on one of those hot summer nights the ferry ride over from the Battery is the best nickel's worth in town.

**Mary.**

Is that all it costs—a nickel?

**John.**

Yes. Municipal ferry. Look, there's one of the boats now. That big red tub. See it?

**Mary.**

Oh, yes! And what's that large white boat? That must be an ocean liner.

**John.**

I think she's on the South American service. I wouldn't mind being on her, right this very minute.

**Mary.**

Oh, neither should I! I want to travel like mad and I'm going to some day too—though goodness knows when or how.

**John.**

Well, as far as I've got is reading the travel folders. If you can't have the real experiences, it helps a little to imagine yourself having them.

**Mary.**

Yes, I know.

**John.**

Tell me, where have I seen you before?

**Mary.**

(*looking at him*) Is that a line? Because I was really enjoying the illustrated lecture.

**John.**

If that's what I were doing, I'd try to think up something a little more original. You don't remember ever seeing me?

**Mary.**

Sorry. But I don't.

**John.**

Well, I've seen you. But I'll be damned if I can remember where. I'll think of it in a minute. All right, let's go back to Brooklyn.

**Mary.**

Yes, that's a wonderful idea. Is that Brooklyn straight ahead?

**John.**

Yes, that's all Brooklyn.

**Mary.**

I'm ashamed to say I've never been to Brooklyn either. Unless Coney Island is Brooklyn.

**John.**

Well, technically speaking it is. Seeing Brooklyn is a career in itself. As nearly as I can figure out, it's about as complicated as China. They even speak different languages in different parts of it. But I've been around a little: Williamsburg, Flatbush, Columbia Heights, the Navy Yard—

**Mary.**

It sounds fascinating. I wish I had the energy to go around like that.

**John.**

Well, I wasn't going entirely on my own energy. For a while I was driving a delivery truck for a bakery on Atlantic Avenue.

**Mary.**

Oh, were you?

**John.**
Well, truck driving isn't really my profession. Just sort of an avocation.

**Mary.**
Well, that's what I thought.

**John.**
Thanks. Some of the time I go through the motions of pretending I'm a writer. I've got it!

**Mary.**
What?

**John.**
Ormont!

**Mary.**
Ormont?

**John.**
Yes, that's where I saw you—coming out of the Silver Bar with Larry Ormont. Late one night—two or three weeks ago. Somebody called him back and for a moment you stood there alone. Remember?

**Mary.**
Yes, but I— Do you know Larry Ormont?

**John.**
A little. I almost spoke to you.

**Mary.**
Why to me?

**John.**
Just that you looked like the kind of a girl who might give a panhandler a dime.

**Mary.**
A panhandler? You mean you were—

**John.**
Yes. Begging. You look shocked.

**Mary.**
No. I'm shockproof by now. But a little surprised.

**John.**
Yes, I know. I guess I don't look that part either. Maybe that's why I've never made a great success of it.

**Mary.**
It sounds as if you've been having fierce hard luck.

**John.**
Well—that's charitable of you. Are you convinced now that I've seen you before?

**Mary.**
Yes. Thoroughly convinced. But—

**John.**
Good! Just so long as I've re-established myself as a

lecturer without ulterior motives. That low, flat place is Governor's Island.

**Mary.**

What do you write—stories?

**John.**

Yes. Cent-a-word for the pulps. But I had intentions of being a playwright.

**Mary.**

So that's how you happen to know Ormont?

**John.**

Yes. That's Battery Park, where you took the boat.

**Mary.**

He won't buy your plays?

**John.**

Nobody will buy my plays. Ever been to the Aquarium?

**Mary.**

No. My name's Mary Ward.

**John.**

John Thompson.

**Mary.**

My grandmother was a Thompson. Do you spell it with a "p"?

**John.**

Yes. My folks came from Massachusetts—about a hundred years ago.

**Mary.**

Well, so did Grandmother's family. Around North Adams, I think.

**John.**

Maybe we're related.

**Mary.**

That's a thought.

**John.**

By the way, have you ever met anyone who was born in New York?

**Mary.**

No, I don't think I have.

**John.**

Neither have I.

**Mary.**

There must be some though.

**John.**

Yes, there certainly must be. You know, of all the New York days I've known, I like these clear October ones best.

**Mary.**

So do I. Only they get me thinking a little wistfully about the lovely New Hampshire woods—all the colors of the rainbow now.

**John.**

Well, if I were back in Iowa today, I'd be out in corduroys and a windbreaker, hunting rabbits over the corn stubble and the frozen lumps of brown earth.

**Mary.**

Listen, I haven't very much money of my own, but if you're broke I can lend you a little—five dollars or so.

**John.**

Well, thanks! But I'm comparatively rich. This morning I collected seventy-five dollars for two stories I sold some time ago.

**Mary.**

Seventy-five dollars!

**John.**

It happens I have only fifty left. I gave twenty-five to a girl who helped me out when I needed help. But that leaves more than enough to get me back to Iowa.

**Mary.**

Oh, you're going to Iowa?

**John.**

Yes. Tomorrow morning. That's why I've come up here. To kiss New York good-by.

**Mary.**

You mean you're going for good?

**John.**

Well, for better or worse. You know, it's a funny thing—but that skyline still gets me. I've seen so much of what goes on behind that magnificent front that I thought I'd developed an immunity to it.

**Mary.**

Why are you going back home?

**John.**

I'm going into business with my brother. He has the Chevrolet agency in Waterloo and he's been urging me to come back ever since I landed in New York, over two years ago.

**Mary.**

Well, my folks keep urging me to come back too, but I'll never go back, no matter what I have to do to stay here. New York's got me, I guess.

**John.**

That's what I'm afraid of——that it'll get *me*. Have you ever been on the Bowery?

**Mary.**

Yes. I took one of those sightseeing trips.

**John.**

I've been there often. A lot of promising boys there, who put off going home until it was too late and they were ashamed to go. I don't want to slouch along under the El and be a guinea pig in a hair-cutting college.

**Mary.**

But if you have fifty dollars——!

**John.**

Yes, I can live for four weeks on that——six if I have to. By that time I might sell another story or get a job somewhere.

**Mary.**

Yes, of course, you will!

**John.**

But I might not sell another story. Or I might not find a job——not even washing dishes. It'll be rainy next month, and then the cold weather begins. So far, I've always managed to hang on to my typewriter and one fairly decent suit of clothes. Next time, I don't know. And if I were hungry enough, I might not even hold out a few dollars for room rent. That would mean nights in flophouses or in the subway. And pretty soon I'd begin to get a little careless about shaving, and not bothering much when buttons started falling off.

**Mary.**

But, listen——

**John.**

Well, let's skip it. How did we ever get started on this anyhow?

**Mary.**

Well, we were just talking and——

**John.**

Yes. And the old male ego suddenly ran amok. You know, you're an awfully good listener. God knows, I haven't struck any of those since I landed here.

**Mary.**

Well, neither have I! Back home there'd always be somebody who cared enough to listen, but here——well, you know how it is. Honestly, I sometimes don't know what to do with myself——just longing for somebody to talk to.

**John.**

You're having troubles of your own, I take it.

**Mary.**

Not exactly. Just puzzled, that's all. I have to make up my mind about something and I don't know what to do about it. You see— (*Breaking off*) This is perfectly silly! You don't go around spilling yourself to total strangers. Not if you grew up in New England, you don't.

**John.**

Well, my God, I've just been baring my soul to you! Anyhow, I thought we decided that we're related. Has this got something to do with Ormont?

**Mary.**

How did you guess that?

**John.**

Oh, just from the way you reacted when I first mentioned his name.

**Mary.**

He's offered me a job—a good part in a good play. Just the chance I've been waiting for. Oh, but I didn't tell you that I'm an actress.

**John.**

I figured that out for myself.

**Mary.**

Well, that's more than the managers seem able to do.

**John.**

But you just said that Ormont has—

**Mary.**

Yes. But if I take the job— You see, I've worked for him before and I know what he's like. Besides, he practically told me so. That's all.

**John.**

I see. And you don't feel that way about him.

**Mary.**

No, I couldn't possibly ever! But, if I turn this down, I just don't know how I'm going to get along—and I'm beginning to think that maybe I'm crazy to attach so much importance to certain ideas of my own about things.

**John.**

Well, I don't see how a man can help a girl decide a thing like that. But if you don't mind my saying so, I don't like it at all—the idea of you and Ormont. You're not the type.

**Mary.**

Thanks. (*Suddenly*) Well, let's not talk about that any more.

**John.**

But, look—

**Mary.**

No, please! No more! Do you really mean you think there's no hope for anybody in New York—that we all might as well give up and go home?

**John.**

I didn't say that.

**Mary.**

Well, that's what it sounded like.

**John.**

No, it didn't! It's like that problem of yours—something everybody has to decide for himself. All I'm saying is that New York is a tough nut that only one in a thousand can crack. And I don't seem to be that one. So, while I still have the chance, I'm going back where I belong, back among the people I know, where I can see the shape of my environment and find myself a place in it.

**Mary.**

You mean you'd really rather spend the rest of your life selling Chevrolets to small-town folks than be here where things are happening, here in the world of art and the theater and all the great things of life?

**John.**

Not if I can be a part of it. But I've been here over two years now and I'm still on the outside looking in. And I say it's better to have a small identity of your own on Main Street than to be an anonymous pedestrian on the avenues of Manhattan.

**Mary.**

But maybe if you stayed a little while longer, things would begin breaking your way.

**John.**

No, I've made up my mind. Listen, would you do something for me? We haven't known each other very long and I guess I have no right to ask it of you. But we seem to understand each other pretty well.

**Mary.**

Well, what is it?

**John.**

Well, it's that fifty dollars. I'll need about half of it to get me back to Iowa. But that still leaves twenty-five or

so. I've been thinking that I'd like to have one big blow-
out on my last night in New York. Cocktails in some
fancy bar, dinner at the Waldorf or the Plaza, orchestra
seats for some good show. All the things I've always
wanted to do but have never been able to afford. Only it
wouldn't be much fun doing them alone, and I don't know
anybody I care enough about to ask. Will you come along
and keep me company?

**Mary.**

No, I won't!

**John.**

Why not?

**Mary.**

Because I think a person like you—young and creative
and with everything to live for—has no right to get discouraged and quit. I think you should be ashamed of
yourself for running away like this. I know it's none of
my business, but I just can't help saying what I think.

**John.**

And will you be ashamed of yourself for giving in to
Ormont?

**Mary.**

I'm *not* giving in to Ormont!

**John.**

You've decided that?

**Mary.**

Yes, I have!

**John.**

Well, that's an important decision. * * * [*They hear a
sightseeing party coming up the stairs.*]

**John.**

Tourists! Look, we could sit at one of those tables, down
there, and have a Coca-Cola. That would only cost a dime.

**Mary.**

Well, I'm willing to go that far with you.

**John.**

Thanks. All right, let's go.

from
# THE GLASS MENAGERIE
by Tennessee Williams

Act II, scene 8
LAURA, JIM

"The play," says Tom, the narrator, "is memory." And as
he speaks the wall of a brick tenement in St. Louis fades
away, revealing a flat and the people who live (or lived)
there—Tom's mother, Amanda, and his sister, Laura, and
Tom himself. Amanda is a southern belle grown middle-
aged; deserted by a husband who was more dashing than
reliable, she lives now in her own memories of balls and
parties and dozens of "gentlemen callers," and in her
children. Laura, shy and painfully self-conscious of a limp
that came with a childhood sickness, is frightened of
people and of the world outside the flat; she lives instead
in a private world which she shares with her collection of
little glass animals. Tom is restless, a poet trapped by the
prosaic realities of the tenement, his dull job, and his
mother's efforts to make a future for her children, a future
involving only subsisting. In the end, Tom runs away, as
his father did; he becomes a merchant seaman, but, no
matter how far he travels, St. Louis and the memories
go with him.

The scene below comes near the end of the play. (For
other excerpts from *The Glass Menagerie*, see pages 91
181, and 308.) Amanda, concerned because Laura has no
suitors, has persuaded Tom to bring home a friend, a
"gentleman caller." She has dressed Laura in the best of
her own old finery, prepared a special dinner, frantically
kept the conversation moving and light. But Laura is
nervous and ill at ease. She flees the table and goes into
the living room. She sits there alone in the half-light as
Jim, the Gentleman Caller, enters.

**Laura.**

Oh . . . (*Puts wine-glass on telephone table, hands him pillow, sits left on day-bed*)

**Jim.**

How about you? Don't you like to sit on the floor?

**Laura.**

Oh, yes.

**Jim.**

Well, why don't you?

**Laura.**

I—will.

**Jim.**

Take a pillow! (*Throws pillow as she sits on floor*) I can't see you sitting way over there. (*Sits on floor again*)

**Laura.**

I can—see you.

**Jim.**

Yeah, but that's not fair. I'm right here in the limelight. (*Laura moves a little closer to him*) Good! Now I can see you! Are you comfortable?

**Laura.**

Yes. Thank you.

**Jim.**

So am I. I'm comfortable as a cow! Say, would you care for a piece of chewing-gum? (*Offers gum*)

**Laura.**

No, thank you.

**Jim.**

I think that I will indulge. (*Musingly unwraps it and holds it up*) Gee, think of the fortune made by the guy that invented the first piece of chewing-gum! It's amazing, huh? Do you know that the Wrigley Building is one of the sights of Chicago?—I saw it summer before last at the Century of Progress.—Did you take in the Century of Progress?

**Laura.**

No, I didn't.

**Jim.**

Well, it was a wonderful exposition, believe me. You know what impressed me most? The Hall of Science. Gives you an idea of what the future will be like in America. Oh, it's more wonderful than the present time is! Say, your brother tells me you're shy. Is that right, Laura?

**Laura.**

I—don't know.

**Jim.**

I judge you to be an old-fashioned type of girl. Oh, I think that's a wonderful type to be. I hope you don't think I'm being too personal—do you?

**Laura.**

Mr. O'Connor?

**Jim.**

Huh?

**Laura.**

I believe I *will* take a piece of gum, if you don't mind. (*Jim peels gum—gets on knees, hands it to Laura. She breaks off a tiny piece. Jim looks at what remains, puts it in his mouth, and sits again.*) Mr. O'Connor, have you—kept up with your singing?

**Jim.**

Singing? Me?

**Laura.**

Yes. I remember what a beautiful voice you had.

**Jim.**

You heard me sing?

**Laura.**

Oh, yes! Very often . . . I—don't suppose—you remember me—at all?

**Jim.**

(*smiling doubtfully*) You know, as a matter of fact I did have an idea I'd seen you before. Do you know it seemed almost like I was about to remember your name. But the name I was about to remember—wasn't a name! So I stopped myself before I said it.

**Laura.**

Wasn't it—Blue Roses?

**Jim.**

(*grinning*) Blue Roses! Oh my gosh, yes—Blue Roses! You know. I didn't connect you with high school some-how or other. But that's where it was, it was high school. Gosh, I didn't even know you were Shakespeare's sister! Gee, I'm sorry.

**Laura.**

I didn't expect you to.—You—barely knew me!

**Jim.**

But, we did have a speaking acquaintance.

**Laura.**

Yes; we—spoke to each other.

**Jim.**

Say, didn't we have a class in something together?

**Laura.**

Yes, we did.

**Jim.**

What class was that?

**Laura.**

It was—singing—chorus!

**Jim.**

Aw!

**Laura.**

I sat across the aisle from you in the auditorium. Mondays, Wednesdays and Fridays.

**Jim.**

Oh yeah! I remember now—you're the one who always came in late.

**Laura.**

Yes, it was so hard for me, getting upstairs. I had that brace on my leg then—it clumped so loud!

**Jim.**

I never heard any clumping.

**Laura.**

(*wincing at recollection*) To me it sounded like—thunder!

**Jim.**

I never even noticed.

**Laura.**

Everybody was seated before I came in. I had to walk in front of all those people. My seat was in the back row. I had to go clumping up the aisle with everyone watching!

**Jim.**

Oh, gee, you shouldn't have been self-conscious.

**Laura.**

I know, but I was. It was always such a relief when the singing started.

**Jim.**

I remember now. And I used to call you Blue Roses. How did I ever get started calling you a name like that?

**Laura.**

I was out of school a little while with pleurosis. When I came back you asked me what was the matter. I said I had pleurosis and you thought I said Blue Roses. So that's what you always called me after that!

**Jim.**

I hope you didn't mind?

**Laura.**

Oh, no—I liked it. You see, I wasn't acquainted with many—people . . .

**Jim.**

Yeah. I remember you sort of stuck by yourself.

**Laura.**

I never did have much luck at making friends.

**Jim.**

Well, I don't see why you wouldn't.

**Laura.**

Well, I started out badly.

**Jim.**

You mean being—?

**Laura.**

Well, yes, it—sort of—stood between me . . .

**Jim.**

You shouldn't have let it!

**Laura.**

I know, but it did, and I—

**Jim.**

You mean you were shy with people!

**Laura.**

I tried not to be but never could—

**Jim.**

Overcome it?

**Laura.**

No, I—never could!

**Jim.**

Yeah. I guess being shy is something you have to work out of kind of gradually.

**Laura.**

Yes—I guess it—

**Jim.**

Takes time!

**Laura.**

Yes . . .

**Jim.**

Say, you know something, Laura? (*Rises to sit on day-bed right.*) People are not so dreadful when you know them. That's what you have to remember! And everybody has problems, not just you but practically everybody has problems. You think of yourself as being the only one who is disappointed. But just look around you and what do you see—a lot of people just as disappointed as you are. You take me, for instance. Boy, when I left high school I thought I'd be a lot further along at this time than I am now. Say, you remember that wonderful write-up I had in "The Torch"?

**Laura.**

Yes, I do! (*She gets year-book from under pillow left of day-bed.*)

**Jim.**

Said I was bound to succeed in anything I went into! Holy Jeez! "The Torch"! (*She opens book, shows it to him and sits next to him on day-bed.*)

**Laura.**

Here you are in "The Pirates of Penzance"!

**Jim.**

"The Pirates"! "Oh better far to live and die under the brave black flag I fly!" I sang the lead in that operetta.

**Laura.**

So beautifully!

**Jim.**

Aw . . .

**Laura.**

Yes, yes—beautifully—beautifully!

**Jim.**

You heard me then, huh?

**Laura.**

I heard you all three times!

**Jim.**

No!

**Laura.**

Yes!

**Jim.**

You mean all three performances?

**Laura.**

Yes.

**Jim.**

What for?

**Laura.**

I—wanted to ask you to—autograph my program. (*Takes program from book*)

**Jim.**

Why didn't you ask me?

**Laura.**

You were always surrounded by your own friends so much that I never had a chance.

**Jim.**

Aw, you should have just come right up and said Here is my—

**Laura.**

Well. I—thought you might think I was—

**Jim.**

Thought I might think you was—what?

**Laura.**

Oh—

**Jim.**

(*with reflective relish*) Oh! Yeah. I was beleaguered by females in those days.

**Laura.**

You were terribly popular!

**Jim.**

Yeah . . .

**Laura.**

You had such a—friendly way—

**Jim.**

Oh, I was spoiled in high school.

**Laura.**

Everybody liked you!

**Jim.**

Including you?

**Laura.**

I—why yes. I did, too . . .

**Jim.**

Give me that program, Laura. (*She does so, and he signs it.*) There you are—better late than never!

**Laura.**

My—what a surprise!

**Jim.**

My signature's not worth very much right now. But maybe some day—it will increase in value! You know, being disappointed is one thing and being discouraged is something else. Well, I may be disappointed but I am not discouraged. Say, you finished high school?

**Laura.**

I made bad grades in my final examinations.

**Jim.**

You mean you dropped out?

**Laura.**

(*rises*) I didn't go back. (*Crosses right to menagerie. Jim lights cigarette still sitting on day-bed. Laura puts yearbook under menagerie. Rises, picks up unicorn—small glass object—her back to Jim. When she touches unicorn*) How is Emily Meisenbach getting along?

**Jim.**

That kraut-head!

**Laura.**

Why do you call her that?

**Jim.**
Because that's what she was.
**Laura.**
You're not still—going with her?
**Jim.**
Oh, I never even see her.
**Laura.**
It said in the Personal section that you were—engaged!
**Jim.**
Uh-huh. I know, but I wasn't impressed by that—propaganda!
**Laura.**
It wasn't—the truth?
**Jim.**
It was only true in Emily's optimistic opinion!
**Laura.**
Oh . . . (*Turns right of Jim. Jim lights a cigarette and leans indolently back on his elbows smiling at Laura with a warmth and charm which lights her inwardly with altar candles. She remains by the glass menagerie table and turns in her hands a piece of glass to cover her tumult.*)
**Jim.**
What have you done since high school? Huh?
**Laura.**
What?
**Jim.**
I said what have you done since high school?
**Laura.**
Nothing much.
**Jim.**
You must have been doing something all this time.
**Laura.**
Yes.
**Jim.**
Well, then, such as what?
**Laura.**
I took a business course at business college . . .
**Jim.**
You did? How did that work out?
**Laura.**
(*turns back to Jim*) Well, not very—well . . . I had to drop out, it gave me—indigestion . . .
**Jim.**
(*laughs gently*) What are you doing now?
**Laura.**
I don't do anything—much . . . Oh, please don't think

I sit around doing nothing! My glass collection takes a good deal of time. Glass is something you have to take good care of.

**Jim.**

What did you say—about glass?

**Laura.**

(*she clears her throat and turns away again, acutely shy*) Collection. I said—I have one.

**Jim.**

(*puts out cigarette. Abruptly*) Say! You know what I judge to be the trouble with you? (*Rises from day-bed and crosses right.*) Inferiority complex! You know what that is? That's what they call it when a fellow low-rates himself! Oh, I understand it because I had it, too. Uh-huh! Only my case was not as aggravated as yours seems to be. I had it until I took up public speaking and developed my voice, and learned that I had an aptitude for science. Do you know that until that time I never thought of myself as being outstanding in any way whatsoever!

**Laura.**

Oh, my!

**Jim.**

Now I've never made a regular study of it—(*Sits armchair right*)—mind you, but I have a friend who says I can analyze people better than doctors that make a profession of it. I don't claim that's necessarily true, but I can sure guess a person's psychology. Excuse me, Laura. (*Takes out gum*) I always take it out when the flavor is gone. I'll just wrap it in a piece of paper. (*Tears a piece of paper off the newspaper under candelabrum, wraps gum in it, crosses to day-bed, looks to see if Laura is watching. She isn't. Crosses around day-bed.*) I know how it is when you get it stuck on a shoe. (*Throws gum under day-bed, crosses around left of day-bed. Crosses right to Laura.*) Yep—that's what I judge to be your principal trouble. A lack of confidence in yourself as a person. Now I'm basing that fact on a number of your remarks and on certain observations I've made. For instance, that clumping you thought was so awful in high school. You say that you dreaded to go upstairs? You see what you did? You dropped out of school, you gave up an education all because of a little clump, which as far as I can see is practically non-existent! Oh, a little physical defect is all you have. It's hardly noticeable even! Magnified a thousand times by your imagination! You

know what my strong advice to you is? You've got to
think of yourself as *superior* in some way! (*Crosses left
to small table right of day-bed. Sits. Laura sits in armchair.*)

**Laura.**

In what way would I think?

**Jim.**

Why, man alive, Laura! Look around you a little and
what do you see? A world full of common people! All
of 'em born and all of 'em going to die! Now, which of
them has one-tenth of your strong points? Or mine? Or
anybody else's for that matter? You see, everybody excels
in some one thing. Well—some in many! You take me,
for instance. My interest happens to lie in electro-dy-
namics. I'm taking a course in radio engineering at night
school, on top of a fairly responsible job at the warehouse.
I'm taking that course *and* studying public speaking.

**Laura.**

Ohhhh. My!

**Jim.**

Because I believe in the future of television! I want to be
ready to go right up along with it. (*Rises, crosses right.*)
I'm planning to get in on the ground floor. Oh, I've al-
ready made the right connections. All that remains now
is for the industry itself to get under way—full steam!
You know, *knowledge*—ZSZZppp! *Money*—Zzzzzzpp!
*POWER!* Wham! That's the cycle democracy is built on!
(*Pause*) I guess you think I think a lot of myself!

**Laura.**

No—o-o-o, I don't.

**Jim.**

(*kneels at arm-chair right*) Well, now how about you?
Isn't there some one thing that you take more interest in
than anything else?

**Laura.**

Oh—yes . . .

**Jim.**

Well, then, such as what?

**Laura.**

Well, I do—as I said—have my—glass collection . . .

**Jim.**

Oh, you do. What kind of glass is it?

**Laura.**

(*takes glass ornament off shelf*) Little articles of it,
ornaments mostly. Most of them are little animals made

out of glass, the tiniest little animals in the world. Mother calls them the glass menagerie! Here's an example of one, if you'd like to see it! This is one of the oldest, it's nearly thirteen. (*Hands it to Jim*) Oh, be careful—if you breathe, it breaks!

**Jim.**

I'd better not take it. I'm pretty clumsy with things.

**Laura.**

Go on, I trust you with him! (*Jim takes horse.*) There— you're holding him gently! Hold him over the light, he loves the light! (*Jim holds horse up to light.*) See how the light shines through him?

**Jim.**

It sure does shine!

**Laura.**

I shouldn't be partial, but he is my favorite one.

**Jim.**

Say, what kind of a thing is this one supposed to be?

**Laura.**

Haven't you noticed the single horn on his forehead?

**Jim.**

Oh, a unicorn, huh?

**Laura.**

Mmmm-hmmmmm!

**Jim.**

Unicorns, aren't they extinct in the modern world?

**Laura.**

I know!

**Jim.**

Poor little fellow must feel kind of lonesome.

**Laura.**

Well, if he does he doesn't complain about it. He stays on a shelf with some horses that don't have horns and they all seem to get along nicely together.

**Jim.**

They do. Say, where will I put him?

**Laura.**

Put him on the table. (*Jim crosses to small table right of day-bed, puts unicorn on it.*) They all like a change of scenery once in a while!

**Jim.**

(*center, facing upstage, stretching arms*) They do. Hey! Look how big my shadow is when I stretch.

**Laura.**

(*crossing to left of day-bed*) Oh, oh, yes—it stretched across the ceiling!

**Jim.**

(*crosses to door right, exits, leaving door open, and stands on fire escape landing. Sings to music. [Popular record of day for dance-hall] When Jim opens door, music swells.*) It's stopped raining. Where does the music come from?

**Laura.**

From the Paradise Dance Hall across the alley.

**Jim.**

(*re-entering room, closing door right, crosses to Laura*) How about cutting the rug a little, Miss Wingfield? Or is your program filled up? Let me take a look at it. (*Crosses back center. Music, in dance-hall, goes into a waltz. Business here with imaginary dance-program card.*) Oh, say! Every dance is taken! I'll just scratch some of them out. Ahhhh, a waltz! (*Crosses to Laura*)

**Laura.**

I can't dance!

**Jim.**

There you go with that inferiority stuff!

**Laura.**

I've never danced in my life!

**Jim.**

Come on, try!

**Laura.**

Oh, but I'd step on you!

**Jim.**

Well, I'm not made out of glass.

**Laura.**

How—how do we start?

**Jim.**

You hold your arms out a little.

**Laura.**

Like this?

**Jim.**

A little bit higher. (*Takes Laura in arms*) That's right. Now don't tighten up, that's the principal thing about it, just relax.

**Laura.**

It's hard not to.

**Jim.**

Okay.

**Laura.**

I'm afraid you can't budge me.

**Jim.**

(*dances around left of day-bed slowly*) What do you bet I can't?

**Laura.**

Goodness, yes, you can!

**Jim.**

Let yourself go, now, Laura, just let yourself go.

**Laura.**

I'm—

**Jim.**

Come on!

**Laura.**

Trying!

**Jim.**

Not so stiff now—easy does it!

**Laura.**

I know, but I'm—!

**Jim.**

Come on! Loosen your backbone a little! (*When they get to upstage corner of day-bed—so that the audience will not see him lift her—Jim's arm tightens around her waist and he swings her around center with her feet off floor about three complete turns before they hit the small table right of day-bed. Music swells as Jim lifts her.*) There we go! (*Jim knocks glass horse off table*) (*Music fades*)

**Laura.**

Oh, it doesn't matter—

**Jim.**

(*picks horse up*) We knocked the little glass horse over.

**Laura.**

Yes.

**Jim.**

(*hands unicorn to Laura*) Is he broken?

**Laura.**

Now he's just like all the other horses.

**Jim.**

You mean he lost his—?

**Laura.**

He's lost his horn. It doesn't matter. Maybe it's a blessing in disguise.

**Jim.**

Gee, I bet you'll never forgive me. I bet that was your favorite piece of glass.

**Laura.**

Oh, I don't have favorites—(*Pause*)—much. It's no tragedy. Glass breaks so easily. No matter how careful you are. The traffic jars the shelves and things fall off them.

**Jim.**

Still I'm awfully sorry that I was the cause of it.

**Laura.**

I'll just imagine he had an operation. The horn was removed to make him feel less—freakish! (*Crosses left, sits on small table*) Now he will feel more at home with the other horses, the ones who don't have horns . . .

**Jim.**

(*sits on arm of arm-chair right, faces Laura*) I'm glad to see that you have a sense of humor. You know—you're —different than anybody else I know? Do you mind me telling you that? I mean it. You make me feel sort of— I don't know how to say it! I'm usually pretty good at expressing things, but—this is something I don't know how to say! Did anybody ever tell you that you were pretty? (*Rises, crosses to Laura*) Well, you are! And in a different way from anyone else. And all the nicer because of the difference. Oh boy, I wish that you were my sister. I'd teach you to have confidence in yourself. Being different is nothing to be ashamed of. Because other people aren't such wonderful people. They're a hundred times one thousand. You're one times one! They walk all over the earth. You just stay here. They're as common as—weeds, but—you, well you're—*Blue Roses!*

**Laura.**

But blue is—wrong for—roses . . .

**Jim.**

It's right for you!—You're pretty!

**Laura.**

In what respect am I pretty?

**Jim.**

In all respects—your eyes—your hair. Your hands are pretty! You think I'm saying this because I'm invited to dinner and have to be nice. Oh, I could do that! I could say lots of things without being sincere. But I'm talking to you sincerely. I happened to notice you had this inferiority complex that keeps you from feeling comfortable with people. Somebody ought to build your confidence up—way up! and make you proud instead of shy and turning away and—blushing— (*Jim lifts Laura up on small table on "way up".*) Somebody—ought to— (*Lifts her down*) Somebody ought to—kiss you, Laura! (*They kiss. Jim releases her and turns slowly away, crossing a little down right. As Jim turns away, music ends. Then, quietly, to himself:*) Gee, I shouldn't have done that—That was way off the beam. (*Gives way down right. Turns to Laura. Laura sits on small table.*) Would you care for a cigarette? You don't smoke, do you? How about a mint? Peppermint—Life-Saver? My pocket's a regular drug-store . . . Laura, you know, if I had a sister like you, I'd do the same thing as Tom. I'd bring fellows home to meet you. Maybe I shouldn't be saying this. That may not have been the idea in having me over. But what if it was? There's nothing wrong with that.—The only trouble is that in my case—I'm not in a position to—I can't ask for your number and say I'll phone. I can't call up next week end—ask for a date. I thought I had better explain the situation in case you—misunderstood and I hurt your feelings . . .

**Laura.**

(*faintly*) You—won't call—again?

**Jim.**

(*crossing to the right of day-bed, and sitting*) No, I can't. You see, I've—got strings on me. Laura, I've been going steady! I go out all the time with a girl named Betty. Oh, she's a nice quiet home girl like you and Catholic and Irish, and in a great many ways we—get along fine. I met her last summer on a moonlight boat trip up the river to Alton, on the *Majestic*. Well—right away from the start it was—love! Oh boy, being in love has made a new man of me! The power of love is pretty tremendous! Love is something that—changes the whole world. It happened that Betty's aunt took sick and she got a wire and had to go to Centralia. So naturally when Tom asked me to dinner—naturally I accepted the invitation, not knowing—I mean—not knowing. I wish that you would —say something. (*Laura gives Jim unicorn.*) What are you doing that for? You mean you want me to have him? What for?

**Laura.**

A—souvenir. (*She crosses right to menagerie. Jim rises.*)

from
# OH DAD, POOR DAD, MAMA'S HUNG YOU IN THE CLOSET AND I'M FEELIN' SO SAD
by Arthur Kopit

Scene 2
ROSALIE, JONATHAN

"I ask you," says Madame Rosepettle, Poor Dad's wife, at the end of the play, "what is the meaning of this?" Audiences and actors have also asked the question, for the play is a potpourri of serious notions, half-stated themes, comic turns, and sensational revelations stitched together haphazardly, like a crazy quilt. Yet the audiences have enjoyed *Oh Dad . . .* , and the actors have discovered that much of the play—in individual scenes, at least—comes surprisingly clear when played for truth of character and situation. The scene below lends itself particularly well to this truthful approach.

The setting is a lavish hotel room on a Caribbean island. There are doors, left, to the hallway, and, right, to a bedroom. A pair of French windows opens onto a balcony. In the bedroom, though they cannot be seen, are Madame Rosepettle and her husband; he is dead, stuffed, and hung in the closet. On stage are Madame Rosepettle's son, Jonathan, "a boy seventeen years old but dressed like a child of ten," and Rosalie, "a girl some two years older than he and dressed in sweet girlish pink." On the balcony is a group of plants—Venus'-flytraps, flourishing and well-fed —and upstage, on a table, is a fishbowl occupied by Rosalinda, a carnivorous fish that eats only Siamese cats.

Rosalie.
But if you've been here two weeks, why haven't I seen you?
Jonathan.
I've . . . I've been in my room.

74

**Rosalie.**

All the time?

**Jonathan.**

Yes. . . . All the time.

**Rosalie.**

Well, you must get out sometimes. I mean, sometimes you simply must get out. You just couldn't stay inside all the time . . . could you?

**Jonathan.**

Yyyyyes.

**Rosalie.**

You never get out at all? I mean, never at all?

**Jonathan.**

Some-sometimes I do go out on the porch. M-Ma-Mother has some . . . Venus'-flytraps which she bra-brought back from the rain forest of Va-Va-Va-Venezuela. They're va-very rrrrrare and need a . . . a lot of sunshine. Well sir, she ka-keeps them on the porch and I . . . I feed them. Twice a day, too.

**Rosalie.**

Oh.

**Jonathan.**

Ma-Ma-Mother says everyone must have a vocation in life. (*With a slight nervous laugh.*) I ga-guess that's . . . my job.

**Rosalie.**

I don't think I've ever met anyone before who's fed . . . uh . . . Venus'-flytraps.

**Jonathan.**

Ma-Ma-Mother says I'm va-very good at it. That's what she . . . says. I'm va-very good at it. I . . . don't know . . . if . . . I am, but . . . that's . . . what she says so I . . . guess I am.

**Rosalie.**

Well, uh, what . . . what do you . . . feed them? You see, I've never met anyone before who's fed Venus'-flytraps so . . . that's why I don't know what . . . you're supposed to feed them.

**Jonathan.**

(*Happy that she asked*) Oh, I fa-feed them . . . l-l-lots of things. Ga-ga-green peas, chicken feathers, rubber bands. They're . . . not very fussy. They're . . . nice, that way. Ma-Ma-Mother says it it it ga-gives me a feeling of a-co-co-complishment. Iffffff you would . . . like to to see them I . . . could show them to you. It's . . . almost

fa-feeding time. It is, and . . . and I could show them to
you.

**Rosalie.**

No. That's all right. (*Jonathan looks away, hurt.*) Well,
how about later?

**Jonathan.**

Do-do-do you ra-really wwwwwwant to see them?

**Rosalie.**

Yes. Yes I really think I would like to see them . . . later.
If you'll show them to me then, I'd really like that.
(*Jonathan looks at her and smiles. There is an awkward
silence while he stares at her thankfully.*) I still don't
understand why you never go out. How can you just sit
in—?

**Jonathan.**

Sometimes, when I'm on the porch . . . I do other things.

**Rosalie.**

*What?*

**Jonathan.**

Sa-sa-sometimes, when I'm . . on the porch, you know,
when I'm on the porch? Sssssssssome-times I . . . do *other
things,* too.

**Rosalie.**

What sort of things? (*Jonathan giggles.*) What sort of
things do you do?

**Jonathan.**

Other things.

**Rosalie.**

(*Coyly*) What do you mean, "Other things"?

**Jonathan.**

Other things besides feeding my mother's plants. Other
things besides that. That's what I mean. Other things
besides that.

**Rosalie.**

What kind of things . . . *in particular?*

**Jonathan.**

Oh, watching.

**Rosalie.**

Watching?

**Jonathan.**

Yes. Like . . . watching.

**Rosalie.**

Watching what? (*He giggles.*) *Watching what!?*

**Jonathan.**

You. (*Short pause. She inches closer to him on the couch.*)

**Rosalie.**

What do you mean . . . watching me?

**Jonathan.**

I . . . watch you from the porch. That's what I mean. I watch you from the porch. I watch you a lot, too. Every day. It's . . . it's the truth. I . . . I swear it . . . is. I watch you ev-ry day. Do you believe me?

**Rosalie.**

Of course I believe you, Albert. Why—

**Jonathan.**

Jonathan!

**Rosalie.**

What?

**Jonathan.**

Jonathan. Ca-ca-call me Ja-Jonathan. That's my na-na-na—

**Rosalie.**

But your mother said your name was—

**Jonathan.**

Nooooo! Call . . . me Jonathan. Pa-pa-please?

**Rosalie.**

All right . . . Jonathan.

**Jonathan.**

(*Excitedly*) You *do* believe me! You rrrrreally do believe me! I-I-I can tell!

**Rosalie.**

Of course I believe you. Why shouldn't—?

**Jonathan.**

You want me to tell you how I watch you? You want me to tell you? I'll bet you'll na-never guess.

**Rosalie.**

How?

**Jonathan.**

*Guess.*

**Rosalie.**

(*Ponders*) Through a telescope?

**Jonathan.**

How did you guess?

**Rosalie.**

I . . . I don't know. I was just joking. I didn't really think that was—

**Jonathan.**

I'll bet everyone watches you through a telescope. I'll bet

everyone you go out with watches you through a telescope.
That's what I'll bet.

**Rosalie.**

No. Not at all.

**Jonathan.**

Well, that's how I watch you. Through a telescope.

**Rosalie.**

I never would have guessed that—

**Jonathan.**

I thought you were . . . ga-going to say I . . . I watch
you with . . . with love in my eyes or some . . . thing like
that. I didn't think you were going to guess that I . . .
watch you through a telescope. I didn't think you were
going to guess that I wa-watch you through a telescope
on the fa-first guess, anyway. Not on the *first guess*.

**Rosalie.**

Well, it was just a guess.

**Jonathan.**

(*Hopefully*) Do you watch *me* through a telescope?

**Rosalie.**

I never knew where your room was.

**Jonathan.**

Now you know. Now will you watch me?

**Rosalie.**

Well I . . . don't have a telescope.

**Jonathan.**

(*Getting more elated and excited*) You can make one.
That's how I got mine. I made it. Out of lenses and
tubing. That's all you need. Lenses and tubing. Do you
have any lenses?

**Rosalie.**

No.

**Jonathan.**

Do you have any tubing?

**Rosalie.**

No.

**Jonathan.**

Oh. (*Pause.*) Well, would you like me to tell you how
I made mine in case you find some lenses and tubing?
Would you like that?

**Rosalie.**

(*Disinterestedly*) Sure, Jonathan. I think that would be
nice.

**Jonathan.**

Well, I made it out of lenses and tubing. The lenses I had
because Ma-Ma-Mother gave me a set of lenses so I

could see my stamps better. I have a fabulous collection of stamps, as well as a fantastic collection of coins and a simply unbelievable collection of books. Well sir, Ma-Ma-Mother gave me these lenses so I could see my stamps better. She suspected that some were fake so she gave me the lenses so I might be . . . able to see. You see? Well, sir, I happen to have nearly a billion sta-stamps. So far I've looked closely at 1,352,769. I've discovered three actual fakes! Number 1,352,767 was a fake. Number 1,352,768 was a fake, and number 1,352,769 was a fake. They were stuck together. Ma-Mother made me feed them im-mediately to her flytraps. Well . . . (*He whispers.*) one day, when Mother wasn't looking . . . that is, when she was out, I heard an airplane flying. An airplane . . . somewhere . . . far away. It wasn't very loud, but still I heard it. An airplane. Flying . . . somewhere, far away. And I ran outside to the porch so that I might see what it looked like. The airplane. With hundreds of people inside it. Hundreds and hundreds and hundreds of people. And I thought to myself, if I could just see . . . if I could just see what they looked like, the people, sitting at their windows looking out . . . and flying. If I could see . . . *just once* . . . if I could see *just once* what they looked like . . . then I might . . . know what I . . . what I . . . (*Slight pause.*) So I . . . built a telescope in case the plane ever . . . came back again. The tubing came from an old blowgun (*He reaches behind the bureau and produces a huge blowgun, easily a foot larger than he.*) Mother brought back from her last hunting trip to Zanzibar. The lenses were the lenses she had given me for my stamps. So I built it. My telescope. A telescope so I might be able to see. And . . . (*He walks out to the porch.*) and . . . and I *could* see! I could! I COULD! I really could. For miles and miles I could see. For miles and miles and *miles!* (*He begins to lift it up to look through but stops, for some reason, before he's brought it up to his eye.*) Only . . . (*He hands it to Rosalie. She takes it eagerly and scans the horizon and the sky. She hands it back to him.*)

**Rosalie.**

(*With annoyance*) There's nothing out there to see.

**Jonathan.**

(*Sadly.*) I know. That's the trouble. You take the time to build a telescope that can sa-see for miles, then there's nothing out there to see. Ma-Mother says it's a lesson in Life. (*Pause.*) But I'm not sorry I built my telescope. And you know why? Because I saw you. Even if I didn't see anything else, I did see you. And . . . and I'm . . . very glad. (*Rosalie moves slightly closer to him on the couch. She moistens her lips.*) I . . . I remember, you were standing across the way in your penthouse garden playing blind man's buff with ten little children. (*After a short pause, fearfully.*) Are . . . are they by any chance . . . yours?

**Rosalie.**

(*Sweetly*) Oh, I'm not married.

**Jonathan.**

Oh!

**Rosalie.**

I'm a baby sitter.

**Jonathan.**

(*With obvious relief*) Oh.

**Rosalie.**

I work for the people who own the penthouse.

**Jonathan.**

I've never seen them around.

**Rosalie.**

I've never seen them either. They're never home. They just mail me a check every week and tell me to make sure I keep the children's names straight.

**Jonathan.**

If you could tell me which way they went I could find them with my telescope. It can see for miles.

**Rosalie.**

They must love children very much. I'll bet she's a marvelous woman. (*Pause.*) There's going to be another one, too! Another child is coming! I got a night letter last night.

**Jonathan.**

By airplane?

**Rosalie.**

I don't know.

**Jonathan.**

I bet it was. I can't see at night. Ma-Mother can but I can't. I'll bet that's when the planes fly.

**Rosalie.**

(*Coyly*) If you like, I'll read you the letter. I have it with me. (*She unbuttons the top of her blouse and turns around in a coquettish manner to take the letter from her brassiere. Reading.*) "Have had another child. Sent it yesterday. Will arrive tomorrow. Call it Cynthia."

**Jonathan.**

That will make eleven. That's an awful lot of children to take care of. I'll bet it must be wonderful.

**Rosalie.**

They do pay very well.

**Jonathan.**

They pay you?

**Rosalie.**

Of course . . . What did you think? (*Pause. Softly, seductively.*) Jonathan? (*He does not answer but seems lost in thought. With a feline purr.*) Jonathan?

**Jonathan.**

Yyyyyes?

**Rosalie.**

It gets very lonesome over there. The children go to sleep early and the parents are never home so I'm always alone. Perhaps . . . well Jonathan, I thought that perhaps you might . . . visit me.

**Jonathan.**

Well . . . well . . . well, you . . . you see . . . I . . . I . . .

**Rosalie.**

We could spend the evenings together . . . at my place. It gets so lonesome there, you know what I mean? I mean, I don't know what to do. I get so lonesome there.

**Jonathan.**

Ma-ma-ma-maybe you . . . you can . . . come over . . . here? Maybe you you can do . . . that.

**Rosalie.**

Why are you trembling so?

**Jonathan.**

I'm . . . I'm . . . I'm . . . I'm . . .

**Rosalie.**

Are you afraid?

**Jonathan.**

Nnnnnnnnnnnnnnnnnnnnno. Whaaaaaaaaaa-why . . . should I . . . be . . . afraid?

**Rosalie.**

Then why won't you come visit me?

**Jonathan.**

I . . . I . . . I . . . I . . .

**Rosalie.**

I don't think you're allowed to go out. That's what I think.

**Jonathan.**

Nnnn-o. I . . . I can . . . can . . . can . . .

**Rosalie.**

Why can't you go out, Jonathan? I want to know.

**Jonathan.**

Nnnnnnnnn—

**Rosalie.**

Tell me, Jonathan!

**Jonathan.**

I . . . I . . .

**Rosalie.**

I said I want to know! *Tell me.*

**Jonathan.**

I . . . I don't . . . know. I don't know why. I mean, I've . . . nnnnnnnever really thought . . . about going out. I . . . guess it's . . . just natural for me to . . . stay inside. (*He laughs nervously as if that explained everything.*) You see . . . I've got so much to do. I mean, all my sssssstamps and . . . ca-coins and books. The pa-pa-plane might fffffly overhead while I was was going downstairs. And then thhhhere are . . . the plants ta-to feeeeeeed. And I enjoy vvvery much wa . . . watching you and all yyyyy-your chil-dren. I've . . . really got so ma-many things . . . to . . . do. Like . . . like my future, for instance. Ma-Mother says I'm going to be great. That's . . . that's . . . that's what she . . . says. I'm going to be great. I sssswear. Of course, she doesn't know ex-actly what I'm . . . going to be great *in* . . . so she sits every afternoon for . . . for two hours and thinks about it. Na-na-naturally I've . . . got to be here when she's thinking in case she . . . thinks of the answer. Otherwise she might forget and I'd never know . . . what I'm ga-going to be great in. You . . . see what I mean? I mean, I've . . . I've gggggot so many things to do I . . . just couldn't possibly get *anything* done if I ever . . . went . . . out-side. (*There is a silence. Jonathan stares at Rosalie as if he were hoping that might answer her question sufficiently. She stares back at him as if she knows there is more.*) Besides, Mother locks the front door.

**Rosalie.**

I thought so.

**Jonathan.**

No! You-you don't understand. It's not what you think. She doesn't lock the door, to ka-ka-keep me in, which would be malicious. She . . . locks the door so I can't get out, which is for my own good and therefore . . . beneficent.

**Clock.**

(*From the master bedroom*) Cuckoo! Cuckoo! Cuckoo!

**Rosalie.**

What's that?

**Jonathan.**

(*Fearfully*) A warning.

**Rosalie.**

What do you mean, a warning?

**Jonathan.**

A warning that you have to go. Your time is up.

**Rosalie.**

My time is what?

**Jonathan.**

Your time is up. You have to go. Now. At once. Right away. You can't stay any longer. You've got to go!

**Rosalie.**

Why?

**Jonathan.**

(*Puzzled: as if this were the first time the question had ever occurred to him*) I don't really know.

**Clock.**

(*Louder*) Cuckoo! Cuckoo! Cuckoo! (*Jonathan freezes in terror. Rosalie looks at him calmly.*)

**Rosalie.**

Why did your mother ask me to come up here?

**Jonathan.**

What?

**Rosalie.**

Why did your mother ask me—?

**Jonathan.**

So I . . . I could meet you.

**Rosalie.**

Then why didn't you ask me yourself? Something's wrong around here, Jonathan. I don't understand why you didn't ask me yourself.

**Jonathan.**

Ma-Mother's so much better at those things.

**Clock.**

(*Very loudly*) CUCKOO! CUCKOO! CUCKOO!

**Jonathan.**

You've got to get out of here! That's the third warning. (*He starts to push her toward the door.*)

**Rosalie.**

Will you call me on the phone?

**Jonathan.**

Please, you've got to go!

**Rosalie.**

Instead of your mother telling me to come, will you come and get me yourself? Will you at least call me? Wave to me?

**Jonathan.**

Yes-yes—I'll do that. Now get out of here!

**Rosalie.**

I want you to promise to come and see me again.

**Jonathan.**

Get out!

**Rosalie.**

(*Coyly*) Promise me.

**Jonathan.**

GET OUT! (*He pushes her toward the door.*)

**Rosalie.**

Why do you keep looking at that door?

**Jonathan.**

(*Almost in tears*) Please.

**Rosalie.**

Why do you keep looking at that door?

**Jonathan.**

*Please!* You've got to go before it's too late!

**Rosalie.**

There's something very wrong here. I want to see what's behind that door. (*She starts toward the master bedroom. Jonathan throws his arms about her legs and collapses at her feet, his face buried against her thighs.*)

**Jonathan.**

(*Sobbing uncontrollably*) I love you. (*Rosalie stops dead in her tracks and stares down at Jonathan.*)

**Rosalie.**

What did you say?

**Jonathan.**

I-I-I lllllllove you. I love you, I love you, I love you I— (*The Cuckoo Clock screams, cackles, and goes out of its mind, its call ending in a crazed, strident rasp as if it had broken all its springs, screws, and innards. The door to the master bedroom opens. Madame Rosepettle appears.*)

**Jonathan.**

(*Weakly*) *Too late.*

# CHAPTER II

## 'ACTING MEANS BELIEVING

Scenes in which the actor exercises his memory, emotional memory, and imagination to act "as if it were real."

Always and forever, when you are on the stage, you must play yourself. But it will be in an infinite variety of combinations of objectives, and given circumstances which you have prepared for your part, and which have been smelted in the furnace of your emotional memory.

Constantin Stanislavski,
*An Actor Prepares*

Napoleon was able to imagine himself an emperor, and, circumstances conspiring with him, he became one. His enemies thought they were belittling him by calling him an actor.

Herbert Beerbohm Tree,
*Thoughts and Afterthoughts*

from
# THE DARK AT THE TOP OF THE STAIRS
by William Inge

Act II
SAMMY

Sammy Goldenbaum's mother is in the movies; his father,
who was also an actor, is dead; and Sammy has spent his
life in military academies and summer camps. He is seventeen, "darkly handsome, with lustrous black hair, black
eyes, and a captivating smile." When he turns up as the
blind date of a shy little girl in a midwestern town, he
seems "a little foreign, . . . a Persian prince, strayed from
his native kingdom. But he has become adept over the
years in adapting himself, and he shows an eagerness to
make friends and to be liked." Indeed, while he waits for
his date to come downstairs, he rattles talk at her aunt and
mother—talk about the academy, his mother, and himself. He explains carefully that, though his mother is not
Jewish, he is—at least, his father was and he has his
father's name and looks. The women quickly say that this
has nothing to do with what he really is, as a person, and
Sammy is relieved. Later, however, at the country club
dance, a matron stops him from dancing with her daughter
and tells him that Jews are not allowed in the club. Sammy's date, shy because this is her first time at a dance and
certain that Sammy is ashamed of her for being a wall-
flower, runs home—and he thinks that she is ashamed of
him. That night he kills himself.

The speech below is a part of Sammy's first conversation with Reenie, his blind date. The setting is Reenie's
home, a comfortable, solidly respectable family house in
Oklahoma City in the early 1920's. With Sammy and
Reenie are her mother, her aunt and uncle, her little
brother, and another young couple bound for the dance.

**Sammy.**

It's awfully nice of you to let me take you to the party. I know just how a girl feels, going out with some crazy guy she doesn't even know.

§ **Reenie.**

Oh . . . that's all right. After all, you don't know anything about me, either. §

**Sammy.**

You know, I've never been to many parties, have you?

§ **Reenie.**

Not many. §

**Sammy.**

I always worry that maybe people aren't going to like me, when I go to a party. Isn't that crazy? Do you ever get kind of a sick feeling in the pit of your stomach when you dread things? Gee, I wouldn't want to miss a party for anything. But every time I go to one, I have to reason with myself to keep from feeling that the whole world's against me. See, I've spent almost my whole life in military academies. My mother doesn't have a place for me, where she lives. She . . . she just doesn't know what else to do with me. But you mustn't misunderstand about my mother. She's really a very lovely person. I guess every boy thinks his mother is very beautiful, but my mother really is. She tells me in every letter she writes how sorry she is that we can't be together more, but she has to think of her work. One time we were together, though. She met me in San Francisco once, and we were together for two whole days. She let me take her to dinner and to a show and to dance. Just like we were sweethearts. It was the most wonderful time I ever had. And then I had to go back to the old military academy. Every time I walk into the barracks, I get kind of a depressed feeling. It's got hard stone walls. Pictures of generals hanging all over . . . oh, they're very fine gentlemen, but they all look so kind of hard-boiled and stern . . . you know what I mean. (*Cora and Lottie stand together, listening to Sammy's speech with motherly expressions. Flirt is bored. Punky is half asleep, and now he gives a sudden, audible yawn that startles everyone*) Well, gee! I guess I've bored you enough, telling you about myself.

from
# A LOSS OF ROSES
by William Inge

Act II, scene 3
LILA

The play, William Inge wrote, "deals with individuals who, like people today seeking an inner peace in the midst of terrifying social change, must come to deal with evil in their lives, either to be destroyed or find themselves strengthened." The leading characters are Helen Baird, a widowed mother who has labored not to love her son too much, not to ask him to take the place of his father; the son, whose personality has been warped all the same, for he is devoted to his mother and feels that she has never loved him; and Lila, a road-show actress, who comes to stay for a time in the mother's home. Lila "is an extraordinarily beautiful woman of thirty-two, blond and voluptuous, still with the form and vitality of a girl. . . . One feels immediately a sincerity about her and a generosity of spirit." When Lila is afraid and unhappy, she needs someone, and for the protection a man can give her she gives of herself without thought of the hurt that may follow. She gives herself to her friend's son, though he is ten years younger than she, and she is crushed by the revulsion he feels for her afterward.

*A Loss of Roses* was not a success on Broadway. The speeches reprinted here and on page 183 are taken from a revised version of the play which Inge wrote after the New York production had closed. They are speeches of recollection and help to explain Lila as she is now.

The setting is a small house in a town outside Kansas City. It is morning. Lila, standing on the front porch, sees a mother leading a child to her first day of school.

**Lila.**

I remember *my* first day at school. Mother took me by
the hand and *I* carried a bouquet of roses, too. Mama
had let me pick the loveliest roses I could find in the
garden, and the teacher thanked me for them. Then
Mama left me and I felt kinda scared, 'cause I'd never
been any place before without her; but she told me
Teacher would be Mama to me at school and would treat
me as nice as she did. So I took my seat with all the
other kids, their faces so strange and new to me. And
I started talking with a little boy across the aisle. I din
know it was against the rules. But Teacher came back
and slapped me, so hard that I cried, and I ran to the
door 'cause I wanted to run home to Mama quick as I
could. But Teacher grabbed me by the hand and pulled
me back to my seat. She said I was too big a girl to be
running home to Mama and I had to learn to take my
punishment when I broke the rules. But I still cried.
I told Teacher I wanted back my roses. But she wouldn't
give them to me. She shook her finger and said, when I
gave away lovely presents, I couldn't expect to get them
back . . . I guess I never learned that lesson very well.
There's so many things I still want back.

from
THE GLASS MENAGERIE
by Tennessee Williams

Two Monologues from Act I, scene 6 and Act II, scene 7
TOM, AMANDA

"Memory takes a lot of poetic license," Tennessee Williams says in his introduction to *The Glass Menagerie*. "It omits some details; others are exaggerated, according to the emotional value of the articles it touches, for memory is seated predominantly in the heart." Here are two monologues, two memories, from the play which itself is a study in memory and contains many fine reflective solo speeches. Tom's monologue is one of several narrations which link and frame the scenes. During these speeches, Tom stands beside the fire escape, overlooking the alley beside the tenement. (For introductory notes about *The Glass Menagerie*, see page 59.)

The setting is the tenement flat—a living room downstage and, above it, curtained off, a small dining room.

**Tom.**

(*enters down right and stands leaning against grille-work, with cigarette, wearing merchant sailor coat and cap*) Across the alley was the Paradise Dance Hall. Evenings in spring they'd open all the doors and windows and the music would come outside. Sometimes they'd turn out all the lights except for a large glass sphere that hung from the ceiling. It would turn slowly about and filter the dusk with delicate rainbow colors. Then the orchestra would play a waltz or a tango, something that had a slow and sensuous rhythm. The young couples would come outside, to the relative privacy of the alley. You could see them kissing behind ashpits and telephone poles. This was the compensation for lives that passed like mine, without change or adventure. Changes and adventure, however, were imminent this year. They were waiting around the corner for all these dancing kids. Suspended

91

in the mist over Berchtesgaden, caught in the folds of Chamberlain's umbrella—In Spain there was Guernica! Here there was only hot swing music and liquor, dance halls, bars, and movies, and sex that hung in the gloom like a chandelier and flooded the world with brief, deceptive rainbows . . . While these unsuspecting kids danced to "Dear One, the World Is Waiting for the Sunrise." All the world was really waiting for bombardments.

## SECOND MONOLOGUE

Amanda's recollection of the gay times of her girlhood comes as she is getting ready to entertain her daughter's first "gentleman caller." She has dressed herself in an old ball gown and, suddenly filled with nostalgia, she calls for Laura to come and look at her.

**Amanda.**

(*off*) I found an old dress in the trunk. But what do you know? I had to do a lot to it but it broke my heart when I had to let it out. Now, Laura, just look at your mother. Oh no! Laura, come look at me now! (*Enters dining-room left door. Comes down through living-room curtain to living-room center, stands holding flowers*) * * * It used to be [lovely]. It used to be. It had a lot of flowers on it, but they got awful tired so I had to take them all off. I led the cotillion in this dress years ago. I won the cake-walk twice at Sunset Hill, and I wore it to the Governor's ball in Jackson. You should have seen your mother. You should have seen your mother how she just sashayed around (*Crossing around left of day-bed back to center*) the ballroom, just like that. I had it on the day I met your father. I had malaria fever, too. The change of climate from East Tennessee to the Delta—weakened my resistance. Not enough to be dangerous, just enough to make me restless and giddy. Oh, it was lovely. Invitations poured in from all over. My mother said, "You can't go any place because you have a fever. You have to stay in bed." I said I wouldn't and I took quinine and kept on going and going. Dances every evening and long rides in the country in the afternoon and picnics. That country—that country—so lovely—so lovely in May, all lacy with dogwood and simply flooded with jonquils. My mother said, "You can't bring any more jonquils in this house."

I said, "I will," and I kept on bringing them in anyhow. Whenever I saw them I said, "Wait a minute, I see jonquils," and I'd make my gentlemen callers get out of the carriage and help me gather some. To tell you the truth, Laura, it got to be a kind of a joke. "Look out," they'd say, "here comes that girl and we'll have to spend the afternoon picking jonquils." My mother said, "You can't bring any more jonquils in the house, there aren't any more vases to hold them." "That's quite all right," I said, "I can hold some myself." Malaria fever, your father and jonquils. (*Amanda puts jonquils in Laura's lap and goes out on to fire-escape landing*) (*Thunder heard*) I hope they get here before it starts to rain. I gave your brother a little extra change so he and Mr. O'Connor could take the service car home.

from
# DEATH OF A SALESMAN
by Arthur Miller

Requiem
LINDA

The tragedy of Willy Loman (see comments on page 135) ends with a brief epilogue which Arthur Miller calls "Requiem." Willy has killed himself by smashing up his car. Still dreaming, he had hoped that his insurance money would give his son Biff the start he needed to become the great man that Willy insisted always that he must be.

The family and an old friend have watched Willy's burial and spoken their farewells. Gradually they move away from the grave, but Linda, Willy's wife, wants to stay a moment longer. She sits at the graveside.

**Linda.**
I'll be with you in a minute. Go on, Charley. I want to, just for a minute. I never had a chance to say good-by. (*Linda sits there, summoning herself.*) Forgive me, dear. I can't cry. I don't know what it is, but I can't cry. I don't understand it. Why did you ever do that? Help me, Willy, I can't cry. It seems to me that you're just on another trip. I keep expecting you. Willy, dear, I can't cry. Why did you do it? I search and search and I search, and I can't understand it, Willy. I made the last payment on the house today, dear. And there'll be nobody home. (*A sob rises in her throat*) We're free and clear. (*Sobbing more fully, released*) We're free. (*Biff comes slowly toward her*) We're free . . . We're free . . . (*Linda sobs quietly* [*and turns to walk off right to her sons.*])

from
# I REMEMBER MAMA
by John van Druten

**Two Monologues and a Scene from Acts I and II
KATRIN, MAMA**

Like *The Glass Menagerie* (page 59), "the play is
memory"—but in *I Remember Mama,* memory recalls
to life a house that was warmed by love and a family
whose members not only managed not to destroy each
other but liked each other. These memories were the subject
of Kathryn Forbes' collection of short stories, *Mama's
Bank Account,* in which she told of her childhood in San
Francisco and of her parents, aunts, and uncles who had
come to America from Norway. When John van Druten
set out to weave the stories into a play, he chose Kathryn
(Katrin) to be his narrator so that the house, the family,
and the San Francisco on his stage would be seen as she
saw them in her memory.

At the opening of the play, Katrin, a young woman, begins to read from a manuscript—the first of her stories
about her family. As she reads, the places she describes
appear on the stage, and the people—Mama, Papa, Katrin's
brothers and sisters, and the rest. Katrin leaves her desk,
seems to grow younger, and joins the others. Now and
again she returns to read the beginning of another chapter
in the manuscript and to draw from her memory another
episode in the story of her family.

The first of Katrin's narrations is reprinted below, followed by a narration from Act II and the scene it introduces, a scene in which Mama, like Katrin, remembers.

**Katrin.**

(*Reading*) "For as long as I could remember, the house
on Steiner Street had been home. Papa and Mama had
both been born in Norway, but they came to San Fran-

cisco because Mama's sisters were here. All of us were born here. Nels, the oldest and the only boy—my sister Christine—and the littlest sister, Dagmar." (*She puts down the manuscript and looks out front*) It's funny, but when I look back, I always see Nels and Christine and myself looking almost as we do today. I guess that's because the people you see all the time stay the same age in your head. Dagmar's different. She was always the baby—so I see her as a baby. Even Mama—it's funny, but I always see Mama as around forty. She couldn't *always* have been forty. (*She picks up her manuscript and starts to read again*) "Besides us, there was our boarder, Mr. Hyde. Mr. Hyde was an Englishman who had once been an actor, and Mama was very impressed by his flowery talk and courtly manners. He used to read aloud to us in the evenings. But first and foremost, I remember Mama." * * * "It wasn't very often that I could get Mama to talk—about herself, or her life in the old country, or what she felt about things. You had to catch her unawares, or when she had nothing to do, which was very, very seldom. I don't think I can ever remember seeing Mama unoccupied." (*Laying down the manuscript and looking out front*) I do remember one occasion, though. It was the day before Dagmar came home from the hospital. And as we left, Mama suggested treating me to an ice-cream soda. (*She rises, gets her hat from beside her— a schoolgirl hat—puts it on and crosses center while she speaks the next lines*) She had never done such a thing before, and I remember how proud it made me feel—just to sit and talk to her quietly like a grown-up person. It was a kind of special *treat*-moment in my life that I'll always remember—quite apart from the soda, which was *wonderful.* (*She has reached center stage now. Mama has come from between the curtains, and starts down the steps*)

**Mama.**

Katrin, you like we go next door, and I treat you to an ice-cream soda?

**Katrin.**

(*Young now, and overcome*) Mama—do you mean it?

**Mama.**

Sure. We celebrate. We celebrate that Dagmar is well, and coming home again. (*They cross to the left, where the turntable represents a drugstore, with a table and two chairs at which they seat themselves*) What you like to have, Katrin?

**Katrin.**

I think a chocolate . . . no, a strawberry . . . no, a chocolate soda.

**Mama.**

(*Smiling*) You are sure?

**Katrin.**

(*Gravely*) I think so. But, Mama, can we *afford* it?

**Mama.**

I think this once we can afford it. (*The soda clerk appears from left.*)

**§ Soda Clerk.**

What's it going to be, ladies? §

**Mama.**

A chocolate ice-cream soda, please—and a cup of coffee. (*The soda clerk goes.*)

**Katrin.**

Mama, he called us "ladies"! (*Mama smiles*) Why aren't you having a soda, too?

**Mama.**

Better I like coffee.

**Katrin.**

When can I drink coffee?

**Mama.**

When you are grown up.

**Katrin.**

When I'm eighteen?

**Mama.**

Maybe before that.

**Katrin.**

When I graduate?

**Mama.**

Maybe. I don't know. Comes the day you are grown up, Papa and I will know.

**Katrin.**

Is coffee really nicer than a soda?

**Mama.**

When you are grown up, it is.

**Katrin.**

Did you used to like sodas better . . . before you were grown up?

**Mama.**

We didn't have sodas before I was grown up. It was in the old country.

**Katrin.**
(*Incredulous*) You mean they don't have sodas in Norway?

**Mama.**
Now, maybe. Now I think they have many things from America. But not when I was little girl. (*The soda clerk brings the soda and the coffee*) * * *

**Katrin.**
(*After a good pull at the soda*) Mama, do you ever want to go back to the old country?

**Mama.**
I like to go back once to look, maybe. To see the mountains and the fjords. I like to show them once to you all. When Dagmar is big, maybe we all go back once . . . one summer . . . like tourists. But that is how it would be. I would be tourist there now. There is no one I would know any more. And maybe we see the little house where Papa and I live when we first marry. And . . . (*Her eyes grow misty and reminiscent*) something else I would look at.

**Katrin.**
What is that? (*Mama does not answer*) What would you look at, Mama?

**Mama.**
Katrin, you do not know you have brother? Besides Nels?

**Katrin.**
No! A brother? In Norway? Mama. . . .

**Mama.**
He is my first baby. I am eighteen when he is born.

**Katrin.**
Is he there now?

**Mama.**
(*Simply*) He is dead.

**Katrin.**
(*Disappointed*) Oh. I thought you meant . . . I thought you meant a real brother. A long-lost one, like in stories. When did he die?

**Mama.**
When he is two years old. It is his grave I would like to see again. (*She is suddenly near tears, biting her lip and stirring her coffee violently, spilling a few drops on her suit. She gets her handkerchief from her pocketbook, dabs at her skirt, then briefly at her nose, then she returns the*

*handkerchief and turns to Katrin again*) (*Matter-of-factly*) Is good, your ice-cream soda?

**Katrin.**

(*More interested now in Mama than in it*) Yes. Mama . . . have you had a very *hard* life?

**Mama.**

(*Surprised*) Hard? No. No life is easy all the time. It is not meant to be.

**Katrin.**

But . . . rich people . . . aren't *their* lives easy?

**Mama.**

I don't know, Katrin. I have never known rich people. But I see them sometimes in stores and in the streets, and they do not *look* as if they were easy.

**Katrin.**

Wouldn't you like to be rich?

**Mama.**

I would like to be rich the way I would like to be ten feet high. Would be good for some things—bad for others.

**Katrin.**

But didn't you come to America to *get* rich?

**Mama.**

(*Shocked*) No. We come to America because they are all here—all the others. Is good for families to be together.

**Katrin.**

And did you like it right away?

**Mama.**

Right away. When we get off the ferry boat and I see San Francisco and all the family, I say: "Is like Norway," only it is better than Norway. And then you are all born here, and I become American citizen. But not to get rich.

**Katrin.**

*I* want to be rich. Rich and famous. I'd buy you your warm coat. When are you going to get that coat, Mama?

**Mama.**

Soon now, maybe—when we pay doctor, and Mr. Hyde pay his rent. I think now I *must* ask him. I ask him tomorrow, after Dagmar comes home.

**Katrin.**

When I'm rich and famous, I'll buy you lovely clothes. White satin gowns with long trains to them. And jewelry. I'll buy you a pearl necklace.

**Mama.**

We talk too much! (*She signs to the soda clerk*) Come, finish your soda. We must go home.

from
A CLEARING IN THE WOODS
by Arthur Laurents

Two Scenes from Act I
VIRGINIA, BARNEY

"I think the man who is lonely is the man who is lonely with himself because he has not accepted himself for the imperfect human being he is," Arthur Laurents wrote in a preface to his play. "Until he makes that difficult acceptance, . . . he cannot feel very much, he cannot have very much. This is the theme of *A Clearing in the Woods.*"

Critics and many others in the audience felt that the play was a compressed acting-out of the psychoanalysis of the central character, Virginia. Laurents says that this is not so. The actual theme, here as in any good play, he says, is in the story. "A woman suddenly finds herself in a clearing in the woods which seems familiar. Various people turn up, including three girls of different ages whom she does not recognize even though they recognize her and joyously announce their pleasure that she will now take care of them. At first, these girls merely confuse the woman; then they irritate her; then they goad her into doing things she hates. Finally furious, she attempts to drive them away, but at that moment they trap her and force her to the realization that they are she. This is the first act. In the second, the woman is led to the moment of choice: whether to continue fighting these girls who are less perfect than she would have them be and thus to live in perpetual torment, or whether to accept them as they are and thus be able to move onward."

Laurents also offers comments on the style of the play. It is nonrealistic because the story is nonrealistic. However, it is not a drama of flashbacks, dreams, or ghosts. Everything that happens does happen in the clearing. "The line of action is direct. It springs from the story and it flows on the *one reality in the play: emotion.*" The playwright's explanation of this structure of emotions that "must drive

100

the actors so that they are constantly running to catch up with it" is important to any performer who sets out to act the play or a scene. It is too lengthy to quote here, but can be found in the preface to the Random House edition of the play.

The two scenes below are for Virginia and her father, Barney. Virginia is still young, still attractive, though her hair is rather disheveled. She wears a soft, flowing negligee. "Barney is lean, tanned, crew-cut, . . . an 'old boy' with an infectious, charming grin which he uses to dull the edge of his remarks. He wears casual clothes with a rather bright tie, and carries a golf club." The setting, of course, is the clearing in the woods. (Another scene from the play will be found on page 528.)

**Barney.**

What's bothering you?

**Virg.**

Nothing.

**Barney.**

You could tell me. But you never do. You never come to see me. After your divorce, you moved out and you haven't spent one night here since.

**Virg.**

It's difficult, Barney, living in town, working . . . (*A pause. He looks at her, then loosens his tie angrily, turns away, then back.*)

**Barney.**

Last night I dreamt I was dead, laid out in the dining room up at the house. The windows were wide open to the rain and the wind. You wouldn't believe a dead man could get cold and wet. He can; I did. No one to shut those windows. You wouldn't believe a dead man could be thinking. He can; I was. I was thinking: "I've never done anything: all right. I've never even done one small thing I really wanted to: also all right: a waste—no tragedy . . . But I've never made anyone happy." (*Pause*) Your mother wouldn't let me, either.

**Virg.**

I am not Mother!

**Barney.**

No.

**Virg.**
And you've told me that dream before.

**Barney.**
It's a recurrent dream! (*Belligerently*) Most people are glad, very glad, to see me. I entertain them. That means I make them happy for a short time, anyway, doesn't it?

**Virg.**
(*As he picks up his club*) If you wanted to, you could . . .

**Barney.**
What?

**Virg.**
I said— (*Clears her throat*)—if you wanted to, you could.

**Barney.**
Could what?

**Virg.**
(*Almost choking, it is so difficult to say the words*) —Help—me . . .

**Barney.**
Oh, you're one of the strong ones, Virginia. They never need—

**Virg.**
(*Interrupting angrily*) I am not strong! And I am exhausted from pretending to be! I am human; I am vulnerable; I hurt!

**Barney.**
Oh? Bad luck with love?

**Virg.**
That pain has an identity—not mine. Mine is one enormous zero in the dead center of nothing! I awake by reflex, not desire. I am so strong that four days ago I went to my office, to the same door I have been opening for over three years— (*He has begun, nervously, to swing his club. She strides over*) The door was not locked, Barney— (*She grabs the club from him*) but I could not open it. (*Drops the club on the ground*) I could not make my hand touch the knob! I pretended to be searching my purse as one of the secretaries opened the door for me. That day, and the next and the next after that, I sat, staring at the gilded sign that had been painted for me. When the room was entered, I picked up a telephone and recited jargon. When alone, I began staring at the open window . . . Then I dropped a piece of paper out, then a cup, then an ash tray. My office is on the sixteenth floor now. Yesterday I took off my shoes and crouched on the window sill. How long? Sense of time and place have

gone. Then one of the phones rang, shrilled like an air-raid alarm—and I ran. To my apartment? Because then I was standing in the ugly light of the medicine chest with a handful of neon-colored sleeping pills. I think I screamed—and ran: down halls and stairs. Then riding, driving down a houseless road that stopped at a footpath through trees. The path, I knew; the path brought me here: home. (*Cries out*) Why isn't it pretty here? (*Smiles*) Probably because that absurd feeling has followed me.

**Barney.**

What feeling?

**Virg.**

(*Lightly*) That something terrible is going to happen to me.

**Barney.**

Like what?

**Virg.**

It has no shape.

**Barney.**

Now, how can you be afraid and not know of what?

**Virg.**

Ah, that's the very best kind of fear. Your blood can stop at the sound of a leaf. Your heart— (*Stops, whirls toward the trees*) Someone is listening!

### SECOND SCENE

**Virg.**

Years and years ago, not long after Mother died, I wrote you a letter that you still quote as a great joke. I was even younger than that child. And I was in love with you then. (*The lighting begins to turn to haze around them. Nostalgic music is heard.*)

**Barney.**

You should have loved your mother more.

**Virg.**

You loved her so much, how could I? She was always out with you or away with you. You were both away on one of those trips when she died. (*He turns away*) When you returned, you told me she was still away. It was only long after, after I had accepted her absence, that I learned the truth from a schoolteacher. Then—I hopefully stole Mother's old wedding ring. But even though she was gone, you were still trying to find her.

**Barney.**

(*Rattling in embarrassment*) She loved me completely:
you were a child, you didn't understand: what letter do I
quote as a joke?

**Virg.**

"Dearest Daddy. You never want me around because I
am not pretty. Therefore, I am a stepchild and so I am
running away. Your loving daughter, Virginia."

**Barney.**

Don't you think that's funny coming from a kid of seven
or eight?

**Virg.**

I put it on your desk and sat in my room with the door
open, waiting for you. Company came. You read them
the letter. Everyone laughed. You called to the maid,
"Pack a bag for Miss Virginia." She put me out on the
verandah, with my little red suitcase. A clear, bright
autumn day. I pull the shades on days like that now. Oh,
she gave me a sandwich, too, an apple and a pear. I
didn't know where to go. Then I heard everyone inside
laugh again, you loudest of all. I rang the bell and the
maid opened the door. "I thought you were running
away," she said, and I said, "Just because he wants me
to, I won't."

**Barney.**

I was watching from behind the curtains. I wouldn't have
let you get very far.

**Virg.**

Why didn't you say something when I came in? Why
didn't you even look at me? Why did you laugh? (*The
music ends; the lighting returns*) That night, I cut your
new trousers.

**Barney.**

(*Bewildered*) But I've always had great success with that
story. If it isn't funny, why does everyone laugh?

**Virg.**

Don't tell it any more, Daddy. It isn't good for you to
tell it.

**Barney.**

I don't understand why. Now I *will* be late for my game.
(*Goes toward trees, then stops*) One of these days, I'll
surprise you.

**Virg.**

Yes, Daddy. You do that.

from
BLUE DENIM
by James Leo Herlihy and William Noble

Act I
JANET, ARTHUR

The ads were sensational: "Too young to marry, not too young to love!" But the play itself was a valid, touching, and perceptive study of parents and children, of the fears and misunderstandings that led to and followed a high school couple's experiments with sex. The authors, one of the New York critics wrote, "hammered into focus the possibility that any and every American home may be sharply divided by unthinking deafness." But the play was still a play, not a social document; its message, as well as its explosive subject, was presented in vigorously written scenes whose realism, like the truthfulness in fine acting, was shaped to the requirements of effective theater. One of these scenes is reprinted here.

Arthur is fifteen, tall, thin, and rather serious. Janet is a year or so older and attractive. They are "nice kids" from "nice families." The setting is the basement of Arthur's house. "The walls are of concrete block, and all the windows—which begin at ground level—are high. The furnishings consist of an old day bed, a night stand, a workbench with a small radio, a rickety table, two old dining chairs whose backs have been broken or sawed off. There are a bicycle with flat tires, an old B-B gun, several abandoned toys, and a punching bag." This is Arthur's refuge. Here he and his friend Ernie play endless games of poker and enjoy the adult pleasures of cigarettes and beer. Tonight, however, Janet has interrupted the card game. She and Ernie never seem to get along very well— her comments on his efforts to play the "big man" annoy him—and this time he has stomped out the cellar door. His exit line was, he hoped, withering: "Janet is the type of girl which, when she grows up, wonders why her husband goes to stag parties."

For a moment there is silence. Arthur tosses the deck of cards onto the table, walks to the punching bag and gives it a couple of hard rights.

**Janet.**
  You sore?

**Arthur.**
  Naw!

**Janet.**
  For breaking up the game, I mean.

**Arthur.**
  Well, okay then! *Why?*

**Janet.**
  I just don't like to see you—the way you act when Ernie's around.

**Arthur.**
  And how's that?

**Janet.**
  Oh—*pretending* so!

**Arthur.**
  Who's pretending? Ernie and me happen to like a couple of beers and a hand of poker. Why do you have to act like somebody's mother?

**Janet.**
  I'm sorry. (*As he does not answer*) I'm sorry, Arthur.

**Arthur.**
  Why don't you call me Art, like everybody else?

**Janet.**
  All right. I'm sorry, Art.

**Arthur.**
  Forget it.

**Janet.**
  (*Searching for a topic*) Want to go down to the drugstore?

**Arthur.**
  For what?

**Janet.**
  I don't know—Coke, soda . . .

**Arthur.**
  On top of beer!

**Janet.**
  Oh. (*A rather strained pause. Janet joins Arthur near the punching bag. She makes him uneasy. He goes to the table, gathers the cards. Janet hits the punching bag with her fist*) Ow!

**Arthur.**

Janet. What'd you mean, when you said you wished your father was different? (*As she does not answer*) The way he's so funny about lipstick and stuff? And doesn't like you to date guys?

**Janet.**

I wish I lived downtown with Norma! I'm going to, the minute I graduate!

**Arthur.**

What the hell, lots of parents are old-fashioned and raise cain with their kids. 'Specially girls.

**Janet.**

Yes, but *my* father *doesn't* raise cain. He says: "How can you *hurt* me this way? How *can* you?" And then he— cries.

**Arthur.**

Cries?

**Janet.**

(*Nodding*) Real tears.

**Arthur.**

But your dad's a grown-up man, a college professor!

**Janet.**

I know. And he makes me feel so *sorry* for him, I— (*Looking around desperately*) Does your radio still work?

**Arthur.**

O' course. Why shouldn't it?

**Janet.**

(*Switching it on*) Good. Let's find some real crazy music!

**Arthur.**

You won't find anything at that end. (*Dialing for her*) How's this? Not very crazy, though. (*Dance music comes on*)

**Janet.**

It's fine— Arthur, dance with me.

**Arthur.**

You know I can't!

**Janet.**

It's no big mystery. (*Walking to him, taking charge*) Now—just walk in time to the music! (*After a moment*) It'll never work if you keep on being so stand-offish. Here, like this! (*Walks into his arms. As he draws back*) No, goofy, closer! (*She presses tightly against him. After a moment*) You catching on?

**Arthur.**

(*Breathlessly*) Yeah, I—think so. (*Acutely conscious of her*) We—we better stop pretty soon, huh?

**Janet.**

You're doing fine. Everybody's self-conscious at first.

**Arthur.**

(*Painfully*) No—I think we better— (*He breaks from her, hurries to the radio and turns it off*)

**Janet.**

What's the matter?

**Arthur.**

Nothing. I told you—I'm no good at that stuff.

**Janet.**

You'll never learn if you won't try!

**Arthur.**

Too bad Ernie isn't here. He goes to dances all the time. Real ones, downtown.

**Janet.**

I wanted to dance with you, not Ernie.

**Arthur.**

I'd give anything if I could be like him.

**Janet.**

Now why?

**Arthur.**

He's really got a smooth tongue on him. I admire that. With me things get all twisted up . . .

**Janet.**

Arthur, what sort of things?

**Arthur.**

Things I wonder about—One thing, it bothers me a lot. I tried to tell Mom about it once, but . . .

**Janet.**

But what?

**Arthur.**

Aw, every time my mother looks at me I feel like she's seeing something small and pink and wrapped up in a blanket.

**Janet.**

(*Moving closer to him*) Try telling me, Art.

**Arthur.**

See . . . I've got this feeling I ought to be somebody—special!

**Janet.**

Who doesn't? I want to be a poet, and what's sillier than that?

**Arthur.**

Yeah, but you got what it takes. I'm just—ordinary.

**Janet.**

Ordinary! You think I'd hang around with you if I didn't think you were going to be—special?

**Arthur.**

You do?

**Janet.**

O' course. That's why you and I can talk.

**Arthur.**

I guess we do talk better than most people. All the kids at school—even Ernie . . . I mean, I figured it out, I don't really *know* anybody at all. Not even my own folks. Does that sound bats?

**Janet.**

Not to *me!*

**Arthur.**

Hunh?

**Janet.**

It seems to me the only people who really know each other are—people in love.

**Arthur.**

Maybe so.

**Janet.**

Arthur, how d'you suppose it feels to be in love with someone?

**Arthur.**

Don't ask me!

**Janet.**

(*Bravely*) Because—because I think *I'm* in love. With you.

**Arthur.**

You . . . ! (*Sharply*) Whadd'ya want to kid like that for?

**Janet.**

I'm not!

**Arthur.**

You are. And I thought we were talking serious.

**Janet.**

Well, if that's your attitude, I'm sorry I told you! (*Janet starts to leave but Arthur's voice stops her*)

**Arthur.**

Janet! Weren't you kidding? (*She turns slowly to face him, shakes her head*) But Lordie, Janet . . .

**Janet.**

Don't worry about it. At my age it's perfectly natural to have crushes on people.

**Arthur.**

Yeah, but—why me?

**Janet.**

Frankly, I don't know. You're not the handsomest boy in the world.

**Arthur.**

Thanks!

**Janet.**

You see, I'm very objective about you, Arthur. My mistake was I told you. Norma says never let a boy know you really like him.

**Arthur.**

Norma doesn't know everything.

**Janet.**

She knows plenty!

**Arthur.**

(*Stunned*) When did you find out? I mean, about me?

**Janet.**

(*Turning to him, excited*) I can tell you the exact second. It was this morning. Remember the English test? I saw you trying to decide whether or not to copy from Billy Robinson's paper . . . Turning sideways, leaning back . . . And all you had to do was look over! But you didn't. I started to laugh. At least I thought I was—but I was starting to cry. Now, almost everything you do is funny . . . and at the same time . . . *not* funny . . . (*She turns away*) Well—*say* something!

**Arthur.**

I don't know what to say!

**Janet.**

I guess you don't— (*She wanders away from him*)

**Arthur.**

(*Joining her, taking her arm*) Don't be—mad.

**Janet.**

I'm not mad.

**Arthur.**

Yes you are.

**Janet.**

I really made a fool of myself, didn't I?

**Arthur.**

No. God no. If you feel like that, and if—

**Janet.**

Norma was right.

**Arthur.**

No! (*He kisses her quickly, awkwardly. Then, laughing self-consciously*) Our noses got in the way.

**Janet.**

(*Softly*) Goofy. Like this. (*She tilts her head slightly, kisses him on the lips*)

**Arthur.**

(*Joking breathlessly*) You seem to know a lot about kissing.

**Janet.**

(*Also breathless and joking*) Enough to keep my nose out of the way. (*They stand holding each other at arm's length, each on the verge of hysteria. Then Janet draws a sharp breath. As though this were a signal, they move suddenly together and cling*) Arthur . . . (*Into his shoulder*) I bet you like me a lot more than you think you do!

**Arthur.**

Maybe—I do. (*She draws back, smiles at him, then self-consciously pushes away and wanders to the table, where she sits*) I feel—funny. Do you?

**Janet.**

Kind of. (*Arthur sits at the table*)

**Arthur.**

Janet. I want to ask you something personal. Only don't get sore.

**Janet.**

I won't.

**Arthur.**

Well—a guy's bound to *wonder!*

**Janet.**

(*Pleased*) You're jealous!

**Arthur.**

You're crazy!

**Janet.**

Yes you are! Well, you don't have to worry, Arthur.

**Arthur.**

You've never?—Not that I'd *blame* you, understand, I'm broad-minded.

**Janet.**

I've thought about it for a long time, though. (*Flaring*) And that's perfectly biologically normal, too! Lots of countries' kids our age are already married and raising families.

**Arthur.**

Sure they are.

**Janet.**

(*Quietly*) With me, I always get to a certain point— listening to somebody's line and kissing, and petting—

then I get scared or disgusted and . . . (*A helpless gesture*)
Do you think I've got a sex blockade or something?

**Arthur.**

O' course not! (*Then, treading softly*) You simply didn't
love those other guys.

**Janet.**

Arthur. Have you slept with lots of girls?

**Arthur.**

Oh, the—the regular amount for a guy fifteen, I guess.

**Janet.**

Is it—was it like you thought it'd be?

**Arthur.**

(*After a moment's deliberation*) More or less.

**Janet.**

When it happened, were you in love with those girls?

**Arthur.**

Hell, no! (*Explaining*) A man doesn't have to be.

**Janet.**

That's not fair! (*Suddenly*) Art, let's not talk about it
any more!

**Arthur.**

(*Following*) What's the matter?

**Janet.**

I think if we talk about it, it's going to spoil something.

**Arthur.**

Okay, Jan.

**Janet.**

(*Sitting on the cot, frowning, her tone violent*) I wish I
was eighteen right this minute and knew all about everything!

**Arthur.**

'F you were, you wouldn't like *me* any more.

**Janet.**

I suppose. (*Looking at him*) That's so hard to believe,
though . . . (*They stare at each other for a long moment*)

**Arthur.**

You're so— (*Unable to find a fine enough word*) Why
didn't I know before what you were like? (*They kiss
tenderly, then nuzzle, forehead to forehead*)

**Janet.**

(*After a moment, softly*) Are your eyes closed?

**Arthur.**

Yes.

**Janet.**

I love you, Arthur!

**Arthur.**

(*Crooning*) Janet, little Janet, Jan . . .

**Janet.**

Arthur . . . Teach me how to love you? . . . (*He draws back and looks at her, slowly comprehending her meaning*)

**Arthur.**

Jan, you don't mean?— (*Janet reaches up, covers his eyes with her hand so that he can't see her face*)

**Janet.**

Yes, Arthur. (*Then, to Arthur's mortification and surprise, he starts to cry, knuckles fiercely at his eyes*) Why, dearest . . . What's the matter?

**Arthur.**

(*Sharply*) Nothing! Don't look at me. (*After a moment he draws a long, shuddering breath, wipes his eyes, and tries to smile at her*) Now, why'd I do a crazy thing like that?

**Janet.**

Is it my fault?

**Arthur.**

(*Strongly*) No!

**Janet.**

Then what? . . .

**Arthur.**

(*Whispering, panic-stricken, his face averted*) Janet—I don't know about anything!

**Janet.**

What do you mean?

**Arthur.**

I made it all up. About other girls.

**Janet.**

(*Tenderly, her voice shaking slightly*) Why, you—you big phony! (*She breaks into a slight hysterical laugh. After a moment they are laughing together, briefly, softly, with panic underneath. Then Arthur's breath goes out of him in a long sigh. He kisses her, straining his body against hers.*)

from
HOTEL UNIVERSE
by Philip Barry

Act I
PAT, NORMAN, TOM, (HOPE)

Three men, three friends, play at being little boys and,
carried away with the game, become as unthinkingly vicious
as children are before experience and hurt have taught
them that human-kindness that grownups call being civi-
lized. This is but one of the strange and jarring happenings
in Barry's psychologically oriented, philosophical play.
*Hotel Universe*, in a sense, is introspection made dramatic.
It is also a fantasy. The setting is the terrace of a house
in Europe, an odd old house that hangs above the sea;
beyond the terrace wall "sea meets sky without a line to
mark the meeting" and "the angle of the terrace is like a
wedge into space." Once the house was a small hotel, the
Hôtel de l'Univers, which was vacated because "things
began to happen there." "People began to resemble other
people and the place itself other places. And time went sort
of funny. Their pasts kept cropping up." That is also what
happens to the people in Barry's play. A group of friends
has come to visit and to cheer up the new tenant of the
Hotel Universe, Ann, a young woman who has come here
with her elderly father, Stephen Field. Mr. Field is a
world-famous physicist, but he is ill and said to "behave
strangely." "He can't take people casually," someone explains. "He's supposed to have some kind of power over
them . . . because he always seems so close to death." In
the play, Stephen Field seems to have the power to be
many people—people who have been important in the
pasts of the men and women who have gathered at the old
house above the sea. With him and with each other they
act out the problems and disappointments they have had
before, and they find the answers and hope which enable
them to go on.

The scene below, which occurs early in the play, presents
a problem, not a solution. The time is evening and the

114

visitors have collected on the terrace. Among them are Tom Ames, who is forty and of "amiable good looks," and his wife, Hope, four years younger and "in full bloom." Pat Farley is thirty-two, "medium tall, slight, and likable looking." Norman Rose, the handsomest of the men, is about thirty-eight.

The conversation has lagged for a moment, then Tom finds a new topic.

**Tom.**

(*After a pause*) I unearthed a marble tablet in the lower garden today. It was in Latin and said: "To Semptronius who, at age 12, danced here, and pleased."

**Hope.**

But how charming that is!—Can't you see him?— Semptronius— (*Tom rises. All at once he is as excited as a child.*)

**Tom.**

I'd like to dance here too. (*To Pat.*) Will you play? And would anyone mind?

**Hope.**

—Now that's what I mean! Really, we're not acting at all sensibly, don't you realize it? (*Tom looks at her, and returns to the wall.*)

**Tom.**

—Ten years ago I wouldn't even have asked. It's a rotten feeling, knowing your youth's gone—knowing that all the brave things you once dreamed of doing, somehow just won't get done.

**Pat.**

(*As a small boy would say it*) I wanna go out to the South Seas like Father Damien!

**Tom.**

(*Soberly*) I did, at that.

**Alice.** [*In classroom presentation, Hope can speak the line. Ed.*]

Who is Father Damien?

**Tom.**

(*Reciting*) Father Damien was a noble priest who went to the South Seas to help the lepers and got it himself.

**Hope.**

Sometimes I don't know his voice from little Tommy's. (*Suddenly Tom stands up upon the wall.*)

**Tom.**

Look, Mummy! Look where *I* am!

**Hope.**

Get down, Tom, you'll fall.

**Tom.**

Don't punish me, Mummy.—Reason with me.

**Hope.**

—Acting like that! I don't know where you think you are. (*Tom descends from the wall.*)

**Tom.**

—Under the piano. (*He moves away from them, toward the table.*)—Under the apple tree— (*He seats himself cross-legged beside the table, whistling a tune softly through his teeth and trying to wrench the top from a wooden champagne-stick. A moment, then he calls, as a small boy would.*) Hey, Pat! Pat! C'mon over! (*Pat comes forward to him.*)

**Pat.**

Hello, Tom.

**Tom.**

Hello, yourself.

**Pat.**

Where're the other fellows?

**Tom.**

How should I know? I got better things to do than follow them all over everywheres. (*He examines his stick with interest. Pat seats himself on the ground beside him.*)

**Hope.**

Don't, Tom.—Make them stop, Ann. They go too far with it. (*But Ann is silent, watching them intently.*)

**Pat.**

—Gosh, I feel good, don't you?

**Tom.**

I feel all right.

**Pat.**

—But don't you ever feel—gosh, I don't know—*good?*

**Tom.**

You don't feel very good when you've got things the matter with you, like I have.

**Pat.**

What have you got? (*No answer.*) Aw, come on, Tom— is it really bad? (*Tom's head bends lower over his stick.*)

**Tom.**

It's awful.

**Pat.**

Aw gosh, I'm sorry—tell me, Tom— (*A moment, then:*)

**Tom.**

Will you promise never so long as you live— (*Pat nods eagerly.*) —I think I've got something, Pat.

**Pat.**

What?

**Tom.**

I think I got the leprosy.

**Pat.**

(*Appalled*) You've—? Gosh, Tom, why do you think that?

**Tom.**

I read a book last night about Father Damien in the South Seas and he got the leprosy and I think I've got it.

**Pat.**

How—how do you suppose you ever—

**Tom.**

I gave a old woman a dime the other day, and she went and kissed my hand, and I think it must of been her that gave it to me.

**Pat.**

But didn't you wash or anything?

**Tom.**

I couldn't till I got home. And it takes awful fast. Look at that— (*He shows his wrist.*)

**Pat.**

Where? (*He almost touches Tom's wrist—but draws his hand back, fearfully.*)

**Tom.**

Doesn't it look sort of—white to you?

**Pat.**

It does, sort of.

**Tom.**

—And scaly. That's the way it starts. My foot's the same way. I could tell for sure by putting it in hot water.

**Pat.**

Hot water!

**Tom.**

If you've got it, you don't feel anything, not even the water, even. Father Damien didn't. That's the way he knew. (*Norman is drawn over to them. He, too, has begun whistling softly. His tune is "Pony Boy."*)

**Pat.**

Oh, he was prob'ly just a crazy ole priest.—H'lo Norman. (*Tom scowls. Norman gestures "Hello," and goes on whistling, hands in pockets.*)

**Tom.**
—A *what,* did you say?

**Pat.**
Well, there *are* crazy priests. Anyways, I bet there have been, some time.

**Tom.**
Never. Never one. God wouldn't let there be.

**Norman.**
What about Theo-philus?

**Tom.**
Who?

**Norman.**
Theo-philus.

**Tom.**
What did he do was so crazy?

**Norman.**
Just burnt the library at Alexandria, that's all.

**Tom.**
I never even heard of it.

**Pat.**
I did. Alexander the Great built it, quite a long time ago, to please his vanity.

**Norman.**
(*Reciting*)—And Theo-philus was a crazy Christian monk that burnt up the library which was the greatest in the whole world and which history tells us contained over seventy thousand volumes.

**Tom.**
Well, if he did, I bet he had some good reason. I bet they were impure books, or something.

**Norman.**
He was crazy.

**Tom.**
I bet he knew they were good and lashivious and he just burnt 'em to the honor and glory of God.

**Norman.**
He was crazy.

**Pat.**
(*Pointedly*) Of course you'd say so, anyway. I guess you'd say any Christian holy man of God was crazy.

**Norman.**
I wouldn't either. (*A moment.*) *Why* would I?

**Pat.**
I suppose you think we didn't notice you didn't eat that ham sandwich the other day and asked for a sardine.

**Norman.**

I wanted a sardine. I like sardines better. I like their taste better.

**Pat.**

Yes, you do!

**Tom.**

(*To Pat*)—Any one says sardines taste better'n ham says so for some good alterior reason, you bet.

**Norman.**

You know what *you* are, don't you?

**Tom.**

What?

**Norman.**

Cath'lic! Cath'lic!

**Tom.**

(*Soberly*) I am a Catholic. Yes. I am proud to be a Catholic.

**Norman.**

Yes—well, before *I'd* go to confession and things—

**Tom.**

You know why?—You wouldn't get the chance. They wouldn't let you in. See, Mr. Jew?

**Pat.**

You are a Jew, aren't you? (*Norman raises his head proudly.*)

**Norman.**

Of course I am. What about it?

**Tom.**

You crucified our Lord, that's what about it.

**Norman.**

Oh, no I didn't.

**Pat.**

Who did, then?

**Norman.**

.—The Roman soldiers. See?

**Pat.**

Oh, you think you know everything. All you do is sit around and read books, little Ikey.

**Norman.**

I'm not an Ikey! Don't you call me that!

**Tom.**

(*To Pat*)—You're just as bad as he is. A heretic's what *you* are—Protestant dog-sit-on-a-log-and-eat-meat-on-*Friday!*

**Pat.**

I'll eat anything I like any day I like—see? *And* ham.

**Tom.**
It's all right now, only wait'll you die. Just wait'll then.

**Pat.**
(*To Norman*) Pooh, "when I die." That's what the priest tells him—

**Tom.**
Well, just let me tell *you:* when I grow up maybe *I'm* going to be a priest. See? Maybe I've got a vacation right this minute. See?

**Pat.**
A what?

**Tom.**
A vacation—a call. (*Pat looks at him in wonder.*)

**Pat.**
Gosh.

**Tom.**
(*Closer to him*) Just think that over, Mr. Fresh.—And when you hear of me going out to the South Seas and places like Father Dami— (*Awestruck, he remembers his malady. In fear he peers at his wrist again.*)

**Pat.**
Is it any worse?

**Tom.**
I—I think it's spread a little.

**Pat.**
Listen—

**Tom.**
What—

**Pat.**
I know a fellow's got a doctor-book. Only he won't lend it. You got to look at it at his house. Shall we—?

**Tom.**
All right. (*A moment. Then:*) Pat—

**Pat.**
What?

**Tom.**
What would you do if *you* had the—the you-know?

**Pat.**
(*After thought*) I'd kill myself.

**Tom.**
You couldn't. You'd go straight to hell. And the tortures of the you-know are as nothing to the tortures of hell.

**Pat.**
Just the same I'd do it, though. I certainly wouldn't go around with the lepr— (*Tom claps his hand over his mouth.*) Let go!

**Tom.**

—You promised! (*To Norman.*)—You get out. Get out, now!—If you know what's good for you— (*Norman leaves them. Pat struggles.*)

**Pat.**

Let go! I'm—I can't breathe. Let go—! (*Still Tom holds him. Pat struggles harder. He begins to beat at him with his fists. Finally freeing himself, he goes at him more violently. Tom retaliates. They go up and down the terrace, advancing, retreating, clinching, separating, raining blows upon each other in dead earnest. Hope suddenly realizes that they are no longer playing, and cries:*)

**Hope.**

Stop it! (*But they go on. She begins to strike at Pat.*) Stop! Stop it, do you hear me? (*She turns imploringly to Norman.*) Norman! (*Norman goes to Tom.*)

**Norman.**

Come on, now—that's enough! (*He holds his arms from behind.*) What's got into you two? (*Hope stands between Pat and Tom, protecting Tom. They are gasping for breath.*)

from
# SUNRISE AT CAMPOBELLO
by Dore Schary

Act II, scene 1
ELEANOR, F.D.R.

Dore Schary's dramatization of a critical period in the life of Franklin D. Roosevelt begins with the picture of a confident young politician well on his way to becoming an important man in his party. It shows him struck down by polio, his battle to learn simply to move at all, and the more difficult struggle to recover his spirit. It ends with a triumph, Roosevelt's appearance as a speaker at a national convention. Schary's portrait is of the Roosevelt family as well as of F.D.R., and it is painted with humor as well as admiration. There are also portrayals of anger and of a fear which is almost too strong to be overcome.

The scene below occurs at the middle of the play. The setting is the downstairs living room of the Roosevelt town house in New York City. Roosevelt, in a wheel chair, has been attempting to get back to work. Discouraged and easily tired, he finds it difficult to keep his temper. He has just apologized about this to his secretary as Eleanor enters the room. The secretary exits.

**Eleanor.**
I had a rather tense chore a few minutes ago. I had to let the upstairs maid go. She complained so much about all the work she had to do—most of which she never did anyway.
**FDR.**
(*Crossing to her*) Sorry, Babs. You've had a big turnover on maids this year. It's been a busy household.
**Eleanor.**
It's been a nice household.
**FDR.**
(*Rolling his chair about the room and putting some of*

122

*his things away*) I'm getting expert with this chair. It moves easily. See that. (*He executes a sharp turn*) We have to get a couple like this for Hyde Park. None of those conventional invalid wheel chairs. (*He takes another turn or two in the chair*) This exercise is stimulating—takes some of the loneliness away. (*He crosses to the couch and picks up a sailboat*)

**Eleanor.**

Loneliness, dear?

**FDR.**

Invalidism—(*Quickly*)—even temporary—is very lonely. I remember reading: "A sick man wishes to be where he is not." (*After a moment*) When you're forced to sit a lot—and watch others move about—you feel apart—lonely—because you can't get up and pace around. I find myself irritated when people come in here and parade all over the place. I have to keep exercising self-control to prevent screaming at them to sit down—quiet down—stand still.

**Eleanor.**

I'll remember.

**FDR.**

You're quiet and restful.

**Eleanor.**

(*She continues straightening out the room*) I am just tired. Is Louie in his room?

**FDR.**

He said he was going out for a feel of the pulse of the city. What he really means—he's going out to buy newspapers. Loves the Teapot Dome stories. Adores political scandals—if they embarrass Republicans.

**Eleanor.**

(*A moment*) Franklin—are there other things I should know that you haven't told me?

**FDR.**

(*Lightly*) You mean like about Louie going out to get the papers?

**Eleanor.**

I mean about your—loneliness.

**FDR.**

(*Not joking now*) Often when you're alone, certain fears seek you out and hunt for a place in your mind. Well, you know, I've always had a small fear about fire. Since this—(*Indicates his legs*) that fear sometimes overwhelms me. I've nightmares about being trapped and unable to move. I've been practicing crawling so I can be sure that in case of fire I could get to a window by myself—or to a door or a flight of steps.

**Eleanor.**

I didn't know you had been—crawling.

**FDR.**

I've been trying—and I can do fairly well—by now. But soon I'll be back on my feet. The back muscles came around—and so will the legs.

**Eleanor.**

Of course they will.

**FDR.**

(*Suddenly turns to the ship model and lifts it in one hand*) Do you like her?

**Eleanor.**

She's lovely.

**FDR.**

She'll really sail, you know—she's not just a toy. (*He places it back on the couch*) I miss the sea. (*He wheels his chair close to Eleanor and takes her hand as his words come wrenching out of him*) Eleanor, I must say this—once to someone. Those first few days at Campobello when this started, I had despair—deep, sick despair. It wasn't the pain—there was much more of that later on when they straightened the tendons in my legs. No, not the pain—it was the sense that perhaps I'd never get up again. Like a crab lying on its back. I'd look down at my fingers and exert every thought to get them to move. I'd send down orders to my legs and my toes—they didn't obey.

**Eleanor.**

(*As he halts his speech for a moment, she goes to him, her head on his lap*) Darling—

**FDR.**

I turned to my faith, Babs—for strength to endure. I feel I have to go through this fire for some reason. Eleanor, it's a hard way to learn humility—but I've been learning by crawling. I know what is meant—you must learn to crawl before you can walk.

(*They embrace. After a moment, the front door is heard slamming and FDR straightens as a voice is heard.*)

from
MARY, MARY
by Jean Kerr

Act I
MARY, BOB, OSCAR
and
ACT II
MARY, DIRK

In Jean Kerr's vastly successful comedy about the reglu-
ing of a marriage that has come unstuck, an old Broadway
comedy situation was somehow transformed into an original and riotous evening in the theater. The magic that
worked this transformation was twofold: Mrs. Kerr writes
splendid, dryly comic dialogue and she has a priceless
gift for noticing and pointing out the extraordinary humor
in ordinary things. With irony, zest, and subtle exaggera-
tion she makes the real more real and very funny. In this
case, the real is a broken marriage. Bob and Mary McKella-
way have been divorced, but unfinished business—last year's
income tax return—requires that they meet, so Mary comes
to the old apartment which Bob now occupies alone. Bob
already has plans to marry a second wife and, before Act
I is done, Mary has begun a flirtation with Dirk Winston,
a movie actor who is the schoolgirl's dream of a romantic
male. But when the curtain falls on Act III, Bob and
Mary have decided to marry each other again. On the
way to this happy conclusion they have discussed and re-
fought their old battles, coped with the problem of Mary's
too ready wit (she was a wife, Bob complains, "on and
off—between jokes"), and done a considerable amount of
remembering.

The two scenes below are sparked by memories. The
first occurs near the beginning of the play. The setting is
a living room in a New York apartment building. Bob "is
a publisher by profession, heading his own company, and
he has a cluttered desk at one side of the room." Though
there is a room, off right, that he calls the office, his office
work seems to have overrun the living room. Mary has
been in the room for about five minutes and already her
sharp-edged remarks (this time about her former husband's

future wife) have Bob spluttering with irritation. He strides to a doorway and calls for Oscar, the tax lawyer, who has come to go over the old checkbooks with Mary.

**Bob.**
(*striding to office door*) Oscar, have you fallen asleep in there?

**Oscar.**
(*off*) Coming!

**Bob.**
(*moving away from Mary as Oscar appears from office*) Shall we get on with this? (*To Mary*) I know you have to get back to Philadelphia—

**Mary.**
I'm staying in town tonight, so you may consider that my time is your time.

**Oscar.**
(*sits at the desk, handing Mary a batch of canceled checks*) Okay, Mary, will you look through these checks? Most of them you've signed.

**Mary.**
Oh, dear—I'm not going to remember *any* of these, Oscar—

**Oscar.**
It'll come. Just give yourself time. You understand that we're particularly looking for items that might be deductible. Business entertaining, professional gifts, and so forth.

**Mary.**
(*working her way through the checks*) L. Bernstein— seventy-eight dollars. That's impossible. The only L. Bernstein I know is Leonard Bernstein and I don't know Leonard Bernstein.

**Oscar.**
(*pointing it out*) This is L. Bernstein, D.D.S. A dentist.

**Bob.**
(*shaking his head*) I told you—Sidney Bauer is my dentist.

**Mary.**
Dentist, dentist, dentist. (*Snapping her fingers*) Listen— it's that man in Boston!

**Bob.**
What man in Boston?

**Mary.**

Don't you remember that crazy restaurant where you go down all the stairs? And you thought you got a stone in the curry—but it was your inlay?

**Bob.**

Oh.

**Mary.**

And we drove all the way out to Framingham because he was the only dentist who'd take you on Sunday?

**Bob.**

Yeah, yeah, yeah.

**Mary.**

By the way, how is that inlay?

**Bob.**

Just grand. How are your crowns? (*They turn from each other.*)

**Oscar.**

(*stopping this*) *And* we have Mrs. Robert Connors—three hundred dollars.

**Bob.**

Mrs. Connors?

**Mary.**

I thought so long as you walked this earth you'd remember Mrs. Connors. Bootsie Connors and her fish?

**Bob.**

Oh, God. That ghastly weekend in Greenwich.

**Oscar.**

Okay, tell Daddy.

**Bob.**

Do you remember that young English critic, Irving Mannix?

**Oscar.**

The angry young man?

**Bob.**

This was two years ago, when he was just a cross young man. At that time he was writing long scholarly articles proving that Shakespeare was a homosexual.

**Mary.**

Sort of the intellectual's answer to *Photoplay*.

**Bob.**

Anyway, he was staying here. And we'd been invited to a party at the Connors'.

**Mary.**

So we brought along dear old Irving.

**Bob.**

Do you know the Connors' place in Greenwich?

**Oscar.**

No.

**Bob.**

Well, the living room is about the size of the ballroom at the St. Regis. You feel it would be just the place to sign a treaty. (*As they become interested in the details of the story Bob and Mary gradually forget their present situation and relax.*) Anyway, it was all too rich for Irving and he started to lap up martinis. In fifteen minutes he was asking our hostess if it was true that the Venetian paneling had been brought over piece by piece from Third Avenue.

**Oscar.**

Why didn't you take this charmer home?

**Bob.**

Because he passed out. In the library.

**Mary.**

(*it comes back*) On that damn velvet sofa.

**Bob.**

But he came to just long enough to light a cigarette. Presently the sofa was on fire—really on fire. Our hero jumped up and, with stunning presence of mind, put out the blaze with a tank of tropical fish.

**Mary.**

And these were no run-of-the-bowl goldfish. They came from Haiti and were friends of the family. I mean, they had *names*.

**Oscar.**

Well, he was a writer. I think we can call that professional entertainment. Okay—we have twenty-five dollars to the Beach Haven Inn.

**Mary.**

That must be yours.

**Bob.**

Nonsense! I was never in . . . (*And then he remembers.*) The Booksellers—

**Mary and Bob.**

(*together*) Convention.

**Bob.**

That awful hotel with the iron deer in front.

**Mary.**

(*nodding, her eyes lighting up*) With the night clerk who looked like Norman Vincent Peale and was so suspicious.

**Bob.**

No wonder he was suspicious! (*To Oscar, indicating*

*Mary*) He turns around to get the key and this one says just loud enough for him to hear, "Darling, are we doing the right thing? Maybe we ought to *wait*."

**Mary.**

He was *delighted* to come face to face with sin.

**Bob.**

That's probably why he charged us four bucks to bring up three bottles of beer.

**Mary.**

(*To Oscar*) He forgot the bottle opener, and we had to pry them open on the handle of the radiator.

**Bob.**

And one of them was warm or something, so it shot up to the ceiling and all over one of the beds. So we both had to sleep in the other twin bed. . . . (*His voice has slowed down on this last thought. The remembering is suddenly a bit painful. There is a short, awkward silence before Mary gets to her feet, deliberately breaking the mood.*)

**Mary.**

Oscar, we're being inefficient. We don't need total recall —just the facts. I'll take these checks into the office and make notes on the ones I can remember.—(*Almost before they realize it, she has left them. Oscar and Bob look at one another, then Bob looks away.*)

## SECOND SCENE

It is shortly after midnight. Mary and Dirk Winston, the film actor, have been out to dinner. She is on her way home—the hotel where she is staying in New York— but she has had to come to the apartment to collect her suitcase. It is snowing outside and Dirk suggests a drink before they begin the battle to find a taxi. Mary agrees. They are new friends, not old; they met this afternoon when Dirk came to collect the manuscript of his autobiography, which Bob is not going to publish. Mary encourages Dirk by telling him that Bob sometimes makes mistakes in choosing which manuscripts to print and reject. When Dirk tells Mary that she is pretty, she answers with a joke and changes the subject. Dirk asks if she always turns off compliments and she replies that probably she does since, after all, she is not pretty. For a moment the talk is about

Dirk's book again, then, as he comes back from the bar with a drink, he turns to Mary:

**Dirk.**

Mary—

**Mary.**

What?

**Dirk.**

You just said Bob makes mistakes. But how did he ever let you slip through his fingers?

**Mary.**

Just lucky, I guess.

**Dirk.**

I think I am beginning to see the clue to this little puzzle.

**Mary.**

What puzzle?

**Dirk.**

You.

**Mary.**

I'd love to think I was a puzzle. A woman of mystery. Smiling and enigmatic on the surface—but underneath, a tigress. (*Change of mood, straightforward*) I hate to admit it, but what you see is all there is. Underneath this plain, girlish exterior, there's a very plain girl.

**Dirk.**

Ah, but what happened to make you *decide* it was such a plain exterior? It was the divorce, wasn't it? It was Bob.

**Mary.**

Bob? I decided *that* when I was thirteen years old. We can't blame Bob for everything.

**Dirk.**

At thirteen, all by yourself, you decided that?

**Mary.**

(*sitting on the ottoman*) Oh, there were people around, but I can't say they gave me any argument. Do you ever look at little girls?

**Dirk.**

How little?

**Mary.**

(*rather intensely, as she remembers and thinks about it. The intensity is perhaps increased by the amount she's had to drink*) You take two little girls. One of them is pink and round, with curly hair and yards of eyelashes.

The other one is pale and bony, with thin, wispy hair
and two little ears poking through—like the handles on
a sugar bowl. Okay, which one of these little girls is
going to have to wear braces on her teeth?

**Dirk.**

The wispy one.

**Mary.**

(*as though awarding him a prize*) You've got it. (*Seeing
herself again, taking a sip of her drink*) That was me.
Braces on my teeth, Band-Aids on my knees, freckles on
my nose. All elbows and shoulder blades. For two years
running I got picked to play the consumptive orphan in
*Michael O'Halloran*.

**Dirk.**

That was talent.

**Mary.**

That was typecasting.

**Dirk.**

All adolescents go through something. I had the worst
case of acne in the history of the world. For three years
I was a Technicolor marvel. You wouldn't remember
when Fleischmann's Yeast was the big thing. I used to
eat Fleischmann's Yeast and drink water until I couldn't
move without gurgling. I imagine I was actually ferment-
ing.

**Mary.**

I never ate yeast, but once I sent away secretly for Still-
man's freckle cream. I guess I used too much, because I
just peeled and peeled. I had to pretend it was a sunburn.

**Dirk.**

I used to pretend I hated everybody. Especially girls,
because I was too self-conscious to talk to them.

**Mary.**

You made a spectacular recovery.

**Dirk.**

I may even have overdone it. But why didn't you—

**Mary.**

Make a recovery? Well, it was sort of different with me.
When I was a kid, I mean really a kid, I never worried
about the way I looked, because I thought—I *knew*—I'd
grow up to be beautiful just like my sister Clara.

**Dirk.**

Was she so beautiful?

**Mary.**

Clara? She had bright red hair and brown eyes and she

always had a faintly startled look, as if she'd just come out of a dark theater into the sunlight. People who met her would be so busy staring they'd forget to finish their sentences.

**Dirk.**

I can see that would have been something of a cross for you.

**Mary.**

No, I thought it was insurance. Clara was six years older than I was, and I thought "I'll grow up to look just like that." One day I was measuring myself—I was about fourteen—and I realized I hadn't grown at all, not an inch, in a whole year. And then it came to me. I wasn't going to grow any more. I was *up*. And I didn't look anything at all like Clara.

**Dirk.**

And you weren't satisfied to look like Mary?

**Mary.**

I certainly was not. I went rushing to my father, and I asked him when I was going to look like Clara. Poor man. He didn't know what to say.

**Dirk.**

What did he say?

**Mary.**

He said "Darling, we wouldn't want two Claras. You're the bright one." That did it. I could have faced being plain, but to be plain *and* bright! In the high school I went to, that was a beatable combination.

**Dirk.**

So you decided to get on the debating team.

**Mary.**

How did you know?

**Dirk.**

Girls who feel they are not going to be invited to dances always get on the debating team.

**Mary.**

And I worked on the school newspaper. And I imagined all the time that I was really Catherine Earnshaw.

**Dirk.**

Catherine who?

**Mary.**

The girl in *Wuthering Heights*. Cathy.

**Dirk.**

Oh, Merle Oberon.

**Mary.**

That's right. I used to dream that somewhere there was a strange, dark man whose heart was quietly breaking for me. On rainy nights I'd open the window and imagine I could hear him calling—"Oh, my wild, sweet Cathy!" The colds I got! And of course the only dark man I ever saw was the middle-aged dentist who used to adjust the braces on my teeth.

**Dirk.**

And you're still cross about it.

**Mary.**

Is that how I sound? I don't feel that way. I feel wistful. I think of that sappy little girl and I wonder what happened to her.

**Dirk.**

Nothing happened. She hasn't changed at all.

**Mary.**

You mean I haven't changed at all? That's a hell of a thing to say.

**Dirk.**

Oh, I'm certain you've changed in appearance. That's clear enough. But you yourself haven't changed. Somewhere inside you, you're *still* wearing braces on your teeth.

**Mary.**

Oh, come, come. I came to the big city. I learned to tip waiters. I read *The New Yorker*. I got married.

**Dirk.**

And nothing took. Do you know what's strange?

**Mary.**

What?

**Dirk.**

Here you are—so lovely. And nobody falls in love with you.

**Mary.**

Oh, is that so? And where did you get that idea?

**Dirk.**

From you.

**Mary.**

You're crazy. I never said—listen, lots of people—well, Bob certainly was in love with me—

**Dirk.**

You really thought so?

**Mary.**
Of course! Why else would he marry me? There was no dowry, or anything.

**Dirk.**
I don't know. Why did he?

**Mary.**
(*seriously unsettled beneath her insistent assurance*) Because he felt that—because we both—listen, what is this? (*Rises.*) I haven't answered so many idiotic questions since I tried to open a charge account at Saks! (*Moves away to the fireplace.*) There must be a genteel, ladylike way of telling you that it's none of your damn business!

**Dirk.**
I knew I'd get a rise out of you when I said that about Bob.

**Mary.**
Then why did you say it?

**Dirk.**
Of course Bob was in love with you. But you don't believe it. You never believed it.

**Mary.**
(*turns to him, alert*) What did he tell you?

**Dirk.**
Nothing. You're the evidence. Women who believe they're attractive have a certain air about them. You don't. Your reflexes are off.

**Mary.**
(*now furious*) I will match my reflexes with your manners any old day! And now, unless you have some other little speech all rehearsed, I suggest you go upstairs or downstairs or wherever it is you call home!

**Dirk.**
Now you're mad.

**Mary.**
Oh, you *are* the quick one! Nothing is wasted on you. Of course I'm mad! What did you expect I'd be?

**Dirk.**
I didn't know. I never met anybody quite like you before.

**Mary.**
We're even. I never met anybody like you, either.

from
DEATH OF A SALESMAN
by Arthur Miller

Act I
LINDA, WILLY

The play, a modern classic almost from the day it opened on Broadway, is the tragedy of Willy Loman, the salesman who believes that the secret of life is "to be liked—not just liked, but well liked." Willy's lifelong pursuit of success has brought him only frustration and failure—the friends he labored to win desert him and the sons he hoped to make great men are ne'er-do-wells. So Willy dreams: of the past, when his boys were full of promise, and of the future in which they will triumph. Between the dreams and the reality, which Willy faces with increasing terror, are memory and truth—Willy's pursuit of goals that were false; the ruin of his sons, destroyed by a father who promised too much and lived up to too little; and the helplessness of his wife, Linda, who must stand by and watch as Willy retreats into his dreams and contemplates suicide, a final escape. It is Linda who recognizes the tragic importance which Miller sees in the destruction of a seemingly little man. She cries out at the world—and the sons—that can show such indifference: "Willy Loman . . . is a human being and a terrible thing is happening to him. So attention must be paid. He's not to be allowed to fall into his grave like an old dog. Attention, attention must finally be paid to such a person."

The opening scene of *Death of a Salesman*, reprinted here, introduces Willy and Linda. Almost from the first, actors and audience are involved in the shifting play of reality, memory, and dream through which the playwright reveals his characters and story. The setting is as plastic as the play itself—a house whose walls can fade away to unveil other rooms and other times.

(Other scenes from *Death of a Salesman* will be found on pages 94 and 479.)

*A melody is heard, played upon a flute. It is small and fine, telling of grass and trees and the horizon. The curtain rises.* * * *

*From the right, Willy Loman, the Salesman, enters, carrying two large sample cases. The flute plays on. He hears but is not aware of it. He is past sixty years of age, dressed quietly. Even as he crosses the stage to the doorway of the house, his exhaustion is apparent. He unlocks the door, comes into the kitchen, and thankfully lets his burden down, feeling the soreness of his palms. A word-sigh escapes his lips—it might be "Oh, boy, oh, boy." He closes the door, then carries his cases out into the living-room, through the draped kitchen doorway.*

*Linda, his wife, has stirred in her bed at the right. She gets out and puts on a robe, listening. Most often jovial, she has developed an iron repression of her exceptions to Willy's behavior—she more than loves him, she admires him, as though his mercurial nature, his temper, his massive dreams and little cruelties, served her only as sharp reminders of the turbulent longings within him, longings which she shares but lacks the temperament to utter and follow to their end.*

**Linda.**

    (*hearing Willy outside the bedroom, calls with some trepidation*) Willy!

**Willy.**

    It's all right. I came back.

**Linda.**

    Why? What happened? (*Slight pause*) Did something happen, Willy?

**Willy.**

    No, nothing happened.

**Linda.**

    You didn't smash the car, did you?

**Willy.**

    (*with casual irritation*) I said nothing happened. Didn't you hear me?

**Linda.**

    Don't you feel well?

**Willy.**

    I'm tired to the death. (*The flute has faded away. He sits on the bed beside her, a little numb*) I couldn't make it. I just couldn't make it, Linda.

**Linda.**

(*very carefully, delicately*) Where were you all day? You look terrible.

**Willy.**

I got as far as a little above Yonkers. I stopped for a cup of coffee. Maybe it was the coffee.

**Linda.**

What?

**Willy.**

(*after a pause*) I suddenly couldn't drive any more. The car kept going off onto the shoulder, y'know?

**Linda.**

(*helpfully*) Oh. Maybe it was the steering again. I don't think Angelo knows the Studebaker.

**Willy.**

No, it's me, it's me. Suddenly I realize I'm goin' sixty miles an hour and I don't remember the last five minutes. I'm—I can't seem to—keep my mind to it.

**Linda.**

Maybe it's your glasses. You never went for your new glasses.

**Willy.**

No, I see everything. I came back ten miles an hour. It took me nearly four hours from Yonkers.

**Linda.**

(*resigned*) Well, you'll just have to take a rest, Willy, you can't continue this way.

**Willy.**

I just got back from Florida.

**Linda.**

But you didn't rest your mind. Your mind is overactive, and the mind is what counts, dear.

**Willy.**

I'll start out in the morning. Maybe I'll feel better in the morning. (*She is taking off his shoes*) These goddam arch supports are killing me.

**Linda.**

Take an aspirin. Should I get you an aspirin? It'll soothe you.

**Willy.**

(*with wonder*) I was driving along, you understand? And I was fine. I was even observing the scenery. You can imagine, me looking at scenery, on the road every week of my life. But it's so beautiful up there, Linda, the trees are so thick, and the sun is warm. I opened the wind-

shield and just let the warm air bathe over me. And then
all of a sudden I'm goin' off the road! I'm tellin' ya, I
absolutely forgot I was driving. If I'd've gone the other
way over the white line I might've killed somebody. So I
went on again—and five minutes later I'm dreamin'
again, and I nearly— (*He presses two fingers against his
eyes*) I have such thoughts, I have such strange thoughts.

**Linda.**

Willy, dear. Talk to them again. There's no reason why
you can't work in New York.

**Willy.**

They don't need me in New York. I'm the New England
man. I'm vital in New England.

**Linda.**

But you're sixty years old. They can't expect you to keep
traveling every week.

**Willy.**

I'll have to send a wire to Portland. I'm supposed to see
Brown and Morrison tomorrow morning at ten o'clock to
show the line. Goddammit, I could sell them! (*He starts
putting on his jacket*)

**Linda.**

(*taking the jacket from him*) Why don't you go down to
the place tomorrow and tell Howard you've simply got
to work in New York? You're too accommodating, dear.

**Willy.**

If old man Wagner was alive I'd a been in charge of New
York now! That man was a prince, he was a masterful
man. But that boy of his, that Howard, he don't appreciate. When I went north the first time, the Wagner
Company didn't know where New England was!

**Linda.**

Why don't you tell those things to Howard, dear?

**Willy.**

(*encouraged*) I will, I definitely will. Is there any cheese?

**Linda.**

I'll make you a sandwich.

**Willy.**

No, go to sleep. I'll take some milk. I'll be up right away.
The boys in?

**Linda.**

They're sleeping. Happy took Biff on a date tonight.

**Willy.**

(*interested*) That so?

**Linda.**

It was so nice to see them shaving together, one behind the other, in the bathroom. And going out together. You notice? The whole house smells of shaving lotion.

**Willy.**

Figure it out. Work a lifetime to pay off a house. You finally own it, and there's nobody to live in it.

**Linda.**

Well, dear, life is a casting off. It's always that way.

**Willy.**

No, no, some people—some people accomplish something. Did Biff say anything after I went this morning?

**Linda.**

You shouldn't have criticized him, Willy, especially after he just got off the train. You mustn't lose your temper with him.

**Willy.**

When the hell did I lose my temper? I simply asked him if he was making any money. Is that a criticism?

§ **Linda.**

But, dear, how could he make any money?

§ **Willy.**

(*worried and angered*) There's such an undercurrent in him. He became a moody man. Did he apologize when I left this morning?

§ **Linda.**

He was crestfallen, Willy. You know how he admires you. I think if he finds himself, then you'll both be happier and not fight any more.

§ **Willy.**

How can he find himself on a farm? Is that a life? A farmhand? In the beginning, when he was young, I thought, well, a young man, it's good for him to tramp around, take a lot of different jobs. But it's more than ten years now and he has yet to make thirty-five dollars a week!

§ **Linda.**

He's finding himself, Willy.

§ **Willy.**

Not finding yourself at the age of thirty-four is a disgrace!

§ **Linda.**

Shh!

§ **Willy.**

The trouble is he's lazy, goddammit!

§ **Linda.**
Willy, please!

§ **Willy.**
Biff is a lazy bum!

§ **Linda.**
They're sleeping. Get something to eat. Go on down.

§ **Willy.**
Why did he come home? I would like to know what brought him home.

§ **Linda.**
I don't know. I think he's still lost, Willy. I think he's very lost.

§ **Willy.**
Biff Loman is lost. In the greatest country in the world a young man with such—personal attractiveness, gets lost. And such a hard worker. There's one thing about Biff—he's not lazy.

§ **Linda.**
Never.

§ **Willy.**
(*with pity and resolve*) I'll see him in the morning; I'll have a nice talk with him. I'll get him a job selling. He could be big in no time. My God! Remember how they used to follow him around in high school? When he smiled at one of them their faces lit up. When he walked down the street . . . (*He loses himself in reminiscenses*) §

**Linda.**
(*trying to bring him out of it*) Willy, dear, I got a new kind of American-type cheese today. It's whipped.

**Willy.**
Why do you get American when I like Swiss?

**Linda.**
I just thought you'd like a change—

**Willy.**
I don't want a change! I want Swiss cheese. Why am I always being contradicted?

**Linda.**
(*with a covering laugh*) I thought it would be a surprise.

**Willy.**
Why don't you open a window in here, for God's sake?

**Linda.**
(*with infinite patience*) They're all open, dear.

**Willy.**
The way they boxed us in here. Bricks and windows, windows and bricks.

**Linda.**

We should've bought the land next door.

**Willy.**

The street is lined with cars. There's not a breath of fresh air in the neighborhood. The grass don't grow any more, you can't raise a carrot in the back yard. They should've had a law against apartment houses. Remember those two beautiful elm trees out there? When I and Biff hung the swing between them?

**Linda.**

Yeah, like being a million miles from the city.

**Willy.**

They should've arrested the builder for cutting those down. They massacred the neighborhood. (*Lost*) More and more I think of those days, Linda. This time of year it was lilac and wisteria. And then the peonies would come out, and the daffodils. What fragrance in this room!

**Linda.**

Well, after all, people had to move somewhere.

**Willy.**

No, there's more people now.

**Linda.**

I don't think there's more people. I think—

**Willy.**

There's more people! That's what's ruining this country! Population is getting out of control. The competition is maddening! Smell the stink from that apartment house! And another one on the other side . . . How can they whip cheese? (*On Willy's last line, Biff and Happy raise themselves up in their beds, listening.*)

**Linda.**

Go down, try it. And be quiet.

**Willy.**

(*turning to Linda, guiltily*) You're not worried about me, are you, sweetheart?

**§ Biff.**

What's the matter?

**Happy.**

Listen! §

**Linda.**

You've got too much on the ball to worry about.

**Willy.**

You're my foundation and my support, Linda.

**Linda.**
Just try to relax, dear. You make mountains out of mole-hills.

**Willy.**
I won't fight with him any more. If he wants to go back to Texas, let him go.

**Linda.**
He'll find his way.

**Willy.**
Sure. Certain men just don't get started till later in life. Like Thomas Edison, I think. Or B. F. Goodrich. One of them was deaf. (*He starts for the bedroom doorway*) I'll put my money on Biff.

**Linda.**
And, Willy—if it's warm Sunday we'll drive in the country. And we'll open the windshield, and take lunch.

**Willy.**
No, the windshields don't open on the new cars.

**Linda.**
But you opened it today.

**Willy.**
Me? I didn't. (*He stops*) Now isn't that peculiar! Isn't that remarkable—(*He breaks off in amazement and fright as the flute is heard distantly*)

**Linda.**
What, darling?

**Willy.**
That is the most remarkable thing.

**Linda.**
What, dear?

**Willy.**
I was thinking of the Chevy. (*Slight pause*) Nineteen twenty-eight . . . when I had that red Chevy— (*Breaks off*) That's funny! I coulda sworn I was driving that Chevy today.

**Linda.**
Well, that's nothing. Something must've reminded you.

**Willy.**
Remarkable. Ts. Remember those days? The way Biff used to Simonize that car? The dealer refused to believe there was eighty thousand miles on it. (*He shakes his head*) Heh! (*To Linda*) Close your eyes, I'll be right up. (*He walks out of the bedroom*)

from
HOTEL UNIVERSE
by Philip Barry

Act I
ANN, PAT

At the Hotel Universe people remember things—so vividly
that they actually seem to relive old loves and hates and
fears. (For notes on the play, see page 114.) For Pat
Farley, a bright and likable young man, the memories
are of love—of a girl, Ann, whom he cannot love though
she loves him, and of another girl whose death he feels
was his fault. His fear is of failure, which he has already
acknowledged, and his hatred is for himself. He makes
wry jokes and shallow conversation, plays the cynic, and
makes plans to commit suicide. Pat's discovering a new
faith in himself and his acceptance that "things go on," a
change of heart influenced by the curious atmosphere of the
Hotel Universe and the wisdom of its master, old Stephen
Field, are the deepest and most fully developed of the
several character-plots in the play. And, when Pat is able
to declare his love for Ann, the play ends.

The scene below comes near the middle of the play.
The memories which haunt Pat and stand between him
and Ann are at their strongest. Not only has he con-
templated killing himself but he has planned the way he
will do it. All evening he has been at his wittiest and
most cynical. Ann has watched him, and his bitterness
and uncaring have frightened her. When the others leave
the terrace to go into the house, Ann closes the door behind them and turns to look at Pat. He stands beside the
wall above the sea, staring into space. For a moment Ann
watches him in silence. Then suddenly, swiftly, she goes
to him, takes him by the shoulders and turns him about,
facing her.

143

**Pat.**
Oh, hello, Ann. (*From the distance piano-music begins to be heard.*)

**Ann.**
(*Lowly, intensely*) I won't have it, Pat. I just will not have it!

**Pat.**
It?—What's that you won't have?

**Ann.**
Something's burning you up. Tell me what it is!

**Pat.**
I'm afraid you're imagining things. Where's the music from?

**Ann.**
Réné Mayer has a house up the road. It's always full of musicians.—You've got to listen to me. I—

**Pat.**
Have you heard Sandy Patch's new song? (*He moves toward the piano.*) —It's called "Drunk and Disorderly." It goes like this—

**Ann.**
Don't, Pat—we haven't time—

**Pat.**
Then let's get the others down, shall we?—And enjoy what there is left. (*He makes a move toward the house. Her hand upon his arm stops him.*)

**Ann.**
Wait! (*She looks away, to control herself, her hand still upon his arm.*)

**Pat.**
I'm all right, my dear. Really I am.

**Ann.**
We've known each other quite a few years, now—

**Pat.**
We have, haven't we? I feel pretty spry, though, don't you?

**Ann.**
We've always been able to talk.

**Pat.**
They say I could talk when I was only— (*Her hand tightens upon his arm.*)

**Ann.**
—Which we've always done directly, and honestly.

**Pat.**
Yes?

**Ann.**

Shan't we now?

**Pat.**

If you like. Why not?

**Ann.**

When you leave tonight I shan't see you again for at least a year—maybe more—

**Pat.**

Oh—before I forget— (*From his pocket, in a fold of tissue paper, he takes a very simple and old ruby pendant, and gives it to her.*)

**Ann.**

What is it?

**Pat.**

It was Mother's. I'm sure she'd want you to have it. I know I do.

**Ann.**

Beautiful—

**Pat.**

I think so.

**Ann.**

But Pat—it's priceless—

**Pat.**

So was she. So is Ann.

**Ann.**

Oh, thank you for it! Put it on for me— (*He catches it around her throat. She turns again, facing him, then stands for a moment with her forehead against his breast.*) Pat—my dear Pat—

**Pat.**

Things don't go the way we'd like them to, Ann. (*A moment, then she leaves him.*)

**Ann.**

—You've been dodging around corners, to get away from me.

**Pat.**

I didn't know it.

**Ann.**

I won't bite you, Pat.—What's been happening to you these past three years? I'm still a little interested.

**Pat.**

It's been pretty much the same sort of life, thanks.

**Ann.**

What are you doing with all that money?

**Pat.**

Oh—spending some of it—giving away quite a lot of it.

It's an awful pile to make a dent in.

**Ann.**

You never found the job we used to talk so much about—
(*Pat smiles.*)

**Pat.**

How well she knows me.

**Ann.**

There are only two people in this world who are really
important to me, you and Father.

**Pat.**

I'm—thanks, Ann. That's good to know.

**Ann.**

I've been able to help him a little—

**Pat.**

I should think you had.

**Ann.**

I'd give the eyes right out of my head, if I could help you.
(*He lifts her hand to his lips, kisses it, and turns away.*)
Oh, Pat, *Pat*—whatever has happened to you?

**Pat.**

Myself.

**Ann.**

—Don't you go telling yourself you're no good! You're
the best there is.

**Pat.**

You don't know.

**Ann.**

Oh, yes I do!

**Pat.**

Anyhow, let's not get solemn about—

**Ann.**

—And what do you suppose it means to me to know that
a person I love as I love you is breaking up into little
pieces over something I've no share in?

**Pat.**

But Ann—you don't love me any more.

**Ann.**

I do, though. I've never got over it—never. I love you
with all my heart. (*A silence. She smiles uncertainly.*)
—I don't suppose by any chance you love me back—

**Pat.**

(*With difficulty*) There's something in the way. Nothing
can ever come of you and me now. There's something in
the— (*He turns away, with an exclamation.*)

**Ann.**

Tell me.

**Pat.**

I can't.

**Ann.**

—You'll be shocked to hear I'm living with you in my mind. I've taught myself to dream about you nearly every night. That gives me—rights.

**Pat.**

Ah, Ann—let it go—please let it go.

**Ann.**

I can't. I simply can't.—You've always been a life-and-death person. You take things terribly hard. I'm sure it's not as hopeless as it seems. (*But he does not answer.*)— Do you remember the first time we met, on the Westbury Road?—me lost, with a sprained ankle, and you—

**Pat.**

—When I forget anything about you and me—

**Ann.**

I wish we could get back there. I wish we could start from the Westbury Road again.

**Pat.**

—But we can't.

**Ann.**

—Such a dear, serious boy you were. All the time you were in college you used to come to me with your little troubles— (*He laughs.*)

**Pat.**

—Would I row on the Crew?—I didn't make the Dramatic Club.—What if they passed me up on Tap Day.— Poor Ann—

**Ann.**

I was important to you then—

**Pat.**

You still are.

**Ann.**

Come to me now with your big trouble, Pat.

**Pat.**

I'm just a flop, darling.

**Ann.**

It's a little soon to decide that, don't you think?

**Pat.**

I told you my schedule was different.

**Ann.**

Pat, whatever happened, happened four years ago. You came back from a year in England, and you were changed. It was a girl, wasn't it? I saw her picture in your study. What was it—wouldn't she have you? (*Pat smiles.*)

**Pat.**

I forget. What did she look like?

**Ann.**

Very young, quite English, very fair. A lovely face—pretty, oh, so pretty.

**Pat.**

Funny—I've forgotten.

**Ann.**

I haven't.—Then you went over again the next winter—for how long was it?

**Pat.**

I don't know—three weeks—

**Pat.**

That's when I had my hunch about you. It wasn't long after you'd sailed. I was walking up Madison Avenue and in a florist's window I saw a lot of hawthorn blossoms. (*Pat starts slightly.*)

**Pat.**

Hawthorn—

**Ann.**

Yes. They were lovely, and I was going in to get some when all at once I began to feel terribly queer. It was as if the bottom had dropped out of everything. I knew it had something to do with you, and I love you and I just went on home without them.

**Pat.**

I don't get it at all.

**Ann.**

Nor do I.—But the next morning I passed the same shop and saw that the hawthorn was gone. Somehow, that was terrible. I couldn't get warm again all day. I love you and I had to cable you.

**Pat.**

I don't get it.

**Ann.**

I've never known such a change in a person, as in you when you came back. Suddenly you were as hard as nails, and so bitter. I hated leaving you that way when I came here with Father. But I was sure you'd get through it somehow, back to yourself. Now I see that you haven't. I see that it's worse than it ever was, it's destroying you. Oh, Pat—it can't be just some fool of a girl who wouldn't have you.—What has done it?

**Pat.**

Honestly, Ann—it's all so long ago.

**Ann.**

But I've *got* to know. Tell me! (*Pat shakes his head.*)

**Pat.**

It's all too ridiculous. Really. I never even think of it any more.

**Ann.**

Whether you do or not, it's got you still. Something awful's got you. Tell me—it will help to tell me. Ah, *please* —because I love you—

**Pat.**

I would if I could. I want to. I simply can't.

**Ann.**

I'll find out!

**Pat.**

All right, Ann.

**Ann.**

—But can't you *accept* it, somehow? Can't you take life whole—all of it—for what it is, and be glad of it? Why do you have to go at it with a tin box of paints, daubing it up pretty? You're grown-up, now.—Why, my dear! What have I said? What is there in that, to hurt you so?

**Pat.**

Listen: you can have your marvelous life. I'm not taking any.

**Ann.**

What are you talking about?!

**Pat.**

—The lot of you—clutching, grabbing at some little satisfaction that lasts a day or two—a swell business.

**Ann.**

You dare talk to me about my life like that!

**Pat.**

Yours—theirs—anyone's—

**Ann.**

Oh, you're horrible— (*Pat looks at her intently.*)

**Pat.**

So you're the last to go. You fail me too—

**Ann.**

(*A cry*) —You?—And who are you, that you shouldn't be failed sometime?

**Pat.**

I don't know, Ann. I've often wondered. (*Again he moves to the wall and stands looking out over it, the light from the lighthouse breaking over his head. Ann sinks into a corner of the sofa. From the distance, the piano-music begins to be heard more clearly. For a long time they are silent. Then Pat speaks. His voice is one of wonder, almost of fright.)* —They're right about this place—it *is* so, you know—it's really so—

**Ann.**

What is?

**Pat.**

—Like other places—like another place—

**Ann.**

Where?

**Pat.**

—A house my mother had in Florida, four years ago, when I came back from England—

**Ann.**

That was the second time—

**Pat.**

Yes. It was in March. I came straight down here from New York—I mean straight down there. Mother was in the patio all alone, having coffee—(*Still he looks out over the wall, without turning.*)—I had so much to tell her— I'll never forget it—I thought if only I could talk to some one who—

(*Ann speaks, softly:*)

**Ann.**

Hello, Son. It's good to have you back.

**Pat.**

—Could talk to some one who might, just might, have some little faint idea of what I—

**Ann.**

Hello, Son. It's good to have you back. (*A moment. Then:*)

**Pat.**

(*A murmur*) Hello, Mother. It's good to be back. (*He comes forward to her, slowly.*)

**Ann.**

I didn't expect you quite so soon.

**Pat.**

I know. (*He sinks down upon a cushion on the floor beside her. The eyes of both are straight ahead, not looking at each other.*)

**Ann.**

You're looking tired.

**Pat.**

It was a rotten trip. (*He goes on in a low voice, almost mechanically.*)—I think I'll stay a while this time.

**Ann.**

I'm glad.

**Pat.**

It seems like a pleasant place.

**Ann.**

It's peaceful.

**Pat.**

That's good.

**Ann.**

Ah, Pat—what is it, dear? I've worried so about you.

**Pat.**

Yes. I suppose.

**Ann.**

I've wanted to ask, but—

**Pat.**

I know. I just couldn't talk.

**Ann.**

Are you so very much in love?

**Pat.**

Yes.

**Ann.**

Tell me about her. Who is she?

**Pat.**

Oh, it's all over now.

**Ann.**

Over?

**Pat.**

Yes.

**Ann.**

But are you sure?

**Pat.**

I'm certain. (*A moment. Then:*)

**Ann.**

Who was she, then?

**Pat.**

—Mary Carr—the niece of one of my dons at Cambridge. (*A moment. His voice hardens.*)—Cambridge—another of Father's fake ideas. Finish me off, eh? Turn me into the little gentleman. Every inch a Farley— God!

**Ann.**

Hush, Pat—

**Pat.**

—Be good at everything. Shine! Always shine! And if you can't don't play.—I can still hear his voice.

**Ann.**

—Mary Carr, I've seen her photograph. She's very lovely.

**Pat.**

Yes.

**Ann.**

—And young.

**Pat.**

She was eighteen in November. (*A pause. Then suddenly.*) God, that is young. Father was right *there*, at least.

**Ann.**

What happened when he went over to you last year—

**Pat.**

I cabled I wanted to get married. He cabled me to wait, he was coming. I waited. He came. He talked me out of it. (*Bitterly.*) —She wasn't suitable.

**Ann.**

But that wasn't *your* reason—

**Pat.**

I tell you I let him talk me out of it!

**Ann.**

You agreed to put it off, that's all.

**Pat.**

Yes—that's what I told myself—and that's what I told Mary.—That's what the little swine I was, grunted at Mary—just put it off a while, that's all. But somehow the point missed Mary—somehow she didn't get me.— She just stopped talking in the middle of a word, and went into the house. And I took a train, and sailed with *him*. He was ill then—or said he was—we couldn't wait a day.

**Ann.**

(*Hesitantly, after a pause*) You—I suppose you and she —you'd been a good deal to each other.

**Pat.**

We'd been everything.

**Ann.**

I see.

**Pat.**

—But there wasn't to be a baby, if that's what you mean— (*Again the bitter voice returns.*) Wise boy, young Farley. *He* knows his way around!

**Ann.**

But you wrote her. Surely you wrote her.

**Pat.**

All the time, but I never had one little word from her. A dozen times I'd have gone over, but how could I with Father dying and then all that tangle settling the estate?

*(He concludes, lowly.)*—It was a year and three months since I'd seen her, when I'd sailed. I didn't even wire—I was afraid she'd run away somewhere.

**Ann.**

But she hadn't, had she?

**Pat.**

No.

**Ann.**

She was there—

**Pat.**

She was there. *(A moment. Then:)*

**Ann.**

—And she just won't have you. *(Her hand reaches to comfort him. He turns to her.)*

**Pat.**

Mother, she just won't have me. *(Suddenly he stares at her.)* You're not—oh, damn you, Ann— *(He rises, and leaves her. She follows him.)*

**Ann.**

All right! But tell me. You've got to finish now! *(In another voice.)*—Surely it isn't hopeless. Surely you can—

**Pat.**

But it is, you see.

**Ann.**

I don't believe it. Where is she now?

**Pat.**

Down in the ground.

**Ann.**

Pat—she isn't—?

**Pat.**

She is, though—as a doornail.

**Ann.**

Oh, my poor boy—

**Pat.**

My poor Mary.

**Ann.**

But listen to me—listen—!

**Pat.**

No. *You* do. *(He points his finger at her, and speaks.)* Three days before I came, she walked out under a tree where—she'd walked out under a hawthorn tree at the end of a very sweet lane we knew, and stood there and shot herself.

**Ann.**

Pat—Pat— *(He moves away from her.)*

**Pat.**
  You wanted to know, didn't you? (*She looks at him. Then:*)

**Ann.**
  —So I lose you to a dead girl.

**Pat.**
  I've lost myself to her.

**Ann.**
  You loved me first!

**Pat.**
  But she died— (*He goes to the piano and seats himself, running his fingers silently over the keys.*)—If only I could get back to her somehow. If I could just let her know I did come back.

**Ann.**
  How much of it is losing her—and how much the loss of yourself?

**Pat.**
  I don't understand that.

**Ann.**
  —You used to have a fair opinion of Pat Farley. That was essential to you—that was you.

**Pat.**
  All I know is that nothing's been any good to me since. I'm licked, Ann.

**Ann.**
  Well, what are you going to do about it? * * *

**Pat.**
  What is there to?

**Ann.**
  (*Suddenly, sharply*) Pat!

**Pat.**
  (*Without turning*) What?

**Ann.**
  You said you'd tell me this the day before you died— (*As she reaches the word, he strikes a chord and drowns it.*)

**Pat.**
  —But I changed my mind, didn't I?—I told you now! (*He turns toward the house and calls:*) What'll I play? Call your tunes, gents—almost closing-time! * * *

**Ann.**
  Pat!

**Pat.**
  I don't know what [you're] talking about. * * *

**Ann.**

Oh, my poor Sweet, why do you want to do it? (*She shakes his shoulders.*) Why?

**Pat.**

Why not?—Maybe you can tell me that!—Why not?—I should have three years ago, but I was too yellow then. (*Still she stares. Another silence, then he pulls away from her, mumbling:*)—All right. Don't worry about me. It's all right. Small brain-storm, that's all.—Over now—

**Ann.**

Promise it! (*He gestures vaguely, * * * turns to her and sings, beating time with his finger.*)

**Pat.**

—Rat-a-plan, rat-a-plan, rat-a-plan-plan-plan-plan— (*He stops on the high note, holds out his arms, and cries:*) Yes! (*And goes to the point of the wall, where he stands with his back to her.*)

from
# BELL, BOOK AND CANDLE
by John van Druten

### Act I
### GILLIAN, MISS HOLROYD

In his comedy about witches in New York, John van Druten makes the fantastic believable and delightful by presenting it in the most matter-of-fact way. His witches exchange the formulas for potions like clubwomen trading recipes. Their professional society is split into groups of petty feuders. There is little that is airy and almost nothing eerie. The plot follows an old formula (almost): witch meets boy, witch loses boy, witch gets boy. Of course, the witch has to lose her occult powers and become just another woman before she can win the man.

The scene below occurs early in the play, while the audience is getting used to the idea of witches in modern dress—and to believing what the actors believe. It provides good exercise for the imagination.

The place is the living room of a first-floor apartment in a brownstone in New York. The time is Christmas Eve. Gillian Holroyd, a small, attractive witch of twenty-seven, has had an uncomfortable conversation with the man from upstairs—her aunt, it seems, keeps turning up in his apartment even when the door is bolted. Gillian has apologized and promised that it will not happen again. As the man leaves, the aunt, Miss Holroyd, enters. She is "an odd-looking woman, vague, fluttery, and eccentric," not at all like Gillian, whose dress and appearance are simple if a little arty. Miss Holroyd "is dressed in a wispy evening gown, bitty and endy, with a trailing scarf, bangles, and a long necklace. When she talks, it is in a high, feathery voice, and a trilling little laugh."

As Gillian closes the door behind the man from upstairs, "Miss Holroyd walks away with exaggerated nonchalance, aware of the scolding that is coming to her, and trying only to postpone it. Gillian stands watching her, like a cat waiting to pounce."

**Miss H.**

So you've met him, after all. Do you still think he's attractive?

**Gillian.**

(*quietly*) Yes, I do. Very.

**Miss H.**

Did you—bring him here?

**Gillian.**

No. He came here to talk to me. (*Pause. Then, springing it*) About *you.*

**Miss H.**

(*naïvely*) Me?

**Gillian.**

Yes, and it's no good acting innocent. I'm angry. *Really* angry.

**Miss H.**

Why, what have I done?

**Gillian.**

You know. Broken into his apartment—played tricks with his telephone . . .

**Miss H.**

That was because he reported me to the agents. That was just to pay him out.

**Gillian.**

I don't care *what* it was. You *promised* when I let you move in here . . .

**Miss H.**

I promised to be careful.

**Gillian.**

And do you call that being careful? Getting caught in his apartment? Twice!

**Miss H.**

What harm did I do? I didn't *take* anything. Yes, I read his letters, but it's not as if I were going to make *use* of them. Though I'm tempted to now—now that he's told on me—to you.

**Gillian.**

(*menacingly, and quite frighteningly*) Auntie, if you do— well, you'll be sorry. And you know I can *make* you sorry, too.

**Miss H.**
(*defensively*) He'd never suspect, darling. Not in a million years. No matter *what* I did. Honestly, it's amazing the way people don't. Why, they don't believe there *are* such things. I sit in the subway sometimes, or in busses, and look at the people next to me, and I think: What would you say if I told you I was a witch? And I know they'd never believe it. They just wouldn't believe it. And I giggle and giggle to myself.

**Gillian.**
Well, you've got to stop giggling here. You've got to swear, swear on the Manual . . .

**Miss H.**
(*retreating a step*) Swear what?

**Gillian.**
That you'll stop practicing—in this house—ever.

**Miss H.**
*You* practice here.

**Gillian.**
I can be discreet about it. You can't.

**Miss H.**
(*very hurt*) I shall move to a hotel.

**Gillian.**
Very well. But if you get into trouble there, don't look to *me* to get you out.

**Miss H.**
(*huffily*) I've other people I can turn to.

**Gillian.**
(*scornfully*) Mrs. de Pass, I suppose.

**Miss H.**
Yes, she's done a lot for me.

**Gillian.**
Well, I wouldn't count on Mrs. de Pass, if *I* turn against you. I'm a lot better than *that* old phony. Now . . . (*She gets a large white-bound book from a closet*)

**Miss H.**
(*really scared*) Oh, please—not on the Manual.

**Gillian.**
(*relentlessly*) On the Manual. (*She brings it*) Now, put your hand on it. (*Miss Holroyd does so, terrified*) Now, then, I swear that I will not practice witchcraft ever in this house again. So help me Tagla, Salamandrae, Brazo and Vesturiel. Say, "I swear."

**Miss H.**
(*after a moment*) I swear.

**Gillian.**

Good. (*She replaces the book*)

**Miss H.**

I think you're very cruel.

**Gillian.**

(*returning, somewhat softened*) Oh, Auntie, if you'd only have a little sense!

**Miss H.**

(*continuing*) *And* hypocritical. Sometimes I think you're *ashamed* of being what you are.

**Gillian.**

Ashamed? I'm not in the least ashamed. No, it's not a question of that, but . . . (*Suddenly*) Auntie, don't you ever wish you *weren't?*

**Miss H.**

(*amazed*) No.

**Gillian.**

That you were like those people you sit next to in the busses?

**Miss H.**

Ordinary and humdrum? No, I *was*. For years. Before I came into it.

**Gillian.**

Well, you came in late. And, anyway, I don't *mean* humdrum. I just mean unenlightened. And I don't hanker for it all the time. Just sometimes.

**Miss H.**

Darling, you're depressed. . . .

**Gillian.**

I know. I expect it's Christmas. It's always upset me.

**Miss H.**

You wait till you get to Zoe's party, and see all your old friends again.

**Gillian.**

I don't *want* to see all my old friends again. I want something different.

**Miss H.**

Well, come with me to Mrs. de Pass's, then. She's got some very interesting people. Some French people. From the Paris chapter.

**Gillian.**

(*laughing*) I didn't mean *that*, when I said I wanted something different. I think maybe I'd like to spend the evening with some everyday people for a change, instead of *us*.

**Miss H.**
(*archly*) With Mr. Henderson?

**Gillian.**
I wouldn't mind.

**Miss H.**
It's too bad he's getting married. Still, I suppose . . .

**Gillian.**
He's getting married?

**Miss H.**
Yes, quite soon. They're announcing it New Year's Eve.

**Gillian.**
How do you know that? Oh, the telephone, I suppose.

**Miss H.**
Yes, dear.

**Gillian.**
Who's he getting married to? Do you know?

**Miss H.**
I don't know her last name. Her first name's Merle.

**Gillian.**
Merle? The only Merle I ever knew was a girl I was in college with. Merle Kittredge. She used to write poison-pen letters. I caught her writing one about me, once. That's why we had all those thunderstorms that spring. She was terrified of them. (*Smiling at the recollection*) We had one every day for a month. It was most extraordinary.

**Miss H.**
You mean that that was *you*? (*Delighted*) Oh, Gillian, you were naughty!

**Gillian.**
She was a nervous wreck by the end of the term.

**Miss H.**
And you think this might be the same girl? What was she like?

**Gillian.**
Southern, and blonde, and helpless . . .

**Miss H.**
This one's blonde. He's got her picture on his bureau.

**Gillian.**
(*continuing her catalogue*) And appealing. And underneath, a liar and a sneak and a beau-snatcher.

**Miss H.**
Did you ever hear what happened to her?

**Gillian.**
I think she became a decorator.

**Miss H.**

This one's a decorator.

**Gillian.**

(*after a moment's pause*) Well, there's probably more than one decorator in New York called Merle. And, if he's engaged, that rules him out.

**Miss H.**

I don't see why.

**Gillian.**

I'm not a Southern belle. I don't take other women's men. Though I would, if it *were* Merle Kittredge.

**Miss H.**

I could find out for you.

**Gillian.**

But—New Year's. That wouldn't leave me much time.

**Miss H.**

You wouldn't *need* time. Just a quick little potion. Or—four words to Pyewacket, you once told me.

**Gillian.**

Yes, but I wouldn't want him that way. That would take the challenge out of it. Especially with her. Other girls can make men like them in a week, without that. Why can't I?

**Miss H.**

Did he seem to like you this afternoon?

**Gillian.**

(*with rueful humor*) Not very much. No.

**Miss H.**

(*with sudden alarm*) Gillian, you—you haven't fallen in love with him, and lost your powers, have you? That isn't what this is all about?

**Gillian.**

(*laughing*) No, of course not.

**Miss H.**

Oh, thank goodness!

**Gillian.**

You don't *believe* that old wives' tale?

**Miss H.**

Of course I do! It's true. They say it's true.

**Gillian.**

It's the other way around. We can't fall in love. (*Pause*) Merle Kittredge. I haven't thought of her in years. (*Pause again*) Do you think—if it were she—I could do it in a week—without tricks?

**Miss H.**

Darling, it's no good asking me. I never could do it at

all. But if it is, why don't you pull a quick one, and have done with it?

**Gillian.**

No. I don't say I wouldn't be tempted, but if I've got a week—I'd like to see how good I am, the other way.

from
# TIME REMEMBERED
by Jean Anouilh  (translated by Patricia Moyes)

Act I, scene 2
AMANDA, THE TAXI DRIVER,
THE ICE-CREAM MAN

The setting is a clearing in a park which surrounds a splendid old house not far from Paris. "It is wild and overgrown. There is a small obelisk encircled by a stone bench. At one side of the scene, pulled up near a large tree, stands an ancient taxi. Two legs stick out from under it. A closer inspection reveals that this is a mere caricature of a taxi—filthy and antiquated, and overgrown with ivy and honeysuckle. A cock crows from the vantage point of its roof. Not far away stands an ice-cream cart, displaying its gaudy pictorial representations of strawberry and vanilla cones and bars. Two legs are also visible under the cart."

This park, with its assortment of things that don't belong together and things that ought to work but don't, seems a setting for *Alice in Wonderland*. And into the clearing rushes a young girl who might be Alice. In Anouilh's gentle and only somewhat fantastic comedy, the girl is not Alice, however; she is Amanda, a little milliner who has been called to the estate by its owner, the Duchess, and offered a rather peculiar job. She has been asked to pretend to be Leocadia, the magnificent ballerina, now dead, who was the beloved of the Duchess' favorite nephew. Since Leocadia's death, the young man has lived only to remember her; he has surrounded himself with the things that he and Leocadia knew together: the café in which they dined, the taxi in which they rode, the ice-cream cart they saw, and the inn where once they had breakfast. So there is, after all, a logic to the hodgepodge in the park. Taxi, cart, and the rest are mementos, and Amanda, if she takes the job, will become a part of the collection—it seems that in appearance she bears a striking resemblance to Leocadia.

163

But Amanda does not yet know the story of Leocadia. She was brought here from Paris, welcomed by a mad old woman (the Duchess), who chatted with a husband who was not there, dashed in and out of the room (a drawing room "of stupefying elegance"), and shouted incomprehensible orders to Amanda to eat more, fidget less, and please be patient. Amanda took advantage of the Duchess' rushes-out to flee the house. She ran into the park and now she is looking for a way to get back to Paris. As she runs into the clearing, carrying her little cardboard suitcase, she sees the taxi, stops, and exclaims joyfully.

**Amanda.**
Oh, thank heavens! A taxi! (*She looks round, sees no one, and then notices the legs.*) Oh . . . excuse me . . .

**A Voice.**
Who are you talking to?

**Amanda.**
I . . . I don't know . . . are these your legs?
(*A benevolent old man appears from behind the ice-cream cart. He adjusts his spectacles, and says:*)

**Man.**
Which legs? (*Amanda, mute with embarrassment, indicates the legs which protrude from under the taxi.*) (*Simply.*) No. Those aren't mine. (*He disappears behind his cart again, newspaper in hand.*)

**Amanda.**
(*as he goes*) Oh, sir . . . please. . . . (*He reappears.*) Am I still in the park? I've been walking for ever so long.

**Man.**
(*lugubrious*) Yes, miss. You can walk as long as you like and you'll still be in the park.
(*A mockingbird's song shrills out as though to taunt Amanda. Suddenly she snatches up her case and runs to the taxi.*)

**Amanda.**
Taxi! Taxi! Driver, are you free? (*At these words, the Driver emerges from under his cab, furious.*)

**Driver.**
Of course I am free. Am I not a Socialist?

**Amanda.**
Oh, thank goodness, I am saved. (*She opens the door of the taxi and jumps in, crying:*) Take me to the railway

station, please! As fast as you can! (*The Driver watches
her get into the taxi with mingled astonishment and
amusement. She emerges almost immediately from the
door on the other side.*)

**Amanda.**

Driver!

**Driver.**

Yes?

**Amanda.**

(*angry*) There are rabbits in your taxi!

**Driver.**

Of course there are rabbits in my taxi! (*He grows very
angry.*) So now I'm not allowed to keep rabbits, is that it?
Eh? Have I or have I not got a right to keep rabbits if I
want to?

**Amanda.**

(*retreating a step*) Of course you have a right to keep
rabbits. . . .

**Driver.**

(*advancing angrily*) Am I a human being or am I not?
I'm only asking. Getting at me just because they pay me
thirty thousand francs a month for doing nothing? Well,
I'm not denying it, am I? That has absolutely nothing to
do with it. Anyway, I always said I'd never be a private
chauffeur . . . that's what they call me. Huh! Well?

**Amanda.**

(*retreating rapidly*) I assure you I never meant——

**Driver.**

All right then.

(*Amanda takes another step back and trips. She cries out,
for by now everything scares her. Then she smiles timidly
at the Driver, as if to excuse her exclamation.*)

**Amanda.**

I'm sorry . . . I'm a bit nervy today. . . . (*She sees what
she has tripped over, and breathes again.*) Oh . . . it's only
a bit of ivy. . . .

**Driver.**

(*calmer*) Of course it's ivy. Any objection? (*He goes
back to his motor.*) It's easy to grow, ivy is. I tried rambler
roses once, pruned 'em, watered 'em every day—no good.
Wouldn't grow. So now I stick to ivy; it's pretty and it
grows quick.

**Amanda.**

It must be awkward when you want to drive away.

**Driver.**
What d'you mean, awkward?

**Amanda.**
Well . . . the . . . the ivy . . . (*By now anything seems possible. She asks with a timid smile:*) Do you . . . take it with you?

**Driver.**
(*delighted at the idea*) You're a comic, you are. What d'you think the ivy's made of then—elastic? (*He calls:*) Hey! Giuseppe! (*The Ice-Cream Man reappears.*) D'you know what she just said? Asked if the ivy follows me around! She's a proper scream, she is. Can't you just see me taking it out for a walk every day. (*Calls, as if to a dog.*) Come along, then! (*Whistles.*) There's a good little ivy . . . heel, sir, heel! (*He roars with laughter.*)

**Amanda.**
(*continuing her inspection*) But your taxi can't possibly go at all! There are creepers growing all over it!

**Driver.**
What's that? My taxi not go! D'you hear that, Giuseppe? So my taxi won't go, won't it? (*He rushes to the taxi, livid, and turns the handle viciously. A hiccough, and the motor starts.*) There! Now who says it won't go!

**Amanda.**
No! No, please! Don't make it move! Not with the ivy! I couldn't bear it! I think I'm going mad . . . everything is absolutely crazy today . . . (*To the Ice-Cream Man.*) You . . . are you really an ice-cream man?

**Man.**
'Course I am, miss.

**Amanda.**
Well, sell me an ice-cream then. I'm terribly thirsty.

**Man.**
An ice-cream! My dear young lady, it's two years since I last made an ice-cream. I doubt if I could remember how.

**Amanda.**
Just as I expected. Thank you. You've set my mind at rest. I am beginning to see a mad sort of sense in all this. I'd only have been worried if you'd *had* an ice-cream to sell—a real, freezing ice-cream. Will you do one more thing for me? (*She hands him something.*)

**Man.**
What's this? A pin? What d'you expect me to do with a pin?

**Amanda.**

Prick me, please—not too hard, just enough to make sure I'm not dreaming.

**Man.**

(*pricking her*) She's a character all right.

**Driver.**

(*lugubrious*) She's worse than a character. She's looney.

**Amanda.**

Ow! Thank you. May I have my pin back, please? (*She takes the pin, and pricks her own hand, gently, experimentally, as if to confirm her previous opinion that she is awake. Having done so, she suddenly turns to the two men, desperately defiant.*) I *am* awake—and alive! D'you hear? I'm alive and when I'm pricked with a pin, I feel it. I've got two legs and two feet, and I can walk on them. I'm not even going to ask you the way to the railway station. I'm going to walk straight ahead and follow my nose till I find the main road. And on the road I'll find a signpost—because in the world I come from—the real world —there are real signposts on the road, pointing to real places! And I'll read it with my own two eyes and then I'll walk to the station, and I'll find the station master— and he'll be a real live station master, made of flesh and blood! (*She picks up her case with a sigh which is very close to tears, and adds:*) I hope.

# CHAPTER III

## CONCENTRATION, COMMUNICATION, CONFLICT, AND CHARACTERIZATION

Ten monologues and twenty-four scenes in which the actor "gets into character," relates to his fellow players, and finds the "beats" or "units and objectives" which carry him through the scene and play.

You must look at me when you speak, fix your eye on my eye!
> Charles Macklin (1697?–1797),
> to his students

. . . An actor must proceed, not by a multitude of details, but by those important units which, like signals, mark his channel and keep him in the right creative line.
> Constantin Stanislavski,
> *An Actor Prepares*

from
# THE RAINMAKER
by N. Richard Nash

Act I
LIZZIE

Lizzie Curry lives on a ranch with her father and two brothers. (For introductory comments on the play, see page 346.) As the playwright describes Lizzie, "At first glance, she seems a woman who can cope with all the aspects of her life. She has the world of materiality under control; she is a good housekeeper; pots and pans, needles and thread—when she touches them, they serve. She knows well where she fits in the family—and she enjoys the manifold elements of her position. She has a sure ownership of her own morality, for the tenets of right and wrong are friendly to her—and she is comfortably forthright in living by them. A strong and integral woman in every life function—except one. Here she is, twenty-seven years old and no man outside the family has loved her or found her beautiful. And, yet, ironically, it is this one unfulfilled part of Lizzie that is the most potentially beautiful facet of the woman, this yearning for romance, this courageous searching for it in the desert of her existence. . . . But she is at great pains to conceal these hungers—by an open display of good humor, by laughter at herself—and by behaving, in a western world of men, as if she were as much a man as any of them. Lizzie, the Tomboy. But if some day a man should find her, he will find no tomboy but a full and ready woman, willing to give herself with the totality of her rich being."

But at this point in the play, near the beginning of Act I, no man has found Lizzie. Last night she came home from Sweetriver, where she was visiting a family with six sons, three of them old enough to marry. Her father sent her on the trip in the hope that one of the three would choose Lizzie. Now she is expected to tell what happened. She

171

does in the speeches below, taken from a scene with her father and brothers.

It is morning. Lizzie has come down to breakfast late—she did not sleep well.

**Lizzie.**
[What did I do in Sweetriver?] Well, the first three or four days I was there—I stayed in my room most of the time.
§ **Noah.**
What'd you do that for? §
**Lizzie.**
Because I was embarrassed!
§ **Noah.**
Embarrassed about what?
**Lizzie.**
Noah, use your head! § I knew what I was there for—and the whole family knew it too. And I couldn't stand the way they were looking me over. So I'd go downstairs for my meals—and rush right back to my room. I packed—I unpacked—I washed my hair a dozen times—I read the Sears, Roebuck catalog from cover to cover. And finally I said to myself: "Lizzie Curry, snap out of this!" Well, it was a Saturday night—and they were all going to a rodeo dance. So I got myself all decked out in my highest heels and my lowest cut dress. And I walked down to that supper table and all those boys looked at me as if I was stark naked. And then for the longest while there wasn't a sound at the table except for Uncle Ned slupping his soup. And then suddenly—like a gunshot—I heard Ned Junior say: "Lizzie, how much do you weigh?"
§ **H.C.**
What'd you say to that? §
**Lizzie.**
(*Squaring off*) I said, "I weigh a hundred and nineteen pounds, my teeth are all my own and I stand seventeen hands high."
§ **Noah.**
That wasn't very smart of you. §
**Lizzie.**
He was just tryin' to open the conversation. (*Wryly*) Well, I guess I closed it. . . . Then, about ten minutes later little Peter came hurrying in to the supper table. He was carrying a geography book and he said: "Hey, Pop—

where's Madagascar?" Well, everybody ventured an opinion and they were all dead wrong. And suddenly I felt I
had to make a good impression and I heard my own voice
talking as if it didn't belong to me. I said: "It's an island
in the Indian Ocean off the coast of Africa right opposite
Mozambique." (*With a wail*) Can I help it if I was good
in geography?

§ **H.C.**

What happened?

**Lizzie.**

Nothing. Not a doggone thing. § Everything was so
quiet it sounded like the end of the world. Then I heard
Ned Junior's voice: "Lizzie, you fixin' to be a school-
marm?"

§ **H.C.**

Oh, no! §

**Lizzie.**

Yes. And suddenly I felt like I was way back at the high-
school dance—and nobody dancing with me. And I had
a sick feeling that I was wearing eyeglasses again the
way I used to. And I knew from that minute on that it was
no go. So I didn't go to the rodeo dance with them—I
stayed home and made up poems about what was on sale
at Sears, Roebuck's.

§ **H.C.**

You and little Pete?

**Lizzie.**

Yes . . . § And the day I left Sweetriver little Peter was
bawling. And he said: "You're the beautifulest girl that
ever was!"

from
DREAM GIRL
by Elmer Rice

Act I
GEORGINA

Georgina dreams—extravagantly, melodramatically, and in
lurid detail. She is a quiet girl who lives with her parents,
owns half of a not very successful bookshop, writes novels
which no publisher buys, and has a hopeless crush on her
brother-in-law. In Georgina's imagination, however, the
people of her everyday life become heroes and villains and
she herself assumes many dramatic roles. The daydreams,
the actual happenings around them, and Georgina's search
for something (and someone) real as well as exciting are
the subject of the play.

The scene below occurs at the opening of Act I. It is
morning and Georgina is fighting her daily battle to get
up, get dressed, and get going. Offstage, her mother calls:
"Georgina! Are you daydreaming in there? It's almost
nine!"

**Georg.**
(*leaping up*) All right, Mother. I'm practically dressed.
(*The lights fade on the scene and come up, at the left, on
Georgina's bathroom, which she enters, talking all the
while.*) Maybe your mother is right, Georgina. Maybe it's
time you cut out the daydreaming—time you stopped
mooning around and imagining yourself to be this extraordinary creature with a strange and fascinating psy-
chological life. (*She has removed her negligee and donned
a bathing cap; and she now goes around behind the bathroom, invisible but still audible. The sound of a shower
is heard.*) Oh, damn it! Cold as ice! There, that's better!
(*She sings "Night and Day" lustily. Then the shower is
turned off, and she reappears wrapped in a large bath towel*

174

*and stands, her back to the audience, rubbing herself vigorously.*) Still, to be honest, I must admit that, compared to the average girl you meet, I'm really quite complex. Intelligent and well informed too; and a good conversationalist. (*Indignantly as, over her shoulder, she sees someone looking in at her*) Well, for heaven's sake! Honestly, some people! (*She pulls down an imaginary window shade and the scene is blacked out, her voice coming out of the darkness.*) And my looks are nothing to be ashamed of either. I have a neat little figure and my legs are really very nice. Of course, my nose is sort of funny, but my face definitely has character—not just one of those magazine-cover deadpans. (*With a yawn*) Oh, I never seem to get enough sleep! (*The lights come up as she raises the imaginary shade. She is dressed now in her shoes, stockings, and slip. She seats herself at her dressing table, facing the audience, and brushes her hair.*) If I could only stop lying awake for hours, dreaming up all the exciting things that could happen but never do. Well, maybe this is the day when things really will begin to happen to me. Maybe Wentworth and Jones will accept my novel. They've had it over a month now, and all the other publishers turned it down in less than two weeks. It certainly looks promising. And especially with Jim's recommendation. Wouldn't that be wonderful! With a published novel, I'd really be somebody. Reviews in all the book sections; royalty checks coming in; women nudging each other at Schrafft's and whispering, "Don't look now, but that girl over there—the one with the smart hat —that's Georgina Allerton, the novelist." (*Going to the washbasin*) Gee, that would be thrilling! To feel that I'd accomplished something. To feel that I had a purpose in life. To feel that— (*She busies herself with a toothbrush, becoming momentarily unintelligible.*) Ubble-ba-glug-ab-lub-mum. Only it wouldn't make up for Jim. (*Going back to the dressing table*) Fifty novels wouldn't make up for Jim. If Miriam only appreciated him. But she doesn't. She doesn't understand him. All his fine sensitive qualities—they're completely lost on her. It's really ironic. (*Baring her teeth*) Gosh, my teeth could certainly stand a good cleaning. It's awful the way I put off going to the dentist. Maybe that's psychopathic too. What to do? What to do? Here I am twenty-three years old—no, let's face it, twenty-four next month! And that's practically thirty. Thirty years old—and nothing to show for it. Suppose nothing ever does happen to me. That's a frightening thought! Just to go on and on like this, on through middle age, on to senility, never experiencing anything—what a prospect! (*Putting on her make-up*) Of course I suppose that up to a certain point there's nothing abnormal about virginity. But the question is, how can you ever be sure you haven't passed that point? Heavens, is that a gray hair? No, thank goodness. What a scare! Still, there must be a lot of women who go right on being virgins until the very day they die. It can be done, I guess. Doesn't sound like much fun though. (*She rises and gets into her dress.*) Well, that brings me right smack back to George Hand. Maybe I shouldn't have accepted his invitation for today. He really is rushing me. Of course, he may not have any intentions at all. No, he's too busy a man to keep on dating up a girl, without having something on his mind. So that puts it squarely up to me. Well, anyhow, if I'm going to play with fire, I may as well look my best. So here goes.

§ **Mother.**

(*off right*) Georgina, I'm getting tired of keeping the coffee hot. §

**Georg.**

Coming! Coming!

from
# THE MEMBER OF THE WEDDING
by Carson McCullers

Act I
FRANKIE

The play is about Frankie, a girl of twelve who has a
difficult time growing into adolescence, and about her attempts to "belong." Frankie has a father but no mother.
She is a tomboy to whom other girls, with their chatter
about clothes and boys, are curiosities she prefers to ignore.
Frankie's special world includes only two other people:
Berenice, the gruff and understanding colored housekeeper,
and John Henry, the sober little boy from next door. With
these two, Frankie plays endless games of cards, talks of
Serious Things, and puts together plays of the most
romantic, swashbuckling kind. Then Frankie's brother
comes home from the army to be married and Frankie
falls in love with the idea of the wedding. She will be a
part of it, she decides, and share the "belonging" of the
bride and groom. Her efforts to join the wedding and
to accompany the couple on their honeymoon are dis-
astrous, but the experience gives Frankie new ideas about
herself. Her father remarries, she is at last a member of an
"us," and girls are no longer curiosities to her but people
she wants to be like and is.

In the monologue, taken from a scene with John Henry,
Frankie comes to her decision to be a member of the
wedding.

The setting is a part of a southern back yard and kitchen.
At stage left there is a scuppernong arbor. There is an elm
tree. Frankie and John Henry are in the yard. It is early
evening.

**Frankie.**

(*looking at the house*) I wonder when that Papa of mine
is coming home. He always comes home by dark. I don't

177

want to go into that empty, ugly house all by myself.
§ **John H.**
Me neither. §
**Frankie.**
(*standing with outstretched arms, and looking around
her*) I think something is wrong. It is too quiet. I have
a peculiar warning in my bones. I bet you a hundred
dollars it's going to storm.
§ **John H.**
I don't want to spend the night with you. §
**Frankie.**
A terrible, terrible dog-day storm. Or maybe even a
cyclone.
§ **John H.**
Huh. §
**Frankie.**
I bet Jarvis and Janice are now at Winter Hill. I see them
just plain as I see you. Plainer. Something is wrong. It
is too quiet. (*A clear horn begins to play a blues tune
in the distance.*)
§ **John H.**
Frankie? §
**Frankie.**
Hush! It sounds like Honey. (*The horn music becomes
jazzy and spangling, then the first blues tune is repeated.
Suddenly, while still unfinished, the music stops. Frankie
waits tensely.*) He has stopped to bang the spit out of
his horn. In a second he will finish. (*After a wait*) Please,
Honey, go on finish!
§ **John H.**
(*softly*) He done quit now. §
**Frankie.**
(*moving restlessly*) I told Berenice that I was leavin' town
for good and she did not believe me. Sometimes I honestly think she is the biggest fool that ever drew breath. You
try to impress something on a big fool like that, and it's
just like talking to a block of cement. I kept on telling
and telling and telling her. I told her I had to leave this
town for good because it is inevitable. Inevitable. (*Mr.
Addams enters the kitchen from the house, calling:
"Frankie, Frankie."*)
§ **Mr. A.**
(*calling from the kitchen door*) Frankie, Frankie. §
**Frankie.**
Yes, Papa.

§ **Mr. A.**

(*opening the back door*) You had supper? §

**Frankie.**

I'm not hungry.

§ **Mr. A.**

Was a little later than I intended, fixing a timepiece for a railroad man. (*He goes back through the kitchen and into the hall, calling: "Don't leave the yard!"*)

**John H.**

You want me to get the weekend bag? §

**Frankie.**

Don't bother me, John Henry. I'm thinking. About the wedding. About my brother and the bride. Everything's been so sudden today. I never believed before about the fact that the earth turns at the rate of about a thousand miles a day. I didn't understand why it was that if you jumped up in the air you wouldn't land in Selma or Fairview or somewhere else instead of the same back yard. But now it seems to me I feel the world going around very fast. (*Frankie begins turning around in circles with arms outstretched.*) I feel it turning and it makes me dizzy.

§ **John H.**

I'll stay and spend the night with you. §

**Frankie.**

(*suddenly stopping her turning*) I just now thought of something.

§ **John H.**

You just a little while ago was begging me. §

**Frankie.**

I know where I'm going. * * * It's like I've known it all my life. Tomorrow I will tell everybody.

§ **John H.**

Where? §

**Frankie.**

(*dreamily*) After the wedding I'm going with them to Winter Hill. I'm going off with them after the wedding.

§ **John H.**

You serious? §

**Frankie.**

Shush, just now I realized something. The trouble with me is that for a long time I have been just an "I" person. All other people can say "we." When Berenice says "we" she means her lodge and church and colored people.

Soldiers can say "we" and mean the army. All people belong to a "we" except me.

**§ John H.**

What are we going to do? §

**Frankie.**

Not to belong to a "we" makes you too lonesome. Until this afternoon I didn't have a "we," but now after seeing Janice and Jarvis I suddenly realize something.

**§ John H.**

What? §

**Frankie.**

I know that the bride and my brother are the "we" of me. So I'm going with them, and joining with the wedding. This coming Sunday when my brother and the bride leave this town, I'm going with the two of them to Winter Hill. And after that to whatever place that they will ever go. (*There is a pause*) I love the two of them so much and we belong to be together. I love the two of them so much because they are the *we* of me.

from
# THE GLASS MENAGERIE
by Tennessee Williams

Act I, scene 3
AMANDA

Amanda Wingfield sells magazine subscriptions and she works at it with an almost frantic determination. It may not be a matter of life or death to her, but it does mean paying the grocery bills. (For introductory comments about the play, see pages 59 and 91.)

For an actress, the speech below involves special problems of concentration and communication: the other "character" on stage, the one to whom Amanda's scene is played, is a telephone.

Amanda is discovered at the phone in the living room.

**Amanda.**

Ida Scott? This is Amanda Wingfield. We missed you at the D.A.R. last Monday. Oh, first I want to know how's your sinus condition? You're just a Christian martyr. That's what you are. You're just a Christian martyr. Well, I was just going through my little red book, and I saw that your subscription to the "Companion" is about to expire just when that wonderful new serial by Bessie Mae Harper is starting. It's the first thing she's written since "Honeymoon for Three." Now, that was unusual, wasn't it? Why, Ida, this one is even lovelier. It's all about the horsey set on Long Island and a debutante is thrown from her horse while taking him over the jumps at the—regatta. Her spine—her spine is injured. That's what the horse did —he stepped on her. Now, there is only one surgeon in the entire world that can keep her from being completely paralyzed, and that's the man she's engaged to be married to and he's tall and he's blond and he's handsome. That's unusual, too, huh? Oh, he's not perfect. Of course he has a weakness. He has the most terrible weakness in the

181

entire world. He just drinks too much. What? Oh, no, Honey, don't let them burn. You go take a look in the oven and I'll hold on . . . Why, that woman! Do you know what she did? She hung up on me.

from
A LOSS OF ROSES
by William Inge

Act I, scene 3
LILA

Lila Green, a tent-show actress, is out of place in the mid-western bungalow of her friend Helen Baird. (For introductory notes about the play, see page 89.) Helen knew Lila as a child and, when she learned that Lila was down on her luck, offered to give her a place to stay, at least for a while. She found Lila considerably changed—glamorous and chipper. But her make-up and offhand manner barely hide the fear and sense of defeat beneath. In the scene from which the excerpts below have been taken Lila tells Helen about her marriage and the chain of events that have left her as she is.

**Lila.**

Helen, I can't really tell you what my marriage to Ed Comiskey was like. You've never known people like those Comiskey brothers. They're just out of another world entirely. You wouldn't believe the things I told you.
§ **Helen.**
Was he . . . peculiar in some way?
§ **Lila.**
Oh no. Ed was very sweet to me. But he was weak. You see, the other Comiskey, Vincent, was not Ed's real brother. No. They called their show the Comiskey Brothers Comedians, but Vincent wasn't Ed's brother at all. Vincent was Ed's *father*.
§ **Helen.**
(*Appalled*) No! §
Lila.
But I din know it for quite a while after we were married. Then I found out that old Vincent Comiskey dyed

183

his hair to keep the gray from showing. He wanted to stay young and keep on playing the leading man. Vincent was the real boss of the show. And a few months after we were married, he started sending Ed out on booking trips . . . Ed wasn't a very good actor. And then, when Ed was gone, old Vincent started coming to my room, trying to force himself on me. * * * I told you you'd never heard of people like them. Oh, he was a horrible old man. I just couldn't stand him. He tried to force me to make love to him . . . in all sorts of ways that . . . that just made me sick, Helen.

§ **Helen.**

Well, I'd have gone straight to his wife and told her that . . . §

**Lila.**

Oh, Mrs. Comiskey knew all about him. She din care what he did. She was in love with another man, a man who played the xylophone between the acts, and he had a wife, too, and two little kids.

§ **Helen.**

Oh, that's shocking. §

**Lila.**

And the xylophone player's wife was in love with the crew boss, the man who had charge of putting up the tent and taking it down.

§ **Helen.**

I've never heard of such people. §

**Lila.**

I told you you wouldn't believe me.

§ **Helen.**

Then you should have reported that Mr. Comiskey to the police. That man was a degenerate. §

**Lila.**

We were in a new town every week, Helen, and I never knew anyone. But old Vincent knew everyone in every town we went to. And people just loved him, too. I couldn't have gone to the police and told them to arrest Vincent Comiskey. The police would have arrested me for being a troublemaker.

§ **Helen.**

But you told Ed, I hope. §

**Lila.**

I tried to tell [Ed] after he got back from his first booking trip, but he wouldn't believe me.

§ **Helen.**

He wouldn't? §

**Lila.**

He didn't wanta believe me. He was scared of his father, and he wouldn't have known how to protect me. It . . . almost made me sorry for Ed. * * * [You and I, Helen—] living back there in that little Oklahoma town where everybody was so honest and friendly, we never guessed there were people like Vincent Comiskey in the world. * * * I just ran away one day. I hardly knew what I was doing, I was so fearful and anxious; but I managed to get on a train somehow, and ended up in Bismarck, North Dakota, in the middle of winter. I just locked myself up in a hotel room and din see anyone, I felt so terrible. Then . . . some people found me.

§ **Helen.**

*Found* you? §

**Lila.**

Well, I . . . I guess I'd tried to kill myself, Helen.

§ **Helen.**

(*shocked*) Lila! §

**Lila.**

Oh now, don't sound so horrified, Helen. I din really mean it. It was just a half-hearted attempt I made, with some sleeping medicine a doctor gave me. It's never gonna happen again. I've learned a lot since then. They took me to a big hospital, a . . . a mental institution. Oh, it scared me to go to such a place, but after I'd been there awhile, I began to feel a lot different. They kept me there for three months, seeing a doctor, and making pottery and sewing. I learned a lot from that doctor. Men don't scare me any more, like they did then. I was just too goody-good in lotsa ways, Helen. . . . [I couldn't write home, of course.] * * * Imagine Mama getting a postcard saying, "Dear Mama, I'm in the loony bin. Love, Lila." Why, they'da had to take her to one, too. No. I just wrote Mama that I was visiting a friend up in North Dakota. She musta wondered where I ever met anyone in North Dakota, but I guess Mama wondered about a lotta things in my life. I'm kinda relieved she's dead now. I don't feel I have to account to anyone any more.

from
WINTERSET
by Maxwell Anderson

Act I, scene 3
MIO

"Plays in verse are a rarity in our theater," Maxwell Anderson wrote, "and perhaps that's as it should be." Some of his critics have agreed: they have questioned his style as a poet and his romanticism as a dramatist. They could not, however, deny the power of his plays, their success, nor the fact that almost singlehandedly Anderson saw to it that poetry had a place on the American stage at all. Not once, but half a dozen times at least, he wrote verse-plays that filled Broadway theaters, university and civic playhouses, exciting audiences and actors alike. In the twentieth-century English-speaking theater, only Britain's Christopher Fry has matched that record—and Fry, like Anderson, has had his detractors, critics who find flaws in his poetry or in his playwriting.

Perhaps, as some of the critics suggest, poetic drama is an impossibility in today's theater. Perhaps the two ways of writing have so diverged in purpose and method that one man cannot succeed with both. Of the many modern poets who have attempted to write dramas and the fewer dramatists who have tried their hands at poetry, most have failed.

Maxwell Anderson began as a playwright, but as he was in love with poetry, he was not concerned with the critics' speculations on the limitations of poetry or drama. "Without doing much theorizing," he said, "I began to write plays in verse, and, since I was canny enough to choose subjects either far away and long ago or with romantic and colorful backgrounds, they were sometimes successful." Certainly the historical settings and heroic characters of his first successful poetic dramas, *Elizabeth the Queen* and *Mary of Scotland,* made it easier for his audiences to accept language that was not the stuff of modern, realistic theater (excerpts from these plays appear on pages 216 and 488). However, as a serious playwright (and a former journalist), Anderson was concerned with the ideas of his own time as well as history, and, in 1935, he wrote a truly "modern" verse-play—its characters were not monarchs and noblemen but East Siders and thugs; its background was not the pageant of history but the immediate controversy of the Sacco and Vanzetti case. If Anderson's approach was again romantic, his story was candid and hard-hitting, and his language echoed the words, if not always the cadences, of the "real" world of the naturalistic dramatists of the 1930's. The play was *Winterset*. In nearly thirty years, as the ideas and problems of American society—the things on which the play relied for its immediate effect with an audience—have changed, *Winterset* has lost some of its impact. Its poetry is not always easy to speak. Yet the play is much more than a "period piece," and it is well worth the study of an actor who is concerned about language, the words which link together performers and playwrights and audiences, and about the division between poetry and drama, which, when they were one, gave our theater its greatest plays.

The setting is New York, "the bank of a river under a bridgehead. A gigantic span starts from the rear of the stage and appears to lift over the heads of the audience and out to the left. At the right rear is a wall of solid supporting masonry. To the left an apartment building abuts against the bridge and forms the left wall of the stage with a dark basement window and a door in the brick wall." There are two sheds, shelter for waifs and strays, and, in the foreground, is the river bank, "black rock worn smooth by years of tramping."

To this place comes Mio, a young man—a boy—whose father was put to death for a crime he did not commit. Mio has come seeking truth, evidence of the conspiracy against justice that dishonored and killed the father and made the son an outcast. In effect, Mio has also come seeking death, for the gangsters who framed the case against his father will kill again to escape their punishment. Mio finds both truth and death, but first he finds Miriamne, the young sister of a man who might have told the truth in court but was afraid. Mio finds Miriamne, loves her, and turns her away. Here he tries to explain to her the

sense of alienation and death which haunts him, separating
him from other men and from her.

Miriamne has asked Mio about his odd-sounding name.
He replies that it is short for Bartolomeo. "My mother's
name was Miriam," she says, "so they called me Miriamne."
"Meaning little Miriam?" he asks. "Yes."

**Mio.**

So now little Miriamne will go in
and take up quietly where she dropped them all
her small housewifely cares.—When I first saw you,
not a half-hour ago, I heard myself saying,
this is the face that launches ships for me—
and if I owned a dream—yes, half a dream—
we'd share it. But I have no dream. This earth
came tumbling down from chaos, fire and rock,
and bred up worms, blind worms that sting each other
here in the dark. These blind worms of the earth
took out my father—and killed him, and set a sign
on me—the heir of the serpent—and he was a man
such as men might be if the gods were men—
but they killed him—
as they'll kill all others like him
till the sun cools down to the stabler molecules,
yes, till men spin their tent-worm webs to the stars
and what they think is done, even in the thinking,
and they are the gods, and immortal, and constellations
turn for them all like mill wheels—still as they are
they will be, worms and blind. Enduring love,
oh gods and worms, what mockery!—And yet
I have blood enough in my veins. It goes like music,
singing, because you're here. My body turns
as if you were the sun, and warm. This men called love
in happier times, before the Freudians taught us
to blame it on the glands. Only go in
before you breathe too much of my atmosphere
and catch death from me.

from
WHO'S AFRAID OF VIRGINIA WOOLF?
by Edward Albee

Act II
GEORGE

Edward Albee's controversial drama might have been titled
"Long Night's Journey into Day," though the dawn which
brings the play to its close is bleak and reveals more
sharply the scars and imperfections of things half-seen by
night. Throughout the night (and the play) four characters—a middle-aged university professor, a young instructor, and their wives—circle around each other in a vicious
social game without rules or compassion. They drink,
laugh, argue, make love, hate, and rub one another's souls
raw. Masks are torn off, old illusions blasted, and dreams
made to seem ridiculous or gross until, in the morning, the
woman who had delighted in getting laughs from a cocktail party crowd by singing "Who's afraid of Virginia
Woolf?" whispers, "I am." Like O'Neill (see page 192),
Albee has understanding for his people but, unlike O'Neill,
little forgiveness or pity.

Critics have argued over the merits of the play, its
meaning, and its viciousness. Few have denied its violent
power or relentless intensity. In form, technique, and
subject matter, it is less experimental than Albee's earlier
plays (see pages 204 and 540). Yet the play is realism
with a difference: to the naturalistic theater Albee brought
the questioning, paradoxical balancing of illusion and truth,
mask and reality, of the "theater of the absurd." When one
of his characters begins to speak of himself or to tell a
tale of something that once happened, there is no certainty
that what he will say will be true—indeed, he may not
believe it himself. Here is none of the directness with
which O'Neill's four Tyrones struggle to describe what
they think, hope, or fear is so. In Albee's play, one must
look for what is so in the reason behind the telling,
whether the thing told is true, false, or a confusion of

189

both. In these reasons, or so it seems to me, lie the revelations of character (and theme) which resolve the play and for which it was written. The brief excerpt below is a case in point—an intriguing as well as a difficult exercise for an actor. It should not be attempted without a thorough reading of the play.

George—the professor—is forty-six; he is thin and his hair is growing gray. The setting is the living room of a house on the campus of a small New England college.

**George.**
When I was sixteen and going to prep school, during the Punic Wars, a bunch of us used to go into New York on the first day of vacations, before we fanned out to our homes, and in the evening this bunch of us used to go to this gin mill owned by the gangster-father of one of us—for this was during the Great Experiment, or Prohibition, as it is more frequently called, and it was a bad time for the liquor lobby, but a fine time for the crooks and the cops—and we would go to this gin mill, and we would drink with the grownups and listen to the jazz. And one time, in the bunch of us, there was this boy who was fifteen, and he had killed his mother with a shotgun some years before—accidentally, completely accidentally, without even an unconscious motivation, I have no doubt, no doubt at all—and this one evening this boy went with us, and we ordered our drinks, and when it came his turn he said, I'll have bergin . . . give me some bergin, please . . . bergin and water. Well, we all laughed . . . he was blond and he had the face of a cherub, and we laughed, and his cheeks went red and the color rose in his neck, and the assistant crook who had taken our order told people at the next table what the boy had said, and then they laughed, and then more people were told and the laughter grew, and more laughter, and no one was laughing more than us, and none of us more than the boy who had shot his mother. And soon, everyone in the gin mill knew what the laughter was about, and everyone started ordering bergin, and laughing when they ordered it. And soon, of course, the laughter became less general, but it did not subside, entirely, for a very long time, for always at this table or that someone would

order bergin and a new area of laughter would rise. We drank free that night, and we were bought champagne by the management, by the gangster-father of one of us. And, of course, we suffered the next day, each of us, alone, on his train, away from New York, each of us with a grownup's hangover . . . but it was the grandest day of my . . . youth. § (*Hands Nick a drink on the word*)
§ **Nick.**

(*very quietly*) Thank you. What . . . what happened to the boy . . . the boy who shot his mother?
§ **George.**

I won't tell you.
§ **Nick.**

All right. §
**George.**

The following summer on a country road, with his learner's permit in his pocket and his father on the front seat to his right [the boy who had shot his mother] swerved the car, to avoid a porcupine, and drove straight into a large tree.
§ **Nick.**

(*faintly pleading*) No. §
**George.**

He was not killed, of course. And in the hospital, when he was conscious and out of danger, and when they told him that his father *was* dead, he began to laugh, I have been told, and his laughter grew and he would not stop, and it was not until after they jammed a needle in his arm, not until after that, until his consciousness slipped away from him, that his laughter subsided . . . stopped. And when he was recovered from his injuries enough so that he could be moved without damage should he struggle, he was put in an asylum. That was thirty years ago.
§ **Nick.**

Is he . . . still there? §
**George.**

Oh, yes. And I'm told that for these thirty years he has . . . not . . . uttered . . . one . . . sound.

from
LONG DAY'S JOURNEY INTO NIGHT
by Eugene O'Neill

Three Monologues, from Acts III and IV
MARY TYRONE; JAMES TYRONE;
EDMUND TYRONE

The play is autobiographical, a play, O'Neill said, "of old sorrow, written in tears and blood." The four Tyrones—Mary and James and their sons, James, Jr., and Edmund—are the playwright's parents, his brother, and O'Neill himself. Their tragedy was his tragedy—the love that was not enough, the misunderstandings, the injuries and recriminations, the dashed hopes, and the desperate escape into illusions that consumed and ultimately trapped. Often bitter memories of these things and these people found their ways into O'Neill's plays. Then, toward the end of his life, he was, he said, able "to face my dead at last and write this play—write it with deep pity and understanding and forgiveness for *all* the four Tyrones." *Long Day's Journey into Night,* though it is a drama of powerful conflicts, is peopled by characters who struggle to explain themselves to each other—and, in so doing, to themselves.

Mary Cavan Tyrone "is fifty-four, about medium height. She still has a young, graceful figure, a trifle plump, but showing little evidence of middle-aged waist and hips, although she is not tightly corseted. Her face is distinctly Irish in type. It must once have been extremely pretty, and is still striking. It does not match her healthy figure but is thin and pale with the bone structure prominent. Her nose is long and straight, her mouth wide with full, sensitive lips. She uses no rouge or any sort of make-up. Her high forehead is framed by thick, pure white hair. Accentuated by her pallor and white hair, her dark brown eyes appear black. They are unusually large and beautiful, with black brows and long curling lashes. What strikes one immediately is her extreme nervousness. Her hands are never still. They were once beautiful hands, with long, tapering fingers, but rheumatism has knotted the joints and warped the fingers, so that now they have an ugly crippled look. One avoids looking at them, the more so because one is conscious she is sensitive about their appearance and humiliated by her inability to control the nervousness which draws attention to them. She is dressed simply but with a sense of what becomes her. Her hair is arranged with fastidious care. Her voice is soft and attractive. When she is merry, there is a touch of Irish lilt in it. Her most appealing quality is the simple, unaffected charm of a shy convent-girl youthfulness she has never lost—innate unworldly innocence."

At times, there is a special unworldliness about Mary—the haze that comes from narcotics. Dosed with cocaine when she was ill, she became addicted. She has fought against it, but time and again she has lost the battle. Today she and the maid, Cathleen, have driven to town and she has had a prescription filled. Now the pleasant, freeing haziness has begun to come over her.

The setting is the living room of the Tyrones' summer home; the time, an early evening of a day in August, 1912.

**Mary.**

Before I met Mr. Tyrone I hardly knew there was such a thing as a theater. I was a very pious girl. I even dreamed of becoming a nun. I've never had the slightest desire to be an actress.

**§ Cath.**

(*Bluntly.*) Well, I can't imagine you a holy nun, Ma'am. Sure, you never darken the door of a church, God forgive you. §

**Mary.**

I've never felt at home in the theater. Even though Mr. Tyrone has made me go with him on all his tours, I've had little to do with the people in his company, or with anyone on the stage. Not that I have anything against them. They have always been kind to me, and I to them. But I've never felt at home with them. Their life is not my life. It has always stood between me and— (*She gets up—abruptly.*) But let's not talk of old things that couldn't be helped. (*She goes to the porch door and stares out.*) How thick the fog is. I can't see the road. All the people in the world could pass by and I would never know. I

wish it was always that way. It's getting dark already.
It will soon be night, thank goodness. (*She turns back
—vaguely.*) It was kind of you to keep me company this
afternoon, Cathleen. I would have been lonely driving
uptown alone.

§ **Cath.**

Sure, wouldn't I rather ride in a fine automobile than stay
here and listen to Bridget's lies about her relations? It
was like a vacation, Ma'am. (*She pauses—then stupidly.*)
There was only one thing I didn't like.

§ **Mary.**

(*Vaguely.*) What was that, Cathleen?

§ **Cath.**

The way the man in the drugstore acted when I took in
the prescription for you. (*Indignantly.*) The impidence
of him! §

**Mary.**

(*With stubborn blankness.*) What are you talking about?
What drugstore? What prescription? (*Then hastily, as
Cathleen stares in stupid amazement.*) Oh, of course, I'd
forgotten. The medicine for the rheumatism in my
hands. § What did the man say? (*Then with indifference.*)
Not that it matters, as long as he filled the prescription.

**Cath.**

It mattered to me, then! I'm not used to being treated
like a thief. He gave me a long look and says insultingly,
"Where did you get hold of this?" and I says, "It's none
of your damned business, but if you must know, it's for
the lady I work for, Mrs. Tyrone, who's sitting out in the
automobile." That shut him up quick. He gave a look
out at you and said, "Oh," and went to get the medicine.

**Mary.**

(*Vaguely.*) Yes, he knows me. § (*She sits in the armchair
at right rear of table. She adds in a calm, detached voice.*)
I have to take it because there is no other that can stop
the pain—*all* the pain—I mean, in my hands. (*She raises
her hands and regards them with melancholy sympathy.
There is no tremor in them now.*) Poor hands! You'd
never believe it, but they were once one of my good
points, along with my hair and eyes, and I had a fine
figure, too. (*Her tone has become more and more far-off
and dreamy.*) They were a musician's hands. I used to
love the piano. I worked so hard at my music in the Convent—if you can call it work when you do something
you love. Mother Elizabeth and my music teacher both

said I had more talent than any student they remembered.
My father paid for special lessons. He spoiled me. He
would do anything I asked. He would have sent me to
Europe to study after I graduated from the Convent. I
might have gone—if I hadn't fallen in love with Mr.
Tyrone. Or I might have become a nun. I had two
dreams. To be a nun, that was the more beautiful one.
To become a concert pianist, that was the other. (*She
pauses, regarding her hands fixedly. Cathleen blinks her
eyes to fight off drowsiness and a tipsy feeling.*) I haven't
touched a piano in so many years. I couldn't play with
such crippled fingers, even if I wanted to. For a time
after my marriage I tried to keep up my music. But it
was hopeless. One-night stands, cheap hotels, dirty trains,
leaving children, never having a home—(*She stares at
her hands with fascinated disgust.*) See, Cathleen, how
ugly they are! So maimed and crippled! You would
think they'd been through some horrible accident! (*She
gives a strange little laugh.*) So they have, come to think
of it. (*She suddenly thrusts her hands behind her back.*)
I won't look at them. They're worse than the foghorn
for reminding me—(*Then with defiant self-assurance.*)
But even they can't touch me now. (*She brings her hands
from behind her back and deliberately stares at them—
calmly.*) They're far away. I see them, but the pain has
gone.

§ **Cath.**

(*Stupidly puzzled.*) You've taken some of the medicine?
It made you act funny, Ma'am. If I didn't know better,
I'd think you'd taken a drop. §

**Mary.**

(*Dreamily.*) It kills the pain. You go back until at last
you are beyond its reach. Only the past when you were
happy is real. (*She pauses—then as if her words had
been an evocation which called back happiness she
changes in her whole manner and facial expression. She
looks younger. There is a quality of an innocent convent
girl about her, and she smiles shyly.*) If you think Mr.
Tyrone is handsome now, Cathleen, you should have
seen him when I first met him. He had the reputation of
being one of the best looking men in the country. The
girls in the Convent who had seen him act, or seen his
photographs, used to rave about him. He was a great
matinee idol then, you know. Women used to wait at

the stage door just to see him come out. You can imagine how excited I was when my father wrote me he and James Tyrone had become friends, and that I was to meet him when I came home for Easter vacation. I showed the letter to all the girls, and how envious they were! My father took me to see him act first. It was a play about the French Revolution and the leading part was a nobleman. I couldn't take my eyes off him. I wept when he was thrown in prison—and then was so mad at myself because I was afraid my eyes and nose would be red. My father had said we'd go backstage to his dressing room right after the play, and so we did. (*She gives a little excited, shy laugh.*) I was so bashful all I could do was stammer and blush like a little fool. But he didn't seem to think I was a fool. I know he liked me the first moment we were introduced. (*Coquettishly.*) I guess my eyes and nose couldn't have been red, after all. I was really very pretty then, Cathleen. And he was handsomer than my wildest dream, in his make-up and his nobleman's costume that was so becoming to him. He was different from all ordinary men, like someone from another world. At the same time he was simple, and kind, and unassuming, not a bit stuck-up or vain. I fell in love right then. So did he, he told me afterwards. I forgot all about becoming a nun or a concert pianist. All I wanted was to be his wife. (*She pauses, staring before her with unnaturally bright, dreamy eyes, and a rapt, tender, girlish smile.*) Thirty-six years ago, but I can see it as clearly as if it were tonight! We've loved each other ever since. And in all those thirty-six years, there has never been a breath of scandal about him. I mean, with any other woman. Never since he met me. That has made me very happy, Cathleen. It has made me forgive so many other things.

## SECOND MONOLOGUE

James Tyrone "is sixty-five but looks ten years younger. About five feet eight, broad-shouldered and deep-chested, he seems taller and slenderer because of his bearing, which has a soldierly quality of head up, chest out, stomach in, shoulders squared. His face has begun to break down but he is still remarkably good looking—a big, finely shaped head, a handsome profile, deep-set light-brown eyes. His gray hair is thin with a bald spot like a monk's tonsure. The stamp of his profession is unmistakably on him. Not that he indulges in any of the deliberate temperamental posturings of the stage star. He is by nature and preference a simple, unpretentious man, whose inclinations are still close to his humble beginnings and his Irish farmer forebears. But the actor shows in all his unconscious habits of speech, movement and gesture. These have the quality of belonging to a studied technique. His voice is remarkably fine, resonant and flexible, and he takes great pride in it. . . . He has never been really sick a day in his life. He has no nerves. There is a lot of stolid, earthy peasant in him, mixed with streaks of sentimental melancholy and rare flashes of intuitive sensibility."

It is midnight. James, wrapped in an old brown dressing gown, has spent most of the evening alone with a pack of cards and a bottle of whisky. Edmund, his younger son, came home and James persuaded him to play a game of cards. It is an awkward, uncomfortable time for both of of them. Occasionally they hear Mary moving about upstairs—she is completely under the euphoric spell of her drug now. Edmund, who has been told today that he has tuberculosis, has learned today that his father, always a pennypincher, has decided to send him to the state farm rather than to a private hospital—the care is just as good, James says, and much less expensive. Edmund, in a fit of anger, calls him "a stinking old miser. . . ." Under this attack, James "shrinks back into his chair, . . . his guilty contrition greater than his anger. He stammers."

**Tyrone.**

(*Pours himself a big drink, which empties the bottle, and drinks it. His head bows and he stares dully at the cards on the table—vaguely.*) Whose play is it? (*He goes on dully, without resentment.*) A stinking old miser. Well, maybe you're right. Maybe I can't help being, although all my life since I had anything I've thrown money over the bar to buy drinks for everyone in the house, or loaned money to sponges I knew would never pay it back—(*With a loose-mouthed sneer of self-contempt.*) But, of course, that was in barrooms, when I was full of whisky. I can't feel that way about it when I'm sober in my home. It was at home I first learned the value of a dollar and the fear of the poorhouse. I've never been able to believe in my luck since. I've always feared it would change and everything I had would be taken away. But still, the more property you own, the safer you think you are. That may not be logical, but it's the way I have to feel. Banks fail, and your money's gone, but you think you can keep land beneath your feet. (*Abruptly his tone becomes scornfully superior.*) You said you realized what I'd been up against as a boy. The hell you do! How could you? You've had everything—nurses, schools, college, though you didn't stay there. You've had food, clothing. Oh, I know you had a fling of hard work with your back and hands, a bit of being homeless and penniless in a foreign land, and I respect you for it. But it was a game of romance and adventure to you. It was play.

§ **Edmund.**

(*Dully sarcastic.*) Yes, particularly the time I tried to commit suicide at Jimmie the Priest's, and almost did.

§ **Tyrone.**

You weren't in your right mind. No son of mine would ever—You were drunk.

§ **Edmund.**

I was stone cold sober. That was the trouble. I'd stopped to think too long.

§ **Tyrone.**

(*With drunken peevishness.*) Don't start your damned atheist morbidness again! I don't care to listen. I was trying to make plain to you— § (*Scornfully.*) What do you know of the value of a dollar? When I was ten my father deserted my mother and went back to Ireland to die. Which he did soon enough, and deserved to, and I hope he's roasting in hell. He mistook rat poison for flour, or sugar, or something. There was gossip it wasn't by mistake but that's a lie. No one in my family ever—

§ **Edmund.**

My bet is, it wasn't by mistake.

**Tyrone.**

More morbidness! Your brother put that in your head. The worst he can suspect is the only truth for him. But never mind. § My mother was left, a stranger in a strange land, with four small children, me and a sister a little

older and two younger than me. My two older brothers
had moved to other parts. They couldn't help. They were
hard put to it to keep themselves alive. There was no
damned romance in our poverty. Twice we were evicted
from the miserable hovel we called home, with my
mother's few sticks of furniture thrown out in the street,
and my mother and sisters crying. I cried, too, though I
tried hard not to, because I was the man of the family.
At ten years old! There was no more school for me. I
worked twelve hours a day in a machine shop, learning
to make files. A dirty barn of a place where rain dripped
through the roof, where you roasted in summer, and
there was no stove in winter, and your hands got numb
with cold, where the only light came through two small
filthy windows, so on grey days I'd have to sit bent over
with my eyes almost touching the files in order to see!
You talk of work! And what do you think I got for it?
Fifty cents a week! It's the truth! Fifty cents a week!
And my poor mother washed and scrubbed for the
Yanks by the day, and my older sister sewed, and my
two younger stayed at home to keep the house. We never
had clothes enough to wear, nor enough food to eat. Well
I remember one Thanksgiving, or maybe it was Christmas, when some Yank in whose house mother had been
scrubbing gave her a dollar extra for a present, and on
the way home she spent it all on food. I can remember
her hugging and kissing us and saying with tears of joy
running down her tired face: "Glory be to God, for
once in our lives we'll have enough for each of us!" (*He
wipes tears from his eyes.*) A fine, brave, sweet woman.
There never was a braver or finer.
§ **Edmund.**

(*Moved.*) Yes, she must have been. §
**Tyrone.**

Her one fear was she'd get old and sick and have to die
in the poorhouse. (*He pauses—then adds with grim
humor.*) It was in those days I learned to be a miser. A
dollar was worth so much then. And once you've learned
a lesson, it's hard to unlearn it. You have to look for
bargains. If I took this state farm sanatorium for a good
bargain, you'll have to forgive me. The doctors did tell
me it's a good place. You must believe that, Edmund.
And I swear I never meant you to go there if you didn't
want to. (*Vehemently.*) You can choose any place you

like! Never mind what it costs! Any place I can afford. Any place you like—within reason. (*At this qualification, a grin twitches Edmund's lips. His resentment has gone. His father goes on with an elaborately offhand, casual air.*) There was another sanatorium the specialist recommended. He said it had a record as good as any place in the country. It's endowed by a group of millionaire factory owners, for the benefit of their workers principally, but you're eligible to go there because you're a resident. There's such a pile of money behind it, they don't have to charge much. It's only seven dollars a week but you get ten times that value. (*Hastily.*) I don't want to persuade you to anything, understand. I'm simply repeating what I was told.

§ **Edmund.**

(*Concealing his smile—casually.*) Oh, I know that. It sounds like a good bargain to me. I'd like to go there. So that settles that. (*Abruptly he is miserably desperate again—dully.*) It doesn't matter a damn now, anyway. Let's forget it! (*Changing the subject.*) How about our game? Whose play is it?

§ **Tyrone.**

(*Mechanically.*) I don't know. Mine, I guess. No, it's yours. (*Edmund plays a card. His father takes it. Then about to play from his hand, he again forgets the game.*) § Yes, maybe life overdid the lesson for me, and made a dollar worth too much, and the time came when that mistake ruined my career as a fine actor. (*Sadly.*) I've never admitted this to anyone before, lad, but tonight I'm so heartsick I feel at the end of everything, and what's the use of fake pride and pretense. That God-damned play I bought for a song and made such a great success in—a great money success—it ruined me with its promise of an easy fortune. I didn't want to do anything else, and by the time I woke up to the fact I'd become a slave to the damned thing and did try other plays, it was too late. They had identified me with that one part, and didn't want me in anything else. They were right, too. I'd lost the great talent I once had through years of easy repetition, never learning a new part, never really working hard. Thirty-five to forty thousand dollars net profit a season like snapping your fingers! It was too great a temptation. Yet before I bought the damned thing I was considered one of the three or four young actors with the greatest artistic promise in America. I'd worked like hell. I'd left a good job as a machinist to take supers' parts because I loved the theater. I was wild with ambition. I read all the plays ever written. I studied Shakespeare as you'd study the Bible. I educated myself. I got rid of an Irish brogue you could cut with a knife. I loved Shakespeare. I would have acted in any of his plays for nothing, for the joy of being alive in his great poetry. And I acted well in him. I felt inspired by him. I could have been a great Shakespearean actor, if I'd kept on. I know that! In 1874 when Edwin Booth came to the theater in Chicago where I was leading man, I played Cassius to his Brutus one night, Brutus to his Cassius the next, Othello to his Iago, and so on. The first night I played Othello, he said to our manager, "That young man is playing Othello better than I ever did!" (*Proudly.*) That from Booth, the greatest actor of his day or any other! And it was true! And I was only twenty-seven years old! As I look back on it now, that night was the high spot in my career. I had life where I wanted it! And for a time after that I kept on upward with ambition high. Married your mother. Ask her what I was like in those days. Her love was an added incentive to ambition. But a few years later my good bad luck made me find the big money-maker. It wasn't that in my eyes at first. It was a great romantic part I knew I could play better than anyone. But it was a great box office success from the start—and then life had me where it wanted me—at from thirty-five to forty thousand net profit a season! A fortune in those days—or even in these. (*Bitterly.*) What the hell was it I wanted to buy, I wonder, that was worth—Well, no matter. It's a late day for regrets. (*He glances vaguely at his cards.*) My play, isn't it?

## THIRD MONOLOGUE

Edmund Tyrone is twenty-three, thin and wiry. Where his elder brother, James, "takes after his father, with little resemblance to his mother, Edmund looks like both his parents, but is more like his mother. Her big, dark eyes are the dominant feature in his long, narrow Irish face. His mouth has the same quality of hypersensitiveness hers possesses. His high forehead is hers accentuated, with dark brown hair, sunbleached to red at the ends, brushed straight back from it. But his nose is his father's and his face in profile recalls Tyrone's. Edmund's hands are noticeably like his mother's, with the same exceptionally long fingers. They even have to a minor degree the same nervousness. It is in the quality of extreme nervous sensibility that the likeness of Edmund to his mother is most marked.

"He is plainly in bad health. Much thinner than he should be, his eyes appear feverish and his cheeks are sunken. His skin, in spite of being sunburned a deep brown, has a parched sallowness."

After James Tyrone's reminiscence (above), the card game and the arguments continue, until Edmund, with alcoholic talkativeness and spurred on by his father's saying that he has the makings of a poet in him, launches into his own spoken memoirs. Edmund, of course, is the character who parallels Eugene O'Neill.

### Edmund.

(*Then with alcoholic talkativeness.*) You've just told me some high spots in your memories. Want to hear mine? They're all connected with the sea. Here's one. When I was on the Squarehead square rigger, bound for Buenos Aires. Full moon in the Trades. The old hooker driving fourteen knots. I lay on the bowsprit, facing astern, with the water foaming into spume under me, the masts with every sail white in the moonlight, towering high above me. I became drunk with the beauty and singing rhythm of it, and for a moment I lost myself—actually lost my life. I was set free! I dissolved in the sea, became white sails and flying spray, became beauty and rhythm, became moonlight and the ship and the high dim-starred sky! I belonged, without past or future, within peace and unity and a wild joy, within something greater than my own life, or the life of Man, to Life itself! To God, if you want to put it that way. Then another time, on the American Line, when I was lookout on the crow's nest in the dawn watch. A calm sea, that time. Only a lazy ground swell and a slow drowsy roll of the ship. The passengers asleep and none of the crew in sight. No sound of man. Black smoke pouring from the funnels behind and beneath me. Dreaming, not keeping lookout, feeling alone, and above, and apart, watching the dawn creep like a painted dream over the sky and sea which slept together. Then the moment of ecstatic freedom came. The peace, the end of the quest, the last harbor, the joy of belonging to a fulfillment beyond men's lousy, pitiful, greedy fears and hopes and dreams! And several other times in my life, when I was swimming far out, or lying alone on a beach, I have had the same experience. Became the sun, the hot sand, green seaweed anchored to a rock, swaying in the tide. Like a saint's vision of beatitude. Like the veil of things as they seem drawn back by an unseen hand. For a second you see—and seeing the secret, are the secret. For a second there is meaning! Then the hand lets the veil fall and you are alone, lost in the fog again, and you stumble on toward nowhere, for no good reason! (*He grins wryly.*) It was a great mistake, my being born a man, I would have been much more successful as a sea gull or a fish. As it is, I will always be a stranger who never feels at home, who does not really want and is not really wanted, who can never belong, who must always be a little in love with death!

§ **Tyrone.**

(*Stares at him—impressed.*) Yes, there's the makings of a poet in you all right. (*Then protesting uneasily.*) But that's morbid craziness about not being wanted and loving death. §

**Edmund.**

(*Sardonically.*) The *makings* of a poet. No, I'm afraid I'm like the guy who is always panhandling for a smoke. He hasn't even got the makings. He's got only the habit. I couldn't touch what I tried to tell you just now. I just stammered. That's the best I'll ever do. I mean, if I live. Well, it will be faithful realism, at least. Stammering is the native eloquence of us fog people. (*A pause. Then they both jump startledly as there is a noise from outside the house, as if someone had stumbled and fallen on the front steps. Edmund grins.*) Well, that sounds like the absent brother. He must have a peach of a bun on.

from
# THE ZOO STORY
by Edward Albee

## JERRY, PETER

When it was produced off Broadway in 1960, this play brought Edward Albee to the attention of New Yorkers and the critics, who heralded him as America's most promising young playwright. Two years later, Albee had a smash hit on Broadway—*Who's Afraid of Virginia Woolf?* (see page 189). *The Zoo Story* is a short play and an odd one. It opens with the tentative conversation of a pair of strangers, Peter and Jerry, who meet in Central Park (the scene reprinted below). It ends with Jerry's goading Peter into killing him; that, it seems, was what came into his mind when he was at the zoo.

Peter is "a man in his early forties, neither fat nor gaunt, neither handsome nor homely. He wears tweeds, smokes a pipe, carries horn-rimmed glasses. Although he is moving into middle age, his dress and his manner would suggest a man younger." Jerry is "in his late thirties, not poorly dressed, but carelessly. What was once a trim and lightly muscled body has begun to go to fat; and while he is no longer handsome, it is evident that he once was. His fall from physical grace should not suggest debauchery; he has, to come closest to it, a great weariness."

The scene is Central Park, a Sunday afternoon in summer. "There are two park benches, one toward either side of the stage; they both face the audience. Behind them: foliage, trees, sky. At the beginning, Peter is seated on one of the benches. . . . He is reading a book. He stops reading, cleans his glasses, goes back to reading. Jerry enters."

**Jerry.**

I've been to the zoo. (*Peter doesn't notice*) I said, I've been to the zoo. MISTER, I'VE BEEN TO THE ZOO!

**Peter.**

Hm? . . . What? . . . I'm sorry, were you talking to me?

**Jerry.**

I went to the zoo, and then I walked until I came here. Have I been walking north?

**Peter.**

(*Puzzled*) North? Why . . . I . . . I think so. Let me see.

**Jerry.**

(*Pointing past the audience*) Is that Fifth Avenue?

**Peter.**

Why yes; yes, it is.

**Jerry.**

And what is that cross street there; that one, to the right?

**Peter.**

That? Oh, that's Seventy-fourth Street.

**Jerry.**

And the zoo is around Sixty-fifth Street; so, I've been walking north.

**Peter.**

(*Anxious to get back to his reading*) Yes; it would seem so.

**Jerry.**

Good old north.

**Peter.**

(*Lightly, by reflex*) Ha, ha.

**Jerry.**

(*After a slight pause*) But not due north.

**Peter.**

I . . . well, no, not due north; but, we . . . call it north. It's northerly.

**Jerry.**

(*Watches as Peter, anxious to dismiss him, prepares his pipe*) Well, boy; *you're* not going to get lung cancer, are you?

**Peter.**

(*Looks up, a little annoyed, then smiles*) No, sir. Not from this.

**Jerry.**

No, sir. What you'll probably get is cancer of the mouth, and then you'll have to wear one of those things Freud wore after they took one whole side of his jaw away. What do they call those things?

**Peter.**
   (*Uncomfortable*) A prosthesis?

**Jerry.**
   The very thing! A prosthesis. You're an educated man, aren't you? Are you a doctor?

**Peter.**
   Oh, no; no. I read about it somewhere; *Time* magazine, I think. (*He turns to his book*)

**Jerry.**
   Well, *Time* magazine isn't for blockheads.

**Peter.**
   No, I suppose not.

**Jerry.**
   (*After a pause*) Boy, I'm glad that's Fifth Avenue there.

**Peter.**
   (*Vaguely*) Yes.

**Jerry.**
   I don't like the west side of the park much.

**Peter.**
   Oh? (*Then, slightly wary, but interested*) Why?

**Jerry.**
   (*Offhand*) I don't know.

**Peter.**
   Oh. (*He returns to his book*)

**Jerry.**
   (*He stands for a few seconds, looking at Peter, who finally looks up again, puzzled*) Do you mind if we talk?

**Peter.**
   (*Obviously minding*) Why . . . no, no.

**Jerry.**
   Yes you do; you do.

**Peter.**
   (*Puts his book down, his pipe out and away, smiling*) No, really; I don't mind.

**Jerry.**
   Yes you do.

**Peter.**
   (*Finally decided*) No; I don't mind at all, really.

**Jerry.**
   It's . . . it's a nice day.

**Peter.**
   (*Stares unnecessarily at the sky*) Yes. Yes, it is; lovely.

**Jerry.**
   I've been to the zoo.

**Peter.**
   Yes, I think you said so . . . didn't you?

**Jerry.**

You'll read about it in the papers tomorrow, if you don't see it on your TV tonight. You have TV, haven't you?

**Peter.**

Why yes, we have two; one for the children.

**Jerry.**

You're married!

**Peter.**

(*With pleased emphasis*) Why, certainly.

**Jerry.**

It isn't a law, for God's sake.

**Peter.**

No . . . no, of course not.

**Jerry.**

And you have a wife.

**Peter.**

(*Bewildered by the seeming lack of communication*) Yes!

**Jerry.**

And you have children.

**Peter.**

Yes; two.

**Jerry.**

Boys?

**Peter.**

No, girls . . . both girls.

**Jerry.**

But you wanted boys.

**Peter.**

Well . . . naturally, every man wants a son, but . . .

**Jerry.**

(*Lightly mocking*) But that's the way the cookie crumbles?

**Peter.**

(*Annoyed*) I wasn't going to say that.

**Jerry.**

And you're not going to have any more kids, are you?

**Peter.**

(*A bit distantly*) No. No more. (*Then back, and irksome*) Why did you say that? How would you know about that?

**Jerry.**

The way you cross your legs, perhaps; something in the voice. Or maybe I'm just guessing. Is it your wife?

**Peter.**

(*Furious*) That's none of your business! (*A silence*) Do you understand? (*Jerry nods. Peter is quiet now*) Well, you're right. We'll have no more children.

**Jerry.**
(*Softly*) That *is* the way the cookie crumbles.
**Peter.**
(*Forgiving*) Yes . . . I guess so.
**Jerry.**
Well, now; what else?
**Peter.**
What were you saying about the zoo . . . that I'd read about it, or see . . . ?
**Jerry.**
I'll tell you about it, soon. Do you mind if I ask you questions?
**Peter.**
Oh, not really.
**Jerry.**
I'll tell you why I do it; I don't talk to many people—except to say like: give me a beer, or where's the john, or what time does the feature go on, or keep your hands to yourself, buddy. You know—things like that.
**Peter.**
I must say I don't . . .
**Jerry.**
But every once in a while I like to talk to somebody, really *talk*; like to get to know somebody, know all about him.
**Peter.**
(*Lightly laughing, still a little uncomfortable*) And am I the guinea pig for today?
**Jerry.**
On a sun-drenched Sunday afternoon like this? Who better than a nice married man with two daughters and . . . uh . . . a dog? (*Peter shakes his head*) No? Two dogs. (*Peter shakes his head again*) Hm. No dogs? (*Peter shakes his head, sadly*) Oh, that's a shame. But you look like an animal man. CATS? (*Peter nods his head, ruefully*) Cats! But, that can't be your idea. No, sir. Your wife and daughters? (*Peter nods his head*) Is there anything else I should know?
**Peter.**
(*He has to clear his throat*) There are . . . there are two parakeets. One . . . uh . . . one for each for my daughters.
**Jerry.**
Birds.
**Peter.**
My daughters keep them in a cage in their bedroom.

**Jerry.**

Do they carry disease? The birds.

**Peter.**

I don't believe so.

**Jerry.**

That's too bad. If they did you could set them loose in the house and the cats could eat them and die, maybe. (*Peter looks blank for a moment, then laughs*) And what else? What do you do to support your enormous household?

**Peter.**

I . . . uh . . . I have an executive position with a . . . a small publishing house. We . . . uh . . . we publish textbooks.

**Jerry.**

That sounds nice; very nice. What do you make?

**Peter.**

(*Still cheerful*) Now look here!

**Jerry.**

Oh, come on.

**Peter.**

Well, I make around eighteen thousand a year, but I don't carry more than forty dollars at any one time . . . in case you're a . . . a holdup man . . . ha, ha, ha.

**Jerry.**

(*Ignoring the above*) Where do you live? (*Peter is reluctant*) Oh, look; I'm not going to rob you, and I'm not going to kidnap your parakeets, your cats, or your daughters.

**Peter.**

(*Too loud*) I live between Lexington and Third Avenue, on Seventy-fourth Street.

**Jerry.**

That wasn't so hard, was it?

**Peter.**

I didn't mean to seem . . . ah . . . it's that you don't really carry on a conversation; you just ask questions. And I'm . . . I'm normally . . . uh . . . reticent. Why do you just stand there?

**Jerry.**

I'll start walking around in a little while, and eventually I'll sit down. (*Recalling*) Wait until you see the expression on his face.

**Peter.**
  What? Whose face? Look here; is this something about the zoo?

**Jerry.**
  (*Distantly*) The what?

**Peter.**
  The zoo; the zoo. Something about the zoo.

**Jerry.**
  The zoo?

**Peter.**
  You've mentioned it several times.

**Jerry.**
  (*Still distant, but returning abruptly*) The zoo? Oh, yes; the zoo. I was there before I came here.

from
BILLY BUDD
by Louis O. Coxe and Robert Chapman

Act I, scene 2
BILLY BUDD, JOHN CLAGGART

The play is an adaptation of Herman Melville's sea novel
*Billy Budd*—a rather free adaptation in which the symbolic
elements in the novelist's story are emphasized and the
theme is more sharply and specifically defined. "This is
a morality play," the adaptors wrote, "and we do not
apologize for its being such." Thus the action follows a
pattern set by the theme; the personifications of absolute
good and evil walk the stage, speak, meet in conflict, and
ultimately destroy one another to prove the writers' thesis
that absolutes cannot survive in a world which is comfortable only with the middle way, with a compound rather
than pure elements.

The world of the play is the British naval ship *H.M.S.
Indomitable*, at sea in August, 1798. It is manned by men
of average virtues and faults, and commanded by officers
who know that, if the ship—the world—is to survive, they
must enforce its rules without swerving, unmoved by
compassion for the most deserving of exceptional men or
anger against the most evil of villains. But among the officers and men of the *Indomitable* there are two exceptional
men, an "angel" and a "devil," who do not act according to
the usual rules. Billy Budd, the new foretopman pressed into
service from the merchant ship *Rights of Man*, is so good-
humored, so naïve in his refusal to recognize ill will, even
when it is directed against him, that he hardly seems real.
John Claggart, the Master-at-Arms, is equally "unreal";
inhumanly cruel, "he lives," one crewman says, "on hurting people." Unable to compromise, unyielding in their
different ways, Billy and Claggart are inevitable adversaries.
Each is fascinated by the other and each seems to know
that, if he himself is to continue to live, the other must
change or be destroyed. Billy, who sees the loneliness in

211

Claggart, tries to make him his friend. Claggart, feeling himself charmed by Billy's ingenuousness, determines to treat him with greater viciousness than he has shown to any other crewman. When Billy is driven at last to react to Claggart's goading, rage takes away his voice; unable to defend himself with words, he strikes out at the Master-at-Arms and kills him. No one doubts the justice of his act. "He was tempted . . . past endurance," the captain says. But Billy has broken the ship's law and the officers must sentence him to be executed.

The scene below occurs near the beginning of the play. Claggart has already singled out the new foretopman and ordered Squeak, the Master-at-Arms' man, to find or manufacture a reason for reporting Billy for punishment. Billy has been told many tales of Claggart's cruelty, but he has not joined his shipmates in their whispered tirades against the Master-at-Arms.

The setting is a part of the maindeck of the ship. It is early evening. Billy stands alone staring over the side as Claggart enters. He does not see Billy, but stops near the quarterdeck ladder and gazes fixedly seaward.

**Billy.**

Good evening, sir.

**Clag.**

(*startled, then subtly sarcastic*) Good evening.

**Billy.**

Will it be all right if I stay topside a bit to watch the water?

**Clag.**

I suppose the Handsome Sailor may do many things forbidden to his messmates.

**Billy.**

Yes, sir. The sea's calm tonight, isn't it? Calm and peaceful.

**Clag.**

The sea's deceitful, boy: calm above, and underneath, a world of gliding monsters preying on their fellows. Murderers, all of them. Only the sharpest teeth survive.

**Billy.**

I'd like to know about such things, as you do, sir.

**Clag.**

You're an ingenuous sailor, Billy Budd. Is there, behind

that youthful face, the wisdom pretty virtue has none
of? Even the gods must know their rivals, boy; and Christ
had first to recognize the ills before he cured 'em.

**Billy.**

What, sir?

**Clag.**

Never mind. But tell me this, how have you stomach to
stand here and talk to me? Are you so innocent and
ignorant of what I am? You know my reputation. Jenkins
and the rest are witnesses and certainly you've heard them
talking to me. Half of them would knife me in the back
some night and do it gladly. Jenkins is thinking of it.
Doubtless he'll try one day. How do you dare, then?
Have you not intelligence enough to be afraid of me? To
hate me as all the others do?

**Billy.**

Why should I be afraid of you, sir? You speak to me
friendly when we meet. I know some of the men . . . are
fearful of you, sir, but I can't believe they're right about
it.

**Clag.**

You're a fool, fellow. In time you'll learn to fear me like
the rest. Young you are, and scarcely used to the fit of
your man's flesh.

**Billy.**

I know they're wrong, sir. You aren't like they say. Nobody could be so.

**Clag.**

So . . . ? So what, boy? Vicious, did you mean to say, or
brutal? But they aren't wrong, and you would see it but
for those blue eyes that light so kindly on your fellow
men.

**Billy.**

Oh, I've got no education. I know that. There must be a
lot of things a man misses when he's ignorant. But learning's hard. Must be sort of lonely, too.

**Clag.**

What are you prating of, half-man, half-child? Your
messmates crowd around, admire your yellow hair and
your blue eyes, do tricks and favors for you out of love,
and you talk about loneliness!

**Billy.**

I just noticed the way you were looking off to leeward
as I came up, sir. Kind of sad, you were looking.

**Clag.**

Not sadness, boy. Another feeling, more like . . . pleasure. That's it. I can feel it now, looking at you. A certain . . . pleasure.

**Billy.**

(*flattered*) Thank you, sir.

**Clag.**

(*annoyed at Billy's incomprehension*) Pah.

**Billy.**

Just talking with you, sir, I can tell they're wrong about you. They're ignorant, like me.

**Clag.**

Compliment for compliment, eh, boy? Have you no heart for terror, fellow? You've seen this stick in use. Have you not got sense and spleen and liver to be scared, even to be cowardly?

**Billy.**

No, sir, I guess not. I like talking to you, sir. But please, sir, tell me something.

**Clag.**

I wonder if I can. Well, ask it.

**Billy.**

Why do you want us to believe you're cruel, and not really like everybody else?

**Clag.**

I think you are the only child alive who wouldn't understand if I explained; or else you'd not believe it.

**Billy.**

Oh, I'd believe you, sir. There's much I could learn from you: I never knew a man like you before.

**Clag.**

(*slowly*) Do you—like me, Billy Budd?

**Billy.**

You've always been most pleasant with me, sir.

**Clag.**

Have I?

**Billy.**

Yes, sir. In the mess, the day I came aboard? And almost every day you have a pleasant word.

**Clag.**

And what I have said tonight, are these pleasant words?

**Billy.**

Yes, sir. I was wondering . . . could I talk to you between watches, when you've nothing else to do?

**Clag.**

You're a plausible boy, Billy. Aye, the nights are long, and talking serves to pass them.

**Billy.**

Thank you, sir. That would mean a lot to me.

**Clag.**

Perhaps to me as well. (*Drops his rattan. Billy picks it up and hands it back to him. Claggart stares at it a moment, then at Billy*) No. No! Charm me, too, would you! Get away!

**Billy.**

(*surprised and puzzled*) Aye, sir. (*He exits down the hatchway. After a pause in which he recovers his self-control, Claggart calls out to Squeak.*)

**Clag.**

[Squeak!] Come here. I thought I told you to put that new seaman Budd on report. Why was it not done?

from
ELIZABETH THE QUEEN
by Maxwell Anderson

Act II, scene 1
PENELOPE, THE FOOL

The play, the first and most successful of Anderson's verse-dramas, holds closely to the tradition of English history plays—it is Elizabethan in approach as well as subject matter. Against a background of regal pomp, of guards, courtiers, politicians and ambitious noblemen, figures of public eminence play out their private joys and loves and griefs. And there are moments, like side-glances, in which the lives and interrelations of minor figures are briefly but sharply revealed. With these briefly glimpsed subplots, the playwright gives reality and substance to his less important characters—they become more than spear-carriers or walking scenery for the eminences—and the structure of the play, like the pattern of a tapestry, is enriched by the colors of myriad, interwoven details.

Act II begins with a "side-glance"—a scene, almost a formal *pas de deux,* in which the fool woos Penelope, first among the ladies-in-waiting to the queen. In itself the scene is a charming and touching vignette. In the context of the entire play it is a repetition of a pattern, ultimately tragic, of love's "foolishness" posed against rank or responsibility. The fool made man by love is "doubly foolish"; the lady who rejects him is also a fool for love's sake, for she loves a favorite of the queen; and he, the favorite, plays love's fool by adoring Elizabeth, who will not, dares not allow the foolishness of loving any man to take precedence over her responsibilities as queen.

The scene is the queen's study. "Penelope is sitting reading. The Fool enters. She does not see him."

**Fool.**

Sh! Make no noise.

**Penel.**

What do you mean?

**Fool.**

Silence! Quiet!

**Penel.**

I am silent, fool.

**Fool.**

You silent? And even as you say it you are talking!

**Penel.**

You began it.

**Fool.**

Began what?

**Penel.**

Talking.

**Fool.**

Oh, no. Talking began long before my time. It was a woman began it.

**Penel.**

Her name?

**Fool.**

Penelope, I should judge.

**Penel.**

Fool.

**Fool.**

(*Looking away*) No, for with this same Penelope began also beauty and courage and tenderness and faith . . . all that a man could desire or a woman offer . . . and all that this early Penelope began has a later Penelope completed.

**Penel.**

(*Rising*) It lacked only this . . . that the court fool should make love to me.

**Fool.**

I am sorry to have been laggard. But truly I have never found you alone before.

**Penel.**

How lucky I've been!

**Fool.**

Are you angered?

**Penel.**

At what?

**Fool.**

At my loving you.

**Penel.**

I've learned to bear nearly everything.

**Fool.**
  A lover's absence?
**Penel.**
  Among other things.
**Fool.**
  The presence of suitors undesired?
**Penel.**
  That, too.
**Fool.**
  I am not a suitor, my lady. I ask nothing. I know where your heart lies. It is with my lord Essex in Ireland. I do not love you.
**Penel.**
  Good.
**Fool.**
  I lied to you. I do love you.
**Penel.**
  I am sorry.
**Fool.**
  You will not laugh at me?
**Penel.**
  No.
**Fool.**
  Then there is yet some divinity in the world . . . while a woman can still be sorry for one who loves her without return.
**Penel.**
  A woman is sadly aware that when a man loves her it makes a fool of him.
**Fool.**
  And if a fool should love a woman . . . would it not make a man of him?
**Penel.**
  No, but doubly a fool, I fear.
**Fool.**
  And the women . . . how of the women?
**Penel.**
  They have been fools, too.
**Fool.**
  The more fool I, I tried to save Lord Essex from Ireland . . . but he needs must go . . . the more fool he.
**Penel.**
  Let us not talk of that.
**Fool.**
  May I kiss you?

**Penel.**
 No.
**Fool.**
 Your hand?
**Penel.**
 Yes. (*He kisses her hand*)
**Fool.**
 I thank you. (*She touches his fool's cap gently with her hand*)
**Penel.**
 The more fool you, poor boy.

from
MORNINGS AT SEVEN
by Paul Osborn

Act I
IDA, HOMER

The setting is the back porches and back yards of two
houses in a midwestern town. The play concerns the people
who live in the houses: three elderly sisters, two elderly
husbands, and, from down the street, another sister and
her husband. Youth is represented by the son of one of
these couples—Homer, who is thirty-nine and finally (perhaps) going to marry his fiancée of five years. "Homer's
shy," his uncle says. "He can't be rushed into anything."
But Homer's mother has seen a movie about the woes of
a lonely old bachelor and she has insisted that Homer
bring his girl, Myrtle Brown, home to meet the family.
Myrtle's arrival triggers a series of crises in both houses.
Homer's father has one of his "spells" and leaves home in
order to find out "where he stands" in life. Next door,
Aunt Cora decides that it is time that she and her husband
set up housekeeping on their own (that is, without the help
or presence of her sister, who has always lived with them).
Cora wants the house on Sycamore Drive, the house which
Homer's father built for him and which has waited empty
for five years while Homer made up his mind about getting
married. And Homer has not really made up his mind yet.
In the scene below, his mother sets out to persuade him
(Homer and Myrtle themselves discuss the problem in the
scenes reprinted on pages 388 and 393).

The time is a late afternoon in summer—the first day of
Myrtle's visit. Homer has just introduced her to Ida, his
mother, while the aunts, assembled on the porch next door,
looked on. Ida has given the couple a few minutes to be
alone, time enough for an uncomfortable little conversation (page 388). Now she has reappeared, announced
that dinner is nearly ready, and Myrtle has gone inside

to wash up. Homer would like to avoid the chat that he
knows is coming, but Ida starts in before he can get away.

**Ida.**

I want to tell you how much I like Myrtle. I think she's
just as nice as she can be. (*Homer sits stump.*)

**Homer.**

Well, I wish you wouldn't leave me alone with her all the
time.

**Ida.**

Now Homer—!

**Homer.**

I don't care, it's embarrassing. I don't know what to say
to her.

**Ida.**

Well, aren't you the limit. What do you say to her when
you go down to visit her in North Lyons?

**Homer.**

That's different.

**Ida.**

You are a goose, aren't you?

**Homer.**

Well, I just wish you wouldn't leave us alone. She keeps
hinting things when you're not with us.

**Ida.**

What things?

**Homer.**

Oh, she wants to know why I brought her home.

**Ida.**

Well, I should think she'd know that. When a man brings
a girl home to meet his mother—

**Homer.**

Now, Mother, you know I haven't made up my mind
about anything yet!

**Ida.**

Now Homer—!

**Homer.**

(*shaking his head obstinately*) Haven't made up my
mind.

**Ida.**

Well, when are you going to?

**Homer.**

Well, I like it living here at home.

**Ida.**
But that's no excuse. And it isn't as though you'd be going way off somewhere. After all, Sycamore Drive is only half a mile away. You can come down here every night if you want to at first.

**Homer.**
It wouldn't be the same.

**Ida.**
You'll be surprised how quickly you'll feel at home in that new house, Homer.

**Homer.**
But I've got all my things here and everything.

**Ida.**
Well, I just wish you'd seen that movie I saw, Homer. That movie actor even looked a little like you.

**Homer.**
Who was it?

**Ida.**
Oh, nobody important.

**Homer.**
Oh!

**Ida.**
But he certainly gave you a very clear picture of just how lonely an old bachelor can be. (*Pause.*)

**Homer.**
(*turns to Ida*) You'd be awfully lonesome.

**Ida.**
(*turning away from him*) Oh, I don't say it's going to be easy for me either.

**Homer.**
Of course it isn't.

**Ida.**
It'll seem strange not to have you coming home after your day's work. But I've had you a long time. Longer than most mothers.

**Homer.**
I don't know what you'd do with my little room up there.

**Ida.**
I've thought of that too. I think I'll keep it just as it is. And you'll know that it'll be ready for you any time you want it. Perhaps you'll want to spend a night down here sometime—you and Myrtle.

**Homer.**
(*gloomily*) My room's too small for two people.

**Ida.**
We might move in a double bed.

**Homer.**

(*embarrassed*) Oh, Mother! (*Pause. They are both rather embarrassed. Homer rises and crosses left. It starts to grow dark. Homer turns back to face his mother.*) And Myrtle gets so personal sometimes.

**Ida.**

What do you mean?

**Homer.**

Oh, she wants to know all sorts of things. The other day she asked me what size underwear I wore.

**Ida.**

She did? What for?

**Homer.**

I guess she wanted to buy me some.

**Ida.**

Well, that does seem odd.

**Homer.**

She wrote it down in a little book she's got. (*Pause. They are both depressed.*)

**Ida.**

Of course after you're married she'll be buying your underwear. (*Pause.*)

**Homer.**

There's something awful nice about Myrtle though.

**Ida.**

Of course there is.

**Homer.**

She's awfully good-hearted and she does nice little things for you all the time.

**Ida.**

Does she?

**Homer.**

She's awfully lonesome down there in North Lyons too. It isn't that I'm not awfully fond of her, Mother.

**Ida.**

Do you love her, Homer?

**Homer.**

Well, I wouldn't want never to see her again. (*Pause.*) Mother.

**Ida.**

Yes, Homer?

**Homer.**

If I was to marry Myrtle do you think I'd—get used to it?

**Ida.**

(*faintly*) I guess so—

**Homer.**
I don't know. Maybe I would. And you want me to do it so bad— (*Ida is crying.*) Mother, what's the matter! (*Homer crosses to Ida.*)

**Ida.**
Never mind me, Homer!

**Homer.**
Mother, you're crying!

**Ida.**
I never thought of that! That she'd be buying your underwear! (*She has a fresh burst of crying and gets up and starts toward the house.*)

**Homer.**
Mother—

**Ida.**
(*as she exits into house left*) Never mind me, Homer. I'll be all right. I'm just a silly old goose! (*Homer pushes the chair back. Kicks the ground, disgusted with himself for upsetting his mother.*)

from
# I REMEMBER MAMA
by John van Druten

## Act II
## TRINA, MR. THORKELSON

When she wrote about them in her stories, Mama's daughter Katrin simply labeled them "The Aunts" (see introductory comments about the play on page 95). They were Mama's three sisters: Jenny and Sigrid, the outspoken ones who squabbled, and Trina, the shy, unmarried one who was afraid of nearly everyone except Mama. In Mama's kitchen, where they met to gossip and argue over family affairs, the Aunts were like a trio of clucking hens, and their feathers were never more ruffled, their squawks more frenzied, than on the day that Trina announced her engagement to Mr. Thorkelson, the undertaker. Jenny and Sigrid laughed—after all, Mr. Thorkelson was as shy as Trina. But Mama was pleased, and she took on the task of persuading fierce old Uncle Chris, the official head of the family, to give his blessing to the marriage.

It was a good marriage. One of Katrin's warmest memories is of the happiness shared by Trina and her timid husband. From that memory came the scene reprinted here.

The time is a year after the wedding; the place, a park bench beside a hedge. Trina and Mr. Thorkelson are seated together. They are not very young, not very handsome. Mr. Thorkelson is a "black Norwegian," which is to say that his hair is dark, not blond. Trina is fair and, at this moment, her face has a special glow; she is cooing over a baby carriage.

**Trina.**
Who's the most beautiful Norwegian baby in San Francisco? Who's going to be three months old tomorrow?

225

Little Christopher Thorkelson! (*To Mr. Thorkelson*)
Do you know, Peter, I think he's even beginning to *look*
a little like Uncle Chris! Quite apart from his black curls
—and those, of course, he gets from *you*. (*To baby
again*) He's going to grow up to be a black Norwegian,
isn't he, just like his daddy and his Uncle Chris? (*Settling
down beside Mr. Thorkelson*) I think there's something
about his mouth . . . a sort of . . . well . . . *firmness*. Of
course, it's *your* mouth, too. But then I've always thought
you had quite a lot of Uncle Chris about you. (*She looks
back at the baby*) Look—he's asleep!

**Mr. T.**
Trina, do you know what next Thursday is?

**Trina.**
(*Nodding, smiling*) Our anniversary.

**Mr. T.**
What would you think of our giving a little party?

**Trina.**
A party?

**Mr. T.**
Oh, quite a modest one. Nothing showy or ostentatious—
but, after all, we have been married a year, and with
your having been in mourning and the baby coming so
soon and everything, we've not been able to entertain. I
think it's time you . . . took your place in society.

**Trina.**
(*Scared*) What . . . sort of a party?

**Mr. T.**
An evening party. (*Proudly*) A soirée! I should say about
ten people . . . some of the Norwegian colony . . . and
Lars and Marta, of course. . . .

**Trina.**
(*Beginning to count on her fingers*) And Jenny and
Sigrid. . . .

**Mr. T.**
Oh . . . I . . . I hadn't thought of asking Jenny and Sigrid.

**Trina.**
Oh, we'd have to. We couldn't leave them out.

**Mr. T.**
Trina, I hope you won't be offended if I say that I have
never really felt . . . well, altogether comfortable with
Jenny and Sigrid. They have always made me feel that
they didn't think I was . . . well . . . *worthy* of you. Of
course, I know I'm not, but . . . well . . . one doesn't like
to be reminded of it . . . *all* the time.

**Trina.**

(*Taking his hand*) Oh, Peter.

**Mr. T.**

But you're quite right. We must ask them. Now, as to the matter of refreshments . . . what would you suggest?

**Trina.**

(*Flustered*) Oh, I don't know. I . . . what would you say to . . . ice cream and cookies for the ladies . . . and coffee, of course . . . and . . . perhaps port wine for the gentlemen?

**Mr. T.**

(*Anxiously*) Port wine?

**Trina.**

Just a little. You could bring it in already poured out, in *little* glasses. Jenny and Sigrid can help me serve the ice cream.

**Mr. T.**

(*Firmly*) No. If Jenny and Sigrid come, they come as guests, like everyone else. You shall have someone in to help you in the kitchen.

**Trina.**

You mean a waitress? (*Mr. Thorkelson nods, beaming*) Oh, but none of us have *ever* . . . do you really think . . . I mean . . . you did say we shouldn't be ostentatious. . . .

**Mr. T.**

(*Nervously*) Trina, there's something I would like to say. I've never been very good at expressing myself or my . . . well . . . *deeper* feelings—but I want you to know that I'm not only very fond of you, but very . . . well . . . very *proud* of you as well, and I want you to have the best of everything, as far as it's in my power to give it to you. (*As a climax*) I want you to have a waitress!

**Trina.**

(*Overcome*) Yes, Peter. (*They hold hands*)

from
SECOND THRESHOLD
by Philip Barry
(with revisions by Robert E. Sherwood)

Act I, scene 1
MIRANDA BOLTON, TOBY WELLS

Philip Barry's last play concerns a man with a "death wish," a man "at the end of his soul's rope." Josiah Bolton has been a man of affairs, a high official in the government, but in his middle age he has lost the impulse to live and, indeed, seems to have tried to kill himself. In the course of the play, he finds a "second threshold" to life in his discovery of the warmth and love in human relationships. This is a problem play, as deeply philosophical as the playwright's *Hotel Universe* (see pages 114 and 143), yet it is enlivened by the comedy and wit of *The Philadelphia Story* and the other, lighter plays for which Barry was famous.

The scene reprinted here, which occurs at the start of the play, introduces Miranda Bolton, the daughter who becomes the personification of the love that saves Josiah Bolton. Now, however, Miranda is seen merely as a pretty girl in her twenties, graceful, socially at ease, and rather flippant.

The setting is the library of Josiah Bolton's house—"a comfortable, handsome, livable room which has been put away for the summer, chairs and sofa slip-covered, chandelier and the two or three paintings are covered with tarletan. There is a tray with a thermos carafe of milk and a plate of sandwiches on a table behind the sofa. The time is late July, a Friday night, a little after midnight." Amanda comes to the double doors, upstage center, and discovers Toby Wells standing, looking out the French windows, left. Toby "is in his late twenties, spare, rangy, with a humorous, likable face, not at all handsome. He is coatless, with necktie awry and shirt sleeves rolled up." As Miranda enters, he turns to meet her.

**Miranda.**

Oh! Good evening. (*Pleasantly*)

**Toby.**

Good evening.

**Miranda.**

(*She comes closer to Toby, smiles*) Why, I think I know you.

**Toby.**

There was a time—quite a few years ago.

**Miranda.**

I've forgotten your name. Could you help me out on that?

**Toby.**

Gladly. I'm by name of Toby Wells.

**Miranda.**

You're not Dr. Wells's little boy! (*He smiles and nods, extends his hand. She shakes it.*) But of course. That summer at Christmas Cove. You had a crew cut—you were an absolute darling.

**Toby.**

That's right—I did have a crew cut.

**Miranda.**

You used to bring me things: bunches of field flowers and pails of clams. I was so pleased . . .

**Toby.**

Don't mention it.

**Miranda.**

I was flattered—because you were an older man, then.

**Toby.**

Sure. I was pushing twenty-one.

**Miranda.**

And I was pushing sixteen.

**Toby.**

You were—advanced for your age—

**Miranda.**

(*Laughs*) I'm afraid I've always been that. (*She sees the food.*) Food, heaven! (*As she goes to it, she looks around.*) Oh—how I love this house! All my life—the same home base. But it certainly could do with a little brightening right now. (*Miranda pours herself some milk.*)

**Toby.**

You haven't been here much recently . . .

**Miranda.**

Not much. But I always love to come back to it. What have *you* been up to all these years?

**Toby.**
Johns Hopkins—University of Edinburgh—Navy.

**Miranda.**
You're a doctor, too!

**Toby.**
Well, yes.

**Miranda.**
(*Suddenly worried*) Why are you here?

**Toby.**
My father's away on his vacation. I've been dropping in every now and then.

**Miranda.**
Why—is anything the matter—?

**Toby.**
Just friendly visits. Your father tells me you're a Bachelor of Arts now. Congratulations.

**Miranda.**
Thank you.

**Toby.**
Did you like Bennington?

**Miranda.**
Very much. I had some experience with your trade. I spent my winter period in the psychiatric ward at Massachusetts General.

**Toby.**
Oh? I didn't know you were troubled that way.

**Miranda.**
(*Laughs*) Working, stupid. And hard.

**Toby.**
I also gather that further congratulations may be in order.

**Miranda.**
Thanks, they are. I'm sailing tomorrow night. We're being married soon after I land—July thirtieth. Isn't it nice?

**Toby.**
Just lovely. But I thought weddings usually took place *Chez* Bride.

**Miranda.**
Oh, he's much too busy to get away. [*Hearing a sound in the hall, she turns, then calls.*] * * * Oh, Malloy! Bless you. That food was a great idea. Thank Mrs. Malloy for me. [Oh, and don't wait up for my house guest.] * * * I gave her a key to the front door. Good night, you angel. * * * I'm carting a girl to England with me— freshman at Bennington—darling child: Thankful Mather.

That's actually her name—Thankful. Isn't that Boston for you?

**Toby.**

Do people still call you Mandy?

**Miranda.**

No, they do not.

**Toby.**

Too bad. You were awfully nice when you were Mandy. (*She is not quite sure what he meant by that one.*)

**Miranda.**

I'm sorry, Dr. Wells—I'm sorry I've changed so much.

**Toby.**

I used to be known to you as Toby.

**Miranda.**

Whatever you used to be— (*Toby takes hold of her by the shoulders and turns her around.*)

**Toby.**

Would you mind—turning around?

**Miranda.**

(*Smiling, puzzled*) Not at all. Only— (*Toby lifts the back of her dress.*) Aren't we being a trifle familiar?

**Toby.**

I just wanted to see if you still have freckles on your shoulder blades.

**Miranda.**

Of course. I'd forgotten. You're a doctor. (*She smiles and starts toward the door.*) It's been terribly nice seeing you again. Do drop in at any time. And give my best remembrances to your father, won't you?

**Toby.**

Very brisk, aren't you? Where do you think you're going? (*She turns and looks at him. She is now moderately annoyed.*)

**Miranda.**

Now?

**Toby.**

Now.

**Miranda.**

To see my father before I fold for the night.

**Toby.**

Sit down.

**Miranda.**

I beg your pardon?

**Toby.**

The hope is he's asleep.

**Miranda.**
How do you mean the hope?

**Toby.**
He hasn't been getting much lately. Sit down please.

**Miranda.**
Well. All right. (*She sits.*)

**Toby.**
Why have you walked out on your father?

**Miranda.**
(*Astounded*) Why have I walked out . . .

**Toby.**
You needn't repeat my question. All you have to do is answer it!

**Miranda.**
(*Smiles*) When you were at Medical School, dear Doctor, did they include a course in charm?

**Toby.**
Yes. But I flunked it. Must I ask you again—?

**Miranda.**
No. I did not walk out on my father. He deliberately cut himself off from me—from everybody. That was his own choice—and it's his lookout, isn't it?

**Toby.**
He's got no lookout left. That's the trouble.

**Miranda.**
What's the matter with him?

**Toby.**
Your father's hit a blank spot—a very blank spot—where he pulls up short and says, "Well, here I am. But where the hell am I? Where do I go from here?"

**Miranda.**
Or—what do I settle for, maybe?

**Toby.**
Maybe. And what he settles for is the conclusion that life just isn't worth living.

**Miranda.**
I don't believe it.

**Toby.**
I'm sure it's difficult, for the highly intellectual daughter of an even more highly so father—

**Miranda.**
You're trying to tell me that he's cracked up?

**Toby.**
Not precisely that—but something like it.

**Miranda.**
I don't believe it. Not him. A man as big as that.

**Toby.**

It's the big ones—the ones who've been in the so-called high places—who get smacked the hardest. They know what combat really is. They've been in the ring with the champ.

**Miranda.**

Has he been talking about my engagement?

**Toby.**

A little.

**Miranda.**

What has he told you?

**Toby.**

Nothing definite. But I gather that he doesn't like the idea of your going to England to marry a man old enough to be your— (*Her eyes flash at him.*) —a man twice your age.

**Miranda.**

I'm marrying Matthew with my eyes wide open. And his age is my business—or isn't it?

**Toby.**

That's for you to say.

**Miranda.**

You're damned right it is! (*She is now moving about, nervously.*) My father used to be very fond of Matthew. He respected him. They worked together during the war, and after it. It was only when Father quit his job that they drifted apart.

**Toby.**

Would you mind telling me—remember, I'm only a doctor —you know, completely clinical—

**Miranda.**

You want another look at my freckles?

**Toby.**

Not this time. Something deeper . . .

**Miranda.**

Come on—what is it?

**Toby.**

Your relationship with your father—

**Miranda.**

(*She knows in her heart what's coming.*) What about it?

**Toby.**

You and he used to be very close to each other— (*Miranda looks at him sharply.*)

**Miranda.**

Now, listen—dear Doctor—are you suggesting—?

**Toby.**

I'm doing the asking, please. You've worked in a psychiatric ward—you ought to know that the doctor does the asking.

**Miranda.**

But not the guessing! If you're leaping to the obvious conclusion that there's ever been anything Freudian in this family—then you'd better go right back to Johns Hopkins and specialize in osteopathy. There was never anything like that. As a matter of fact, it was the exact opposite. We were friends—companions. Nothing emotional. We were close to each other because I was the only member of the family he could trust *not* to be emotional. After Mother got a divorce, and he lost all hope of making anything out of Jock—you remember my brother, Jock?

**Toby.**

(*Nods*) Sure.

**Miranda.**

Father had me with him in Washington—he took me along to the conferences. I was useful to him: I'll say that for myself—secretary, hostess, courier, sounding board—mostly sounding board. He could talk to me, impersonally, about anything. That's the way it always was between us—impersonal.

**Toby.**

That's the way it is now, apparently.

**Miranda.**

Exactly!

**Toby.**

You didn't come home for Christmas, did you?

**Miranda.**

How did you know I didn't? Has he complained about that?

**Toby.**

Oh, no. I happened to be here on Christmas. I noticed that you weren't.

**Miranda.**

I went to England—a house party—friends of ours. Father knew I was going. He didn't mind in the least. That was when—when Matthew and I got engaged. To tell you the whole truth, dear Doctor, Father has made it increasingly clear that he wanted to be by himself. Ever after the accident, he insisted I shouldn't come down from college.

**Toby.**

Which accident?

**Miranda.**

Last March—when he crashed that little chartered plane. I know it wasn't serious, but—look! Do you suppose there might have been a concussion or something?

**Toby.**

(*Shaking his head*) We went over him like a dog for ticks. Nothing but a sprained wrist, minor abrasions and contusions. It was miraculous. They say the airplane was a wreck.

**Miranda.**

I never could figure out how it happened. He's a marvelous pilot.

**Toby.**

I suppose we all get careless.

**Miranda.**

Not him! (*She looks sharply at Toby.*) Do you want me to believe that perhaps it wasn't an accident?

**Toby.**

(*Ignoring the question*) When did you last hear from him?

**Miranda.**

Oh—a month or so ago. What's he doing—all alone—here—in the middle of the summer?

**Toby.**

He's been doing nothing—but—sitting and thinking—and reading—and eating a little at odd times—and sleeping a little at odder—and occasionally listening to the news on the radio. He hasn't stirred out of this house and its two-by-four garden in eight weeks. It was May thirtieth—Decoration Day—when he drove himself down the Island to Amagansett—"just for a swim"—with you know what results.

**Miranda.**

I'm afraid I don't.

**Toby.**

Ask him. Possibly he may not want people to—anyway, it also turned out not to be serious—

**Miranda.**

Are you trying to scare me?

**Toby.**

Perhaps "arouse" is the better word.

**Miranda.**

But what are *you* doing about it? Isn't it your job as a doctor to take care of him?

**Toby.**
It isn't my job. I don't come in here as a doctor—as a friend. If your father thought I was here in my professional capacity, he'd throw me out. Maybe *you* can persuade him to see a doctor; I can't. And, by the way, I don't send in any bills for visits, which is just as well, since I'm producing no results.

**Miranda.**
What can *I* do?

**Toby.**
You're sailing tomorrow night?

**Miranda.**
I—I might stay on a few days, and fly instead.

**Toby.**
It's a three-months' job, at the very least. Six months would be nearer it. I suppose—there's no chance of postponing the wedding?

**Miranda.**
It's got to be now, or maybe never. Matthew has to go out to the Far East in August and there's no way of telling how long he'll be gone or whether I'd be allowed to follow him out there. (*Toby gathers up his coat preparatory to leaving.*) You're not going?

**Toby.**
Afraid I must. Couple of calls before I go to bed.

**Miranda.**
Do you think I could get Father to go to England with me?

**Toby.**
I doubt it.

**Miranda.**
It would be wonderful for him—he has lots of friends there, people who know how much he really did in the war, and they're grateful to him. And if he and Matthew could only come face to face—

**Toby.**
(*Smiling*) It's a nice idea, Mandy. Go ahead—put it up to him. No harm in trying.

**Miranda.**
You think I'm a stupid child, don't you!

**Toby.**
I happen to be very fond of children. (*He goes to the door.*)

**Miranda.**
Dr. Wells—

**Toby.**
Yes?

**Miranda.**
I don't believe a word of what you've been telling me—

**Toby.**
I'm sorry. You'll just have to find it out for yourself.

**Miranda.**
But— (*Emotional*) I feel lost—helpless. I don't know what to say to him. We're strangers to each other—my own father, and I. There's a great gulf of indifference between us. I don't know how to get across it. I can't even see what he looks like, on the other side.

**Toby.**
Maybe—when that gulf is increased by the width of the Atlantic Ocean—maybe you'll be able to dismiss the whole distasteful matter from your mind. (*He opens the door, listens.*) I think I hear someone.

**Miranda.**
Probably Thankful, in from her party.

**Toby.**
No, it's from upstairs.

**Miranda.**
(*Scared*) Perhaps he's coming down.

**Toby.**
Well—good night.

**Miranda.**
No! Please—please wait just one minute.

**Toby.**
Why?

**Miranda.**
It's just—it's just that I don't want to be alone with him straight off. I've got to think.

**Toby.**
Ever try feeling, instead? (*Toby turns toward the door.*)

from
BIOGRAPHY
by S. N. Behrman

## Act I
MARION FROUDE, LEANDER NOLAN

In his highly successful comedy of character and ideas, S. N. Behrman poses youth against maturity, unrelenting belief in principles against amused tolerance and acceptance of things as they are. His central character, Marion Froude, is in her mid-thirties, a fashionable portrait-painter, who has roamed the world and always felt at home. Marion has "played footie with royalty," fallen in and out of love any number of times, and she has learned that there is a time to take the good things of life that happen by (like love) and a time to let them go without remorse. "Something always turns up for me!" she exclaims at the end of the play. In the lopsided triangle that is the basis of Behrman's plot are Marion, Leander Nolan, whom she knew when she was young, and Richard Kurt, who is very young now. Leander—Marion calls him Bunny—is solid, respectable, and about to run for the Senate. Richard Kurt, a writer for an outspoken little magazine, is carefully and consciously brash, dedicated to absolute beliefs and not averse to martyrdom. Nolan, about to be married to the daughter of his most important political backer, drops in on Marion to ease his conscience of an old and lingering guilt (he discusses it in the scene below). Kurt comes to ask Marion to write her autobiography and stays to become her lover (that development is the subject of the scene on page 354). Nolan and Kurt come into conflict when the would-be senator asks Marion not to write the book and reveal things about him which would ruin him politically. Marion is caught between her own inclination to make a generous compromise—to live and let live—and Kurt's unyielding determination to see justice done, no matter who is hurt. Thus Behrman plays out his theme of the opposition of two rights, the easy-

238

goingness of the mature accepter of the world and the relentlessness of the youthful crusader. But the play *is* a comedy—a high comedy in its brilliant, sharply pointed dialogue, a comedy of character in its perceptively drawn people and neatly developed situations.

In the scene below, the audience meets Leander (Bunny) Nolan and gets to know Marion Froude. "She is one of those women, the sight of whom on Fifth Avenue, where she has just been walking, causes foreigners to exclaim enthusiastically that American women are the most radiant in the world. She is tall, lithe, indomitably alive. . . . The tears in things have warmed without scalding her; she floats life like a dancer's scarf in perpetual enjoyment of its colors and contours." Nolan "is middle-aged, ample, handsome. Like the late Warren Gamaliel Harding. Soberly dressed and wears a waistcoat with white piping on it. The façade is impeccable but in Nolan's eye you may discern, at odd moments, an uncertainty, an almost boyish anxiety to please, to be right, that is rather engaging." He is most uncertain at the moment, for Marion does not know who he is; she had expected him to be a young man who wanted to talk to her about writing a book. The setting is Marion's cavernous, cluttered studio-apartment in an old-fashioned building in New York; the time, about five o'clock of an afternoon in late November, 1932.

(*Marion turns to face Nolan, who is standing with his arms behind his back rather enjoying the surprise he is about to give her.*)

**Nolan.**

How are you, Marion?

**Marion.**

(*delicately*) Er—do I know you?

**Nolan.**

Yes. You know me.

**Marion.**

Oh yes—of course!

**Nolan.**

About time!

**Marion.**

(*brightly insecure*) Lady Winchester's garden party at Ascot—two summers ago. . . .

**Nolan.**
  Guess again!

**Marion.**
  No—I know you perfectly well—it's just that—no, don't tell me . . . (*She covers her eyes with her hand, trying to conjure him out of the past.*)

**Nolan.**
  This is astonishing. If someone had said to me that I could walk into a room in front of Marion Froude and she not know me I'd have told 'em they were crazy!

**Marion.**
  (*desperate*) I do know you. I know you perfectly well—it's just that . . .

**Nolan.**
  You'll be awful sore at yourself—I warn you . . .

**Marion.**
  I can't forgive myself now—I know!

**Nolan.**
  I don't believe it!

**Marion.**
  The American Embassy dinner in Rome on the Fourth of July—last year—you sat on my right. . . .

**Nolan.**
  I did not!

**Marion.**
  (*miserably*) Well, you sat somewhere. Where did you sit?

**Nolan.**
  I wasn't there.

**Marion.**
  Well, I think it's very unkind of you to keep me in suspense like this. I can't bear it another second!

**Nolan.**
  I wouldn't have believed it!

**Marion.**
  Well, give me some hint, will you?

**Nolan.**
  Think of home—think of Tennessee!

**Marion.**
  Oh!

**Nolan.**
  Little Mary Froude . . .

**Marion.**
  (*a light breaking in on her*) No! Oh, no!

**Nolan.**
  Well, it's about time.

**Marion.**

But . . . ! You were—

**Nolan.**

Well, so were you!

**Marion.**

But—Bunny—you aren't Bunny Nolan, are you? You're his brother!

**Nolan.**

I have no brother.

**Marion.**

But Bunny—Bunny dear—how important you've become!

**Nolan.**

I haven't done badly—no.

**Marion.**

Here, give me your coat and hat— (*Marion, taking his coat and hat, crosses upstage to piano, and leaves them there. Laughing, a little hysterical.*) You should have warned me. It's not fair of you. Bunny! Of all people—I can scarcely believe it. . . . (*A moment's pause. He doesn't quite like her calling him Bunny but he doesn't know how to stop it. She sits on model-stand looking up at him as she says:*) You look wonderful. You look like a—like a— Senator or something monumental like that.

**Nolan.**

(*sits on sofa below piano*) That's a good omen. I'll have to tell Orrin.

**Marion.**

What's a good omen? And who is Orrin?

**Nolan.**

Your saying I look like a Senator. Because—I don't want to be premature—but in a few months I may be one.

**Marion.**

A Senator!

**Nolan.**

(*smiling*) Senator. Washington. Not Nashville.

**Marion.**

Do you want to be a Senator or can't you help it?

**Nolan.**

(*to whom this point of view is incomprehensible*) What do you mean?

**Marion.**

I'll paint you, Bunny. Toga. Ferrule. Tribune of the people.

**Nolan.**

Not a bad idea. Not a bad idea at all. I remember now—

you were always sketching me. Sketching everything. Say, you've done pretty well yourself, haven't you?

**Marion.**

Not as well as you have, Bunny. Imagine. Bunny Nolan— a Senator at Washington. Well, well! And tell me—how do I seem to you? You knew me at once, didn't you?

**Nolan.**

Sure I did. You haven't changed so much—a little perhaps . . .

**Marion.**

(*delicately*) Ampler?

**Nolan.**

(*inspecting her*) No . . . not that I can notice.

**Marion.**

(*with a sigh of relief*) That's wonderful.

**Nolan.**

You look just the same. You are just the same.

**Marion.**

Oh, you don't know, Bunny. I'm artful. How long is it since we've seen each other? Twelve years anyway. More than that—fifteen . . .

**Nolan.**

Just about—hadn't even begun to practice law yet.

**Marion.**

We were just kids . . . children. . . . And now look at you! I can see how successful you are, Bunny.

**Nolan.**

How?

**Marion.**

White piping on your vest. That suggests directorates to me. Multiple control. Vertical corporations. Are you vertical or horizontal, Bunny?

**Nolan.**

I'm both.

**Marion.**

Good for you! Married?

**Nolan.**

Not yet . . .

**Marion.**

How did you escape? You're going to be, though.

**Nolan.**

I'm engaged.

**Marion.**

Who's the lucky girl?

**Nolan.**

Slade Kinnicott. Daughter of Orrin Kinnicott.

**Marion.**

Orrin Kinnicott. The newspaper publisher?

**Nolan.**

Yes. He's backing me for the Senate.

**Marion.**

Well, if he's backing you you ought to get in. All that circulation—not very good circulation, is it? Still, one vote's as good as another, I suppose.

**Nolan.**

(*hurt*) In my own state the Kinnicott papers are as good as any.

**Marion.**

Well, I wish you luck. I'm sure you'll have it. My! Senator Nolan!

**Nolan.**

If I get in I'll be the youngest Senator . . .

**Marion.**

And the best-looking too, Bunny . . .

**Nolan.**

(*embarrassed*) Well . . .

**Marion.**

You're fussed! How charming of you! (*She sits beside him.*) Oh, Bunny, I'm very proud of you, really.

**Nolan.**

You see, Marion, I've been pretty successful in the law. Tremendously successful, I may say. I've organized some of the biggest mergers of recent years. I've made a fortune—a sizable fortune. Well, one day I woke up and I said to myself: Look here, Nolan, you've got to take stock. You've got to ask yourself where you're heading. I'd been so busy I'd never had a chance to ask myself these fundamental questions before. And I decided to call a halt. You've got enough, more than enough for life, I said to myself. It's time you quit piling up money for yourself and began thinking about your fellow-man. I've always been ambitious, Marion. You know that. You shared all my early dreams . . .

**Marion.**

Of course I did.

**Nolan.**

Remember I always told you I didn't want money and power for their own sakes—I always wanted to be a big man in a real sense—to do something for my country and my time.

**Marion.**

Yes. Sometimes you sounded like Daniel Webster, darling,
I'm not a bit surprised you're going in the Senate.

**Nolan.**

I never thought—even in my wildest dreams—

**Marion.**

Well, you see, you underestimated yourself. You may go
even higher—the White House—why not?

**Nolan.**

I never let myself think of that.

**Marion.**

Why not? It's no more wonderful than what's happened
already, is it?

**Nolan.**

(*Napoleon at Saint Helena*) Destiny!

**Marion.**

Exactly. Destiny!

**Nolan.**

(*kind, richly human, patronizing*) And you, my dear!

**Marion.**

As you see. Obscure. Uncertain. Alone. Nowhere at all.
Not the remotest chance of my getting into the Senate—
unless I marry into it. Oh, Bunny, after you get to Washington will you introduce me to some Senators?

**Nolan.**

Well, that's premature . . . Naturally if the people should
favor me I'd do what I could. I never forget a friend.
Whatever faults I may have, disloyalty, I hope, is not one
of them.

**Marion.**

Of course it isn't. You're a dear. You always were. (*A
moment's pause.*)

**Nolan.**

Who was that fellow I found you with when I came in?

**Marion.**

An old friend of mine from Vienna, a composer.

**Nolan.**

You've been a lot with foreigners, haven't you?

**Marion.**

A good deal . . .

**Nolan.**

Funny, I don't understand that.

**Marion.**

Foreigners are people, you know, Bunny. Some of 'em
are rather nice.

**Nolan.**

When I'm abroad a few weeks home begins to look pretty good to me.

**Marion.**

I love New York but I can't say I feel an acute nostalgia for Tennessee. (*Another pause. He stares at her suddenly—still incredulous that he should be seeing her at all, and that, after all these years and quite without him, she should be radiant still.*)

**Nolan.**

Little Marion Froude! I can't believe it somehow. . . .

**Marion.**

Oh, Bunny! You're sweet! You're so—ingenuous. That's what I always liked about you.

**Nolan.**

What do you mean?

**Marion.**

The way you look at me, the incredulity, the surprise. What did you expect to see? A hulk, a remnant, a whitened sepulchre—what?

**Nolan.**

(*uncomfortable at being caught*) Not—not at all.

**Marion.**

Tell me, Bunny, what—? I won't be hurt. . . .

**Nolan.**

(*miserably, stumbling*) Well, naturally, after what I'd heard—

**Marion.**

What have you heard? Oh, do tell me, Bunny.

**Nolan.**

Well, I mean—about your life.

**Marion.**

Racy, Bunny? Racy?

**Nolan.**

No use going into that. You chose your own way. Everybody has a right to live their own life, I guess.

**Marion.**

(*Pats his arm*) That's very handsome of you, Bunny. I hope you take that liberal point of view when you reach the Senate.

**Nolan.**

I came here, Marion, in a perfectly sincere mood to say something to you, something that's been on my mind ever since we parted, but if you're going to be flippant

I suppose there's no use my saying anything—I might as well go, in fact. (*But he makes no attempt to do so.*)

**Marion.**

(*seriously*) Do forgive me, Bunny. One gets into an idiom that passes for banter, but really I'm not so changed. I'm not flippant. I'm awfully glad to see you, Bunny. (*An undertone of sadness creeps into her voice.*) After all, one makes very few real friends in life—and you are part of my youth—we are part of each other's youth.

**Nolan.**

You didn't even know me!

**Marion.**

Complete surprise! After all I've been in New York many times during these years and never once—never once have you come near me. You've dropped me all these years. (*With a sigh.*) I'm afraid, Bunny, your career has been too much with you.

**Nolan.**

(*grimly*) So has yours!

**Marion.**

I detect an overtone—faint but unmistakable—of moral censure.

**Nolan.**

(*same tone*) Well, I suppose it's impossible to live one's life in art without being sexually promiscuous! (*He looks at her accusingly.*)

**Marion.**

Oh, dear me, Bunny! What shall I do? Shall I blush? Shall I hang my head in shame? What shall I do? How does one react in the face of an appalling accusation of this sort? I didn't know the news had got around so widely.

**Nolan.**

Well, so many of your lovers have been famous men.

**Marion.**

Well, you were obscure—But you're famous now, aren't you? I seem to be stimulating if nothing else . . .

**Nolan.**

If I had then some of the fame I have now you probably wouldn't have walked out on me at the last minute the way you did—

**Marion.**

Dear, dear Bunny, that's not quite—

**Nolan.**

(*irritated beyond control*) I wish you wouldn't call me Bunny. . . .

**Marion.**

Well, I always did. What is your real name?

**Nolan.**

You know perfectly well—

**Marion.**

I swear I don't. . . .

**Nolan.**

My name is Leander. . . .

**Marion.**

Bunny, really.

**Nolan.**

That is my name.

**Marion.**

Really I'd forgotten that. Leander! Who was he—he did something in the Hellespont, didn't he? What did he do in the Hellespont?

**Nolan.**

(*sharply*) Beside the point.

**Marion.**

Sorry! You say you wanted to tell me something—

**Nolan.**

(*grimly*) Yes!

**Marion.**

I love to be told things.

**Nolan.**

That night you left me—

**Marion.**

We'd quarreled about something, hadn't we?

**Nolan.**

I realized after you left me how much I'd grown to depend on you—

**Marion.**

Dear Bunny!

**Nolan.**

I plunged into work. I worked fiercely to forget you. I did forget you— (*he looks away from her.*) And yet—

**Marion.**

And yet—?

**Nolan.**

The way we'd separated and I never heard from you— it left something bitter in my mind—something— (*He hesitates for a word.*)

**Marion.**

(*supplying it*) Unresolved?

**Nolan.**

(*quickly—relieved that she understands so exactly*) Yes. All these years I've wanted to see you, to get it off my mind—

**Marion.**

Did you want the last word, Bunny dear?

**Nolan.**

(*fiercely*) I wanted to see you, to stand before you, to tell myself—"Here she is and—and what of it!"

**Marion.**

Well, can you?

**Nolan.**

(*heatedly, with transparent overemphasis*) Yes! Yes!

**Marion.**

Good for you, Bunny. I know just how you feel—like having a tooth out, isn't it? (*Sincerely.*) In justice to myself—I must tell you this—that the reason I walked out on you in the summary way I did was not as you've just suggested because I doubted your future—it was obvious to me, even then, that you were destined for mighty things—but the reason was that I felt a disparity in our characters not conducive to matrimonial contentment. You see how right I was. I suspected in myself a—a tendency to explore, a spiritual and physical wanderlust— that I knew would horrify you once you found it out. It horrifies you now when we are no longer anything to each other. Imagine, Leander dear, if we were married how much more difficult it would be—If there is any one thing you have to be grateful to me for it is that instant's clear vision I had which made me see, which made me look ahead, which made me tear myself away from you. Why, everything you have now—your future, your prospects,—even your fiancée, Leander dear—you owe to me—no, I won't say to me—to that instinct—to that premonition.

**Nolan.**

(*nostalgic*) We might have done it together.

**Marion.**

I wouldn't have stood for a fiancée, Bunny dear—not even *I* am as promiscuous as that.

**Nolan.**

Don't use that word!

**Marion.**

But, Leander! It's your own!

**Nolan.**

Do you think it hasn't been on my conscience ever since, do you think it hasn't tortured me—!

**Marion.**

What, dear?

**Nolan.**

That thought!

**Marion.**

Which thought?

**Nolan.**

Every time I heard about you—all the notoriety that's attended you in the American papers—painting pictures of Communist statesmen, running around California with movie comedians!

**Marion.**

I have to practice my profession, Bunny. One must live, you know. Besides, I've done Capitalist statesmen too. And at Geneva—

**Nolan.**

(*darkly*) You know what I mean!

**Marion.**

You mean . . . (*She whispers through her cupped hand.*) You mean promiscuous? Has that gotten around, Bunny? Is it whispered in the sewing-circles of Nashville? Will I be burned for a witch if I go back home? Will they have a trial over me? Will you defend me?

**Nolan.**

(*quite literally, with sincere and disarming simplicity*) I should be forced, as an honest man, to stand before the multitude and say: In condemning this woman you are condemning me who am asking your suffrages to represent you. For it was I with whom this woman first sinned before God. As an honorable man that is what I should have to do.

**Marion.**

And has this worried you—actually!

**Nolan.**

It's tortured me!

**Marion.**

You're the holy man and I'm Thais! That gives me an idea for the portrait which I hope you will commission me to do. I'll do you in a hair shirt. Savonarola. He was a Senator too, wasn't he? Or was he?

**Nolan.**

(_gloomily contemplating her_) I can't forget that it was I who—

**Marion.**

Did you think you were the first, Bunny? Was I so unscrupulously coquettish as to lead you to believe that I— oh, I couldn't have been. It's not like me. (_She crosses to right of model stand._)

**Nolan.**

(_fiercely_) Don't lie to me!

**Marion.**

(_sitting on stand_) Bunny, you frighten me!

**Nolan.**

(_stands over her almost threateningly_) You're lying to me to salve my conscience but I won't have it! I know my guilt and I'm going to bear it!

**Marion.**

Well, I don't want to deprive you of your little pleasures, but—

**Nolan.**

You're evil, Marion. You haven't the face of evil but you're evil—evil!

**Marion.**

Oh, Bunny darling, now you can't mean that surely. What's come over you? You never were like that—or were you? You know perfectly well I'm not evil. Casual— maybe—but not evil. Good heavens, Bunny, I might as well say you're evil because you're intolerant. These are differences in temperament, that's all—charming differences in temperament.

**Nolan.**

(_shakes his head, unconvinced_) Sophistry!

**Marion.**

All right, Dean Inge. Sophistry. By the way, I've met the Gloomy Dean and he's not gloomy at all—he's very jolly. (_Gets up from stand._) Let's have a cup of tea, shall we? Will your constituents care if you have a cup of tea with a promiscuous woman? Will they have to know?

**Nolan.**

I'm afraid I can't, Marion. I have to be getting on.

**Marion.**

Oh, stay and have some tea— (_Makes him sit down._) What do you have to do that can't wait for a cup of tea? (_Calls off._) Minnie—Minnie . . .

from
ANASTASIA
by Marcelle Maurette, English adaptation by Guy
  Bolton

Act II
ANNA, THE EMPRESS

It was said that when the Bolsheviks shot the Tsar and
his family, one little daughter, left for dead, did not die.
Discovered by loyalist peasants who came to care for the
bodies, the little girl was smuggled out of Russia into
another country and there, under a new name, she lived
and grew up. On these facts, or legend, the play is based.
Prince Bounine, an opportunistic Russian exile, learns that
a young woman in a hospital has said that she is Anastasia
Nicolaevna, daughter of the Tsar—the nurses heard her
cry it out when she was delirious. Bounine is interested,
for in banks safely out of Russia there are sizable deposits
of money which can be claimed only by a direct heir of
the Tsar. If the girl in the hospital is really Anastasia—
or if enough people can be convinced that she is—Bounine
can help her to claim the fortune and, of course, collect
a share for himself. When he interviews the girl, Anna,
she denies that she is Anastasia but she does agree to work
with Bounine; her illness and poverty had driven her to
consider suicide and in the prince's game of deception
there is, at least, life. He carefully teaches her the facts
and manners she must know to convince the world and the
remnants of Russian nobility that she is indeed the Tsar's
child. At times, however, the things she says—perhaps
remembers—surprise Bounine, for she speaks of things in
the old court which the prince himself does not really remember. Anna convinces many people, but her final test
is an interview with the Dowager Empress, Anastasia's
grandmother. That conversation is reprinted below.
  Are Anna's claims true? In the play, at least, no one can
be certain. She runs away, perhaps to lead the ordinary life
that has always been hers, perhaps to begin a new life

251

unclouded by memories of people, grandeur, and a time that are gone and cannot be revived.

The time is February, 1926; the place, a room in Prince Bounine's house in Berlin. The big room has been "done up" with an overdone elegance that the prince feels is appropriate to "Her Imperial Highness Anastasia Nicolaevna." Upstage center there is a curtained doorway— the entrance to Anna's room. She has come through this doorway a few moments ago. At Bounine's suggestion, she is dressed in a middyblouse and skirt, her hair arranged in a folded braid at the back. She has been introduced to the Dowager Empress, a small, elderly woman, straightbacked and indomitable. Now they have been left alone. The Empress, seated on a sofa, waits, her hands resting on her tightly furled umbrella. Hesitantly Anna moves toward her, then drops a small curtsy. The Empress turns her head.

**Empress.**

(*After a moment's inspection*) Yes, I can see why the others have believed, especially my romantic-minded nephew. The likeness is good enough for a waxwork gallery.

**Anna.**

I haven't cared whether they recognized me or not. But you—don't you know me?

**Empress.**

(*Turning her gaze away from Anna*) Where were you born?

**Anna.**

In Peterhoff.

**Empress.**

Child, no doubt of Emperor Nicholas the Second and Alexandra, his Empress?

**Anna.**

And grandchild of Maria Feodorovna.

**Empress.**

(*Drily*) You have taken a long time in coming to comfort my bereavement.

**Anna.**

I wrote you letters but you never answered. Perhaps you never got them.

**Empress.**

(*Grim and hard*) Oh, yes, I have received quite a few appeals from resurrected Romanovs. It seems the Bolshevik firing squads were very poor shots.

**Anna.**

Twice I started out to try and find you—only there were many days when I did not know who I was.

**Empress.**

But now you do? You, at least, have accepted yourself . . . Tell me: how long have you been an actress?

**Anna.**

As in your own case, Your Majesty, from earliest childhood.

**Empress.**

Yes, to be a princess is to be an actress, but not necessarily a good one.

**Anna.**

Perhaps I should have learned to be a better one if the curtain hadn't fallen so early.

**Empress.**

You are being flippant about a subject which you must realize is, for me, a great personal sorrow.

**Anna.**

Forgive me, I forgot for a moment you would be regarding that tragedy as more yours than mine. I am trying to keep my courage. But you are making it very hard for me . . . I have been without love for so long. (*Her voice is husky.*)

**Empress.**

Come, have there been no men in your life? I thought the story of your rescue included a Bolshevik guard who had fallen in love with you and who carried you from the shed where the bodies were awaiting burial?

**Anna.**

Yes, he rescued me and took me to Rumania, but he soon decided that a crazy girl was no great prize.

**Empress.**

A rescue from the very edge of the grave; years of lost memory in an asylum—excellent material for melodrama!

**Anna.**

Long empty days in which the consciousness of living came only through pain . . . hardly melodrama, grandmama.

**Empress.**

Did I give you permission to call me that name?

**Anna.**

(*Turning away*) I'm sorry, it slipped out. I will try to guard my tongue.

**Empress.**

You think my answer should be to grant you that privilege? A lonely old woman should be glad to hear someone call her "grandmama."

**Anna.**

(*Turns back*) My loneliness has been as bitter as yours.

**Empress.**

You ask me for recognition, for love. And you do it well; your eyes are moist, your voice full of feeling. But I can only reply that the love you beg for belongs to one who is dead . . . You have chosen to deck yourself in the robes of a specter, *mademoiselle,* and in so doing, have managed to win endorsement from a few poor sentimentalists, dreamers, self-deceivers—but I am none of those things. The shell that was once my heart is not easily pierced.

**Anna.**

(*With tears in her voice*) And so you thrust me from you? I was told you would ask me difficult questions. But you are not interested enough to ask me any.

**Empress.**

Oh, I was going to catechize you, was I? That is what your business associates told you?

**Anna.**

They mean nothing to me, those men, nor the millions about which they dream.

**Empress.**

But they've told you about those millions?

**Anna.**

Oh, yes, they have told me.

**Empress.**

(*On a sudden outburst*) And did you not say that a Romanov may be butchered but is not to be bought? That should have been your answer. For if your blood was truly Romanov you would not let yourself be made a catspaw by Bounine and his crew.

**Anna.**

Tell me to whom this money should be given and I will give it. Then perhaps you will believe me.

**Empress.**

Easily said. But you cannot give the money away until you have it. And you cannot get it without first obtaining my recognition! (*She raps with her umbrella on the floor to give further emphasis to her words.*)

**Anna.**

Yes, you are hard. You are showing your fighting face, the wounding words, barbed like arrows . . . I remember hearing Father say you were the toughest fighter the family had known since Peter the Great . . . That was at the time you and my mother quarreled over a necklace, some emeralds, part of the Imperial treasure, but you wanted to keep them for your lifetime.

**Empress.**

(*Surprised for a moment*) Who told you this? Oh, but there were plenty who must have known about it. Rasputin as a beginning, Alix aired all her grievances to him.

**Anna.**

You wore them with your last court dress, the red velvet one with the long train.

**Empress.**

(*The surprise returns*) Where did you see my portrait, or did someone describe me?

**Anna.**

It's strange, I only remember the large outlines or the little details.

**Empress.**

(*Recollection awakened*) It was the worst of our quarrels . . . the Winter Palace, my private rooms, the snow falling outside the double windowpanes . . . Alix had herself formally announced by one of the lackeys. "Her Imperial Majesty!" Thought she was going to awe me with a title that had been my own for many years . . . I was sitting by the fire with my jewel box on my knees, and, after that pompous nonsense, I didn't even trouble to get up. I merely said— (*She breaks off as, turning her head, she realizes to whom she is talking*) I don't know why I am telling all this to you.

**Anna.**

(*Eagerly*) My father took the side of my mother; they even brought in the Chancellor. They were all lined up against you—but you kept Figgy's jewels!

**Empress.**

How did you learn to call the great Catherine "Figgy"?

**Anna.**

We always called her that. And sometimes we'd give the same nickname to Marie because she had such an eye for the men. Olga used to tease her and—

**Empress.**
Stop! I forbid it! I forbid you to bandy those names!

**Anna.**
(*Choked, indignant*) They're my sisters! I can speak of them if I choose. (*She snatches up the photograph of the royal family that stands on the table beside the settee and clasps it to her bosom.*)

**Empress.**
Impostor!

**Anna.**
(*Recoiling as from a blow*) *You* call me that?

**Empress.**
Yes, and I want it stopped. If you have any decency I demand that you end this masquerade . . . I will pay you, give you more than these blackguards will.

**Anna.**
(*Backing away*) Go away! Leave me!

**Empress.**
I'm offering you money.

**Anna.**
Go away, please. (*She turns and goes, leaving the Empress, as she crosses toward far side of room.*)

**Empress.**
You're giving up, are you?

**Anna.**
So it wasn't enough to have suffered all that, the cellar, the asylum, the horror, the cruelty, the emptiness? . . . It was also necessary that I should meet you again—like this.

**Empress.**
Excellent, excellent! The tragic scene of despair. You're forgetting nothing, are you?

**Anna.**
Oh, how can anyone who has suffered so much have so little heart for suffering?

**Empress.**
I'm sorry, *mademoiselle*, if your failure to win me over is such a cruel disappointment . . . Good-bye. (*She goes to door. Anna drops the picture she is holding into chair beside her and runs to door, blocking the Empress' path.*)

**Anna.**
Don't go!

**Empress.**
(*Indicating over her shoulder*) But you just told me to.

**Anna.**
Not yet. I'll say nothing more to try and convince you.

**Empress.**

Then what do you want of me?

**Anna.**

Just a moment or two longer. Let me touch your dress. Put my hand for a moment in yours. (*She drops on her knees beside the Empress and clasps her dress. The Empress makes a move to disengage herself*) Please, just a moment more to hear your voice, to close my eyes and fancy we are on the terrace at Livadia with the smell of the sea, and an echo of laughter from the tennis courts where Father and Olga are playing. You called me little one, "Malenkaia." It was your own special name for me. You used it for no one else. (*She breaks off, coughing.*)

**Empress.**

Are you ill?

**Anna.**

Nothing serious.

**Empress.**

(*Bending over her*) But have you seen a doctor, a good one?

**Anna.**

Oh, yes, I am well acquainted with doctors! But it is kind of you to ask. And I am not, after all, surprised that you do not recognize me. I know I have changed very much indeed.

**Empress.**

Let me go, please. I must go home.

**Anna.**

What is strange is that you have altered so little. You still seem to me as you did that day that my finger was pinched in your carriage door and you told me to try not to cry because I was the daughter of the Tsar.

**Empress.**

Let me go.

**Anna.**

Look, it is still not quite straight, that finger. Or can't you see the difference from the others?

**Empress.**

(*Trying to go*) You are too clever for me . . . I don't know how you know these things, but, please, *mademoiselle*, I am an old woman . . . I have not the strength—

**Anna.**

(*Releasing her*) Very well, go, if you must. We have met once again after all the years, the only two left of our family.

**Empress.**

I will come back. I will see you once again, *mademoiselle*, when my mind is clearer. But now!—

**Anna.**

(*Overlapping*) No, perhaps you had better not come again. You are kind now; you have softened toward me. But later you will get your balance. You will say, "It was all acting. She is some sort of cheap little actress hired for money." And it is true, grandmama, they did hire me for money. I was starving after I ran away from the asylum. I had nowhere to go, I even went down the steps to the canal . . . Perhaps I should not have let him stop me—(*She rises and goes toward settee.*)

**Empress.**

Good-bye, *mademoiselle*.

**Anna.**

(*Dropping down on settee*) Good-bye, dear grandmama; I will try not to be lonely or frightened . . . Where have I said those words before? . . . Oh, yes, I remember, it was on board the *Standart!* I had waked and found a storm raging, the big waves breaking against the hull. And I cried out, "Grandmama!" And you came to my cabin. (*The Empress stares at Anna. She takes a step toward her, stops, then another step, then another pause, moving as if dragged against her will. Anna lies back against sofa, eyes closed.*)

**Empress.**

(*Brokenly*) Malenkaia! (*She drops down beside Anna and opens her arms to her. Anna drops her head on the Empress' bosom*) Malenkaia! Malenkaia! (*She kisses the top of the bowed head*) I couldn't believe it at first. You've come from so far away, and I've waited so long for you. (*She is pulling off her glove*) Don't cry, just rest yourself and don't speak. You are warm, you are alive, that is enough . . . I can stand no more for now. Can't you hear how that weary old heart of mine is beating? I must go, but don't be afraid. I shall come back . . . I need you. (*She is visibly overcome, leaning over against the settee. She rises; Anna reaches out, clutching her dress*) No, let go of my dress. That is what you used to do as a child . . . (*She is crying and laughing*) Be sensible, Malenkaia, I'll go as I used to, speaking to you as I left the side of your little bed. We will go— tomorrow if you like—to my old palace in Finland. It is still there and it's still mine. There is a very old man there, our lamplighter. Each night he goes from one room to another lighting the empty lamps until, for him, the great, dark rooms are ablaze with light. The other servants take no notice. They realize that he is childish. And perhaps that is true of us all, and we are lighting dead lamps to illumine a grandeur that is gone . . . Good night, Anastasia. (*She makes the sign of the cross as if blessing her*) And please, if it should not be you . . . don't ever tell me! (*She turns, going out with the uncertain step of an old woman. Anna rises, follows toward door, stops, half turns and slumps to the floor in a faint.*)

from
# TWELFTH NIGHT
by William Shakespeare

### Act I, scene 5
### VIOLA, OLIVIA, (MARIA)

Shakespeare and his audience delighted in the comic possibilities of situations in which things and people were not what they seemed to be. *Twelfth Night* abounds with such disguises and confusions, none of them more delightful than the wooing of the Lady Olivia by Viola, a girl pretending to be a boy. Despite her determination to play the part of a man convincingly, Viola cannot altogether control her womanly inclination to poke pins into the inflated ego of a lady who is too pleased with her own beauty. When she views "the picture" of the lady's face, she questions its truth to nature and comments upon its features with candor. It is a scene of repartee that sparkles with delicately barbed innuendoes and puns.

As for the plot that includes this scene, the author of program-notes for opera (the only man in whom such oversimplification is forgivable) might summarize it in three sentences: A girl, shipwrecked on a foreign coast, disguises herself as a boy and obtains employment as a page in the household of a duke with whom she promptly falls in love. When the duke sends her to carry a message of love to the lady he adores, she resolves to do her best for him. But the lady is too proud, the girl grows annoyed, the wooing becomes a contest—a duel fought with words instead of rapiers—until the lady, fascinated by the messenger's disdain, falls hopelessly in love with him (her).

For the rest of the story, it should be noted that Viola has a twin brother, a more appropriate object for the lady's affections; that the duke is more in love with love than with Olivia and is not at all displeased to discover that his loyal page is actually a charming girl; that there is a handful of notable subplots, most of them comic; and that the ending is happy.

Better still, read the play.

The setting for the scene is Olivia's house. A caller, a young person "not yet old enough for a man nor young enough for a boy" has demanded to be allowed to speak with the lady. When he refuses to go away, Olivia covers her face with a veil and asks that the caller be shown into the room. Viola enters, in her page's disguise.

**(Enter VIOLA.)**

**Viola.**

The honourable lady of the house, which is she?

**Olivia.**

Speak to me; I shall answer for her. Your will?

**Viola.**

Most radiant, exquisite, and unmatchable beauty,—I pray you, tell me if this be the lady of the house, for I never saw her. I would be loath to cast away my speech, for besides that it is excellently well penned, I have taken great pains to con it. Good beauties, let me sustain no scorn. I am very comptible, even to the least sinister usage.

**Olivia.**

Whence came you, sir?

**Viola.**

I can say little more than I have studied, and that question's out of my part. Good gentle one, give me modest assurance if you be the lady of the house, that I may proceed in my speech.

**Olivia.**

Are you a comedian?

**Viola.**

No, my profound heart; and yet, by the very fangs of malice I swear, I am not that I play. Are you the lady of the house?

**Olivia.**

If I do not usurp myself, I am.

**Viola.**

Most certain, if you are she, you do usurp yourself; for what is yours to bestow is not yours to reserve. But this is from my commission. I will on with my speech in your praise, and then show you the heart of my message.

**Olivia.**

Come to what is important in't. I forgive you the praise.

**Viola.**

Alas, I took great pains to study it, and 'tis poetical.

**Olivia.**
It is the more like to be feigned. I pray you, keep it in.
I heard you were saucy at my gates, and allowed your
approach rather to wonder at you than to hear you. If
you be not mad, be gone; if you have reason, be brief:
'tis not that time of moon with me to make one in so
skipping a dialogue.

**Maria.**
Will you hoist sail, sir? Here lies your way.

**Viola.**
No, good swabber, I am to hull here a little longer.
Some mollification for your giant, sweet lady. Tell me
your mind. I am a messenger.

**Olivia.**
Sure, you have some hideous matter to deliver, when
the courtesy of it is so fearful. Speak your office.

**Viola.**
It alone concerns your ear. I bring no overture of war,
no taxation of homage: I hold the olive in my hand: my
words are as full of peace as matter.

**Olivia.**
Yet you began rudely. What are you? What would you?

**Viola.**
The rudeness that hath appeared in me have I learned
from my entertainment. What I am, and what I would,
are as secret as maidenhead; to your ears, divinity; to
any other's, profanation.

**Olivia.**
Give us the place alone; we will hear this divinity. (*Exit*
MARIA.) Now, sir, what is your text?

**Viola.**
Most sweet lady—

**Olivia.**
A comfortable doctrine, and much may be said of it.
Where lies your text?

**Viola.**
In Orsino's bosom.

**Olivia.**
In his bosom! In what chapter of his bosom?

**Viola.**
To answer by the method, in the first of his heart.

**Olivia.**
O, I have read it; it is heresy. Have you no more to say?

**Viola.**
Good madam, let me see your face.

**Olivia.**

Have you any commission from your lord to negotiate with my face? You are now out of your text, but we will draw the curtain and show you the picture. Look you, sir, such a one I was this present. Is't not well done? (*Unveiling.*)

**Viola.**

Excellently done, if God did all.

**Olivia.**

'Tis in grain, sir; 'twill endure wind and weather.

**Viola.**

'Tis beauty truly blent, whose red and white
Nature's own sweet and cunning hand laid on.
Lady, you are the cruel'st she alive,
If you will lead these graces to the grave
And leave the world no copy.

**Olivia.**

O, sir, I will not be so hard-hearted; I will give out divers schedules of my beauty. It shall be inventoried, and every particle and utensil labelled to my will: as, item, two lips, indifferent red; item, two grey eyes, with lids to them; item, one neck, one chin, and so forth. Were you sent hither to praise me?

**Viola.**

I see you what you are, you are too proud;
But, if you were the devil, you are fair.
My lord and master loves you. O, such love
Could be but recompens'd, though you were crown'd
The nonpareil of beauty!

**Olivia.**

                              How does he love me?

**Viola.**

With adorations, with fertile tears,
With groans that thunder love, with sighs of fire.

**Olivia.**

Your lord does know my mind; I cannot love him.
Yet I suppose him virtuous, know him noble;
Of great estate, of fresh and stainless youth,
In voices well divulg'd, free, learn'd, and valiant,
And in dimension and the shape of nature
A gracious person: but yet I cannot love him.
He might have took his answer long ago.

**Viola.**

If I did love you in my master's flame,
With such a suff'ring, such a deadly life,

In your denial I would find no sense.
I would not understand it.

**Olivia.**

                              Why, what would you?

**Viola.**

Make me a willow cabin at your gate,
And call upon my soul within the house;
Write loyal cantons of contemned love
And sing them loud even in the dead of night;
Halloo your name to the reverberate hills
And make the babbling gossip of the air
Cry out "Olivia!" O, you should not rest
Between the elements of air and earth,
But you should pity me.

**Olivia.**

                    You might do much.

What is your parentage?

**Viola.**

Above my fortunes, yet my state is well.
I am a gentleman.

**Olivia.**

                    Get you to your lord.

I cannot love him. Let him send no more,—
Unless, perchance, you come to me again
To tell me how he takes it. Fare you well!
I thank you for your pains; spend this for me.

**Viola.**

I am no fee'd post, lady. Keep your purse.
My master, not myself, lacks recompense.
Love make his heart of flint that you shall love;
And let your fervor, like my master's be
Plac'd in contempt! Farewell, fair cruelty. (*Exit.*)

**Olivia.**

"What is your parentage?"
"Above my fortunes, yet my state is well.
I am a gentleman." I'll be sworn thou art.
Thy tongue, thy face, thy limbs, actions, and spirit
Do give thee five-fold blazon. Not too fast! Soft, soft!
Unless the master were the man. How now!
Even so quickly may one catch the plague?
Methinks I feel this youth's perfections
With an invisible and subtle stealth
To creep in at mine eyes. Well, let it be.
What ho, Malvolio!

(*Re-enter* MALVOLIO)

**§ Malvolio.**

Here, madam, at your service. §

**Olivia.**

Run after that same peevish messenger,
The county's man. He left this ring behind him,
Would I or not. Tell him I'll none of it.
Desire him not to flatter with his lord,
Nor hold him up with hopes. I'm not for him.
If that the youth will come this way to-morrow,
I'll give him reasons for't. Hie thee, Malvolio.

**Malvolio.**

Madam, I will. (*Exit.*)

**Olivia.**

I do I know not what, and fear to find
Mine eye too great a flatterer for my mind.
Fate, show thy force; ourselves we do not owe;
What is decreed must be, and be this so. (*Exit.*)

from
NO TIME FOR COMEDY
by S. N. Behrman

Act II
LINDA, AMANDA

In 1938, S. N. Behrman, the very successful author of urbane comedies, wrote a play about the very successful
author of urbane comedies. Gaylord Easterbrook, the
playwright in the play, is dissatisfied with his work and
determined to write a serious drama about disillusion-
ment and death. With the world standing fearful beneath
the shadow of war, it is, Gaylord says, no time for comedy.
At the end of the play, however, Gaylord throws away his
pretentious drama and begins to write a new comedy, one
which he hopes will also reflect "the disturbances and
agonies of our times." That is his answer to the question,
posed by another character in the play, whether "it is
more profound to write of death of which we know nothing than of life which we may illuminate, if only briefly,
with gaiety and understanding."

Comedy was Behrman's answer, too. Though *No Time
for Comedy* touches on the serious matters that troubled
playwrights—and their audiences—in 1938, it is a gay,
sophisticated play; the characters are portrayed with the
understanding candor of the humorist and they speak the
elegant, posed dialogue of which Behrman was the un-
equaled master. Gaylord's choice between serious and
light drama is played out in terms of his choice between
two women. His wife, Linda, an actress who has starred
in his plays, urges him to continue writing comedies.
Amanda, "the other woman," who persuades him that he
owes it to himself to be profound, is a "Lorelei with an
intellectual patter," a woman who adores developing the
latent genius in men of talent.

In Act II (in the scene reprinted here), Linda and
Amanda confront each other for the first time—they have
met before but never, until now, as rivals. The scene is

266

marked by the high-styled fireworks and velvet-gloved dueling that was the specialty of the best of the mannered comedies that flourished on Broadway in the 1930's and early 1940's. Linda has learned of her husband's interest in Mandy—and of Mandy's interest in his work (which makes the situation doubly dangerous). Determined to put up a fight (but subtly), Linda has persuaded her friend Pym, a debonair British bachelor, to take her to pay a call on Mandy. When they are shown into Mandy's drawing room, they discover that Gaylord is in the library working on his new, very serious play. For a few minutes, Mandy and her surprise visitors chat—about Mandy's husband (he is upstairs asleep or she would call him to say hello) and about Gaylord (Mandy has so often asked him to bring Linda along when he came to dinner). Then, at a signal from Linda, Pym hurries away, leaving the two women alone.

Linda is "a glamorous actress, a bit over thirty." She is "sane, sensible, and witty." Amanda is "quiet, slim, and dark; she has what is known as a classic profile, of which she is aware and which she displays unobtrusively without ever a flourish. Her voice is gentle, low, musical—she seldom raises it—it is a rich voice rather, it vibrates with understanding and intimation. She lets it vibrate—she uses it—privately she tells herself that it has a cello quality."

The setting is the upstairs living room, a room all soft green and gold, "luxuriously furnished in perfect taste." Linda will later refer to it as a "dimly-lit oasis."

**Linda.**
 (*As Pym goes out, closing the door.*) I adore Pym, don't you?
**Amanda.**
 (*Looks at Linda*) Yes. I'm *very* fond of him. (*Turns and glares at door through which Pym has gone*) Rather wastes himself, though, doesn't he? (*Looks at Linda.*)
**Linda.**
 That's not necessarily extravagant!
**Amanda.**
 Oh—?
**Linda.**
 I mean—if people want to waste themselves, why shouldn't they?

**Amanda.**

I'm afraid I don't agree—that goes against my profoundest convictions—

**Linda.**

Does it?

**Amanda.**

Yes. I believe that people *have* an obligation—it may sound priggish to say so—but a profound *moral* obligation to live up to the *best* in them.

**Linda.**

Well, don't you think they do?

**Amanda.**

Obviously they don't.

**Linda.**

*Can* one add a cubit to one's stature?

**Amanda.**

People do it all the time. Great *occasions* make them, *crises* make them, *love* makes them. One must unearth one's latent powers—develop them.

**Linda.**

How nice to believe in these psychic trap–doors!

**Amanda.**

You put it *very* well.

**Linda.**

It's all so comforting!

**Amanda.**

History is full of people who have exceeded their capacities.

**Linda.**

No—perhaps they have merely expressed them. (*A moment, then:*)

**Amanda.**

(*Rises and goes to table left*) We disagree. We disagree— (*Picks up cigarette box, turns to Linda*) *fundamentally*. (*Smiles*) Isn't that delightful? (*Offers open box to Linda.*)

**Linda.**

Great fun! (*She shakes her head negatively at offer of cigarette. A pause. She glances at the library door*) I gather—that Gay is in your library working. (*Looks at Amanda*) May I ask—*what* he is working on?

**Amanda.**

(*Lights a cigarette for herself. Innocently, permitting herself the assumption that Linda knows*) His new play. (*Turns to table; places match in ashtray.*)

**Linda.**

Really? I didn't know he had a new play—

**Amanda.**

(*Turns and moves to left of center stool*) Really? Oh, I'm terribly sorry. I—

**Linda.**

(*Breaks in*) It's quite all right. I'm delighted naturally. Do you know what it's about?

**Amanda.**

(*Solemnly*) It's about *immortality*.

**Linda.**

Really?

**Amanda.**

Yes.

**Linda.**

What on earth does Gay know about immortality?

**Amanda.**

What does anyone *know* about immortality?—*except* by intuition.

**Linda.**

But Gay—you *do* know his *other* work?

**Amanda.**

But this is altogether *different* from his other work— profounder—richer! I think it's great. I think you'll be proud.

**Linda.**

(*After a moment*) Why didn't he tell me about it, do you suppose?

**Amanda.**

Because—

**Linda.**

Why?

**Amanda.**

No. (*Looks away*) I mustn't say it.

**Linda.**

Oh, but you *must*. Please—*Mandy*.

**Amanda.**

(*Turns to Linda*) I'm afraid you'll misunderstand my motive.

**Linda.**

But I assure you I won't. I'll understand it *perfectly*.

**Amanda.**

(*Facing her bravely*) Because—there's no part in it for you.

**Linda.**

But that's so silly. I love playing in Gay's plays; I love

speaking his lines. But if he's written a play and it's good I shall be very happy. Surely he knows that and that *I* know it.

**Amanda.**

(*Moves a step toward Linda*) Perhaps he thought that—

**Linda.**

What?

**Amanda.**

That you wouldn't be—sympathetic to *this* play?

**Linda.**

But why shouldn't I be? I am really hurt.

**Amanda.**

(*Goes above stool to below table left*) I'm sorry—I'm terribly sorry—I shouldn't have—

**Linda.**

But you're not in the least sorry. You have probably never in your life been so ecstatically happy as you are at this moment.

**Amanda.**

(*Stops and turns a step toward Linda*) But really, *Mrs. Easterbrook!*

**Linda.**

(*Cheerfully*) Call me *Linda!* Shall we be *honest* with each other? It's enormously difficult, I know. But shall we try? *You* enjoy inspiring Gay.

**Amanda.**

Yes—

**Linda.**

That is to say you enjoy sleeping with him. I understand that perfectly.

**Amanda.**

Oh, but that's not true—we haven't—that's not true.

**Linda.**

If it's not true already then it's imminent. You'll *inspire* him into it. I don't mind telling you I'm intensely jealous. Sleep with him if you like but for pity's sake don't ruin his *style.* (*She rises—moves away to down right. Amanda turns up to right side of table*) Immortality: Oh, really, Mandy!

**Amanda.**

(*Puts out her cigarette on table left. Her cello voice vibrates slowly and richly*) We can't really talk—because we have nothing—(*Turns to Linda*) absolutely *nothing* —in common.

**Linda.**

(*Turns to her*) What about Gay!

**Amanda.**

(*Her hand on chair right side of table*) In my poor puny way I've been trying to bring his work into relation to the period in which he is living. I want him to stop fiddling while Rome burns. I am afraid you are *selfish*, Linda.

**Linda.**

Of course I am. What are you?

**Amanda.**

I feel that Gay might be great—

**Linda.**

What's the matter with him now?

**Amanda.**

His work is brilliant but—I have told him so myself—trivial.

**Linda.**

Why? Because he writes comedy? I'd rather have him write trivial comedy than shallow tragedy. (*Moves to left end of sofa*) The truth is, Mandy—you see yourself as an influence—with a capital *I*!

**Amanda.**

(*Moves a step toward Linda*) I do. I am not ashamed of it. That's the *best* a woman can be. To inspire a brilliant man to become a great one. History is *full* of women who—

**Linda.**

(*Goes to right side of center stool; kneels on it. Breaks in*) I doubt it. Women may have stimulated men—to success—but I don't believe in First Aids to greatness. That's something else again.

**Amanda.**

We're at opposite poles. (*Turns and goes to below left side of table.*)

**Linda.**

(*Looks toward the library door*) We are indeed. I wish I were at *yours*. (*A pause.*)

**Amanda.**

(*Turns to Linda*) You and Philo are so alike. (*Moves to upstage center*) Both isolated in your own strengths, in your own careers, your own egotisms.

**Linda.**

Why don't you inspire Philo?

**Amanda.**

(*Turns and moves down to beside chair right of table*)

You are laughing at me.

**Linda.**

Did you never?

**Amanda.**

But I will answer that. Philo is beyond reach. I have done everything I could to make him—outgiving. In the beginning I thought I could help him. That's why I *married* him.

**Linda.**

(*With unconcealed malice*) Is that the *only* reason?

**Amanda.**

I don't expect *you* to understand.

**Linda.**

Why don't you inspire to greatness someone obscure? Wouldn't that be more exciting? (*Moves to left end of sofa; sits on arm.*)

**Amanda.**

(*Moves down a few steps*) The artist who has arrived and who begins to doubt his talents—there is no more *poignant* tragedy than that.

**Linda.**

If this play you're drawing out of Gay like a bad tooth turns out to be good I'll never forgive you, Mandy!

**Amanda.**

(*Turns and goes to below right end of table; arranges something on table*) Well, you are honest at any rate.

**Linda.**

Yes. Why don't you try it—just for the novelty?

**Amanda.**

(*Turns to Linda. Stiffly—she finds herself suddenly on the verge of tears*) I beg your pardon—!

**Linda.**

You don't believe this act of yours, do you? You can't possibly. You've got Gay through—this rainbow-belief in the profundity of his literary powers—

**Amanda.**

(*Nearer still to tears*) How dare you! How dare you!

**Linda.**

It's all in fun—come clean, Mandy—I wish you could teach me the technique—all this pastel theorizing—wonderful dim lighting for sex.

**Amanda.**

(*Moves a step down. Hurt to the quick, throwing all discretion to the winds suddenly*) I understand—I understand *everything* now!

**Linda.**

What?

**Amanda.**

He's always talking, about your clairvoyance, your critical faculty of which he's afraid, your *pitiless* clarity—

**Linda.**

My God, Mandy, you make me sound like an X-ray!

**Amanda.**

(*Moves a step down*) You are! You've shriveled *him!*

**Linda.**

Is Gay shriveled? He looked awfully well this afternoon.

**Amanda.**

In his *soul!* You don't believe in faith or hope—you don't believe in anything but empty laughter. You're merciless and destructive. (*Moves to above center stool toward Linda*) If I *have* furnished him with an oasis where he can escape to brood and dream I'm happy—do you hear—(*Turns and moves away to below table left*)— proud and happy!

**Linda.**

(*Aloud to herself in a sudden dreadful revelation*) My God! You believe it! I'm sunk!

**Amanda.**

(*Starts right toward library door*) It's inconceivable to you that anyone can be sincere—you don't understand the truth—you attribute the most *sordid* motives to everything—(*Breaks down and weeps. Stops in front of door, her hand on doorknob and turns to Linda*) You're horrid —you're hateful and horrid and I—I—*hate you!* (*Goes out, slamming the door.*)

**Linda.**

(*Looks after her. From her lips escapes involuntarily an exclamation of admiration at her rival's self-absorption, her capacity for self-justification, her talent for being aggrieved. She puts her hands on her hips and stares after Amanda. Below left end of sofa*) And besides all that— you can cry. Well—!

from
SEPARATE TABLES
by Terence Rattigan

"Table by the Window," scene 1
JOHN, ANNE, (DOREEN)

The play is actually two plays, two stories told against the same background—a boarding hotel near Bournemouth in England—and involving many of the same characters. In both, Terence Rattigan deals with aspects of loneliness, a phenomenon frequently on view in a private hotel, the "home" of people who have no homes. He sees the loneliness of living too long, of overindependence, of pride, of the fear of people, and of somehow not being able to break through an invisible barrier to other men or women. Always a master of tightly written scenes, Rattigan develops his theme in a series of telling vignettes and brief scenes for two or three characters. One such scene is reprinted here; others will be found on pages 281 and 363.

"Table by the Window," the first of the two plays, concerns two people whose temperaments, pride, and even their love have driven them apart. Their marriage ended with a murderous, physical fight, another battle in a courtroom, and headlines splashed across the front pages of the papers. The husband's hopeful career as a politician was ruined. He retired to the country, to this out-of-the-way hotel, and here, under an assumed name, he made a new, quiet life for himself as a journalist. Now, eight years after the divorce, his wife unexpectedly appears in the hotel. He finds her sitting in the dining room when he walks in, late for dinner, and, after the other diners have left the room, they have an opportunity to speak.

John "is in the early forties, of rather rugged appearance, untidily dressed, and with unruly hair." Sitting alone at his table, he faces Anne, also alone at another table. She is about forty, and she seems entirely out of place in the Beauregard Private Hotel. "Not that her clothes are unsuitable, although they are smart, nor that her coiffure

274

is too stylish, although it is stylish, but she has brought with her an air of Belgravia and the smarter London restaurants." The waitress, Doreen, has just given John his soup. As she exits, he crumbles a piece of bread, then slowly lifts his eyes from the tablecloth to gaze at Anne.

**John.**

(*At length*) Is this coincidence?

**Anne.**

Of course.

**John.**

What are you doing here?

**Anne.**

A rest cure.

**John.**

Why this place—of all places?

**Anne.**

It was recommended to me.

**John.**

Who by?

**Anne.**

A man I met at a party somewhere.

**John.**

He didn't tell you I was here?

**Anne.**

He did say something about a journalist—called John Malcolm. Is that you?

**John.**

Yes.

**Anne.**

John Malcolm. Oh, yes, of course. Your Christian names.

**John.**

(*Savagely*) Why, for the love of God, didn't you go to the Royal Bath or the Norfolk or the Branksome Towers, or any of the grand hotels—why? (*He stops as Doreen comes in.*)

**Doreen.**

What you having after, 'cause Cook's got to leave it out. Turnover is best.

**John.**

All right.

**Doreen.**

Finished your soup?

**John.**
Yes, thank you.

**Doreen.**
You haven't touched it. I *said* too much liquid— (*She takes the soup into the kitchen.*)

**Anne.**
I couldn't afford a grand hotel.

**John.**
He pays you alimony, doesn't he?

**Anne.**
Seven fifty a year. I don't find it very easy. You see, I'm not getting work these days—

**John.**
I thought he was a rich man.

**Anne.**
Michael? Oh, no. His antique shop lost a lot of money.

**John.**
He gets his name in the papers a lot.

**Anne.**
Oh, yes. Quite a social figure—first nights and all that.

**John.**
How long exactly were you married to him?

**Anne.**
Three years and six months.

**John.**
Beating me by three months? I saw the headlines of the case. They were quite juicy—but not as juicy as ours— you'll admit. It was cruelty again, wasn't it?

**Anne.**
Yes.

**John.**
Did *he* try to kill you too?

**Anne.**
(*Quietly*) No. (*Doreen comes in with John's second course.*)

**Doreen.**
There you are. Usual veg? (*John nods. Doreen helps him*) You look a bit down in the dumps tonight. Anything the matter?

**John.**
No.

**Doreen.**
All right. Don't take long, will you? My friend's waiting— (*She goes out. John makes no attempt to touch his food.*)

**John.**
How did he show *his* cruelty?

**Anne.**

In a lot of ways. Small ways. They can all be summed up by saying that he doesn't really like women.

**John.**

Why did he marry you?

**Anne.**

He wanted a wife.

**John.**

And you wanted a husband? (*She nods*) As wide a contrast as possible from your first, I suppose. Still, couldn't you have done a bit better for yourself?

**Anne.**

I suppose so. But he was gentle and kind and made me laugh and I was fond of him. I went into it with my eyes well open. I thought I could make it work. I was wrong. (*John laughs suddenly*) What's the joke?

**John.**

A nice poser for a woman's magazine. Girls, which husband would you choose? One who loves you too little—or one who loves you too much? (*After a pause*) Third time lucky perhaps.

**Anne.**

Perhaps. (*Pause.*)

**John.**

How long are you staying here?

**Anne.**

I booked for two weeks.

**John.**

I'll go to London.

**Anne.**

No. If you feel like that, then I'll go to another hotel.

**John.**

That might be easier. (*Pause.*)

**Anne.**

John—I don't see why—

**John.**

Do you think these old women don't notice anything? They spend their whole days gossiping. It would take them less than a day to nose out the whole story and wouldn't they have a time with it! They're suspicious enough of me as it is. They know I write in the *New Outlook* under the name of Cato—and how they found that out I'll never know, because none of them would sully their dainty fingers by even touching such a bolshie rag.

**Anne.**

I read it every week.

**John.**

Turning left wing in your old age?

**Anne.**

(*Quietly*) My old age?

**John.**

How old are you now?

**Anne.**

Well—let's just say eight years older than when I last saw you.

**John.**

Yes. You don't look it.

**Anne.**

Thank you. But I feel it. (*Pause.*)

**John.**

Why didn't you come to see me in prison yourself?

**Anne.**

I wanted to. I was stopped.

**John.**

Who by?

**Anne.**

My mother and father.

**John.**

I suppose they told you I might try to strangle you in front of the warden. I nearly did try to strangle your solicitor.

**Anne.**

They thought it would make it easier for you if I kept away.

**John.**

A very well-bred, Christian thought. My dear ex-in-laws. How are they?

**Anne.**

My father's dead. My mother lives in a place rather like this, in Kensington. (*Pause. John is gazing at her intently.*)

**John.**

(*At length*) Then you'll go tomorrow, will you?

**Anne.**

Yes.

**John.**

Thank you. (*Stiffly*) I'm sorry to have to put you to so much inconvenience.

**Anne.**

That's all right. (*He gets up abruptly from his table and walks up to hers. Anne rises quickly.*)

**John.**

Well, what do we do—shake hands?

**Anne.**

I'm very glad to see you again, John. (*She kisses him gently on the cheek.*)

**John.**

It may seem boorish of me not to be able to say the same, Anne. But then I am a boor, as you know. In fact, you must still have a scar on the side of your head to prove it to you.

**Anne.**

It's gone now.

**John.**

Gone? After five stitches and a week in hospital?

**Anne.**

Eight years will cure most scars.

**John.**

Most, I suppose. Not all, though. Well, good night. (*He goes toward the hall door.*)

from
SEPARATE TABLES
by Terence Rattigan

"Table Number Seven," scene 1
MISS COOPER, SIBYL

In "Table Number Seven," the second part of *Separate Tables*, Terence Rattigan writes of a scandal and the reactions it draws from the residents of the Beauregard Private Hotel. (For introductory notes about the play, see page 274.) Major Pollock, who lives at the hotel, has been arrested and has pleaded guilty to the charge of "insulting behavior" in a local cinema—he made advances to a woman seated next to him. Though some of the hotel's residents stand up for the major, the majority of them vote to demand that the management ask him to leave. The manager, Miss Cooper, refuses, but the major himself agrees to check out. He books a room at another hotel and only as he is about to leave does he allow Miss Cooper to persuade him to stay, to face up to the others and to himself. His decision hinges on his friendship with Miss Railton-Bell, another "misfit," a woman whose domineering mother has forced her to remain a frightened child. With Miss Railton-Bell and the major, Rattigan presents another aspect of loneliness: the isolation of those who are locked up in themselves, unable to reach out to others emotionally or physically.

Major Pollock "is in the middle fifties with a clipped military mustache and extremely neat clothes. In fact, both in dress and appearance he is almost too exact a replica of the retired major to be entirely true." And he is not true—he is a phony, who can face the world only by pretending to have attended a "good" school, which he did not attend, and to have served with an esteemed regiment, to which he never belonged. Sibyl Railton-Bell is a "timid-looking, wizened creature, . . . bespectacled, dowdy, and without make-up." She has had a friendship of sorts with the major: they can talk with one another

280

as neither of them can with most other people. The announcement of the major's crime—and the kind of crime it was—horrifies Sibyl; she is literally made sick by it.

The setting for the scene is the lounge of the hotel; the time, shortly after the meeting at which the residents have decided to ask Miss Cooper to send the major away. He and Sibyl have had a brief, uncomfortable conversation and she has heard him ask Miss Cooper to suggest the name of another hotel to which he can move. As he leaves the lounge, Miss Cooper turns to Sibyl.

**Miss C.**

Your mother's gone up to dress for dinner, Miss Railton-Bell. She told me I'd find you in the writing room lying down and I was to tell you that you can have your meal upstairs tonight, if you'd rather.

**Sibyl.**

That's all right.

**Miss C.**

(*Sympathetically*) How are you feeling now?

**Sibyl.**

(*Brusquely*) All right. (*Miss Cooper approaches her.*)

**Miss C.**

(*Quietly*) Is there anything I can do to help you?

**Sibyl.**

(*Angrily*) No. Nothing. And please don't say things like that. You'll make me feel bad again, and I'll make a fool of myself. I feel well now. He's going and that's good. I despise him.

**Miss C.**

Do you? I wonder if you should.

**Sibyl.**

He's a vile, wicked man, and he's done a horrible beastly thing. It's not the first time, either. He admits that.

**Miss C.**

I didn't think it was.

**Sibyl.**

And yet you told him he could stay on in the hotel if he wanted to? That's wicked too.

**Miss C.**

Then I suppose I *am* wicked too. (*She puts her hand on her arm*) Sibyl, dear—

**Sibyl.**

Why is everyone calling me Sibyl this evening? Please stop. You'll only make me cry.

**Miss C.**

I don't mean to do that. I just mean to help you. (*Sibyl breaks down suddenly, but now quietly and without hysteria. Miss Cooper holds her*) That's better. Much better.

**Sibyl.**

It's so horrible.

**Miss C.**

I know it is. I'm very sorry for you.

**Sibyl.**

He says we're alike—he and I.

**Miss C.**

Does he?

**Sibyl.**

He says we're both scared of life and people and sex. There—I've said the word. He says I hate *saying* it even, and he's right. I do. What's the matter with me? There must be something the matter with me.

**Miss C.**

Nothing very much, I should say. Shall we sit down? (*She gently propels her on to the sofa and sits beside her.*)

**Sibyl.**

I'm a freak, aren't I?

**Miss C.**

(*In matter-of-fact tones*) I never knew what that word means. If you mean you're different from other people, then, I suppose, you are a freak. But all human beings are a bit different from each other, aren't they? What a dull world it would be if they weren't.

**Sibyl.**

I'd like to be ordinary.

**Miss C.**

I wouldn't know about that, dear. You see, I've never met an ordinary person. To me all people are extraordinary. I meet all sorts here, you know, in my job, and the one thing I've learnt in five years is that the word normal, applied to any human being, is utterly meaningless. In a sort of a way it's an insult to our Maker, don't you think, to suppose that He could possibly work to any set pattern.

**Sibyl.**

I don't think Mummy would agree with you.

**Miss C.**

I'm fairly sure she wouldn't. Tell me—when did your father die?

**Sibyl.**

When I was seven.

**Miss C.**

Did you go to school?

**Sibyl.**

No. Mummy said I was too delicate. I had a governess some of the time, but most of the time Mummy taught me herself.

**Miss C.**

Yes. I see. And you've never really been away from her, have you?

**Sibyl.**

Only when I had a job, for a bit. (*Proudly*) I was a salesgirl in a big shop in London—Jones & Jones. I sold lampshades. But I got ill, though, and had to leave.

**Miss C.**

(*Brightly*) What bad luck. Well, you must try again, some day, mustn't you?

**Sibyl.**

Mummy says no.

**Miss C.**

Mummy says no. Well, then, you must just try and get Mummy to say yes, don't you think?

**Sibyl.**

I don't know how.

**Miss C.**

I'll tell you how. By running off and getting a job on your own. She'll say yes quick enough then. (*She pats Sibyl's knee sympathetically and gets up*) I have my menus to do. (*She goes toward the door.*)

**Sibyl.**

(*Urgently*) Will he be all right, do you think?

**Miss C.**

The Major? I don't know. I hope so.

**Sibyl.**

In spite of what he's done, I don't want anything bad to happen to him. I want him to be happy. Is it a nice hotel —this one in West Kensington?

**Miss C.**

Very nice.

**Sibyl.**

(*After a pause*) Do you think he'll find a friend there? He told me just now that he'd always be grateful to me for making him forget how frightened he was of people.

**Miss C.**
He's helped you too, hasn't he?

**Sibyl.**
Yes.

**Miss C.**
(*After a pause*) I hope he'll find a friend in the new hotel.

**Sibyl.**
So do I. Oh, God, so do I.

from
COUNSELLOR-AT-LAW
by Elmer Rice

Act II, scene 3
CORA, GEORGE SIMON

George Simon is a very successful lawyer. His cases are
the sort that make headlines in the papers and make Mr.
Simon a wealthy man. Mr. Simon fights hard for his
clients and for himself, for he grew up in a tenement and
it is important to him to win, to attain the things that
symbolize success—his reputation, his busy, well-staffed
office, his homes in the city and the country, and his wife,
Cora, the daughter of an old and socially prominent family.
Despite their different backgrounds, the Simons seem to
get on well enough, though Cora sometimes wishes that
her husband practiced polite business law with her family's
banker-friends, and Mr. Simon sometimes worries that his
full schedule and his wife's social engagements leave them
too little time for each other. He has planned a trip to
Europe, a time for them to be alone together. Then he is
threatened with disbarment. One of the gentlemanly at-
torneys whom Cora knows and admires, a man who de-
tests her husband's ruthless methods in the courtroom, has
discovered that once in his long career George Simon
allowed a witness to take the stand and perjure himself.
The central action of the play concerns Mr. Simon's efforts
to save his career and his turning to his wife for support.
His practice and reputation are saved, his marriage is not.

The scene below marks the turning point in the relationship between George and Cora Simon. He has asked her
to come to his office. She has stopped by in the midst of a
shopping expedition. While they talk, their son and daughter
wait in the outer office.

The setting, Mr. Simon's office, is "a large room simply
furnished in modernistic style." There is a large flat-top
desk—Mr. Simon's—and a smaller desk, a comfortable
sofa. Two windows in the rear wall face south, affording

285

a panoramic view of lower Manhattan. On Mr. Simon's desk are a cigarette box, a cigar box of fine wood, a handsome desk set, telephones, and a photograph of Cora Simon in a large leather frame.

Mr. Simon's secretary leaves the office as Cora enters.

**Simon.**
All right. I'd like not to be disturbed now. * * * Close both doors, will you please? * * * (*Sitting beside Cora on the sofa*): Well, darling, I'm afraid the European trip is off.

**Cora.**
So you said over the telephone.

**Simon.**
I know it's a big disappointment to you. And I assure you it is to me too. I never in my life looked forward so much to anything. But something has come up and I can't get away.

**Cora.**
You were so certain, no longer ago than yesterday, that nothing could keep you from going.

**Simon.**
Yes, I know it. That's the funny part of it. I would have sworn yesterday that nothing in the world could have made me call off the trip—barring something happening to Mamma. And then this thing had to come up.

**Cora.**
What is it; another hundred-thousand-dollar fee?

**Simon.**
Why, darling, you don't think a hundred thousand or five hundred thousand would make me call off our little honeymoon trip, do you? I wouldn't have called it off for a retainer from the United States Steel Corporation.

**Cora.**
Then it's not business that's detaining you?

**Simon.**
Well, it is and it isn't. I don't know just how to tell you.

**Cora.**
Don't tell me, if you don't want to. I didn't mean to be prying.

**Simon.**
Why, darling, of course I want to. You don't think I'd

have any secrets from you, do you? It's just a little hard
to explain, that's all. I'm afraid it's going to upset you
a little.

**Cora.**

Well, tell me, George, what it is. It doesn't help matters
to pile up the suspense.

**Simon.**

(*rising*) No, I guess you're right. (*With a great effort*)
Well, darling, I'm in trouble: the worst trouble I've ever
been in in my whole life. (*He pauses.*)

**Cora.**

Well, tell me.

**Simon.**

Well, I'm threatened with disbarment.

**Cora.**

Oh, how perfectly awful!

**Simon.**

I knew it would be a shock to you. That's why it took me
so long to get it out. And it's been a shock to me, I can
tell you. I didn't know anybody could go through such
hell as I've been going through these last twenty-four
hours.

**Cora.**

But I don't understand it. Disbarment! Why, I thought—

**Simon.**

Of all the things that could have happened to me! God,
you never know from one day till the next!

**Cora.**

But doesn't disbarment imply—?

**Simon.**

Yes, it does more than imply. It establishes that a man
is guilty of conduct which makes him unworthy to practice his profession. That's what I'm faced with this very
minute.

**Cora.**

Then—I mean—I'm quite bewildered—

**Simon.**

Eighteen years I've been a full-fledged lawyer. Eighteen
years and nobody's ever had anything on me. And then
this one thing, this one, little thing, that was dead and
buried, comes up—and bing, out I go like a candle.
God, I can't believe it!

**Cora.**

But, what was it that you did, George?

**Simon.**

Wait until you hear. Then you'll understand the irony of the whole thing. Once, mind you, once in eighteen years—yes, and with a thousand opportunities to get away with murder—once I overstepped the mark, and then it was to save a poor devil from going to prison for life. Do you know what it means to frame up an alibi?

**Cora.**

Yes, I think I do. Getting someone to testify falsely—

**Simon.**

Yes, that's it. I had a hand in framing up an alibi, so that a kid who had committed a number of petty crimes wouldn't have to spend the rest of his life in prison.

**Cora.**

I don't know much about these things. But wasn't that a dishonest thing to do?

**Simon.**

(*seating himself at his desk*) It was conniving at a lie, to prevent a conviction that nobody wanted, not the judge, nor the district attorney, nor the jury; but that the law made inevitable.

**Cora.**

(*rising*) Why do you have anything to do with such people—thieves, criminals?

**Simon.**

I'm a lawyer, darling.

**Cora.**

All lawyers don't have dealings with such people.

**Simon.**

Somebody's got to defend people who are accused of crime.

**Cora.**

This boy was guilty.

**Simon.**

Guilty of stealing a few dollars, yes. I'd known the boy since he was a baby. Why, I never would have had a night's sleep if I'd let that boy go up the river for life.

**Cora.**

And now someone has found out and they are going to disbar you, is that it?

**Simon.**

Yes, someone has found out. And it's just my luck that it happens to be a man who's had it in for me for years: a gentleman by the name of Francis Clark Baird.

**Cora.**

Francis Clark Baird. Why, he's a very eminent lawyer, isn't he? I think I've heard father speak of him. Isn't he one of the Connecticut Bairds?

**Simon.**

He may be, for all I know. But that doesn't mean much to me. All that I know is that he's got the drop on me and he's going to make me pay through the nose.

**Cora.**

Why do you always put things on a personal basis, George? Isn't it the duty of a man like Mr. Baird—?

**Simon.**

No man has to break another man—unless he wants to. I've locked horns with this Baird a good many times, and he's always come out on the short end. He doesn't like taking that from a nobody, from an East Side boy that started in the police court.

**Cora.**

Is a person who began in the police court necessarily superior to one who grew up in an atmosphere of culture and refinement?

**Simon.**

Why, darling, you're not siding with Baird, are you?

**Cora.**

It isn't a matter of siding with anyone. But I can't help resenting a little the constant implication that there's some peculiar merit in having a humble origin.

**Simon.**

I'm not implying that, darling. You ought to know me better than that. I realize my shortcomings. Especially when I compare myself with you. I know that you sacrificed a lot to marry me, and that you've had to put up with a lot of things that you didn't like. And it's because you've been so sweet and understanding about it that I'm putting all my cards on the table: telling you just where I stand and what I'm up against. It's because I know I can count on you to help me through this thing.

**Cora.**

I don't see how I can help you, George.

**Simon.**

I don't mean that I want you to do anything, sweetheart. I'm going to do whatever can be done. I'm in a tough spot, but I'm going to take an awful lot of licking before I throw up the sponge. It's just having you with me and knowing that you're standing by me that's going to make

all the difference to me. Because in you I've got something
worth fighting for.

**Cora.**

(*seating herself*) I really don't know what to say, George.
It's most distressing.

**Simon.**

Yes, it's just about as bad as anything that could have
happened. But there's nothing to do but face it. Maybe
something will break for me—who can tell? I've got
lots of loyal friends, and when you've got your back to
the wall, you can do an awful lot of fighting.

**Cora.**

Yes, that's all very well, George. I understand thoroughly
how you must feel about it. And, of course, I'm quite
willing to accept your explanation of the whole thing.

**Simon.**

I knew you would, Cora.

**Cora.**

I know how you've had to struggle and work and it's all
very admirable. But it's made it possible for you to accept
things that are rather difficult for me to accept.

**Simon.**

What things, darling?

**Cora.**

Oh, I don't know. There's something distasteful—frankly,
something rather repellent—about the whole atmosphere
of the thing. This association with thieves and perjurers,
and all the intrigue and conniving that goes with it. And
now this scandal—it will be a scandal, I'm sure—newspaper publicity and all that.

**Simon.**

Yes, no doubt about it.

**Cora.**

It's a horrible prospect. I suppose I'll have my picture in
the papers too. And reporters knocking at my door.

**Simon.**

I'll try to spare you all I can, darling.

**Cora.**

And what are my friends going to say? How am I going
to face them?

**Simon.**

Do they mean more to you than I do?

**Cora.**

That isn't the point. It's something deeply vital to you:
your career, your reputation, all the rest of it. But what

am I to do? Flutter about pathetically in the background, in an atmosphere of scandal and recrimination? (*She rises.*) No, I can't. The best thing for me to do is to go to Europe, as I had planned. If this thing blows over—and let's hope it will—you can join me abroad, later. If it doesn't—well, then there's time enough to think about that.

**Simon.**

You mean you're going to walk out on me?

**Cora.**

That's a very crude way of putting it. And very unfair to me too. It implies that I'm deserting you when you need me. You know that isn't fair. It isn't as though I could do anything to help you. If there were, I'd be glad to stay. But you've said yourself that there isn't, haven't you now?

**Simon.**

Yes, I guess I did. It was just that at a time like this I thought I'd like to have you around, that's all.

**Cora.**

But isn't that just a little selfish, George: to ask me to stay and be subjected to all that miserable business, because it would give you a little satisfaction to have me here?

**Simon.**

Yes, I guess you're right. I guess it is selfish. I hadn't looked at it in that way. I just thought that maybe you'd want to stay.

**Cora.**

(*going to him and putting her hand on his shoulder*) Please don't misunderstand me, George. Please don't think I'm unsympathetic. I assure you I'm terribly upset about this thing. If there were anything I could do, I should be only too happy to do it. Would you like me to ask father to intercede with Mr. Baird?

**Simon.**

No, I wish you wouldn't do that. (*He goes to his desk.*)

**Cora.**

(*following him*) Well, just whatever you say. I do hope sincerely that everything will turn out for the best. And I give you my word, George, that if I could see how giving up my trip could possibly help you out of this difficulty, I'd give it up in a minute. But you know it couldn't.

**Simon.**

Yes, sure. Just forget about it, darling. It was just a foolish idea of mine. But you're perfectly right. I've got to fight this thing out myself, and there really isn't anybody that can help me.

**Cora.**

If you think of any way at all in which I can be helpful—

**Simon.**

I'll let you know. Thanks, sweetheart.

**Cora.**

I've really got to run now. Both Dorothy and I must be at the hairdresser's at two. Will you be coming out to the country tonight?

**Simon.**

I don't know whether I'll be able to make it or not. I'll phone you if I can't.

**Cora.**

Yes, do. (*She puts her hand on his.*) Au revoir, George, and I do hope that everything is going to be all right.

**Simon.**

(*patting her hand*) Well, we'll see. Good-by, sweetheart. Here, you can go out through Rexie's office.

**Cora.**

Don't bother. I know the way. (*She exits.*)

(*Simon seats himself slowly at his desk, his hands stretched out before him. He looks straight ahead of him. Then his eyes wander to Cora's photograph, and, taking it up, he holds it before him, in both hands, and stares at it.*)

from
ETHAN FROME
by Owen and Donald Davis

Act II, scene 1
ZEENA, ETHAN, MATTIE

After nearly thirty years, this dramatization of Edith Wharton's novel of New England life still stands as a model of the art of adaptation. Though a playwright today might call for a flexible unit set and construct a free-flowing drama broken into fewer separate scenes, he would find it difficult to make a finer translation of the plot of a novel into theatrical terms or to put the novelist's characters on stage as completely and unexaggeratedly. The most outspoken praise of Owen and Donald Davis' dramatization came from Edith Wharton herself. She wrote in an introduction to the play, "I found myself thinking at every page: 'Here at last is a new life for Ethan.' And the discovery moved me more than I can say."

Audiences also were moved by the playwrights' retelling of the tragic tale of Miss Wharton's "hungry lonely New England villagers . . . on their stormy hillside." The story, like those rock-strewn hillsides, is sharply and ruggedly cut—a triangle involving a man, his wife, and a girl. Ethan Frome is married to Zeena, whose imaginary ailments and whining demands make their life together lonely and bitter. When Zeena's cousin Mattie comes to live with them, life and cheer enter the house with her. For Ethan, it becomes easier to put up with Zeena's complaints when Mattie is there to understand. It is easy, too, for him to begin to fall in love with Mattie and to wish that Zeena were not there at all. Zeena is sick, but not blind, and she grows jealous. She does her best to make life impossible for Mattie (as in the scene reprinted below). Then Zeena goes away to consult a doctor, leaving Ethan and Mattie alone and happy with each other. But when she comes home, she insists that Mattie must go away. Helpless to oppose her, Ethan and Mattie declare their love for each

293

other and decide that it would be better to die together than to live apart. They ride a bobsled to a crash against a great elm at the bottom of the long hill. But they are not killed: Mattie, her back broken, must live on as a helpless invalid while Ethan is more than ever tied to Zeena and the desolate farm.

The setting for the scene below is Ethan's and Zeena's bedroom. It is five-thirty in the morning—the morning after Ethan has taken his time walking Mattie home from a church sociable. (Two other scenes from the play appear on pages 414 and 422.)

*Ethan's and Zeena's bedroom. A small bleak room cramped close under the slanting eaves of the roof. There is a tiny snow-encrusted window at right and a door at back center. The room is attic-like and bare. A string stretched across right corner of the room, from which a faded curtain is suspended, marks the space in which the Frome clothing is kept. Between the closet space and the window at right is a plain washstand supporting a cracked pitcher and bowl. The bed, which is cramped under the slanting roof at left, is rickety but apt to be (from an urban point of view) a quite good Colonial bed. It faces the audience. There is a small table beside the bed . . . the top of which is littered with bottles and pharmaceutical boxes and stained tumblers with spoons in them and various other patented medical supplies. Excepting 3 straight-back chairs, there is very little else in the room. A commode up center. It is still quite dark at 5:30 of a New England winter morning. But a pale, wan light is beginning to fight its way through the tightly closed, heavily frosted window, the cracks of which are stuffed with newspaper. Ethan, already dressed except for his shirt, stands in front of the washstand right, shaving with an old-fashioned straight razor— aided more or less by a small piece of broken mirror nailed to the wall. He wears corduroy trousers thrust into the tops of high laced boots, as usual, and a heavy, fleecy woolen undershirt. Zeena (her flannel wrapper is on hook left) sits in bed—the blankets drawn up over her body. She takes her stocking, puts it under the covers, draws it on her leg—she gets it on, then sits there, shuddering with the cold. Ethan is in a generous, voluble mood this morning,*

*suffused with the memory of his talk with Mattie. As he
scrapes away at his chin he hums a tune he heard at the
church sociable last night.*

**Zeena.**

Gettin' a bit light-headed lately, ain't you, Ethan? (*He
is scraping away at his chin. She glares at him for another
moment. Looks at Ethan accusingly.*) That's the third
time't you've shaved this week!

**Ethan.**

(*good-naturedly, but absorbed in screwing up one side of
his face to give a smooth surface to the other*) A-yeah.
Sort of nippy, ain't it? (*Sets razor down on washstand.*)
A-yeah . . . mighty sharp, this mornin'. You know what,
Zeenie . . . I'd stay right under them blankets today . . .
if I was you! I wouldn't get up out of bed at all!

**Zeena.**

(*pettishly*) If I had someone to take care of things proper,
maybe I could stay in bed.

**Ethan.**

Well, Mattie'll do for you all right.

**Zeena.**

(*scornfully*) Mattie!

**Ethan.**

You just tell her anythin' you want she sh'd do . . .
and she'll do it for you right off—you know that, Zeenie!

**Zeena.**

(*whiningly*) That's what's ailin' me . . . followin' her
around . . . showin' her . . . watchin' over her . . .

**Ethan.**

(*cleans razor, puts it away on table*) Well—Mattie's
willin' enough . . . that's one sure thing!

**Zeena.**

(*continues in same tone, as though he hadn't interrupted*)
I'm beginnin' to wonder if she's with it! She can't cook.
She can't scrub—

**Ethan.**

You wanted company!

**Zeena.**

She don't talk to me none.

**Ethan.**

(*has finished shaving and now he plunges his face into
water*) Oh, you're just frettin' yourself, Zeenie! (*Straightens up from washbowl—reaches out blindly for a towel.
There is a pause as he find a towel, rubs his face briskly.
Zeena watches him.*)

**Zeena.**

Well . . . I won't be sorry to see her go. . . . (*Ethan stops abruptly. Zeena glances at him.*) 'Course she will go . . . sooner or later . . . I wouldn't want it said't I'd stood in her way. (*Ethan starts getting into his shirt.*) . . . A poor girl like Mattie Silver . . . it wouldn't be right to stop her leavin' . . . if she got a chance to get married.

**Ethan.**

(*easily*) Well, 'tain't very likely!

**Zeena.**

Don't you go and be too sure now, Ethan! (*He looks at her. She adds, just emphatically enough to be significant:*) Anyway—whatever happens—I ain't goin' to be left alone!

**Ethan.**

What's got into you this morning, Zeena! You must be gone queer in the head!

**Zeena.**

(*violently*) No, I ain't! And don't you never say a thing like that to me again! You hear!

**Mattie.**

(*calls from kitchen below, heartily*) Ethan! Ethan!

**Zeena.**

(*whines*) You never talked that way to me before . . . never . . . why, you never said anythin' like that. . . . (*She is whining.*) I don't know how I c'n go on like this. (*He gets finished with shirt; she takes spoonful of liquid medicine from bottle.*) With you bein' so cruel . . . and me sufferin' and doin' for that girl . . . when she'd ought to be doin' for me! (*Mattie is heard running quickly upstairs. She knocks lightly at door left upper.*)

**Ethan.**

(*quickly*) Come in, Matt!

**Mattie.**

(*enters quickly, crosses center, moving blithefully into room. She is eager and quite gay this morning*) Why, Ethan Frome, do you know it's most 6 o'clock! Breakfast's been ready for hours! (*Then to Zeena pleasantly.*) 'Mornin', Zeena! (*Zeena looks at her without replying.*)

**Ethan.**

(*hastily*) Say, Matt!—fill up that hot-water bottle there— (*She turns to get it from commode up center.*) Zeenie's gone and got herself a terrible chill this mornin'.

**Zeena.**

I got my chill last night—goin' down them drafty stairs

to open that door in the middle of the night! (*Mattie glances at Ethan quickly and then at Zeena.*)

**Mattie.**

Oh, now, ain't that a shame! Just you wait one second . . . Zeena . . . I got water boilin' on the stove . . . and I'll be back before you know it! (*She takes hot-water bottle, exits hurriedly, out left. Slight pause.*)

**Ethan.**

(*as soon at Mattie is gone, puts on sweater and says casually*) Guess that was my fault, Zeenie. . . . I got gabbin' with Ed Varnum about business . . . and first thing you know . . . I was late gettin' to the sociable to fetch Mattie. (*He glances at Zeena, a bit self-consciously reaches for his coat and murmurs:*) Now, Zeenie, don't you go frettin' yourself . . . Mattie's all right, she's doin' fine. . . . (*Smoothly.*) 'Course I know she ain't the house-keeper't you are! . . . But you can't expect that. (*Pointedly as he struggles into sweater.*) One thing I know . . . Mattie ain't leavin's long's she's needed. (*Gets his coat on and buttons it up.*) Well, Jotham's comin' and we're loadin' spruce and startin' to haul over to Andrew Hale's place today. (*Puts coat on.*) I guess't I'm a little late gettin' started.

**Zeena.**

I guess't you're always late . . . now't you shave every mornin'. (*The implication stops Ethan.*)

**Mattie.**

(*enters with the hot-water bottle and a breakfast tray*) Here you are, Zeena! (*Mattie hurries to bed with hot-water bottle, Zeena shifts about petulantly.*)

**Zeena.**

(*grabs hot-water bottle from Mattie*) I'll do for myself!

**Mattie.**

(*Sets tray on chair*) I'm terribly sorry about last night . . . we was just awful late, wasn't we, Zeenie? (*Ethan is standing stock-still . . . nervous and embarrassed, and alarmed at what Mattie is about to say.*) Well . . . it was all my fault, every bit. . . . I went and promised Denis Eady the last dance and he just wouldn't let me go . . . and there was poor Ethan waitin' out in the cold. . . . (*Zeena glances from one to other of them, smiles slightly, Ethan is overwhelmed with embarrassment.*)

**Zeena.**

Ethan, I thought you was late gettin' about your business.

**Ethan.**

A-yeah, well, I'll get there. You see't everythin' gets done, Mattie . . . so's Zeena c'n rest easy. . . . I'll be back in time to give you a hand around the house later on. (*Crosses to door left. Mattie gets tray from chair.*)

**Zeena.**

Ethan! (*He stops.*) You 'tend to the haulin' we'll see to the housework! (*He exits. Mattie sets the tray on Zeena's lap, Zeena is watching her steadily which increases Mattie's uneasiness. Zeena looks at the tray full of food.*) All them things . . . just goin' to waste . . . thk, thk, thk. . . .

**Mattie.**

(*cheerfully*) You always say that, Zeena. Well . . . (*Crosses up to door left.*)

**Zeena.**

(*sharply*) Mattie! (*Mattie turns quickly. Zeena composes herself.*) Oh, I didn't mean to be cross. You know, I didn't sleep much last night. (*Takes sip of coffee, looks up at Mattie.*) You been leadin' quite a lot of dances with Denis Eady—lately, ain't you?

**Mattie.**

(*relieved at the turn of the conversation*) Oh, well—I don't know—I guess he dances a lot with most everybody.

**Zeena.**

(*significantly*) His father owns the Starkfield grocery.

**Mattie.**

(*innocently*) I know, an' folks say they're real well off, too.

**Zeena.**

Denis is quite a catch for some girl.

**Mattie.**

(*center*) My, I should say!

**Zeena.**

(*pleasantly*) If you was to get goin' steady with him you c'd ask him over to the house Wednesday evenin's. Denis is a mighty fine boy, and I wouldn't stand in your way if he was ever to propose to you.

**Mattie.**

(*laughs*) Oh, my—why, he wouldn't never do that!

**Zeena.**

He might . . . if you was to give him the chance.

**Mattie.**

(*center*) Why, gorry, whatever put that into your head, Zeena? And I never thought of him that way at all! I don't like *him!*

**Zeena.**

Paupers can't be choosey. (*Drinks coffee.*)

**Mattie.**

(*quickly*) Oh, I'm not choosey . . . Zeena . . . honest, I'm not. Like I was saying to Ethan only last night . . . I says nobody ain't never asked me yet, I said, and he said, if he wasn't married he might ask me himself . . . so 'course I said, "Sayin' that don't mean anythin'. . . . But still an' all," I says, "it's real nice of you to say it" . . . and it was, too, wasn't it? (*She beams.*) And that's about's near to proposin's anybody ever—got—(*Zeena is sitting rigidly bolt-upright in the bed, and is staring at Mattie fixedly.*)

**Zeena.**

(*indicates tray*) You c'n take this . . . if you're a mind to.

**Mattie.**

(*hastily and frightenedly*) Yes, Zeena. (*Mattie goes to lift the tray. Zeena lurches away from Mattie. Mattie upsets the coffee cup on the tray and the coffee spills out over the blankets. Zeena sits rigidly motionless, staring at the rapidly spreading stain. Mattie is terrified. She suddenly darts forward, sets the cup upright upon the tray.*) Oh, Zeena! Oh, my! . . . if I'd only been thinkin' what I was doin' . . . oh, them blankets is just ruint, simply ruint! (*Puts tray on chest up center, stops, straightens up, glances at Zeena helplessly, and then after a moment, unable to bear Zeena's steady gaze of terrific hatred, she mumbles faster and faster:*) I don't know what I'm going to do! (*She sighs, unconsciously adopting Zeena's perpetually worried manner.*) I got an awful lot needs tendin' to up here today . . . them floors to scrub and the windows want washin' real bad . . . an' them blankets'll have to be washed out and I don't know how I'll ever get things to dry this weather! (*Picks up blankets from bed. Zeena gets up, goes to closet, searches frantically. Mattie, with blankets, crosses center.*) Don't you want I sh'd help, Zeena! I'll get whatever you're looking for! (*She reaches out to help Zeena.*)

**Zeena.**

(*fiercely*) I ain't askin' any favors from you. (*Grabs dress from Mattie.*) You leave that be! That's my wedding dress. Don't you never touch none of my things! You keep you hands off my things! An' don't forget that as long as you live! (*Mattie hesitates. Zeena raises her*

*head, smiles wanly, murmurs quietly:)* Get along downstairs now, Mattie! *(Mattie bolts for the hallway, exits
left. Zeena, her pains forgotten, stares at the dress. Suddenly she buries her face in the dress and sobs.)*

from
# THE WALTZ OF THE TOREADORS
by Jean Anouilh, translated by Lucienne Hill

Act II, scene 2
GENERAL ST. PÉ, MME. ST. PÉ

A French blend of farce, high comedy, ideas, and sentiment, *The Waltz of the Toreadors* concerns a general who refuses, despite his age, to turn from amours to memoirs (though he is writing the memoirs, too). General St. Pé is proud of his conquests on the battlefield and off. His home life, however, leaves much to be desired. His wife is a nagging hypochondriac; his daughters, a bedraggled pair of whiners. To escape these day-to-day annoyances, General St. Pé works sporadically at his memoirs, keeps an eye out for any halfway pretty woman passing by, and remembers Ghislaine, the great love of his life, the woman with whom he danced the Waltz of the Toreadors at the garrison ball at Saumur. The ball was seventeen years ago, and for those seventeen years the lovers—Ghislaine and the general—have stayed apart, sacrificing themselves for the sake of his duty to Emily, his wife, a woman whose worthiness cannot, unfortunately, be questioned or denied. Then Ghislaine appears at the general's house. Their romance can begin at last, she says, for she has evidence that Emily has been unfaithful—love letters to her physician, Dr. Bonfant. A portion (two excerpts) of the general's confrontation with his wife is reprinted below.

As it happens, the general's great love never does blossom, for Ghislaine falls in love with his young male secretary. But that is all right: in a deft twist of plot at the end of the play, it is revealed that the young man is the general's son (a wild oat sprung into an oak tree, the general says). To Ghislaine, the boy is the general as he was seventeen years ago; he is the one she loves and marries.

The setting is General St. Pé's house, the bedroom occupied by his wife. It is afternoon. Emily, in night cap and bedjacket, is sitting up among her pillows in her monumental quilted bed. She has spent a part of the day lying on the railroad tracks—a gesture intended to prove that she was never unfaithful, that her husband is a beast, and that it is all too, too much for a poor sick woman. The general stands beside the bed.

**Gen.**
We must thrash this matter out, Madam, once and for all.

**Wife.**
I tried to kill myself, you monster, isn't that enough for you?

**Gen.**
You were stretched out on the tracks—an awkward position but quite safe. The train had already passed.

**Wife.**
I didn't know! I was waiting for it!

**Gen.**
On that branch line you could reckon on a good twenty-four hours of it.

**Wife.**
Is nothing sacred to you? You brute! I might have died of cold during the night.

**Gen.**
We are well into April, and spring is early this year. We are dying of heat.

**Wife.**
Of sunstroke then—starvation, I don't know. . . . Of sorrow—yes, that's it—quite simply of sorrow, in my state of health.

**Gen.**
Sorrow you can die of in your bed, Madam, at leisure. It was absurd, like everything else you do.

**Wife.**
I am seriously ill. How often has the doctor told you that my condition gives cause for the gravest alarm? I did truly mean to kill myself and that alone should make you fall sobbing at my feet, if your heart were not made of granite!

**Gen.**
My heart is not made of granite, Madam, but I am thrifty with my tears.

**Wife.**

I sacrificed my life for you! (*Screaming.*) Murderer!

**Gen.**

Be quiet, confound you, or I'll leave the room! Let us talk things over calmly.

**Wife.**

I'm too unhappy. You aren't unhappy, not you! You have your health and strength, you have. You're up and dressed each morning, you ride your horse, you walk around the garden, you go drinking with your friends! You live! You jeer at me, on your two legs, while I sit glued to my wheel chair. Aren't you ashamed of being well?

**Gen.**

You are glued to your wheel chair for no other reason than because you want to be. We know that now.

**Wife.**

Do you dare to say that I'm not ill?

**Gen.**

One has to be an idiot like myself, Madam, to go on believing in your aches and pains by this time. As for your poor ailing legs, thank God we'll hear no more about those for a bit. I strongly suspect you of stretching them in your room every night. They helped you keep your balance mighty well down the wisteria and over to the railway line this morning.

**Wife.**

It was the last spasm of the stricken beast who longs for death—Call your accomplice Doctor Bonfant, with his rubber mallet; let him test my reflexes!

**Gen.**

Death and damnation, Madam, that's too easy!

**Wife.**

Too easy for you, I daresay. What have you got to complain about? While I lie here, racked with pain, you who can wander fancy free on your great fat legs, where do you go, eh?

**Gen.**

From my study to the garden, at your beck and call every ten minutes.

**Wife.**

And what is there in the garden? Answer me that, you pig, you satyr, you lascivious goat!

**Gen.**

Well, I dunno . . . roses . . .

**Wife.**

(*Cackling.*) Roses! There's Madame Tardieu on the other side of the privet hedge, that frightful woman who exhibits her bodice as she leans over her flowerbeds. They're a household word hereabouts, Madame Tardieu's breasts! Whalebone, rubber, steel probably—she's propped up like a tumbledown barn. * * *

**Gen.**

Let's change the subject, Madam. I have something very serious to say to you. You are untrue to me, Madam, that's the long and short of it. You wrote to Doctor Bonfant that you were in love with him. I have proof of it here in my wallet, down in black and white with two spelling mistakes which identify your hand. Yes. For you, who have always accused me of being a clodhopper, too lumpish to appreciate Baudelaire or Wagner, can't tell a conjunction from a carrot. You never had a day's schooling in your life.

**Wife.**

How shabby you are! To come on my deathbed and throw my unhappy childhood in my face! For over a year I was a boarder with the daughters of consuls and ambassadors in the most select ladies' college in Paris.

**Gen.**

Where your mother went to do the household mending and where they took you in and fed you out of charity.

**Wife.**

My poor mother and I suffered a great deal, no doubt. But please to remember that my mother was a woman of infinite distinction, not a little provincial housewife like yours.

**Gen.**

One trade is as good as another, but your mother, Madam, was a dresser at the Opera.

**Wife.**

She accepted the post at the earnest request of the Director, solely for love of music. A woman whose hand M. Gounod kissed at a gala matinée for charity.

**Gen.**

Have it your own way. Let us get back to those letters. Did you or did you not write them? Do you or do you not address him as "Armand"? Do you tell him, yes or no, that his hair smells of vanilla when he sounds your chest, and that you pretend to have a belly ache so he can come and feel it for you? It's down in black and white with two spelling mistakes in your own handwriting.

**Wife.**

How could you stoop so low as to come poking about in my correspondence?

**Gen.**

I did not poke about in your correspondence, Madam. I obtained possession of those letters. How? That's none of your business.

**Wife.**

Oh, isn't it? None of my business? Those letters were in the drawer of my bedside table where I keep my curlers and other objects of an intimate nature. You tell me they are in your wallet. And you dare to cross-question *me*? It's past belief! But I did think you were still a gentleman.

**Gen.**

Dammit, Madam, will you stick to the point?

**Wife.**

So you ransack a lady's drawers, do you, my lad? You try to dishonor her, you a senior officer? All right, then, I shall tell, I shall tell everybody. I shall get up, I'll recover, for a day, the use of my poor aching legs, and the night of the reception at the annual Tattoo, in front of all the high ranking military personnel, I shall make a sensational entrance and I shall tell all!

**Gen.**

I repeat I have not ransacked your drawers.

**Wife.**

Have you those letters?

**Gen.**

I have.

**Wife.**

Show them to me.

**Gen.**

Ha ha! Not on your life.

**Wife.**

Very well. If you really have those letters in your wallet, there can be nothing more between us but an ocean of contempt. You may go. I am sleepy. I'm asleep. (*She lies with her eyes closed.*)

**Gen.**

No, Madam, you are not asleep. That would be too easy. Open your eyes. Open your eyes, this instant, do you

here, or I'll open them for you! (*Shaking her.*) Emily!
Do as I say! Open your eyes! (*He shakes her, slaps her,
forces her eyelids up from their white eyeballs, begins to
lose his head.*) Come to your senses, damn you! What
new game are you playing now?

**Wife.**

(*Weakly.*) My heart!

**Gen.**

What about your heart!

**Wife.**

It's shrinking. Good-bye, Leon! I never loved anyone else
but you.

**Gen.**

Oh no, not your heart attack. We haven't even raised
our voices. Your heart attack is for after the big scenes,
Madam. You are warm, your pulse is good. I'm not
falling for that. (*Shaking her.*) Wake up, Emily! You
can't be as rigid as that. You're doing it on purpose. I'll
give you your drops. (*He rummages about among the
bottles on the side tables.*) Holy Moses, what a collection!
It would take a qualified druggist to make head or tail
of this lot! There's enough here to upset the constitution
of a cart horse. Needless to say, no dropper. Where the
devil did Eugenie put the thing? Oh well, here goes—one
drop more, one drop less—the way things are now. . . .
There, Emily, drink this, and if that doesn't do the trick
I'll call the doctor. Unclench your teeth, my love—unclench your teeth, damn you, it's dripping all over you!
Give me strength—what's the matter with you? Your
pulse is all right. There's no getting away from that. I'll
give you your injection.

**Wife.**

(*Feebly.*) You're still rummaging, Leon. You're suspicious
of me even on my deathbed.

**Gen.**

I'm *not* rummaging, I'm looking for your capsules.

**Wife.**

Too late. Call the children.

**Gen.**

What are you raving about, my dear, you aren't going to
die. You're weak, that's all. I'll get the doctor.

**Wife.**

Too late. I implore you, don't move, Leon. Stay with me.
Hold my hand as you did in the old days long ago, when
I was ill. You took care of me then, you were patient with

me. You used to bathe my temples with eau de cologne and murmur sweet nothings in my ears. . . .

**Gen.**

(*Looking for the bottle and mumbling.*) I can still dab you with a bit of cologne. . . .

**Wife.**

But without the sweet nothings! It's that that's killing me —you murderer!

from
THE GLASS MENAGERIE
by Tennessee Williams

Act I, scene 2
AMANDA, LAURA

Amanda Wingfield treasures the past and her memories,
but she has to pay the bills in the present and she worries
about the future. (For introductory comments on the play,
see page 59.) Amanda's daughter, Laura, is the greatest
of her worries. Retiring, crippled, and afraid, Laura hides
from the world, but her mother is determined to draw or
drive her out of hiding.

The setting is the living room of the flat in St. Louis.
The time is midafternoon.


*Laura discovered by menagerie, polishing glass. Crosses
to phonograph, plays record.*

*Enter Amanda down alley right. Rattles key in lock.
Laura crosses guiltily to typewriter and types. (Small typewriter table with typewriter on it is still on stage in living-
room left.) Amanda comes into room right closing door.
Crosses to arm-chair, putting hat, purse and gloves on it.*

*Something has happened to Amanda. It is written in her
face: a look that is grim and hopeless and a little absurd.
She has on one of those cheap or imitation velvety-looking
cloth coats with imitation fur collar. Her hat is five or six
years old, one of those dreadful cloche hats that were worn
in the late twenties and she is clasping an enormous black
patent-leather pocketbook with nickel clasps and initials.
This is her full-dress outfit, the one she usually wears to
the D.A.R.*

*She purses her lips, opens her eyes very wide, rolls
them upward and shakes her head.*

*Seeing her mother's expression, Laura touches her lips
with a nervous gesture.*

**Laura.**

Hello, Mother, I was just . . .

**Amanda.**

I know. You were just practicing your typing, I suppose. (*Behind chair right*)

**Laura.**

Yes.

**Amanda.**

Deception, deception, deception!

**Laura.**

(*shakingly*) How was the D.A.R. meeting, Mother?

**Amanda.**

(*crosses to Laura*) D.A.R. meeting!

**Laura.**

Didn't you go to the D.A.R. meeting, Mother?

**Amanda.**

(*faintly, almost inaudibly*) No, I didn't go to any D.A.R. meeting. (*Then more forcibly*) I didn't have the strength —I didn't have the courage. I just wanted to find a hole in the ground and crawl in it and stay there the rest of my entire life. (*Tears type charts, throws them on floor*)

**Laura.**

(*faintly*) Why did you do that, Mother?

**Amanda.**

(*sits on right end of day-bed*) Why? Why? How old are you, Laura?

**Laura.**

Mother, you know my age.

**Amanda.**

I was under the impression that you were an adult, but evidently I was very much mistaken. (*She stares at Laura*)

**Laura.**

Please don't stare at me, Mother! (*Amanda closes her eyes and lowers her head. Pause*)

**Amanda.**

What are we going to do? What is going to become of us? What is the future? (*Pause*)

**Laura.**

Has something happened, Mother? Mother, has something happened?

**Amanda.**

I'll be all right in a minute. I'm just bewildered—by life . . .

**Laura.**

Mother, I wish that you would tell me what's happened!

**Amanda.**

I went to the D.A.R. this afternoon, as you know; I was to be inducted as an officer. I stopped off at Rubicam's Business College to tell them about your cold and to ask how you were progressing down there.

**Laura.**

Oh . . .

**Amanda.**

Yes, oh—oh—oh. I went straight to your typing instructor and introduced myself as your mother. She didn't even know who you were. Wingfield, she said? We don't have any such scholar enrolled in this school. I assured her she did. I said my daughter Laura's been coming to classes since early January. "Well, I don't know," she said, "unless you mean that terribly shy little girl who dropped out of school after a few days' attendance?" No, I said, I don't mean that one. I mean my daughter, Laura, who's been coming here every single day for the past six weeks! "Excuse me," she said. And she took down the attendance book and there was your name, unmistakable, printed, and all the dates you'd been absent. I still told her she was wrong. I still said, "No, there must have been some mistake! There must have been some mix-up in the records!" "No," she said, "I remember her perfectly now. She was so shy and her hands trembled so that her fingers couldn't touch the right keys! When we gave a speed test— she just broke down completely—was sick at the stomach and had to be carried to the washroom! After that she never came back. We telephoned the house every single day and never got any answer." (*Rises from day-bed, crosses right center.*) That was while I was working all day long down at that department store, I suppose, demonstrating those—(*With hands indicates brassiere*) Oh! I felt so weak I couldn't stand up! (*Sits in armchair*) I had to sit down while they got me a glass of water! (*Laura crosses up to phonograph*) Fifty dollars' tuition. I don't care about the money so much, but all my hopes for any kind of future for you—gone up the spout, just gone up the spout like that. (*Laura winds phonograph up*) Oh, don't *do* that, Laura!—Don't play that victrola!

**Laura.**

Oh! (*Stops phonograph, crosses to typing table, sits*)

**Amanda.**

What have you been doing every day when you've gone

out of the house pretending that you were going to business college?

**Laura.**

I've just been going out walking.

**Amanda.**

That's not true!

**Laura.**

Yes, it is, Mother, I just went walking.

**Amanda.**

Walking? Walking? In winter? Deliberately courting pneumonia in that light coat? Where did you walk to, Laura?

**Laura.**

All sorts of places—mostly in the park.

**Amanda.**

Even after you'd started catching that cold?

**Laura.**

It was the lesser of two evils, Mother. I couldn't go back.
I threw up on the floor!

**Amanda.**

From half-past seven till after five every day you mean
to tell me you walked around in the park, because you
wanted to make me think that you were still going to
Rubicam's Business College?

**Laura.**

Oh Mother, it wasn't as bad as it sounds. I went inside
places to get warmed up.

**Amanda.**

Inside where?

**Laura.**

I went in the art museum and the bird-houses at the Zoo.
I visited the penguins every day! Sometimes I did without lunch and went to the movies. Lately I've been spending most of my afternoons in the Jewel-box, that big glass
house where they raise the tropical flowers.

**Amanda.**

You did all that to deceive me, just for deception! Why?
Why? Why? Why?

**Laura.**

Mother, when you're disappointed, you get that awful
suffering look on your face, like the picture of Jesus'
mother in the Museum! (*Rises*)

**Amanda.**

Hush!

**Laura.**

(*crosses right to menagerie*) I couldn't face it. I couldn't.

**Amanda.**

(*rising from day-bed*) So what are we going to do now, honey, the rest of our lives? Just sit down in this house and watch the parades go by? Amuse ourselves with the glass menagerie? Eternally play those worn-out records your father left us as a painful reminder of him? (*Slams phonograph lid*) We can't have a business career. No, we can't do that—that just gives us indigestion. (*Around right day-bed*) What is there left for us now but dependency all our lives? I tell you, Laura, I know so well what happens to unmarried women who aren't prepared to occupy a position in life. (*Crosses left, sits on day-bed*) I've seen such pitiful cases in the South—barely tolerated spinsters living on some brother's wife or a sister's husband— tucked away in some mouse-trap of a room—encouraged by one in-law to go on and visit the next in-law—little birdlike women—without any nest—eating the crust of humility all their lives! Is that the future that we've mapped out for ourselves? I swear I don't see any other alternative. And I don't think that's a very pleasant alternative. Of course—some girls *do* marry. My goodness, Laura, haven't you ever liked some boy?

**Laura.**

Yes, Mother. I liked one once.

**Amanda.**

You did?

**Laura.**

I came across his picture a while ago.

**Amanda.**

He gave you his picture, too? (*Rises from day-bed, crosses to chair right*)

**Laura.**

No, it's in the year-book.

**Amanda.**

(*sits in arm-chair*) Oh—a high-school boy.

**Laura.**

Yes. His name was Jim. (*Kneeling on floor, gets year-book from under menagerie*) Here he is in "The Pirates of Penzance."

**Amanda.**

(*absently*) The what?

**Laura.**

The operetta the senior class put on. He had a wonderful voice. We sat across the aisle from each other Mondays, Wednesdays and Fridays in the auditorium. Here he is with a silver cup for debating! See his grin?

**Amanda.**

So he had a grin, too! (*Looks at picture of father on wall behind phonograph. Hands year-book back*)

**Laura.**

He used to call me—Blue Roses.

**Amanda.**

Blue Roses? What did he call you a silly name like that for?

**Laura.**

(*still kneeling*) When I had that attack of pleurosis—he asked me what was the matter when I came back. I said pleurosis—he thought that I said "Blue Roses." So that's what he always called me after that. Whenever he saw me, he'd holler, "Hello, Blue Roses!" I didn't care for the girl that he went out with. Emily Meisenbach. Oh, Emily was the best-dressed girl at Soldan. But she never struck me as being sincere . . . I read in a newspaper once that they were engaged. (*Puts year-book back on a shelf of glass menagerie*) That's a long time ago—they're probably married by now.

**Amanda.**

That's all right, honey, that's all right. It doesn't matter. Little girls who aren't cut out for business careers sometimes end up married to very nice young men. And I'm just going to see that you do that, too!

**Laura.**

But, Mother—

**Amanda.**

What is it now?

**Laura.**

I'm—crippled!

**Amanda.**

Don't say that word! (*Rises, crosses to center. Turns to Laura*) How many times have I told you never to say that word! You're not crippled, you've just got a slight defect. (*Laura rises*) If you lived in the days when I was a girl and they had long graceful skirts sweeping the ground, it might have been considered an asset. When you've got a slight disadvantage like that, you've just got to cultivate something else to take its place. You have to cultivate charm—or vivacity—or *charm!* That's the only thing your father had plenty of—charm! (*Amanda sits on day-bed. Laura crosses to arm-chair and sits.*)

from
# SUMMER AND SMOKE
by Tennessee Williams

Part I, scene 1
ALMA, JOHN

The play is an ironic tale of two people whose lives cross
and recross yet never merge, for neither is ready for the
other at the right time. At the outset, John, a young doctor,
is a realist, cynical, "brilliantly and restlessly alive in a stag-
nant society," and given to dissipations to relieve his unrest.
Alma is the minister's daughter, prematurely spinsterish,
self-conscious, and nervous; "people her own age regard
her as quaintly and humorously affected." Each tries to
cure the other—he to teach her to face the realities of life
and sex; she to give him a sense of value and higher purpose as a doctor and a man. They succeed too well in their
lessons, both of them change, and, when they meet at the
end of the play, they are as far apart as they were at the
beginning.

The scene below follows a prologue in which John and
Alma are seen as children. Now they are young adults. It
is the fourth of July in a year shortly before the First
World War. Alma has sung at the band concert, then
joined her mother and father in the part of the city park
which is shown on the stage. Alma's mother, senile and
childish, has created a fuss and been hurried home. Left
alone, Alma sinks onto a park bench, feeling slightly
faint. John is standing nearby, beside a fountain topped
with a stone angel. Noticing a firecracker on the ground,
he "leans over negligently to pick it up. He grins and lights
it and tosses it toward Alma's bench. When it goes off she
springs up with a shocked cry, letting the parasol drop."

**John.**

(*jumping up as if outraged*) Hey! Hey, you! (*He looks off to the right. Alma sinks back weakly on the bench. John solicitously advances*) Are you all right?

**Alma.**

I can't seem to—catch my breath! Who threw it?

**John.**

Some little rascal.

**Alma.**

There ought to be an ordinance passed in this town for-bidding firecrackers.

**John.**

Dad and I treated fifteen kids for burns in the last couple of days. I think you need a little restorative, don't you? (*He takes out a flask*) Here!

**Alma.**

What is it?

**John.**

Applejack brandy.

**Alma.**

No thank you.

**John.**

Liquid dynamite.

**Alma.**

I'm sure. (*John laughs and returns it to his pocket. He remains looking down at her with one foot on the end of her bench. His steady, smiling look into her face is dis-concerting her.*

(*In Alma's voice and manner there is a delicacy and elegance, a kind of "airiness," which is really natural to her as it is, in a less marked degree, to many Southern girls. Her gestures and mannerisms are a bit exaggerated but in a graceful way. It is understandable that she might be accused of "putting on airs" and of being "affected" by the other young people of the town. She seems to belong to a more elegant age, such as the Eighteenth Century in France. Out of nervousness and self-consciousness she has a habit of prefacing and concluding her remarks with a little breathless laugh. This will be indicated at points, but should be used more freely than indicated; however, the characterization must never be stressed to the point of making her at all ludicrous in a less than sympathetic way.*)

**Alma.**

You're—home for the summer? (*John gives an affirma-*

*tive grunt*) Summer is not the pleasantest time of year to renew an acquaintance with Glorious Hill—is it? (*John gives an indefinite grunt. Alma laughs airily*) The Gulf wind has failed us this year, disappointed us dreadfully this summer. We used to be able to rely on the Gulf wind to cool the nights off for us, but this summer has been an exceptional season. (*He continues to grin disconcertingly down at her; she shows her discomfiture in flurried gestures*)

**John.**
(*slowly*) Are you—disturbed about something?

**Alma.**
That firecracker was a shock.

**John.**
You should be over that shock by now.

**Alma.**
I don't get over shocks quickly.

**John.**
I see you don't.

**Alma.**
You're planning to stay here and take over some of your father's medical practice?

**John.**
I haven't made up my mind about anything yet.

**Alma.**
I hope so, we all hope so. Your father was telling me that you have succeeded in isolating the germ of that fever epidemic that's broken out at Lyon.

**John.**
Finding something to kill it is more of a trick.

**Alma.**
You'll do that! He's so positive that you will. He says that you made a special study of bacter—bacter . . .

**John.**
Bacteriology!

**Alma.**
Yes! At Johns Hopkins! That's in Boston, isn't it?

**John.**
No. Baltimore.

**Alma.**
Oh, Baltimore. Baltimore, Maryland. Such a beautiful combination of names. And bacteriology—isn't that something you do with a microscope?

**John.**
Well—partly. . . .

**Alma.**

I've looked through a telescope, but never a microscope. What . . . what do you—see?

**John.**

A—universe, Miss Alma.

**Alma.**

What kind of a universe?

**John.**

Pretty much the same kind that you saw through the lens of a telescope—a mysterious one. . . .

**Alma.**

Oh, yes. . . .

**John.**

Part anarchy—and part order!

**Alma.**

The footprints of God!

**John.**

But not God.

**Alma.**

(*ecstatically*) To be a doctor! And deal with these mysteries under the microscope lens . . . I think it is more religious than being a priest! There is so much suffering in the world it actually makes one sick to think about it, and most of us are so helpless to relieve it. . . . But a physician! Oh, my! With his magnificent gifts and training what a joy it must be to know that he is equipped and appointed to bring relief to all of this fearful suffering— and fear! And it's an expanding profession, it's a profession that is continually widening its horizons. So many diseases have already come under scientific control but the commencement is just—beginning! I mean there is so much more that is yet to be done, such as mental afflictions to be brought under control. . . . And with your father's example to inspire you! Oh, my!

**John.**

I didn't know you had so many ideas about the medical profession.

**Alma.**

Well, I am a great admirer of your father, as well as a patient. It's such a comfort knowing that he's right next door, within arm's reach as it were!

**John.**

Why? Do you have fits?

**Alma.**

Fits? (*She throws back her head with a peal of gay*

*laughter*) Why no, but I do have attacks!—of nervous heart trouble. Which can be so alarming that I run straight to your father!

**John.**

At two or three in the morning?

**Alma.**

Yes, as late as that, even . . . occasionally. He's very patient with me.

**John.**

But does you no good?

**Alma.**

He always reassures me.

**John.**

Temporarily?

**Alma.**

Yes . . .

**John.**

Don't you want more than that?

**Alma.**

What?

**John.**

It's none of my business.

**Alma.**

What were you going to say?

**John.**

You're Dad's patient. But I have an idea . . .

**Alma.**

Please go on! (*John laughs a little*) Now you have to go on! You can't leave me up in the air! What were you going to tell me?

**John.**

Only that I suspect you need something more than a little temporary reassurance.

**Alma.**

*Why?* Why? You think it's more serious than . . . ?

**John.**

You're swallowing air.

**Alma.**

I'm what?

**John.**

You're swallowing air, Miss Alma.

**Alma.**

I'm swallowing air?

**John.**

Yes, you swallow air when you laugh or talk. It's a little trick that hysterical women get into.

**Alma.**

(*uncertainly*) Ha-ha . . . !

**John.**

You swallow air and it presses on your heart and gives you palpitations. That isn't serious in itself but it's a symptom of something that is. Shall I tell you frankly?

**Alma.**

Yes!

**John.**

Well, what I think you have is a *doppelganger*! You have a *doppelganger* and the *doppelganger* is badly irritated.

**Alma.**

Oh, my goodness! I have an irritated *doppelganger*! (*She tries to laugh, but is definitely uneasy*) How awful that sounds! What exactly *is* it?

**John.**

It's none of *my* business. You are not *my* patient.

**Alma.**

But that's downright wicked of you! To tell me I have something awful-sounding as that, and then refuse to let me know what it is! (*She tries to laugh again, unsuccessfully*)

**John.**

I shouldn't have said anything! I'm not your doctor. . . .

**Alma.**

Just how did you arrive at this—diagnosis of my case? (*She laughs*) But of course you're teasing me. Aren't you? . . . There, the Gulf wind is stirring! He's actually moving the leaves of the palmetto! And listen to them complaining. . . .

(*As if brought in by this courier from the tropics, Rosa Gonzales enters and crosses to the fountain. Her indolent walk produces a sound and an atmosphere like the Gulf wind on the palmettos, a whispering of silk and a slight rattle of metallic ornaments. She is dressed in an almost outrageous finery, with lustrous feathers on her hat, greenish blue, a cascade of them, also diamond and emerald earrings.*)

**John.**

(*sharply*) Who is that?

**Alma.**

I'm surprised that you don't know.

**John.**

I've been away quite a while.

**Alma.**

That's the Gonzales girl. . . . Her father's the owner of the gambling casino on Moon Lake. (*Rosa drinks at the fountain and wanders leisurely off*) She smiled at you, didn't she?

**John.**

I thought she did.

**Alma.**

I hope that you have a strong character. (*He places a foot on the end of the bench*)

**John.**

Solid rock.

**Alma.**

(*nervously*) The pyrotechnical display is going to be brilliant.

**John.**

The what?

**Alma.**

The fireworks.

**John.**

Aw!

**Alma.**

I suppose you've lost touch with most of your *old* friends here.

**John.**

(*laconically*) Yeah.

**Alma.**

You must make some *new* ones! I belong to a little group that meets every ten days. I think you'd enjoy them, too. They're young people with—intellectual and artistic interests. . . .

**John.**

(*sadly*) Aw, I see . . . intellectual. . . .

**Alma.**

You must come!—sometime—I'm going to remind you of it. . . .

**John.**

Thanks. Do you mind if I sit down?

**Alma.**

Why, certainly not, there's room enough for two! Neither of us are—terribly large in diameter! (*She laughs shrilly.*) (*A girl's voice is heard calling: "Good-bye, Nellie!" and another answers: "Good-bye!" Nellie Ewell enters—a girl of sixteen with a radiantly fresh healthy quality.*)

**Alma.**

Here comes someone much nicer! One of my adorable little vocal pupils, the youngest and prettiest one with the least gift for music.

**John.**

I know that one.

**Alma.**

Hello, there, Nellie dear!

**§ Nellie.**

Oh, Miss Alma, your singing was so beautiful it made me cry.

**§ Alma.**

It's sweet of you to fib so. I sang terribly.

**§ Nellie.**

You're just being modest, Miss Alma. Hello, Dr. John! Dr. John?

**§ John.**

Yeah?

**§ Nellie.**

That book you gave me is too full of long words.

**§ John.**

Look 'em up in the dictionary, Nellie.

**§ Nellie.**

I did, but you know how dictionaries are. You look up one long word and it gives you another and you look up that one and it gives you the long word you looked up in the first place. (*John laughs*) I'm coming over tomorrow for you to explain it all to me. (*She laughs and goes off*)

**§ Alma.**

What book is she talking about?

**§ John.**

A book I gave her about the facts of nature. § She came over to the office and told me her mother wouldn't tell her anything and she had to know because she'd fallen in love.

**Alma.**

Why the precocious little—imp! (*She laughs.*)

**John.**

What sort of a mother has she?

**Alma.**

Mrs. Ewell's the merry widow of Glorious Hill. They say that she goes to the depot to meet every train in order to make the acquaintance of traveling salesmen. Of course she is ostracized by all but a few of her own type of women in town, which is terribly hard for Nellie. It isn't fair to the child. Father didn't want me to take her as a pupil because of her mother's reputation, but I feel that one has a duty to perform toward children in such—circumstances. . . . And I always say that life is such a mysteriously complicated thing that no one should really presume to judge and condemn the behavior of anyone else! (*There is a faraway "puff" and a burst of golden light over their heads. Both look up. There is a long-drawn "Ahhh . . ." from the invisible crowd. This is an effect that will be repeated at intervals during the scene.*) There goes the first skyrocket! Oh, look at it burst into a million stars! (*John leans way back to look up and allows his knees to spread wide apart so that one of them is in contact with Alma's. The effect upon her is curiously disturbing.*)

**John.**
(*after a moment*) Do you have a chill?

**Alma.**
Why, no!—no. Why?

**John.**
You're shaking.

**Alma.**
Am I?

**John.**
Don't you feel it?

**Alma.**
I have a touch of malaria lingering on.

**John.**
You have malaria?

**Alma.**
Never severely, never really severely. I just have touches of it that come and go. (*She laughs airily*)

**John.**
(*with a gentle grin*) Why do you laugh that way?

**Alma.**
What way? (*John imitates her laugh. Alma laughs again in embarrassment.*)

**John.**
Yeah. That way.

**Alma.**
I do declare, you haven't changed in the slightest. It used to delight you to embarrass me and it still does!

**John.**
I guess I shouldn't tell you this but I heard an imitation of you at a party.

**Alma.**

Imitation? Of what?

**John.**

You.

**Alma.**

I?—I? Why, *what* did they imitate?

**John.**

You singing at a wedding.

**Alma.**

My voice?

**John.**

Your gestures and facial expression!

**Alma.**

How mystifying!

**John.**

No, I shouldn't have told you. You're upset about it.

**Alma.**

I'm not in the least upset, I am just mystified.

**John.**

Don't you know that you have a reputation for putting on airs a little—for gilding the lily a bit?

**Alma.**

I have no idea what you are talking about.

**John.**

Well, some people seem to have gotten the idea that you are just a little bit—affected!

**Alma.**

Well, well, well, well. (*She tries to conceal her hurt*) That may be so, it may seem so to some people. But since I am innocent of any attempt at affectation, I really don't know what I can do about it.

**John.**

You have a rather fancy way of talking.

**Alma.**

Have I?

**John.**

Pyrotechnical display instead of fireworks, and that sort of thing.

**Alma.**

So?

**John.**

And how about that accent?

**Alma.**

Accent? This leaves me quite speechless! I have sometimes been accused of having a put-on accent by people who disapprove of good diction. My father was a Rhodes scholar at Oxford, and while over there he fell into the natural habit of using the long A where it is correct to use it. I suppose I must have picked it up from him, but it's entirely unconscious. Who gave this imitation at this party you spoke of?

**John.**
(*grinning*) I don't think she'd want that told.

**Alma.**
Oh, it was a *she* then?

**John.**
You don't think a man could do it?

**Alma.**
No, and I don't think a lady would do it either!

**John.**
I didn't think it would have made you so mad, or I wouldn't have brought it up.

**Alma.**
Oh, I'm not mad. I'm just mystified and amazed as I always am by unprovoked malice in people. I don't understand it when it's directed at me and I don't understand it when it is directed at anybody else. I just don't understand it, and perhaps it is better not to understand it. These people who call me affected and give these unkind imitations of me—I wonder if they stop to think that I have had certain difficulties and disadvantages to cope with—which may be partly the cause of these peculiarities of mine—which they find so offensive!

**John.**
Now, Miss Alma, you're making a mountain out of a molehill!

**Alma.**
I wonder if they stop to think that my circumstances are somewhat different from theirs? My father and I have a certain—cross—to bear!

**John.**
What cross?

**Alma.**
Living next door to us, you should know what cross.

**John.**
Mrs. Winemiller?

**Alma.**
She had her breakdown while I was still in high school. And from that time on I have had to manage the Rectory and take over the social and household duties that would ordinarily belong to a minister's wife, not his daughter.

And that may have made me seem strange to some of my more critical contemporaries. In a way it may have—deprived me of—my youth. . . . (*Another rocket goes up. Another "Ahhh . . ." from the crowd.*)

**John.**

You ought to go out with young people.

**Alma.**

I am not a recluse. I don't fly around here and there giving imitations of other people at parties. But I am not a recluse by any manner of means. Being a minister's daughter I have to be more selective than most girls about the —society I keep. But I do go out now and then. . . .

**John.**

I have seen you in the public library and the park, but only two or three times have I seen you out with a boy and it was always someone like this Roger Doremus.

**Alma.**

I'm afraid that you and I move in different circles. If I wished to be as outspoken as you are, which is sometimes just an excuse for being rude—I might say that I've yet to see you in the company of a—well, a—reputable young woman. You've heard unfavorable talk about me in your circle of acquaintances and I've heard equally unpleasant things about you in mine. And the pity of it is that you are preparing to be a doctor. You're intending to practice your father's profession here in Glorious Hill. (*She catches her breath in a sob*) Most of us have no choice but to lead useless lives! But you have a gift for scientific research! You have a chance to serve humanity. Not just to go on enduring for the sake of endurance, but to serve a noble, humanitarian cause, to relieve human suffering. And what do you do about it? Everything that you can to alienate the confidence of nice people who love and respect your father. While he is devoting himself to the fever at Lyon you drive your automobile at a reckless pace from one disorderly roadhouse to another! You say you have seen two things through the microscope, anarchy and order? Well, obviously *order* is not the thing that impressed you . . . conducting yourself like some overgrown schoolboy who wants to be known as the wildest fellow in town! And you—a gifted young doctor —*Magna cum Laude!* (*She turns aside, touching her eyelids with a handkerchief*) You know what I call it? I call it a *desecration!* (*She sobs uncontrollably. Then she springs up from the bench. John catches her hand.*)

**John.**

You're not going to run off, are you?

**Alma.**

Singing in public always—always upsets me!—Let go of my hand. (*He holds on to it, grinning up at her in the deepening dusk. The stars are coming out in the cyclorama with its leisurely floating cloud-forms. In the distance the band is playing "La Golondrina"*) Please let go of my hand.

**John.**

Don't run off mad.

**Alma.**

Let's not make a spectacle of ourselves.

**John.**

Then sit back down. (*A skyrocket goes up. The crowd "Ahhh . . . s."*)

**Alma.**

You threw that firecracker and started a conversation just in order to tease me as you did as a child. You came to this bench in order to embarrass me and to hurt my feelings with the report of that vicious—imitation! No, let go of my hand so I can leave, now. You've succeeded in your purpose. I *was* hurt, I *did* make a fool of myself as you intended! So let me go now!

**John.**

You're attracting attention! Don't you know that I really *like* you, Miss Alma?

**Alma.**

No, you don't. (*Another skyrocket.*)

**John.**

Sure I do. A lot. Sometimes when I come home late at night I look over at the Rectory. I see something white at the window. Could that be you, Miss Alma? Or, is it your *doppelganger,* looking out of the window that faces my way?

**Alma.**

Enough about *doppelganger*—whatever that is!

**John.**

There goes a nice one, Roman candle they call it! (*This time the explosion is in back of them. A Roman candle shoots up puffs of rainbow-colored light in back of the stone angel of the fountain. They turn in profile to watch it.*)

**John.**

(*counting the puffs of light*) Four—five—six—that's all? No—seven! (*There is a pause. Alma sits down slowly*)

**Alma.**

(*vaguely*) Dear me . . . (*She fans herself*)

**John.**

How about going riding?

**Alma.**

(*too eagerly*) When . . . now? (*Rosa Gonzales has wandered up to the fountain again. John's attention drifts steadily toward her and away from Alma.*)

**John.**

(*too carelessly*) Oh . . . some afternoon.

**Alma.**

Would you observe the speed limit?

**John.**

Strictly with you, Miss Alma.

**Alma.**

Why then, I'd be glad to—John. (*John has risen from the bench and crosses to the fountain.*)

**John.**

And wear a hat with a plume!

**Alma.**

I don't have a hat with a plume!

**John.**

Get one!

from
# A STREETCAR NAMED DESIRE
by Tennessee Williams

Act I, scene 2
BLANCHE, STANLEY

Blanche du Bois has a delicate beauty "that must avoid strong light." Something about her uncertain manner, as well as her dainty clothes, suggests a moth. Blanche grew up at Belle Reve, a decaying Mississippi mansion that was all that remained of her family's plantation. When her sister married and moved away, Blanche stayed on, surrounded by elderly servants and relations who one by one grew sick and died. Blanche supported herself by teaching English in the high school. The house was mortgaged and mortgaged again and finally lost. Then Blanche was fired. Fleeing to New Orleans to visit her sister, she took a streetcar named Desire, transferred to one called Cemeteries, rode six blocks, and got off at the street called Elysian Fields. That is where the play begins—at a rundown white frame building with "rickety stairs and galleries and quaintly ornamented gables."

On the ground floor of the building Blanche's sister, Stella, lives with her husband, Stanley Kowalski. There are no plantations in Stanley's past and there is nothing uncertain about him. He brawls and makes love and takes from life whatever he can grab. To Blanche, Stanley is rough and animal-like. To her sister, he is a man uninhibited and alive; in loving him she has escaped the air of unreality and death that hung over Belle Reve.

With these three characters—Blanche, Stella, and Stanley—Tennessee Williams plays out a story of kinds of love. Blanche, with her delicacy and illusions, and Stanley, with his roughness and open delight in sex, are at opposite ends of the spectrum of love. Yet each has a fascination for the other. Blanche's clothes and manners, her poses and the little tricks she uses in dealing with men mask a desperate need which she has satisfied physically many times with many men, but never truly met. With Stanley, she is the moth that flies into the flame and destroys itself. She retreats into her illusions, no longer able to bear the harsh light of a fierce and savage world, and she is sent to an asylum.

The scene below presents one of the first encounters between Stanley and Blanche. (For an earlier scene, introducing Blanche and Stella, see page 518.) Stanley has learned of the loss of Belle Reve, which, through his wife's inheritance, should have been half his. Angry, certain that Blanche has cheated him of his property, he is determined to shout or shake the facts out of her.

The setting is the bedroom of the two-room flat. Stanley has torn open Blanche's wardrobe trunk and scattered the clothes, furs, and costume jewelry in a search for the finery on which she may have spent the money that was rightly his. Now he waits for her to finish one of the hour-long baths she takes two or three times a day. She comes out of the bathroom in a red satin robe.

**Blanche.**

(*Airily*) Hello, Stanley! Here I am, all freshly bathed and scented, and feeling like a brand new human being! (*He lights a cigarette*)

**Stanley.**

That's good.

**Blanche.**

(*Drawing the curtains at the windows*) Excuse me while I slip on my pretty new dress!

**Stanley.**

Go right ahead, Blanche. (*She closes the drapes between the rooms*)

**Blanche.**

I understand there's to be a little card party to which we ladies are cordially *not* invited!

**Stanley.**

(*Ominously*) Yeah? (*Blanche throws off her robe and slips into a flowered print dress*)

**Blanche.**

Where's Stella?

**Stanley.**

Out on the porch.

**Blanche.**
I'm going to ask a favor of you in a moment.

**Stanley.**
What could that be, I wonder?

**Blanche.**
Some buttons in back! You may enter! (*He crosses through drapes with a smoldering look*) How do I look?

**Stanley.**
You look all right.

**Blanche.**
Many thanks! Now the buttons!

**Stanley.**
I can't do nothing with them.

**Blanche.**
You men with your big clumsy fingers. May I have a drag on your cig?

**Stanley.**
Have one for yourself.

**Blanche.**
Why, thanks! . . . It looks like my trunk has exploded.

**Stanley.**
Me an' Stella were helping you unpack.

**Blanche.**
Well, you certainly did a fast and thorough job of it.

**Stanley.**
It looks like you raided some stylish shops in Paris.

**Blanche.**
Ha-ha! Yes—clothes are my passion!

**Stanley.**
What does it cost for a string of fur-pieces like that?

**Blanche.**
Why, those were a tribute from an admirer of mine!

**Stanley.**
He must have had a lot of—admiration!

**Blanche.**
Oh, in my youth I excited some admiration. But look at me now! (*She smiles at him radiantly*) Would you think it possible that I was once considered to be—attractive?

**Stanley.**
Your looks are okay.

**Blanche.**
I was fishing for a compliment, Stanley.

**Stanley.**
I don't go in for that stuff.

**Blanche.**
What—stuff?

**Stanley.**

Compliments to women about their looks. I never met a woman that didn't know if she was good-looking or not without being told, and some of them give themselves credit for more than they've got. I once went out with a doll who said to me, "I am the glamorous type, I am the glamorous type!" I said, "So what?"

**Blanche.**

And what did she say then?

**Stanley.**

She didn't say nothing. That shut her up like a clam.

**Blanche.**

Did it end the romance?

**Stanley.**

It ended the conversation—that was all. Some men are took in by this Hollywood glamor stuff and some men are not.

**Blanche.**

I'm sure you belong in the second category.

**Stanley.**

That's right.

**Blanche.**

I cannot imagine any witch of a woman casting a spell over you.

**Stanley.**

That's—right.

**Blanche.**

You're simple, straightforward and honest, a little bit on the primitive side I should think. To interest you a woman would have to— (*She pauses with an indefinite gesture*)

**Stanley.**

(*Slowly*) Lay . . . her cards on the table.

**Blanche.**

(*Smiling*) Well, I never cared for wishy-washy people. That was why, when you walked in here last night, I said to myself—"My sister has married a man!"—Of course that was all that I could tell about you.

**Stanley.**

(*Booming*) Now let's cut the re-bop!

**Blanche.**

(*Pressing hands to her ears*) Ouuuuu!

**Stella.** [*Stella's lines may be read offstage. Ed.*]

(*Calling from the steps*) Stanley! You come out here and let Blanche finish dressing!

**Blanche.**

I'm through dressing, honey.

**Stella.**

Well, you come out, then.

**Stanley.**

Your sister and I are having a little talk.

**Blanche.**

(*Lightly*) Honey, do me a favor. Run to the drugstore and get me a lemon-coke with plenty of chipped ice in it!—Will you do that for me, Sweetie?

**Stella.**

(*Uncertainly*) Yes. (*She goes around the corner of the building*)

**Blanche.**

The poor little thing was out there listening to us, and I have an idea she doesn't understand you as well as I do. . . . All right; now, Mr. Kowalski, let us proceed without any more double-talk. I'm ready to answer all questions. I've nothing to hide. What is it?

**Stanley.**

There is such a thing in this State of Louisiana as the Napoleonic code, according to which whatever belongs to my wife is also mine—and vice versa.

**Blanche.**

My, but you have an impressive judicial air! (*She sprays herself with her atomizer; then playfully sprays him with it. He seizes the atomizer and slams it down on the dresser. She throws back her head and laughs*)

**Stanley.**

If I didn't know that you was my wife's sister I'd get ideas about you!

**Blanche.**

Such as what!

**Stanley.**

Don't play so dumb. You know what!

**Blanche.**

(*She puts the atomizer on the table*) All right. Cards on the table. That suits me. (*She turns to Stanley*) I know I fib a good deal. After all, a woman's charm is fifty per cent illusion, but when a thing is important I tell the truth, and this is the truth: I haven't cheated my sister or you or anyone else as long as I have lived.

**Stanley.**

Where's the papers? In the trunk?

**Blanche.**

Everything that I own is in that trunk. (*Stanley crosses to the trunk, shoves it roughly open and begins to open compartments*)

**Blanche.**

What in the name of heaven are you thinking of! What's in the back of that little boy's mind of yours? That I am absconding with something, attempting some kind of treachery on my sister?—Let me do that! It will be faster and simpler . . . (*She crosses to the trunk and takes out a box*) I keep my papers mostly in this tin box. (*She opens it*)

**Stanley.**

What's them underneath? (*He indicates another sheaf of paper*)

**Blanche.**

These are love-letters, yellowing with antiquity, all from one boy. (*He snatches them up. She speaks fiercely*) Give those back to me!

**Stanley.**

I'll have a look at them first!

**Blanche.**

The touch of your hands insults them!

**Stanley.**

Don't pull that stuff! (*He rips off the ribbon and starts to examine them. Blanche snatches them from him, and they cascade to the floor*)

**Blanche.**

Now that you've touched them I'll burn them!

**Stanley.**

(*Staring, baffled*) What in hell are they?

**Blanche.**

(*On the floor gathering them up*) Poems a dead boy wrote. I hurt him the way that you would like to hurt me, but you can't! I'm not young and vulnerable any more. But my young husband was and I—never mind about that! Just give them back to me!

**Stanley.**

What do you mean by saying you'll have to burn them?

**Blanche.**

I'm sorry, I must have lost my head for a moment. Every-one has something he won't let others touch because of their—intimate nature . . . (*She now seems faint with exhaustion and she sits down with the strong box and puts on a pair of glasses and goes methodically through a*

*large stack of papers*) Ambler & Ambler. Hmmmmm. . . .
Crabtree. . . . More Ambler & Ambler.

**Stanley.**
What is Ambler & Ambler?

**Blanche.**
A firm that made loans on the place.

**Stanley.**
Then it *was* lost on a mortgage?

**Blanche.**
(*Touching her forehead*) That must've been what happened.

**Stanley.**
I don't want no ifs, ands or buts! What's all the rest of them papers? (*She hands him the entire box. He carries it to the table and starts to examine the papers*)

**Blanche.**
(*Picking up a large envelope containing more papers*) There are thousands of papers, stretching back over hundreds of years, affecting Belle Reve as, piece by piece, our improvident grandfathers and father and uncles and brothers exchanged the land for their epic fornications— to put it plainly! (*She removes her glasses with an exhausted laugh*) The four-letter word deprived us of our plantation, till finally all that was left—and Stella can verify that!—was the house itself and about twenty acres of ground, including a graveyard, to which now all but Stella and I have retreated. (*She pours the contents of the envelope on the table*) Here all of them are, all papers! I hereby endow you with them! Take them, peruse them —commit them to memory, even! I think it's wonderfully fitting that Belle Reve should finally be this bunch of old papers in your big, capable hands! . . . I wonder if Stella's come back with my lemon-coke . . . (*She leans back and closes her eyes*)

**Stanley.**
I have a lawyer acquaintance who will study these out.

**Blanche.**
Present them to him with a box of aspirin tablets.

**Stanley.**
(*Becoming somewhat sheepish*) You see, under the Napoleonic code—a man has to take an interest in his wife's affairs—especially now that she's going to have a baby. (*Blanche opens her eyes.*)

**Blanche.**
Stella? Stella going to have a baby? (*Dreamily*) I didn't

know she was going to have a baby! (*She gets up and crosses to the outside door. Stella appears around the corner with a carton from the drugstore. Stanley goes into the bedroom with the envelope and the box. Blanche goes to meet Stella at the foot of the steps to the sidewalk*)

**Blanche.**
Stella, Stella for Star! How lovely to have a baby! It's all right. Everything's all right.

from
PICNIC
by William Inge

Act II
MADGE, HAL

The picnic, an annual Labor Day celebration in a small
town in Kansas, happens offstage. Onstage, a group of
women of varying ages and frustrations circle about an
eligible, magnetic young man who has turned up from
nowhere and charmed them all. Hal Carter, the young
man, is a drifter—not at all like his old college pal, Alan
Seymour, who is reliable, straightforward, and well-to-do.
But there is something about Hal: Millie, a shy, boyish
sixteen-year-old, can talk to him; Mrs. Potts, who is nearly
sixty, bakes cakes for him; Rosemary Sydney, an unmarried schoolteacher who prefers not to think about her
age, is alternately attracted and repelled by him (attracted
when he looks at her, repelled when he pays attention to
someone younger); and Madge, Millie's pretty older sister,
falls in love and elopes with him.

The scene below ends Act II. It is the day of the picnic.
Hal has spent the afternoon sitting on the porch of Madge's
mother's house, entertaining an assortment of neighbors,
most of them women. There was some chatting, some
dancing, some flirting until the pleasant time was spoiled
by Rosemary, who burst out furiously at Hal because he
danced with Madge instead of with her—and because he
and Madge are young. Now Rosemary and the others have
left for the picnic. Hal sits on the porch, defeated and
silent. When Madge, his friend's fiancée, comes quietly onto
the porch, he "shows no recognition of her presence. She
sits on a bench . . . and finally speaks in a soft voice."

**Madge.**

You're a wonderful dancer . . .

**Hal.**

(*Hardly audible*) Thanks.

**Madge.**

. . . and I can tell a lot about a boy by dancing with him.
Some boys, even though they're very smart, or very successful in some other way, when they take a girl in their
arms to dance, they're sort of awkward and a girl feels
sort of uncomfortable.

**Hal.**

(*He keeps his head down, his face in his hands*) Yah.

**Madge.**

But when you took me in your arms—to dance—I had
the most relaxed feeling, that you knew what you were
doing, and I could follow every step of the way.

**Hal.**

Look, baby, I'm in a pretty bad mood. (*He stands suddenly and walks away from her, his hands thrust into
his pockets. He is uncomfortable to be near her, for he
is trembling with insult and rage*)

**Madge.**

You mustn't pay any attention to Miss Sydney. (*Hal is
silent*) Women like her make me mad at the whole female
sex.

**Hal.**

Look, baby, why don't you beat it?

**Madge.**

(*She is aware of the depth of his feelings*) What's the
matter?

**Hal.**

(*Gives up and begins to shudder, his shoulders heaving as
he fights to keep from bawling*) What's the use, baby? I'm
a bum. She saw through me like a goddamn X-ray machine. There's just no place in the world for a guy like
me.

**Madge.**

There's got to be.

**Hal.**

(*With self-derision*) Yah?

**Madge.**

Of course. You're young, and—you're very entertaining.
I mean—you say all sorts of witty things, and I just loved
listening to you talk. And you're strong and—you're very

good-looking. I bet Miss Sydney thought so, too, or she wouldn't have said those things.

**Hal.**

Look, baby, lemme level with you. When I was fourteen, I spent a year in the reform school. How ya like that?

**Madge.**

Honest?

**Hal.**

Yah!

**Madge.**

What for?

**Hal.**

For stealin' another guy's motorcycle. Yah! I *stole* it, I stole it 'cause I wanted to get on the damn thing and go so far away, so fast, that no one'd ever catch up with me.

**Madge.**

I think—lots of boys feel that way at times.

**Hal.**

Then my old lady went to the authorities. (*He mimics his "old lady"*) "I've done everything I can with the boy. I can't do anything more." So off I go to the goddamn reform school.

**Madge.**

(*With all the feeling she has*) Gee!

**Hal.**

Finally some welfare league hauls me out and the old lady's sorry to see me back. Yah! she's got herself a new boy friend and I'm in the way.

**Madge.**

It's awful when parents don't get along.

**Hal.**

I never told that to another soul, not even Seymour.

**Madge.**

(*At a loss*) I—I wish there was something I could say— or *do*.

**Hal.**

Well—that's the Hal Carter story, but no one's ever gonna make a movie of it.

**Madge.**

(*To herself*) Most people would be awfully shocked.

**Hal.**

(*Looking at her, then turning away cynically*) There you are, baby. If you wanta faint—or get sick—or run in the house and lock the doors—go ahead. I ain't stoppin' you. (*There is a silence. Then Madge, suddenly and*

*impulsively, takes his face in her hands and kisses him.
Then she returns her hands to her lap and feels embarrassed. Hal looks at her in amazement*) Baby! What'd you
do?

**Madge.**

I . . . I'm proud you told me.

**Hal.**

(*With humble appreciation*) Baby!

**Madge.**

I . . . I get so tired of being told I'm pretty.

**Hal.**

(*Folding her in his arms caressingly*) Baby, baby, baby.

**Madge.**

(*Resisting him, jumping to her feet*) Don't. We have to
go. We have all the baskets in our car and they'll be waiting. (*Hal gets up and walks slowly to her, their eyes
fastened and Madge feeling a little thrill of excitement as
he draws nearer*) Really—we have to be going. (*Hal takes
her in his arms and kisses her passionately. Then Madge
utters his name in a voice of resignation*) Hal!

**Hal.**

Just be quiet, baby.

**Madge.**

Really . . . We have to go. They'll be waiting.

**Hal.**

(*Picking her up in his arms and starting off. His voice is
deep and firm*) We're not goin' on no goddamn picnic.

from
PICNIC
by William Inge

Act III, scene 1
ROSEMARY, HOWARD

It is after midnight on the night of the Labor Day picnic
(see introductory notes on page 336). "A great harvest
moon shines in the sky, a deep, murky blue. The moon is
swollen and full and casts a pale light on the scene below"
—two porches and the yards between. The time for enjoying the picnic is over, the hangovers have not yet begun;
it is an in-between, edgy time, a time for remembering the
things that went wrong with a day that was meant to be so
pleasant. There is silence, then offstage there is the sound
of a not new Chevrolet chugging to a stop. Howard and
Rosemary enter. He "is a small, thin man, rapidly ap-
proaching middle age. A small-town businessman, he wears
a permanent smile of greeting which, most of the time, is
pretty sincere." She is nearly as old as he, but would never
admit it. Rosemary teaches school, and her social life re-
volves around the group of unmarried teachers whom she
always calls "the girls." Usually her "tone of voice must tell
a man that she is independent of him." But not tonight.
"Wearily, a groggy depression having set in, she makes
her way to the doorstep and drops there, sitting limp." She
"seems preoccupied at first and her responses to Howard
are mere grunts."


**Howard.**
Here we are, honey. Right back where we started from.
**Rosemary.**
(*Her mind elsewhere*) Uhh.
**Howard.**
You were awful nice to me tonight, Rosemary.

340

**Rosemary.**
Uhh.
**Howard.**
Do you think Mrs. Owens suspects anything?
**Rosemary.**
I don't care if she does.
**Howard.**
A businessman's gotta be careful of talk. And after all, you're a schoolteacher. (*Fumbling to get away*) Well, I better be gettin' back to Cherryvale. I gotta open up the store in the morning. Good night, Rosemary.
**Rosemary.**
Uhh.
**Howard.**
(*He pecks at her cheek with a kiss*) Good night. Maybe I should say, good morning. (*He starts off*)
**Rosemary.**
(*Just coming to*) Where you goin', Howard?
**Howard.**
Honey, I gotta get home.
**Rosemary.**
You can't go off without me.
**Howard.**
Honey, talk sense.
**Rosemary.**
You can't go off without me. Not after tonight. *That's* sense.
**Howard.**
(*A little nervous*) Honey, be reasonable.
**Rosemary.**
Take me with you.
**Howard.**
What'd people say?
**Rosemary.**
(*Almost vicious*) To *hell* with what people'd say!
**Howard.**
(*Shocked*) Honey!
**Rosemary.**
What'd people say if I thumbed my nose at them? What'd people say if I walked down the street and showed 'em my pink panties? What do I care what people say?
**Howard.**
Honey, you're not yourself tonight.
**Rosemary.**
Yes, I am. I'm more myself than I ever was. Take me

with you, Howard. If you don't I don't know what I'll do
with myself. I mean it.

**Howard.**
Now look, honey, you better go upstairs and get some
sleep. You gotta start school in the morning. We'll talk
all this over Saturday.

**Rosemary.**
Maybe you won't be back Saturday. Maybe you won't
be back ever again.

**Howard.**
Rosemary, you know better than that.

**Rosemary.**
Then what's the next thing in store for me? To be nice
to the next man, then the next—till there's no one left to
care whether I'm nice to him or not. Till I'm ready for the
grave and don't have anyone to take me there.

**Howard.**
(*In an attempt to be consoling*) Now, Rosemary!

**Rosemary.**
You can't let that happen to me, Howard. I won't let you.

**Howard.**
I don't understand. When we first started going together,
you were the best sport I ever saw, always good for a
laugh.

**Rosemary.**
(*In a hollow voice*) I can't laugh any more.

**Howard.**
We'll talk it over Saturday.

**Rosemary.**
We'll talk it over *now*.

**Howard.**
(*Squirming*) Well—honey—I . . .

**Rosemary.**
You said you were gonna marry me, Howard. You said
when I got back from my vacation, you'd be waitin' with
the preacher.

**Howard.**
Honey, I've had an awful busy summer and . . .

**Rosemary.**
Where's the preacher, Howard? Where is he?

**Howard.**
(*Walking away from her*) Honey, I'm forty-two years old.
A person forms certain ways of livin', then one day it's
too late to change.

**Rosemary.**

(*Grabbing his arm and holding him*) Come back here, Howard. I'm no spring chicken either. Maybe I'm a little older than you think *I* am. I've formed my ways too. But they can be changed. They *gotta* be changed. It's no good livin' like this, in rented rooms, meetin' a bunch of old maids for supper every night, then comin' back home alone.

**Howard.**

*I* know how it is, Rosemary. My life's no bed of roses either.

**Rosemary.**

Then why don't you do something about it?

**Howard.**

I figure—there's some bad things about every life.

**Rosemary.**

There's too much bad about mine. Each year, I keep tellin' myself, is the last. Something'll happen. Then nothing ever does—except I get a little crazier all the time.

**Howard.**

(*Hopelessly*) Well . . .

**Rosemary.**

A *well's* a hole in the ground, Howard. Be careful you don't fall in.

**Howard.**

I wasn't tryin' to be funny.

**Rosemary.**

. . . and all this time you just been leadin' me on.

**Howard.**

(*Defensive*) Rosemary, that's not *so!* I've not been leading you *on*.

**Rosemary.**

I'd like to know what else you call it.

**Howard.**

Well—can't we talk about it Saturday? I'm dead tired and I got a busy week ahead, and . . .

**Rosemary.**

(*She grips him by the arm and looks straight into his eyes*) You gotta marry me, Howard.

**Howard.**

(*Tortured*) Well—honey, I can't marry you *now*.

**Rosemary.**

You can be over here in the morning.

**Howard.**

Sometimes you're unreasonable.

**Rosemary.**

You gotta marry me.

**Howard.**

What'll you do about your job?

**Rosemary.**

Alvah Jackson can take my place till they get someone new from the agency.

**Howard.**

I'll have to pay Fred Jenkins to take care of the store for a few days.

**Rosemary.**

Then get him.

**Howard.**

Well . . .

**Rosemary.**

I'll be waitin' for you in the morning, Howard.

**Howard.**

(*After a few moments' troubled thought*) No.

**Rosemary.**

(*A muffled cry*) Howard!

**Howard.**

I'm not gonna marry anyone that says, "You gotta marry me, Howard." I'm not gonna. (*He is silent. Rosemary weeps pathetic tears. Slowly Howard reconsiders*) If a woman wants me to marry her—she can at least say "please."

**Rosemary.**

(*Beaten and humble*) Please marry me, Howard.

**Howard.**

Well—you got to give me time to think it over.

**Rosemary.**

(*Desperate*) Oh, God! Please marry me, Howard. Please . . . (*She sinks to her knees*) Please . . . Please . . .

**Howard.**

(*Embarrassed by her suffering humility*) Rosemary . . . I . . . I gotta have some time to think it over. You go to bed now and get some rest. I'll drive over in the morning and maybe we can talk it over before you go to school. I . . .

**Rosemary.**

You're not just tryin' to get out of it, Howard?

**Howard.**

I'll be over in the morning, honey.

**Rosemary.**

Honest?

**Howard.**

Yah. I gotta go to the courthouse anyway. We'll talk it over then.

**Rosemary.**

Oh, God, please marry me, Howard. Please.

**Howard.**

(*Trying to get away*) Go to bed, honey. I'll see you in the morning.

**Rosemary.**

Please, Howard!

**Howard.**

I'll see you in the morning. Good night, Rosemary. (*Starting off*)

**Rosemary.**

(*In a meek voice*) Please!

**Howard.**

Good night, Rosemary.

**Rosemary.**

(*After he is gone*) Please.

from
THE RAINMAKER
by N. Richard Nash

Act II
LIZZIE, FILE, (NOAH)

The play is set on a ranch in the West at the time of a
drought, a time when the rich green of the grasslands has
turned a dusty, dead gray and the people are poor and
desperate. Yet the play is a comedy and a romance, and
the playwright insists, "It must never be forgotten that it is
a romance." The hopes of the desperate people are realized
and they are deserving people "filled with love of one
another."

The people are H. C. Curry, his two sons and his
daughter, Lizzie. The ranch is theirs. There is File, the
sheriff's deputy, whom H. C. and his sons have picked as
a likely husband for Lizzie. And there is Starbuck, a
wanderer, a romantic, a mountebank, who claims to be
a rainmaker. His promises are like dreams, but the people
whose lands and lives are touched by drought need
dreams—or belief. Starbuck makes them believe, or hope,
and somehow with belief the dreams, or hopes, are realized. At the end of the play, the rain does come.

No one in the play is more in need of hope than Lizzie
(see notes, page 171). She is unmarried and, she thinks,
unwanted, a woman whom no man will love. Her father
and brothers pin their hopes for her on File. They invite
him to dinner, but he refuses the invitation. Later, he
comes around to apologize—and to make amends for having knocked Lizzie's brother in the eye when the refused
invitation caused a fight. The Currys make certain that
Lizzie and File are left alone. Lizzie has been joking with
her father, pretending to be one of the wide-eyed little girls
who cling to men—and win them. But with File she is
straightforward and serious.

File is a man who wears his thumbs tucked into his belt.
"He is a lean man, reticent, intelligent, in his late thirties.

He smiles wryly at the world and at himself. Perhaps he is a little bitter; if so, his bitterness is leavened by a mischievous humor." However, at the beginning of this scene (two excerpts), he is painfully embarrassed, as is Lizzie. H. C. has walked out of the room, leaving them alone. For a moment, they are unable to meet one another's glance.

The setting is the central downstairs room of the ranch house, a combination of living and dining room.

**Lizzie.**
(*Just to fill the silence*) Would you—do you care for a cup of coffee?

**File.**
No, thank you—I already had my supper.

**Lizzie.**
(*Embarrassed at the mention of "supper"*) Yes—yes, of course.

**File.**
I didn't mean to mention supper . . . sorry I said it.

**Lizzie.**
Lemonade?

**File.**
No, thank you.

**Lizzie.**
(*In agony—talking compulsively*) I make lemonade with limes. I guess if you make it with limes you can't really call it *lemon*-ade, can you?

**File.**
(*Generously—to put her at ease*) You can if you want to. No law against it.

**Lizzie.**
But it's really *lime*-ade, isn't it?

**File.**
Yep—that's what it is. Limeade.

**Lizzie.**
(*Taking his mannish tone*) That's what it is, all right! (*an impasse—nothing more to talk about.*) * * *

**File.**
Was that Jim's drum I been hearin'?

**Lizzie.**
Yes.

**File.**

(*With a dry smile*) Didn't know he was musical.

**Lizzie.**

(*Smiling at his tiny little joke*) Uh—wouldn't you like to sit down—or something?

**File.**

No, thank you . . . (*Referring to the absent Jim and H. C.*) I guess they both knew I was lyin'.

**Lizzie.**

Lying? About what?

**File.**

I didn't come around to apologize to Jim.

**Lizzie.**

What did you come for, File?

**File.**

To get something off my chest. (*His difficulties increasing*) This afternoon—your father—he—uh—(*Diving in*) Well, there's a wrong impression goin' on in the town—that I'm a widower. Well, I'm not.

**Lizzie.**

(*Quietly—trying to ease things for him*) I know that, File.

**File.**

I know you know it—but I gotta say it. (*Blurting it out*) I'm a divorced man.

**Lizzie.**

You don't have to talk about it if you don't . . .

**File.**

(*Interrupting roughly*) Yes, I do! I came to tell the truth. To your father—and to the whole town. I've been denyin' that I'm a divorced man—well, now I admit it. That's all I want to say—(*Angrily*)—and that squares me with everybody.

**Lizzie.**

(*Soberly*) Does it?

**File.**

Yes, it does! And from here on in—if I want to live alone—all by myself—it's nobody's business but my own! (*He has said what he thinks he came to say. And having said it, he turns on his heel and starts to beat a hasty retreat. But Lizzie stops him.*)

**Lizzie.**

(*Sharply*) Wait a minute! (*As he turns*) You're dead wrong!

**File.**

Wrong? How?

**Lizzie.**

(*Hotly*) It's everybody's business!

**File.**

How do you figure that, Lizzie?

**Lizzie.**

Because you owe something to people.

**File.**

I don't owe anything to anybody.

**Lizzie.**

Yes, you do!

**File.**

What?

**Lizzie.**

(*Inarticulate—upset*) I don't know—friendship. If somebody holds out his hand toward you, you've got to reach —and take it.

**File.**

What do you mean I've got to?

**Lizzie.**

(*In an outburst*) Got to! There are too many people alone . . . ! And if you're lucky enough for somebody to want you—for a friend—(*With a cry*) It's an *obligation*! (*Stillness. He is deeply disturbed by what she has said; even more disturbed by her impassioned manner.*)

**File.**

This—this ain't somethin' the two of us can settle by just talkin' for a minute.

**Lizzie.**

(*Tremulously*) No, it isn't.

**File.**

It'll take some time.

**Lizzie.**

Yes. (*A spell has been woven between them. Suddenly it is broken by Noah's entrance. Coming in by way of the front door, he is surprised to see File.*)

**Noah.**

Oh, you here, File?

**File.**

Yeah, I guess I'm here.

**Noah.**

(*Looking for an excuse to leave*) Uh—just comin' in for my feed book. (*He gets one of his ledgers and goes out the front door. It looks as though the charmed moment is lost between them.*)

**File.**

(*Going to the door*) Well.

**Lizzie.**

(*Afraid he will leave*) What were we saying?

**File.**

What were *you* sayin'?

**Lizzie.**

(*Snatching for a subject that will keep him here*) I—you were telling me about your divorce.

**File.**

No—I wasn't . . . (*Then, studying her, he changes his mind*) . . . but I will. (*As he moves a step back into the room*) She walked out on me.

**Lizzie.**

I'm sorry.

**File.**

Yes—with a schoolteacher. He was from Louisville.

**Lizzie.**

(*Helping him get it said*) Kentucky? (*As he nods*) Was she—I guess she was beautiful . . . ?

**File.**

Yes, she was.

**Lizzie.**

(*Her hopes dashed*) That's what I was afr—(*Catching herself*)—that's what I thought.

**File.**

Black hair.

**Lizzie.**

(*Drearily, with an abortive little movement to her un-black hair*) Yes . . . black hair's pretty, all right.

**File.**

I always used to think: If a woman's got pitch-black hair, she's already halfway to bein' a beauty.

**Lizzie.**

(*Agreeing—but without heart*) Oh, yes—at least halfway.

**File.**

And she had black eyes too—and I guess that did the other half. (*Suddenly, intensely—like a dam bursting*) With a schoolteacher, dammit! Ran off with a school-teacher!

**Lizzie.**

What was *he* like?

**File.**

(*With angry intensity*) He had weak hands and near-sighted eyes! And he always looked like he was about ready to faint. And she ran off with *him!* And there *I* was . . . (*A cry of pain and rage*) I'll never understand it!

**Lizzie.**

(*Gently*) Maybe the teacher needed her and you didn't.

**File.**

Sure I needed her!

**Lizzie.**

Did you tell her so?

**File.**

(*Raging*) No, I didn't! Why should I?

**Lizzie.**

(*Astounded*) Why *should* you? Why *didn't* you?

**File.**

Look here! There's one thing I learned. *Be independent!* If you don't *ask* for things—if you don't let on you *need* things—pretty soon you don't need 'em.

**Lizzie.**

(*Desperately*) There are some things you *always* need.

**File.**

(*Doggedly*) I won't ask for anything.

**Lizzie.**

But if you *had* asked her, she might have stayed.

**File.**

I know darn well she mighta stayed. The night she left she said to me: "File, tell me not to go! Tell me don't go!"

**Lizzie.**

(*In wild astonishment*) And you didn't?

**File.**

I tried—I couldn't!

**Lizzie.**

Oh, pride . . . !

**File.**

Look, if a woman wants to go, let her go! If you have to hold her back—*it's no good!*

**Lizzie.**

File, if you had to do it over again . . .

**File.**

(*Interrupting, intensely*) I still wouldn't ask her to stay!

**Lizzie.**

(*In a rage against him*) Just two words—"don't go!" you wouldn't say them?

**File.**

It's not the words! It's beggin'— And I won't beg!

**Lizzie.**

You're a fool! (*It's a slap in the face. A dreadful moment for an overly proud, stubborn man. A dreadful moment*

*for Lizzie. It is a time for drastic measures—or he will
go. Having failed with File on an honest, serious level,
she seizes upon flighty falsity as a mode of behavior.
Precipitously, she becomes Lily Ann Beasley, the flibber-
tigibbet.)*

**Lizzie.**

(*Chattering with false, desperate laughter*) Whatever am
I doing? Getting so serious with you, File! I shoulda
known better—because whenever I do, I put my foot in
it. Because bein' serious— that's not my nature. I'm
really a happy-go-lucky girl—just like any other girl and
I— would you like some grapes?

**File.**

(*Quietly*) No, thank you.

**Lizzie.**

(*Giddily*) They're very good. And so purply and pretty.
We had some right after supper. Oh, I wish you'd been
here to supper. I made such a nice supper. I'm a good
cook—and I just love cookin'. I think there's only one
thing I like better than cookin'. I'll bet you can't guess
what that is! (*As he is silent*) Go on—guess!

**File.**

(*Puzzled at her changed manner*) I don't know.

**Lizzie.**

Readin' a book! I love to read! Do you read very much?

**File.**

(*Watching her as if she were a strange specimen*) No.
Only legal circulars—from Washington.

**Lizzie.**

(*Seizing on any straw to engage him in the nonsensical
chit-chat*) Oh, Washington! I just got through readin' a
book about him! What a great man! Don't you think
Washington was a great man?

**File.**

(*Drily*) Father of our country.

**Lizzie.**

Yes—exactly! And when you think of all he went through!
All that sufferin'! Valley Forge—and all those bleedin'
feet! When you *think* of it!

**File.**

I don't think about it much.

**Lizzie.**

And why should you? A busy man like you! (*More Lily
Ann Beasley than ever*) Oh, my, what a nice tie! I just
die for men in black silk bow ties!

**File.**

(*Quietly—getting angry*) It ain't silk—it's celluloid!

**Lizzie.**

No! I can't believe it! It looks so real—it looks so real!

**File.**

(*Significantly—like a blow*) It ain't real—it's fake!

**Lizzie.**

(*Unable to stop herself*) And when you smile you've got the strongest white teeth!

**File.**

(*Angry*) Quit that!

**Lizzie.**

(*Stunned*) What . . . ?

**File.**

(*Raging*) Quit it! Stop sashayin' around like a dumb little flirt!

**Lizzie.**

(*With a moan*) Oh, no . . .

**File.**

Silk tie—strong white teeth! What do you take me for? And what do you take yourself for?

**Lizzie.**

(*In flight, in despair*) I was trying to—trying to . . .

**File.**

Don't be so damn ridiculous! Be yourself!

from
BIOGRAPHY
by S. N. Behrman

Act II
MARION FROUDE, RICHARD KURT

Marion Froude, a painter of portraits, is writing her autobiography and she is enjoying the job, for the most part
because a chapter dealing with the present would include
her editor-collaborator, Richard Kurt, a young journalist.
(For introductory comments about the play, see page 238.)
There would be conflict, too, in a chapter dealing with
Marion's life at the moment. An old friend, Bunny Nolan,
has asked her to stop writing the book—the things she
could reveal would ruin his chances to be elected to the
Senate. Indeed, Nolan has just stomped out of Marion's
studio after an angry argument with Kurt. Now Marion
must decide what to do about the book. Her collaboration
with the young painter has been a sparring match from the
first. Marion, at thirty-five or so, is relaxed, tolerant, and
mature. Kurt, at twenty-five, is intense and dedicated. "He
has the essential audacity which comes from having seen
the worst happen, from having endured the keenest pain.
He has the hardness of one who knows that he can be dev-
astated by pity, the bitterness which comes from having
seen, in early youth, justice thwarted and tears unavailing,
the self-reliance which comes from having seen everything
go in a disordered world save one, stubborn, unyielding
core of belief—at everything else he laughs, in this alone
he trusts. He has the intensity of a fanatic and the carelessness of a vagabond." He and Marion are different indeed, yet they are also attracted to one another, a situation
which the playwright develops in the scene below. Nolan
has slammed out of the room and Marion turns to Kurt.

**Marion.**

(*really distressed*) This is awful!

**Kurt.**

(*highly elated*) It's wonderful!

**Marion.**

But I'm very fond of Bunny. Oh dear! I'll telephone him tonight—

**Kurt.**

(*grimly*) Over my dead body!

**Marion.**

Can it be, Dickie, that I control the election of senators from Tennessee? (*Sits right end of sofa left.*)

**Kurt.**

(*after a moment*) How could you ever have loved a stuffed-shirt like that!

**Marion.**

He wasn't a stuffed-shirt. That's the funny part. He was charming. He was a charming boy. Rather thin. Rather reticent. He was much nicer than you, as a matter of fact. . . .

**Kurt.**

I'm sure he was!

**Marion.**

He was much less violent!

**Kurt.**

(*sits*) Hypocritical old buccaneer!

**Marion.**

He used to work hard all day and at night he studied law. We used to walk the country lanes and dream about the future. He was scared—he was wistful. How did he emerge into this successful, ambitious, over-cautious—mediocrity? How do we all emerge into what we are? How did I emerge into what I am? I've dug up some of my old diaries. I was a tremulous young girl. I was eager. I believe I was naïve. Look at me now! Time, Dickie . . . What will you be at forty? A bond-holder and a commuter . . . Oh, Dickie!

**Kurt.**

(*tensely*) I'll never be forty!

**Marion.**

(*laughing*) How will you avoid it?

**Kurt.**

(*same tone*) I'll use myself up before I'm forty.

**Marion.**

Do you think so? I don't think so. (*Rises.*) I sometimes

wake up on certain mornings feeling absolutely—immortal! Indestructible! One is perpetually reborn, I think, Dickie. Everyone should write one's life, I think—but not for publication. For oneself. A kind of spiritual spring-cleaning!

**Kurt.**

The Ego preening!

**Marion.**

(*sitting right arm of sofa left*) Well, why not? After all, one's ego is all one really has.

**Kurt.**

Reminiscence is easy. So is anticipation. It's the *present* that's difficult, and most people are too lazy or too indifferent to cope with it.

**Marion.**

It's natural for you to say that—at your age one has no past—and no future either, because the intimation of the future comes only with the sense of the past . . .

**Kurt.**

(*with sudden bitterness*) *I* see the past as an *evil thing*—to be extirpated.

**Marion.**

How awful! (*Pause.*) Why?

**Kurt.**

That's not important.

**Marion.**

(*rises*) You freeze up so whenever I try to find out anything about you. I'm not used to that. Usually people open up to me—I'm a born confidante. But not you. . . . I'm interested too, because in an odd way I've become very fond of you.

**Kurt.**

My life's very dull, I assure you. *My* past lacks completely what you would call *glamour*.

**Marion.**

No, Dickie. I don't believe that. I don't believe that's true of anybody's life.

**Kurt.**

Well, it's true. Moreover, it's true of most people's lives. It's easy for anyone who's lived as you have to make romantic generalizations. It's very pleasant for you to believe them. Well, I shan't disillusion you. (*Turns away from her.*) Why should I? It's not important. (*She is sitting down, smoking a cigarette in a holder, watching him. He becomes conscious that she is studying him.*)

**Marion.**

I had no idea you felt this way about me—you despise me, don't you? (*He doesn't answer.*) Don't you?

**Kurt.**

Yes.

**Marion.**

Why?

**Kurt.**

(*rises. Walks away*) Why did we start this?

**Marion.**

You're annoyed at having even momentarily revealed yourself, aren't you? I'll have your secret, Dickie—I'll pluck out the heart of your mystery.

**Kurt.**

Secret! Mystery! More romantic nonsense. I have no secret. Nobody has a secret. There are different kinds of greed, different kinds of ambition—that's all!

**Marion.**

Oh, you simplify too much—really I'm afraid you do. Tell me—why do you disapprove of me? Is it—as Bunny does—on moral grounds?

**Kurt.**

(*right end of sofa left—angrily*) You're superficial and casual and irresponsible. You take life, which is a tragic thing, as though it were a trivial bedroom-farce. You're a second-rate artist who's acquired a reputation through vamping celebrities to sit for you.

**Marion.**

(*quietly, she continues smoking*) Go on . . .

**Kurt.**

As an unglamorous upstart who has been forced to make my way, I resent parasitism, that's all!

**Marion.**

Isn't there in biology something about benevolent parasites, Dickie? Many great men, I believe, owe a debt of gratitude to their parasites, as many plants do . . . there are varieties. Again, Dickie, you simplify unduly. It is a defect of the radical and the young.

**Kurt.**

To return to the Honorable Nolan—

**Marion.**

I return to him with relief.

**Kurt.**

He may exert pressure on us, you know.

**Marion.**

How? I'm very interested.

**Kurt.**

Well, for one thing, his future father-in-law might get me fired.

**Marion.**

Could he do that?

**Kurt.**

He might. He might easily. (*Marion sits upright and looks at him.*) Some form of bribery. He might go to my chief and offer him a bigger job—anything.

**Marion.**

All on account of my poor little biography—it seems incredible that anyone would take all this trouble.

**Kurt.**

I'd just like to see them try. I'd just like to, that's all.

**Marion.**

What would you do?

**Kurt.**

Do? I'd make the Honorable Nolan the laughing-stock of the country, and his athletic father-in-law, too. I'd just plaster them, that's what I'd do.

**Marion.**

You sound vindictive.

**Kurt.**

Baby, I am vindictive!

**Marion.**

Funny, I'm just amused. . . .

**Kurt.**

Well, everything's a spectacle to you! (*Turns away from her.*) God, how I hate detachment!

**Marion.**

Your desire to break up Bunny is quite impersonal then.

**Kurt.**

Surgical. Just as impersonal as that.

**Marion.**

You're a funny boy, Dickie.

**Kurt.**

(*turns away from her*) I'm not funny and I'm not a boy. You've been around with dilettantes so long you don't recognize seriousness when you see it.

**Marion.**

But it's the serious people who are funny, Dickie! Look at Bunny.

**Kurt.**

(*faces her*) Yes, look at him! An epitome of the brainless muddle of contemporary life, of all the self-seeking second-raters who rise to power and wield power. That's why I'm going to do him in! (*The phone rings—for a moment they pay no attention to it.*) It's the most beautiful chance anybody ever had, and I'd just like to see them try and stop me. (*Phone keeps ringing. Marion answers it.*)

**Marion.**

Yes . . . yes . . . certainly. (*To Kurt—a bit surprised.*) It's for you . . . (*She hands him hand-receiver.*)

**Kurt.**

(*takes phone and talks from rear of sofa*) Yes. Hello . . . sure. Well, what about it? . . . Oh, you want to talk to me about it, do you? . . . I thought you would . . . I'll be around . . . sure . . . so long. (*He hangs up.*) They've begun! (*He is almost gay with the heady scent of battle.*)

**Marion.**

What do you mean?

**Kurt.**

That was my chief. He wants to talk to me about your story. Kinnicott's begun to put the screws on him. He's going to ask me to kill it. All right—I'll kill it!

**Marion.**

(*faintly*) I can't believe it.

**Kurt.**

Neff's had a call from the father-in-law—

**Marion.**

Did he say so?

**Kurt.**

No, but you can bet he has!

**Marion.**

I must say this puts my back up.

**Kurt.**

I'll make a fight for it to keep my job. But if he's stubborn I'll tell him to go to Hell—and go to a publisher with your manuscript. And if I don't get quick action that way I'll publish it myself—I'll put every penny I've saved into it.

**Marion.**

But why should you? Why does it mean so much to you?

**Kurt.**

Do you think I'd miss a chance like this? It'll test the caliber of our magazines, of our press, our Senators, our morality—

**Marion.**

All on account of my poor little story—how Vicki would have laughed!

**Kurt.**

(*a spasm of jealousy again*) Who's Vicki?

**Marion.**

(*aware of it*) An old friend to whom I'm dedicating the biography.

**Kurt.**

Yeah! (*Sits beside her, then speaks.*) Where is he now?

**Marion.**

He's dead. (*A pause. She gets up and crosses to center.*) I've always rather despised these contemporary women who publicize their emotions. (*Another moment. She walks upstage. She is thinking aloud.*) And here I am doing it myself. Too much self-revelation these days. Loud-speakers in the confessional. Why should I add to the noise? I think, as far as this story is concerned, I'll call it a day, Dickie.

**Kurt.**

What!

**Marion.**

Let's forget all about it, shall we?

**Kurt.**

If you let me down now, I'll hate you.

**Marion.**

Will you? Why won't you take me into your confidence then? Why won't you tell me about yourself? What are you after?

**Kurt.**

(*after a moment of inhibition decides to reveal his secret dream*) My ambition is to be critic-at-large of things-as-they-are. I want to find out everything there is to know about the intimate structure of things. I want to reduce the whole system to absurdity. I want to laugh the powers that be out of existence in a great winnowing gale of laughter.

**Marion.**

That's an interesting research. Of course it strikes me it's vitiated by one thing—you have a preconceived idea of what you will find. In a research biased like that from the start, you are apt to overlook much that is noble and generous and gentle.

**Kurt.**
(*challenging and bitter*) Have you found generosity and gentleness and nobility?

**Marion.**
A good deal—yes.

**Kurt.**
Well, I haven't!

**Marion.**
I'm sorry for you.

**Kurt.**
You needn't be. Reserve your pity for weaklings. I don't need it!

**Marion.**
Are you so strong? (*A pause. Kurt doesn't answer.*) How old are you, Dickie?

**Kurt.**
(*Turns away*) What difference does that make?

**Marion.**
Who do you live with?

**Kurt.**
I live alone.

**Marion.**
Are you in love with anybody?

**Kurt.**
No.

**Marion.**
Where are your parents?

**Kurt.**
They're dead.

**Marion.**
Long?

**Kurt.**
My mother is. I hardly remember her. Just barely remember her.

**Marion.**
Your father? (*He doesn't answer.*) Do you remember your father?

**Kurt.**
(*in a strange voice*) Yes. I remember him all right.

**Marion.**
What did your father do?

**Kurt.**
He was a coal miner.

**Marion.**
Oh! Won't you tell me about him? I'd like to know.

**Kurt.**

I was a kid of fourteen. There was a strike. One day my father took me out for a walk. Sunny spring morning. We stopped to listen to an organizer. My father was a mild little man with kind of faded, tired blue eyes. We stood on the outskirts of the crowd. My father was holding me by the hand. Suddenly somebody shouted: The militia! There was a shot. Everybody scattered. My father was bewildered—he didn't know which way to turn. A second later he crumpled down beside me. He was bleeding. He was still holding my hand. He died like that. . . . (*A moment. He concludes harshly—coldly—like steel.*) Are there any other glamorous facts of my existence you would like to know?

**Marion.**

(*Stirred to her heart*) You poor boy . . . I knew there was something . . . I knew . . . !

**Kurt.**

(*hard and ironic*) It's trivial really. People exaggerate the importance of human life. One has to die. (*Turns to her.*) The point is to have fun while you're alive, isn't it? Well, you've managed. I congratulate you!

**Marion.**

(*her heart full*) Dickie darling—why are you so bitter against me? Why against me?

**Kurt.**

Do you want to know that too? Well, it's because—(*His voice rises. She suddenly doesn't want him to speak.*)

**Marion.**

Hush, dearest—hush—don't say any more—I understand—not any more. . . . (*His defenses vanish suddenly. He sinks to his knees beside her, his arms around her.*)

**Kurt.**

Marion, my angel!

**Marion.**

(*infinitely compassionate, stroking his hair*) Dickie—Dickie—Dickie . . . Why have you been afraid to love me?

from
SEPARATE TABLES
by Terence Rattigan

"Table by the Window," scene 3
MISS COOPER, JOHN, (DOREEN)

The desperation of loneliness, that frustration of people
somehow shut off from one another, which provides the
thematic link between the two parts of *Separate Tables,* is
most sharply stated in the scene reprinted below. (For
introductory comments on the play, see page 274.) The
playwright's spokesman is Miss Cooper, the manager of
the boarding house. She is "youngish, with a rather
masculine appearance, and a quiet manner." Alone herself, she has a sympathetic understanding of the separate-
ness which is the affliction and way of life of the men and
women for whom her hotel is, at least, a place to be. Miss
Cooper tries to give them more than that; along with room
and board, she offers, to those who can accept them,
understanding and warmth—a "Good morning" or "How
are you?" that is not the mere mouthing of words. In
doing this, of course, she also fills some of the gaps in
her own life. Her concern for John Malcolm, however, is
quite different. She has given him love and he in turn has
given her at least a grateful affection. When John's former
wife, Anne, seeks him out at the hotel, Miss Cooper
understands why he has had no more than affection to
give. He has not forgotten his love for Anne and, though
he rejects Anne's efforts at a reconciliation, Miss Cooper
resolves to do something about the bitter pride which
stands between him and his wife.

The time is morning; the place, the dining room of
the hotel. Miss Cooper, left alone after breakfast, has
slumped wearily into a chair. She has spent most of the
night talking to Anne, for the conversation between Anne
and John, which began in this room at supper, ended in
a fight. As he had eight years before, John struck out
viciously at Anne, knocking her to the floor. Now Anne is

363

preparing to leave. John has not been seen since the fight.

Miss Cooper pours herself some coffee, "sips it, and then lets her head fall wearily forward on to her chest, in an attitude of utter exhaustion. After a moment John comes in slowly from the hall. After a look around he walks up to her quietly."

**John.**

(*in a low voice*) Pat, I must see you for a moment. (*Miss Cooper opens her eyes and looks up at him. She jumps to her feet and takes him in.*)

**Miss C.**

Are you all right?

**John.**

Yes, I'm all right.

**Miss C.**

Where did you go?

**John.**

I don't know. I walked a long way.

**Miss C.**

Were you out all night?

**John.**

No. I sat in a shelter for a time. Pat, I've got to have some money. I'm broke to the wide. I spent my whole week's check in the Feathers last night—

**Miss C.**

How much do you want?

**John.**

Enough to get me on a train and keep me some place for a few days. Three or four pounds, I suppose. Can you let me have it, Pat?

**Miss C.**

You won't need it, John. She's going.

**John.**

Are you sure?

**Miss C.**

Yes.

**John.**

Where is she now?

**Miss C.**

In my office. It's all right. She won't come in here. (*She feels his clothes*) Did you get very wet?

**John.**
Yes, I suppose so. It's dried off now.

**Miss C.**
You'd better sit down and have some breakfast. Your hands are like ice. (*She rings a bell.*)

**John.**
I don't want anything to eat. Just some tea.

**Miss C.**
All right. Now sit down. Straighten your tie a bit, and turn your collar down. That's better. Now you look quite respectable. (*She pulls out a chair for John to sit down at his table. Doreen comes in.*)

**Doreen.**
Yes, miss? (*Seeing John*) Oh, you back? I suppose you think you can have breakfast at this time?

**Miss C.**
Just some tea, Doreen—that's all.

**Doreen.**
Okey doke. (*She goes into the kitchen.*)

**Miss C.**
She'll have to go, that girl. (*She turn to John*) Well, that was a fine way to behave, dashing out into the night, and scaring us out of our wits—

**John.**
Us?

**Miss C.**
Oh, yes. She was scared too. I stopped her from calling the police.

**John.**
So you talked, did you?

**Miss C.**
Most of the night. She was a bit hysterical and needed quieting. I didn't want to get a docter.

**John.**
Did I—Pat, tell me the truth—did I hurt her?

**Miss C.**
Her throat? No.

**John.**
She fell though, didn't she? I seem to remember pushing her, and her falling and hitting her head—or perhaps I'm confusing it with—

**Miss C.**
(*Firmly*) She's as right as rain. There isn't a mark on her of any kind.

**John.**

(*Murmuring*) Thank God. (*Doreen comes in with a pot of tea and a plate.*)

**Doreen.**

I brought you some digestive biscuits. I know you like them.

**John.**

Thank you. Thank you, Doreen, very much.

**Doreen.**

Had a tumble or something? You've got mud all over your arm.

**John.**

What? Oh, yes. So I have. Yes, I remember now. I fell down last night in the dark.

**Doreen.**

Give it to me after and I'll get it off. (*She goes out.*)

**Miss C.**

I should have seen that. I'm sorry.

**John.**

It's all right. They'll just think I was drunk. How is she this morning?

**Miss C.**

A bit shaky. Quieter, though. Did you know she took drugs?

**John.**

Drugs? What sort of drugs?

**Miss C.**

Oh, just those things that make you sleep. Only she takes about three times the proper dose and takes them in the day too.

**John.**

How long has this been going on?

**Miss C.**

About a year, I gather.

**John.**

The damn little fool. Why does she do it?

**Miss C.**

(*Shrugging*) Why do you go to the Feathers? (*Pause*) Yes—there's not all that much to choose between you, I'd say. When you're together you slash each other to pieces, and when you're apart you slash yourselves to pieces. All told, it's quite a problem. (*Pause.*)

**John.**

Why didn't she tell me about this last night?

**Miss C.**

Because she's what she is, that's why. If she'd shown you

she was unhappy, she'd have had to show you how much she needed you, and that she'd never do—not her—not in a million years. Of course that's why she lied about coming down here. I've got a rather bad conscience about that, you know. I should never have told you. Just a flash of jealousy, I suppose. I'm sorry.

**John.**

What time is she leaving?

**Miss C.**

She's only waiting now to get some news of you. I was just going to start ringing up the hospitals. She asked me to do that.

**John.**

I see. Well, when I've finished this I'll slip out somewhere. You can tell her that I'm all right. Then when she's gone you can give me a ring.

**Miss C.**

You don't think you might tell her that yourself? (*Pause.*)

**John.**

No.

**Miss C.**

It's your business, of course, but I think if I were in your place I'd want to.

**John.**

(*Savagely*) You don't know what it's like to be in my place. You can't even guess.

**Miss C.**

(*Quietly*) I think I can. Gosh, I'm tired. I shouldn't be sitting here gossiping with you. I've got work to do. You'd better let me tell her you're here.

**John.**

No, Pat, don't. Give me one good reason why I should ever see her again. Just one reason—

**Miss C.**

All right. Just one then. And God knows it's not for me to say it. Because you love her and because she needs your help. (*Pause.*)

**John.**

(*Suspiciously*) What went on between you two last night? How did she win you over?

**Miss C.**

She didn't win me over, for heaven's sake. Feeling the way I do, do you think she could? Anyway, to do her justice, she didn't even try. She didn't give me an act and

I could see her as she is, all right. I think all you've ever
told me about her is probably true. She *is* vain and
spoiled and selfish and deceitful. Of course, with you
being in love with her, you look at all those faults like
in a kind of distorting mirror, so that they seem like
monstrous sins and drive you to—well—the sort of
thing that happened last night. Well, I just see them as
ordinary human faults, that's all—the sort of faults a
lot of people have—mostly women, I grant, but some
men too. I don't like them but they don't stop me feeling
sorry for a woman who's unhappy and desperate and
ill and needing help more than anyone I have ever known.
Well? Shall I call her in?

**John.**

No. Pat. No. Don't interfere in this. Just let her go back
to London and her own life, and leave me to live the
rest of mine in peace.

**Miss C.**

(*Quietly*) That'd be fine, John, if you'd just tell me a
little something first. Exactly what kind of peace *are*
you living in down here?

**John.**

A kind of peace, anyway.

**Miss C.**

Is it? Is it even really living? (*He makes no reply*) Is it,
John? Be honest, now. Oh, I know there's your work and
your pals at the Feathers and—well—me—but is it even
living? (*Pause.*)

**John.**

(*Brusquely, at length*) It'll do.

**Miss C.**

(*With a faint laugh*) Thank you. I'm glad you didn't
hand me one of those tactful tarradiddles. I *did* try—
you know—when we first began—you and I—all that
time ago—I *did* try to help you to get back into some
sort of life. As a matter of fact I tried very hard—

**John.**

I know you did.

**Miss C.**

It didn't take me long, though, to see I hadn't a hope.

**John.**

Don't blame me for that, Pat. Circumstances, as they say,
outside my control—

**Miss C.**

Outside your control? Yes. That's right. (*Quite brightly*)

When you think of it it seems really rather a pity you two ever met, doesn't it?

**John.**

Yes. A great pity.

**Miss C.**

(*Brightly*) If you hadn't, she'd have been a millionairess, and you'd have been Prime Minister, and I'd have married Mr. Hopkins from the bank, and then we'd have all been happy. I'm going into my office now and I'm going to tell her you're here. I'll have a word with Mr. Fowler first, about a room he didn't take up, so if you want to skedaddle, you can. The door's through there and the street's outside, and down the street is the Feathers. It's a bit early, but I've no doubt they'll open for you. (*She goes into the lounge. As she goes:*) Oh, Mr. Fowler, I'm so sorry to bother you, but I just want to have a word— (*The door closes behind her. Left alone, John stands in evident doubt and irresolution.*)

from
# THE DARK AT THE TOP OF THE STAIRS
by William Inge

Act II
LOTTIE, CORA

"The dark" is the fear that a child feels when the lights
are out. "Why are you so afraid?" he is asked. He answers,
" 'Cause . . . you can't see what's in front of you. And it
might be something awful."

Men, too, know this fear of the unseen that lies ahead.
That is the theme of the play, and it is resolved when the
man, like the child, can say "I'm not afraid . . . if someone's with me." William Inge uses several characters and
interwoven plots to illustrate and reiterate his theme.
There is Sonny, the little boy who is actually afraid of the
dark at the top of the stairs. There is Sammy, a young
man who has no one to count on and kills himself (see
scene on page 87). The central plot involves Rubin
Flood, a seemingly independent and certainly strong-
tempered man, who has never been able to bring himself
to admit his fears to his wife. Instead Rubin fights with
her—about money and the way to treat their children.
After one such fight, he leaves and it seems that he does
not mean to come back. His wife, Cora, waits as she has
waited before; she leans on her children and calls for the
help of her sister and brother-in-law, Lottie and Morris.
Cora envies Lottie's quiet, reliable husband until Lottie
confesses that her marriage is something less than ideal.
That conversation is in the scene below. Afterwards, Cora
feels less sorry for herself, and, when Rubin comes home
and at last is able to turn to her for support and love, she
is ready to help him face the darkness.

Cora is in her thirties and still pretty. Lottie is bigger,
heavier, and a few years older. Her dress is gaudy and she
wears a great deal of costume jewelry. The setting is the
living room of the Floods' comfortable old house in
Oklahoma City in the early 1920's. The time is midevening.

Lottie's husband, Morris, has decided to go for a walk.
She follows him to the door and calls after him.

**Lottie.**

Oh. Well, don't be gone long. We've got to get started
back soon.

**Cora.**

Oh, please don't talk about going.

**Lottie.**

My God, Cora, we can't stay here all night. (*She peers
out the window now, wondering about Morris*) Morris
is funny, Cora. Sometimes he just gets up like that and
walks away. I never know why. Sometimes he's gone for
hours at a time. He says the walk helps his digestion,
but I think it's because he just wants to get away from
me at times. Did you ever notice how he is with people?
Like tonight. He sat there when all the young people
were here, and he didn't say hardly a word. His mind
was a thousand miles away. Like he was thinking about
something. He seems to be always thinking about something.

**Cora.**

Morris is nice to you. You've got no right to complain.

**Lottie.**

He's nice to me . . . in *some* ways.

**Cora.**

Good heavens, Lottie! He gave you those red patent-
leather slippers, and that fox neckpiece . . . you should
be grateful.

**Lottie.**

I know, but . . . there's *some* things he hasn't given me.

**Cora.**

Lottie! That's not his fault. You've got no right to hold
that against him!

**Lottie.**

Oh, it's just fine for you to talk. You've got two nice
kids to keep you company. What have I got but a house
full of cats?

**Cora.**

Lottie, you always claimed you never wanted children.

**Lottie.**

Well . . . what else can I say to people?

**Cora.**
(*This is something of a revelation to her*) I just never knew.

**Lottie.**
(*Having suddenly decided to say it*) Cora . . . I can't let you and the kids come over and live with us.

**Cora.**
(*This is a blow to her*) Oh . . . Lottie.

**Lottie.**
I'm sorry, Cora. I just can't do it.

**Cora.**
Lottie, I was depending on you . . .

**Lottie.**
Maybe you've depended on me too much. Ever since you were a baby, you've run to me with your problems, and now I've got problems of my own.

**Cora.**
What am I going to do, Lottie?

**Lottie.**
Call up Rubin and ask him to come back. Beg him to come back, if you have to get down on your knees.

**Cora.**
I mustn't do that, Lottie.

**Lottie.**
Why not?

**Cora.**
Because we just can't keep from fighting, Lottie. You know that. I just don't think it's right, our still going on that way.

**Lottie.**
Do you still love him?

**Cora.**
Oh . . . don't ask me, Lottie.

**Lottie.**
Do you?

**Cora.**
Oh . . . yes.

**Lottie.**
Cora, I don't think you should listen to the stories those old Werpel sisters tell you.

**Cora.**
He's as good as admitted it, Lottie.

**Lottie.**
Well, Cora, I don't think it means he likes you any the less, because he's seen Mavis Pruitt a few times.

**Cora.**
No . . . I know he loves me.

**Lottie.**
(*Asking very cautiously*) Does he still want to be intimate?

**Cora.**
That's only animal, Lottie. I couldn't indulge myself that way if I didn't feel he was being honorable.

**Lottie.**
(*Breaks into a sudden raucous laugh*) My God, a big handsome buck like Rubin! Who cares if he's honorable?

**Cora.**
(*A little shocked*) Lottie!

**Lottie.**
(*We see now a sudden lewdness in Lottie that has not been discernible before*) Cora, did you hear what the old maid said to the burglar? You see, the burglar came walking into her bedroom with this big, long billy club and . . .

**Cora.**
Lottie!

**Lottie.**
(*Laughing so hard she can hardly finish the story*) And the old maid . . . she was so green she didn't know what was happening to her, she said . . .

**Cora.**
Lottie! That's enough. That's enough.

**Lottie.**
(*Shamed now*) Shucks, Cora. I don't see what's wrong in having a little fun just telling stories.

**Cora.**
Sometimes you talk shamefully, Lottie, and when I think of the way Mama and Papa brought us up . . .

**Lottie.**
Oh, Mama and Papa, Mama and Papa! Maybe they didn't know as much as we gave them credit for.

**Cora.**
You're changed since you were a girl, Lottie.

**Lottie.**
What if I am!

**Cora.**
I never heard such talk.

**Lottie.**
Well, that's all it is. It's only talk. Talk, talk, talk.

**Cora.**
Lottie, are you sure you can't take us in?

**Lottie.**

It'd mean the end of my marriage too, Cora. You don't understand Morris. He's always nice and quiet around people, so afraid of hurting people's feelings. But he's the most nervous man around the house you ever saw. He'd try to make the best of it if you and the kids came over, but he'd go to pieces. I know he would.

**Cora.**

Honest?

**Lottie.**

I'm not joking, Cora. My God, you're not the only one who has problems. Don't think that for a minute.

**Cora.**

A few moments ago, you said *you* had problems, Lottie . . .

**Lottie.**

Problems enough.

**Cora.**

Tell me, Lottie.

**Lottie.**

Oh, why should I?

**Cora.**

Doesn't Morris ever make love to you any more?

**Lottie.**

(*It takes her several moments to admit it*) . . . No. It's been over three years since he even touched me . . . that way.

**Cora.**

(*Another revelation*) Lottie!

**Lottie.**

It's the God's truth, Cora.

**Cora.**

Lottie! What's wrong?

**Lottie.**

How do I know what's wrong? How does anyone ever know what's wrong with anyone else?

**Cora.**

I mean . . . is there another woman?

**Lottie.**

Not unless she visits him from the spirit world. (*This releases her humor again and she is diverted by another story*) Oh, say, Cora, did I tell you about this woman over in Oklahoma City who's been holding séances? Well, Marietta went to her and . . . (*But suddenly, again, she loses her humor and makes another sad admission*) Oh, no, there isn't another woman. Sometimes I wish there was.

**Cora.**
Lottie, you don't mean that.

**Lottie.**
How the hell do *you* know what I mean? He's around the house all day long, now that he's got his dental office in the dining room. Day and night, day and night. Sometimes I get tired of looking at him.

**Cora.**
Oh, Lottie . . . I'd always felt you and Morris were so devoted to each other. I've always felt you had an almost perfect marriage.

**Lottie.**
Oh, we're still devoted, still call each other "honey," just like we did on our honeymoon.

**Cora.**
But what happened? Something must have happened to . . .

**Lottie.**
Did you notice the way Morris got up out of his chair suddenly and just walked away, with no explanation at all? Well, something inside Morris did the same thing several years ago. Something inside him just got up and went for a walk, and never came back.

**Cora.**
I . . . just don't understand.

**Lottie.**
Sometimes I wonder if maybe I've been too bossy. Could be. But then, I always supposed that Morris *liked* me because I was bossy.

**Cora.**
I always envied you, having a husband you could boss.

**Lottie.**
Yes, I can boss Morris because he just isn't there any more to fight back. He doesn't care any more if I boss him or not.

**Cora.**
Just the same, he never hit you.

**Lottie.**
I wish he would.

**Cora.**
Lottie!

**Lottie.**
I do. I wish to God someone *loved* me enough to hit me.

You and Rubin fight. Oh, God, I'd like a good fight. Anything'd be better than this *nothing*. Morris and I go around always being so sweet to each other, but sometimes I wonder maybe he'd like to kill me.

**Cora.**

Lottie, you don't mean it.

**Lottie.**

Do you remember how Mama and Papa used to caution us about men, Cora?

**Cora.**

Yes, I remember.

**Lottie.**

My God, they had me so afraid of ever giving in to a man, I was petrified.

**Cora.**

So was I.

**Lottie.**

Yes, you were until Rubin came along and practically raped you.

**Cora.**

Lottie! I don't want Sonny to hear talk like that.

**Lottie.**

Why not? Let him hear!

**Cora.**

(*Newly aghast at her sister's boldness*) Lottie!

**Lottie.**

Why do we feel we always have to protect kids?

**Cora.**

Keep your voice down. Rubin never did anything like that.

**Lottie.**

Didn't he?

**Cora.**

Of course not!

**Lottie.**

My God, Cora, he had you pregnant inside of two weeks after he started seeing you.

**Cora.**

Sssh.

**Lottie.**

I never told. I never even told Morris. My God, do you remember how Mama and Papa carried on when they found out?

**Cora.**

I remember.

**Lottie.**

And Papa had his stroke just a month after you were married. Oh, I just thought Rubin was the wickedest man alive.

**Cora.**

I never blamed Rubin for that. I was crazy in love with him. He just swept me off my feet and made all my objections seem kinda silly. He even made Mama and Papa seem silly.

**Lottie.**

Maybe I shoulda married a man like that. I don't know. Maybe it was as much my fault as Morris'. Maybe I didn't . . . respond right . . . from the very first.

**Cora.**

What do you mean, Lottie?

**Lottie.**

Cora, I'll tell you something. Something I've never told another living soul. I never did enjoy it the way some women . . . say they do.

**Cora.**

Lottie! You?

**Lottie.**

Why do you say *me* like that? Because I talk kinda dirty at times? But that's all it is, is talk. I talk all the time just to convince myself that I'm alive. And I stuff myself with victuals just to feel I've got something inside me. And I'm full of all kinds of crazy curiosity about . . . all the things in life I seem to have missed out on. Now I'm telling you the truth, Cora. Nothing ever really happened to me while it was going on.

**Cora.**

Lottie . . .

**Lottie.**

That first night Morris and I were together, right after we were married, when we were in bed together for the first time, after it was all over, and he had fallen asleep, I lay there in bed wondering what in the world all the cautioning had been about. Nothing had happened to me at all, and I thought Mama and Papa musta been makin' things up.

**Cora.**

Oh, Lottie!

**Lottie.**

So, don't come to me for sympathy, Cora. I'm not the person to give it to you.

# Chapter IV

## Character Development in Two or More Scenes

Groups of scenes for the same characters.

To exhibit true action in a part, is to do everything allotted by an author to the character represented, in a manner exactly conformable to what the person himself wou'd or ought to have done in it, under every circumstance and in every situation thro' which the action of the play successively carries him.

John Hill, *The Actor, a Treatise on the Art of Playing* (1750)

# STREET SCENE
## by Elmer Rice

Two Scenes from Acts II and III
ROSE, SAM

The setting for the play is a street in New York, a run-down
street with an ugly brownstone "walk-up" apartment house
flanked by a storage warehouse and the shell of another
apartment building which the wreckers are demolishing.
The characters are the people who live on the street or
pass through it—husbands and wives, children and old
men, Italians, Irish, Germans, Jews, and Russians, lovers
and laborers and dreamers. They are seen against the
background of the street and their voices are heard above
the sounds of the city: "the distant roar of El trains,
automobile sirens and the whistles of boats on the river;
the rattle of trucks and the indeterminate clanking of metal;
fire engines, ambulances, musical instruments, a radio,
dogs barking, and human voices calling, quarreling, and
screaming with laughter. The noises are subdued and in the
background, but they never wholly cease."

The time is June, about 1929. It is summer, hot and
sticky, a time when the street is a refuge from close
rooms and every window of every apartment is open so
that life inside and in the street are mingled and all one.

One of the many plots woven together in *Street Scene*
concerns Sam, the son of a Jewish immigrant family, and
Rose, whose mother is the neighborhood scandal. Sam and
Rose are young; both long to escape the drabness of the
street. Sam is an idealist and a cynic, blessed and cursed
with a brilliant mind, in search of causes and beliefs. Rose
is more realistic; she wants the comfort, security, and
happiness that she believes will come with money and
moving to a better neighborhood, but she has to decide
whether these advantages are worth a marriage—or an
affair—with a man she does not love. Though Sam and
Rose are drawn to each other, many things stand between

381

them. The two scenes below spotlight important moments in the development of their friendship.

It is morning. Rose and Sam's sister have met on the steps of the apartment house and Rose has been warned to stay away from Sam, not to get in the way of his studies and career. Sam appears at a window with a cup of coffee and a piece of coffee cake. His sister hurries away, asking Rose not to mention their conversation. Rose agrees.

**Rose.**
(*rising and turning toward Sam*) Sam—
**Sam.**
(*holding out the coffee cake*) Want some coffee cake?
**Rose.**
No. (*Going up the steps*) Sam, there's something I want to ask you, before I forget: Is there any special way you have to act in a synagogue?
**Sam.**
(*eating throughout*) In a synagogue?
**Rose.**
Yes. The funeral I'm going to is in a synagogue, and I thought there might be some special thing you have to do. Like in church, you know, a girl is always supposed to keep her hat on.
**Sam.**
I don't know. I've never in my life been in a synagogue.
**Rose.**
Didn't you ever go to Sunday school, or anything like that?
**Sam.**
No.
**Rose.**
That's funny. I thought everybody went, once in a while. How about when your mother died?
**Sam.**
She was cremated. My parents were always rationalists.
**Rose.**
Didn't they believe in God or anything?
**Sam.**
What do you mean by God?

**Rose.**

(*puzzled*) Well—you know what I mean. What anybody means—God. Somebody that sort of loves us and looks after us, when we're in trouble.

**Sam.**

(*sitting on the window sill*) That's nothing but superstition—the lies that people tell themselves, because reality is too terrible for them to face.

**Rose.**

But, Sam, don't you think it's better to believe in something that makes you a little happy, than not to believe in anything and be miserable all the time?

**Sam.**

There's no such thing as happiness. That's an illusion, like all the rest.

**Rose.**

Then what's the use of living?

**Sam.**

(*brushing the last crumbs off his hands*) Yes, what is the use?

**Rose.**

Why, you oughtn't to talk like that, Sam—a person with all the talent and brains that you've got. I know things aren't just the way you want them to be. But they aren't for anybody. They aren't for me either.

**Sam.**

Then why don't we get out of it, together?

**Rose.**

I don't see just how we could do that, Sam.

**Sam.**

It would be easy enough—ten cents' worth of carbolic acid.

**Rose.**

Why, Sam, you don't mean kill ourselves!

**Sam.**

Is your life so precious to you that you want to cling to it?

**Rose.**

Well, yes. I guess it is.

**Sam.**

Why? Why? What is there in life to compensate for the pain of living?

**Rose.**

There's a lot. Just being alive—breathing and walking around. Just looking at the faces of people you like and hearing them laugh. And seeing the pretty things in the

store windows. And roughhousing with your kid brother.
And—oh, I don't know—listening to a good band, and
dancing. Oh, I'd hate to die! (*Earnestly*) Sam, promise
you won't talk about killing yourself any more.

**Sam.**

What difference would it make to you if I did?

**Rose.**

Don't talk like that, Sam! You're the best friend I've ever
had. (*She puts her hand on his.*)

**Sam.**

I can't think of anything but you.

**Rose.**

There's something I want to ask your advice about, Sam.
It's about what I started to tell you about, last night. A
man I know wants to put me on the stage.

**Sam.**

(*releasing her hand and drawing back*) What man?

**Rose.**

A man that works in the office. He knows a manager and
he says he'll help me get started. You see, what I thought
was, that if I could only get out of here and have a
decent place to live and make a lot of money, maybe
everything would be different, not only for me, but for
Ma and Pop and Willie.

**Sam.**

But don't you know what he wants, this man?

**Rose.**

Nobody gives you anything for nothing, Sam. If you
don't pay for things in one way, you do in another.

**Sam.**

Rose, for God's sake, you mustn't.

(*Vincent Jones comes out of the house.*)

**Rose.**

(*seeing Vincent in the vestibule*) Look out, Sam, here's
that tough from upstairs. (*She goes over to the left of
the stoop.*)

## SECOND SCENE

It is midafternoon of the same day. The street has been
shaken by a scandal and a disaster. Rose's father, learning
that his wife has been having an affair with another man,
has shot and killed her. He has been captured and taken
away, and Rose must begin to make plans for herself and
her young brother. In the few hours since the tragedy,

she has stayed outside among the sympathetic neighbors of the street. Now she has steeled herself to go upstairs to the apartment. As she starts up the front steps, Sam calls after her.

**Sam.**
I must talk to you! What are you going to do, Rose?

**Rose.**
Well, I haven't really had any time to do much thinking. But I really think the best thing I could do would be to get out of New York. You know, like we were saying, this morning—how things might be different if you only had a chance to breathe and spread out a little. Only when I said it, I never dreamed it would be this way.

**Sam.**
If you go, I'll go with you.

**Rose.**
But, Sam dear—

**Sam.**
I don't care anything about my career. It's you—you—I care about. Do you think I can stay here, stifling to death in this slum, and never seeing you? Do you think my life means anything to me without you?

**Rose.**
But, Sam, we've got to be practical about it. How would we manage?

**Sam.**
I don't care what I do. I'll be a day laborer; I'll dig sewers —anything. (*Taking her passionately in his arms*) Rose, don't leave me!

**Rose.**
I like you so much, Sam. I like you better than anybody I know.

**Sam.**
I love you, Rose. Let me go with you!

**Rose.**
It would be so nice to be with you. You're different from anybody I know. But I'm just wondering how it would work out.

**Sam.**
If we have each other, that's the vital thing, isn't it? What else matters but that?

**Rose.**
Lots of things, Sam. There's lots of things to be considered. Suppose something was to happen—well, suppose

I was to have a baby, say. That sometimes happens even when you don't want it to. What would we do then? We'd be tied down then, for life, just like all the other people around here. They all start out loving each other and thinking that everything is going to be fine—and before you know it, they find out they haven't got anything and they wish they could do it all over again—only it's too late.

**Sam.**

It's to escape all that, that we must be together. It's only because we love each other, and belong to each other, that we can find the strength to escape.

**Rose.**

(*shaking her head*) No, Sam.

**Sam.**

Why do you say no?

**Rose.**

It's what you said just now—about people belonging to each other. I don't think people ought to belong to anybody but themselves. I was thinking, that if my mother had really belonged to herself, and that if my father had really belonged to himself, it never would have happened. It was only because they were always depending on somebody else, for what they ought to have had inside themselves. Do you see what I mean, Sam? That's why I don't want to belong to anybody, and why I don't want anybody to belong to me.

**Sam.**

You want to go through life alone?—never loving anyone, never having anyone love you?

**Rose.**

Why, of course not, Sam! I want love more than anything else in the world. But loving and belonging aren't the same thing. (*Putting her arms around him*) Sam dear, listen. If we say good-by now, it doesn't mean that it has to be forever. Maybe someday, when we're older and wiser, things will be different. Don't look as if it was the end of the world, Sam!

**Sam.**

It *is* the end of my world.

**Rose.**

It isn't, Sam! If you'd only believe in yourself a little more, things wouldn't look nearly so bad. Because once you're sure of yourself, the things that happen to you aren't so important. The way I look at it, it's not what you do that matters so much; it's what you are. (*Warmly*) I'm so fond of you, Sam. And I've got such a lot of confidence in you. (*Impulsively*) Give me a nice kiss! [*He takes her in his arms and kisses her. Then, aware again of the street and its watchful eyes, she draws away and turns to go to collect her suitcase.*]

# MORNINGS AT SEVEN
by Paul Osborn

Two Scenes from Acts I and II
MYRTLE, HOMER

Homer and Myrtle are engaged and have been for five years (see introductory notes about the play on page 220). They have seen each other only in the town where Homer works and Myrtle lives. Now, at last, Homer has brought her home to meet the parents, aunts, and uncles that she has heard about so often. She is to stay for the week end; it is an important occasion and one that is not entirely comfortable for anybody.

The first of the scenes below occurs early in Act I. Myrtle has arrived, been introduced to Homer's mother, and been peered at by the uncles and aunts. Now she and Homer have pointedly been "left alone together"—as alone as they can be in a back yard that adjoins another back yard and is overlooked by two back porches, one of them the roosting place of Homer's aunts.

**Myrtle.**
(*sits on stump*) Oh, I think your mother's too wonderful!
**Homer.**
She's pretty nice, all right.
**Myrtle.**
She's so *friendly!* She's just what a mother should be!
**Homer.**
She's pretty nice. (*He sits in chair left center.*)
**Myrtle.**
Oh, she's more than that. She's so—*human!* (*Pause. Homer sits staring before him. Myrtle rises—crosses up of stump—looks at the house right.*) And that's where your Uncle Thor and Aunt Cora live.

388

**Homer.**

And Aunt Arry.

**Myrtle.**

Oh, yes. She's the maiden aunt, isn't she?

**Homer.**

She's the old maid. (*Myrtle gives a little nervous laugh.*)

**Myrtle.**

How long has she been living with them?

**Homer.**

About forty-five to fifty years.

**Myrtle.**

My goodness, that must be pretty hard on your Aunt Cora.

**Homer.**

Why? They're sisters.

**Myrtle.**

(*sits on stump*) Yes, but wouldn't you think a woman would want to live alone—I mean just alone with her husband.

**Homer.**

Aunt Arry didn't have any other place to go when her mother died so Aunt Cora took her in.

**Myrtle.**

Aunt Cora must be pretty nice, I think, to share her home like that.

**Homer.**

Aunt Cora's nice. Not as nice as mother.

**Myrtle.**

Oh, of course not! Of course not! My goodness—Anyway it must be awfully pleasant for all of them to live so close together now that they're getting older. They must be a lot of company for each other.

**Homer.**

Then there's Aunt Esther, too.

**Myrtle.**

Oh, yes, Aunt Esther.

**Homer.**

(*indicating with his finger*) She lives up the street about a block and a half.

**Myrtle.**

And she's married to—?

**Homer.**

Uncle David.

**Myrtle.**

That's right. He's the one who studies all the time.

**Homer.**
He's a very highly educated man. He doesn't like us.

**Myrtle.**
Why not?

**Homer.**
He thinks we're morons.

**Myrtle.**
Morons? Why does he think that?

**Homer.**
I don't know. He says we don't think about important enough things.

**Myrtle.**
Does he think about important things?

**Homer.**
Practically all of the time.

**Myrtle.**
What does he do?

**Homer.**
Doesn't do anything now. He used to be a college professor. But he couldn't get along with the President.

**Myrtle.**
Oh.

**Homer.**
He said the President was a moron too!

**Myrtle.**
Well, he doesn't think *you're* a moron, Homer?

**Homer.**
He thinks we all are except my father.

**Myrtle.**
Why, what's the matter with your father?

**Homer.**
He says my father has something more than the rest of us. Something that makes him question life sometimes.

**Myrtle.**
Oh, I see.

**Homer.**
But the rest of us are all morons. That's why he never comes down here and never lets any of us come up there.

**Myrtle.**
He sounds awfully odd to me.

**Homer.**
He doesn't let Aunt Esther come down either. He's afraid we'll pull her down to our level.

**Myrtle.**
So she never comes down.

**Homer.**

Just when he doesn't know it. She hasn't been down now for over a week though.

**Myrtle.**

(*rises—crosses left—takes off hat and leaves it on porch*) I'm afraid I wouldn't like your Uncle David very well.

**Homer.**

Oh, I think you would. He's awfully nice. I've always sort of liked Uncle David. (*Pause. Myrtle turns to Homer.*)

**Myrtle.**

Homer—do you think your mother liked me?

**Homer.**

She didn't say anything—I guess so though.

**Myrtle.**

Dear, I hope she did. I tried to make a good impression on her. I liked her so much.

**Homer.**

She's pretty nice all right.

**Myrtle.**

It was terribly sweet of her to ask me to come. (*Pause. She takes a quick look at him. Steps toward him.*) Of course I couldn't help but wonder why it just happened that this time you decided to bring me. Because she has asked you to before, hasn't she?

**Homer.**

(*uncomfortable*) Uh-huh. (*Pause.*)

**Myrtle.**

I mean I wondered if anything happened to change your mind about bringing me. (*Slight pause.*)

**Homer.**

(*suddenly*) My mother saw a movie.

**Myrtle.**

A movie?

**Homer.**

Uh-huh.

**Myrtle.**

Oh! (*Pause.*) I guess she wouldn't think very much of me if she knew about us, would she?

**Homer.**

Well, there's no reason for her to know.

**Myrtle.**

She'd think I wasn't very nice.

**Homer.**

Older people don't understand things like that very well, Myrtle. Maybe we'd better not talk about it here.

**Myrtle.**

(*sits on ledge of porch steps*) Oh, all right. Of course your mother must think it's rather funny about you and me though. Being engaged so long. (*Pause.*) Hasn't she ever asked you anything about it? About when we're going to get married, I mean?

**Homer.**

Uh-huh.

**Myrtle.**

What did you say to her?

**Homer.**

I told her you had a job.

**Myrtle.**

Oh!—Well, I was thinking about my job the other day. I was wondering whether I oughtn't to give it up.

**Homer.**

I thought you liked it.

**Myrtle.**

Oh, I do! It's a good job. But—well, I get awfully sick of it sometimes. And after all, I am thirty-nine years old, you know. (*Pause. Myrtle stares at Homer. Nervously, he looks off left.*)

**Homer.**

(*pointing off left*) My father set out most of these trees himself. Transplanted some of them. That one there I remember when it was just a twig he brought over from a house he was building on Maple Street. It must have been fifteen years ago.

**Myrtle.**

My, you wouldn't think it would get that big in fifteen years.

**Homer.**

They grow awfully fast. (*Pause. Homer is staring before him. Myrtle looks at him, nervously.*)

**Myrtle.**

There isn't anything the matter is there, Homer?

**Homer.**

(*shaking his head*) Un-uh—

**Myrtle.**

You're not mad at me about anything, are you?

**Homer.**

No.

**Myrtle.**

You act so funny here. Are you sorry you brought me after all?

**Homer.**

No, I guess not. (*Myrtle smiles at him and suddenly takes his arm and snuggles to him.*)

**Myrtle.**

You silly!

**Homer.**

(*pulling away*) They'll see you from the other house, Myrtle.

**Myrtle.**

Oh! (*She drops his arm. Pause. Then she rises and moves over by the trees left—stands looking off.*) I get awfully lonesome sometimes about this time of day. Or maybe a little later. I guess it's really not so bad at the office. I'm usually pretty busy. But when I get through and have to go to my room—And then when it starts getting dark —(*Turns to Homer.*) Often when I know you're not going to be coming down I don't bother to get myself any supper. I just go right to bed. (*They laugh—embarrassed. Pause.*) Sometimes I wonder how I ever happened to get stuck with that job. It doesn't seem natural. I guess when you come right down to it what a woman really wants is a home of her own. (*Pause. Homer makes no answer. Arry wanders out from the porch at right, casually, as though she were not aware of the others. * * ***)

**Homer.**

That's Aunt Arry. She knows we're here.

**Myrtle.**

Oh!


## SECOND SCENE

It is early the next morning and things have not gone well. Homer's father has left home, determined to "find himself" before it is too late. His Aunt Cora has wangled a twenty-year lease on the house which was to have belonged to Homer and Myrtle. And Homer himself has decided that, with his father gone, his mother needs him and he cannot marry. Now he has to say something to Myrtle. They meet in the yard after breakfast and, as before, they are left alone to talk.

(It might be appropriate to add that Myrtle, like Homer, has something to announce: she is going to have a baby. She tells Homer during the walk they take after the

scene below. That brings Act II to a rousing conclusion—
and assures a happy resolution in Act III.)

**Myrtle.**
(*turns to him with a bright smile*) Hello.
**Homer.**
Hello.
**Myrtle.**
Did you have a good sleep?
**Homer.**
Not very.
**Myrtle.**
Oh, what a shame. I slept ever so nicely.
**Homer.**
Did you?
**Myrtle.**
That's the softest bed I think I ever slept on.
**Homer.**
I thought about things all night.
**Myrtle.**
Now you shouldn't have done that. I told you when you
went to bed that you were to go right to sleep and not
think about anything.
**Homer.**
(*turns away*) I couldn't help it.
**Myrtle.**
That was bad of you.
**Homer.**
(*turns toward her*) Myrtle.
**Myrtle.**
(*stopping him*) Now don't you feel bad about anything,
Homer. I thought it all out last night. I see just what
you mean about not leaving your mother. And I think it's
nice of you. We can go on just the way we have been.
It's been wonderful this way and—
**Homer.**
No, it's not that. It's something else.
**Myrtle.**
What?
**Homer.**
It's—something I've got to tell you before we go. It
wouldn't be fair not to.
**Myrtle.**
What is it? (*She waits—Homer hesitates.*)
**Homer.**
It's not very nice.

**Myrtle.**

My goodness, it can't be so very bad. Now out with it.

**Homer.**

It's about our house.

**Myrtle.**

(*suddenly alarmed*) Nothing's happened to it, Homer! It hasn't burned down or anything—?

**Homer.**

No, it's—all right.

**Myrtle.**

(*her hand to her heart*) My goodness, you scared me. You shouldn't say things like that.

**Homer.**

It's just that— It isn't our house any more. (*Pause. Myrtle looks at him, puzzled.*)

**Myrtle.**

Our house—isn't our house any more?

**Homer.**

My father just rented it to Aunt Cora. She's got a twenty-year lease on it.

**Myrtle.**

On *our* house?

**Homer.**

Uh-huh. I guess he thought we weren't going to be using it. (*Myrtle, bewildered, puts her hand to her head. She turns away slightly, too stunned to understand it yet. Homer watches her. Anguished.*) Gee, Myrtle, I'm so sorry!

**Myrtle.**

(*in a dazed voice*) It's all right. Of course, it's all right—. It really wasn't our house, was it? Not really. It was your father's house. You couldn't expect him to just keep it empty until—He has kept it empty for five years—. You couldn't expect— (*She turns away from him—trying to reason it out—and to keep back the tears.*)

**Homer.**

(*stepping toward her*) I'll build you one myself, Myrtle. I'll build you a house that'll make that house look like a garage.

**Myrtle.**

Don't be silly! (*She moves over by stump.*)

**Homer.**

(*crossing to chair left—sitting*) Myrtle—I've been thinking things out.

**Myrtle.**

(*wearily*) Yes, you said you had. (*Sits stump.*)

**Homer.**

Not just last night. Today, too. I ought to have got married and had a home of my own a long time ago. I ought to have done it.

**Myrtle.**

(*faintly*) Why didn't you, Homer?

**Homer.**

I got caught. Somehow or other I got caught. But I'd do it now, Myrtle. I'd do it now except—

**Myrtle.**

Except what?

**Homer.**

Except now I really have to stay here with my mother.

**Myrtle.**

What do you mean?

**Homer.**

My father's going away. He said to my mother, "You'll be all right. You've got Homer."

**Myrtle.**

What did he mean?

**Homer.**

He meant she had me to take care of her. She didn't need him.

**Myrtle.**

(*slightly bitter*) She's always depended on you, Homer. You told me that last night.

**Homer.**

Yes, that's what I mean. She's always had me to take care of her. Maybe that's the trouble.

**Myrtle.**

(*pause—then suddenly turns to him*) Homer! Do you mean you really want to marry me now—? (*Rising and crossing to him—rapidly.*) Because if you do—if you really want to—it doesn't matter about our house—and you could be with your mother too. I could come and live here with you in this house. And we could have your little room. It's a darling little room. I looked at it on the way down. And we could all be together. (*Homer turns to her— She pauses.*) That is, if you *wanted* to, of course.

**Homer.**

You mean, you'd live here—with everybody?

**Myrtle.**
Of course I would. I'd just love it.

**Homer.**
You always said a woman wanted a home of her own.

**Myrtle.**
Well, I'd be having it. It'd be even nicer in one way than being up there on Sycamore Drive. We'd never be lonesome here. (*Pause. Homer rises.*)

**Homer.**
(*suddenly*) I'm awfully fond of you, Myrtle.

**Myrtle.**
Are you, Homer?

**Homer.**
I'm fonder of you than anything I could think of. (*Pauses, he stands looking at her.*) I think you're wonderful. (*They stand looking at each other a minute.*)

**Myrtle.**
Thank you, Homer. (*Myrtle looks away a minute—starts to say something—then changes her mind—looks back.*) Shall we take our walk? (*Homer comes to her. He starts to put his arm around her. Hesitates. Looks over at the other house. Puts his arm around her anyway. They exit up center.*)

from

THE RAINMAKER

by N. Richard Nash

Three Scenes from Acts II and III
LIZZIE, STARBUCK

"Bill Starbuck is a big man, lithe, agile—a loud braggart,
a gentle dreamer. He carries a short hickory stick—it is his
weapon, his magic wand, his pride of manhood." Starbuck
turns up at a ranch house in the West and claims to be
a rainmaker. Whether or not he can work magic with the
weather, he has a power over people that is close to magi-
cal. (See introductory comments on pages 171 and 346.)

Below are three scenes in which Starbuck works his
magic—the magic of hope—on Lizzie, a girl who fears
that she is already an old maid. Starbuck had involved
Lizzie's father and one of her brothers in his ritual of
rainmaking. Now he turns to Lizzie, who is suspicious of
his line of talk. They are alone in the ranch house. From
outside comes the sound of a bass drum—following Starbuck's orders, Lizzie's brother is sitting under the stars
drumming. Lizzie, fuming with anger, whirls on Starbuck.

**Lizzie.**
Well! I'll bet you feel real proud of yourself!
**Starbuck.**
(*Smiling evenly*) Kinda proud, sure.
**Lizzie.**
(*Raging*) You're not satisfied to steal our money! You
have to make jackasses out of us! Why'd you send them
out on those fool errands? Why? What for?
**Starbuck.**
Maybe I thought it was necessary.
**Lizzie.**
You know good and well it wasn't necessary—you know
it!

398

**Starbuck.**

Maybe I sent them out so's I could talk to you alone!

**Lizzie.**

(*Off balance*) What?

**Starbuck.**

You heard me.

**Lizzie.**

(*Her rage mounting*) Then why didn't you just say it straight out: Lizzie; I want to talk to you—alone—man to man!

**Starbuck.**

(*Quietly*) Man to man, Lizzie?

**Lizzie.**

(*Bitingly*) Excuse me—I made a mistake—you're not a man! (*Starbuck tenses, then controls his anger.*)

**Starbuck.**

Lizzie, can I ask you a little question?

**Lizzie.**

No!

**Starbuck.**

I'll ask it anyway. Why are you fussin' at the buttons on your dress?

**Lizzie.**

Fussing at the . . . ! I'm not! (*And she stops doing it.*)

**Starbuck.**

Let 'em alone. They're all buttoned up fine—as tight as they'll ever get. . . . And it's a nice dress too. Brand new, ain't it? You expectin' somebody?

**Lizzie.**

None of your business.

**Starbuck.**

A woman gets all decked out—she must be expectin' her beau. Where is he? It's gettin' kinda late.

**Lizzie.**

(*Breaking out*) I'm not expecting anybody!

**Starbuck.**

(*Quietly*) Oh, I see. You were—but now you ain't. Stand you up?

**Lizzie.**

Mr. Starbuck, you've got more gall . . . ! (*And she starts for the stairs. But he grabs her arm.*)

**Starbuck.**

Wait a minute!

**Lizzie.**

Let go of me!

**Starbuck.**

(*Tensely*) The question I really wanted to ask you before —it didn't have nothin' to do with buttons. It's this: The minute I walked into your house—before I hardly said a word—you didn't like me! Why?

**Lizzie.**

I said let go!

**Starbuck.**

(*Letting her go*) You didn't like me—why? Why'd you go up on your hind legs like a frightened mare?

**Lizzie.**

I wasn't frightened!

**Starbuck.**

Yes, you were!

**Lizzie.**

Of you? Of what?

**Starbuck.**

I don't know! Mares get scared by lots of things—fire— lightning—the smell of blood!

**Lizzie.**

I wasn't scared, Mr. Starbuck. You paraded yourself in here—and you took over the place. I don't like to be taken by a con man.

**Starbuck.**

(*Lashing out*) Wait a minute! I'm sick and tired of this! I'm tired of you queerin' my work, callin' me out of my name!

**Lizzie.**

I called you what you are—a big-mouthed liar and a fake!

**Starbuck.**

(*With mounting intensity*) How do you know I'm a liar? How do you know I'm a fake? Maybe I *can* bring rain! Maybe when I was born God whispered a special word in my ear! Maybe He said: "Bill Starbuck, you ain't gonna have much in this world—you ain't gonna have no money, no fancy spurs, no white horse with a golden saddle! You ain't gonna have no wife and no kids—no green little house to come to! But Bill Starbuck—wherever you go— you'll bring rain!" Maybe that's my one and only blessing!

**Lizzie.**

There's no such blessing in the world!

**Starbuck.**

I seen even better blessings, Lizzie-girl! I got a brother who's a doctor. You don't have to tell him where you ache or where you pain. He just comes in and lays his hand on your heart and pretty soon you're breathin' sweet again. And I got another brother who can sing—and when he's singin', that song is there—and never leaves you! (*With an outcry*) I used to think—why ain't *I* blessed like Fred or Arny? Why am I just a nothin' man, with nothin' special to my name? And then one summer comes the drought—and Fred can't heal it away and Arny can't sing it way. But me—I go down to the hollow and I look up and I say: "Rain! Dammit! *Please*—bring rain!" And the rain came! And I knew—I knew I was one of the family! (*Suddenly quiet, angry with himself*) That's a story. You don't have to believe it if you don't want to. (*A moment. She is affected by the story—but she won't let herself be. She pulls herself together with some effort.*)

**Lizzie.**

I don't believe it.

**Starbuck.**

You're like Noah. You don't believe in anything.

**Lizzie.**

That's not true.

**Starbuck.**

Yes, it is. You're scared to believe in anything. You put the fancy dress on—and the beau don't come. So you're scared that nothin'll ever come. You got no faith.

**Lizzie.**

(*Crying out*) I've got as much as anyone!

**Starbuck.**

You don't even know what faith is. And I'm gonna tell you. It's believin' you see white when your eyes tell you black. It's knowin'—with your heart!

**Lizzie.**

And I know you're a fake.

**Starbuck.**

(*In sudden commiseration*) Lizzie, I'm sad about you. You don't believe in nothin'—not even in yourself! You don't even believe you're a woman. And, if you *don't*— you're not! (*He turns on his heel and goes outdoors. Lizzie stands there, still hearing his words. She is deeply perturbed by them.*)

### SECOND SCENE

It is the same evening. Lizzie's older brother, Noah, the family realist, has had a fight with the younger brother, Jim, the one who was beating the bass drum. They fought about

Lizzie, for Noah told her that it was time she faced the fact she is plain—she'll never get a husband. Starbuck overheard the conversation and saw Lizzie's stricken reaction. Now, later in the evening, Starbuck is getting ready to bed down in the tack room.

(*Brightest moonlight—moonlight alone—illuminates the inside of the tack room. It is a rough, picturesque room—a junk room really—at the rear of the house. A slanting ceiling with huge hand-hewn beams: large casement windows which give such a vast expanse of bluest night sky that we feel we are more outdoors than in; a wagon wheel against a wall; leather goods—saddles, horse traces and the like; a wagon seat made into a bench, with faded homemade pillows to fit it; an old castaway cot against the wall. It is a room altogether accidental, yet altogether romantic. . . . Starbuck takes off his boots and his neckerchief, then he stands in the center of the room, not moving, thinking intently. He hurries to the door, closes it and barricades it with the wagon-seat bench. He moves to the windows and tries to open them but they are nailed shut. It's stifling in here. He takes his shirt off and sits on the edge of the cot, suffering the heat. He waves his shirt around to make a breeze. Then he decides to forgo caution—and removes the barricade, opening the door. He lies down on the cot. The stillness is a palpable thing, and the heat. As he relaxes, as he slips back into his solitude, a lonely little humming comes from him. It grows in volume and occasionally we hear the words of the song. He hears a sound and sits bolt upright.*)*

**Starbuck.**

Who's that? (*He rises tautly.*)

(*Lizzie stands in the doorway, trying not to look into the room. She is carrying the bed linens. She knocks on the door frame.*)

**Lizzie.**

(*Trying to sound calm*) It's me—Lizzie.

(*Starbuck starts to put on his shirt. An awkward moment. Then Lizzie, without entering the room, hands the bedding across the threshold.*)

**Lizzie.**

Here.

**Starbuck.**

What's that?

**Lizzie.**

Bed linens—take them.

**Starbuck.**

Is that what you came out for?

**Lizzie.**

(*After a painful moment*) No . . . I came out because . . . (*She finds it too difficult to continue.*)

**Starbuck.**

(*Gently*) Go on, Lizzie.

**Lizzie.**

I came out to thank you for what you said to Noah.

**Starbuck.**

I meant every word of it.

**Lizzie.**

What you said about Jim—I'm sure you meant that.

**Starbuck.**

What I said about you.

**Lizzie.**

I don't believe you.

**Starbuck.**

Then what are you thankin' me for? What's the matter, Lizzie? You afraid that if you stop bein' sore at me you'll like me a little?

**Lizzie.**

No . . . (*And she starts to go.*)

**Starbuck.**

(*Stopping her*) Then stay and talk to me! (*As she hesitates*) It's lonely out here and I don't think I'll sleep much —not in a strange place.

**Lizzie.**

Then I guess you never sleep. Running from one strange place to another.

**Starbuck.**

(*With a smile*) Not runnin'—travelin'.

**Lizzie.**

Well, if that's the kind of life you like . . .

**Starbuck.**

Oh, it's not what a man likes—it's what he's got to do. Now what would a fella in my business be doin' stayin' in the same place? Rain's nice—but it ain't nice all the time.

**Lizzie.**

(*Relaxing a bit*) No, I guess not.

**Starbuck.**

People got no use for me—except maybe once in a lifetime. And when my work's done, they're glad to see me go.

**Lizzie.**

(*Caught by the loneliness in his voice*) I never thought of it that way.

**Starbuck.**

Why would you? You never thought of me as a real rainmaker—not until just now.

**Lizzie.**

I still don't think it! (*Now she starts to go more determinedly than before. Starbuck stops her physically this time.*)

**Starbuck.**

Lizzie—wait! Why don't you let yourself think of me the way you *want* to?

**Lizzie.**

(*Unnerved*) What do you mean?

**Starbuck.**

Think like Lizzie, not like Noah.

**Lizzie.**

I don't know what you're talking about.

**Starbuck.**

What are you scared of?

**Lizzie.**

You! I don't trust you!

**Starbuck.**

Why? What don't you trust about me?

**Lizzie.**

Everything! The way you talk, the way you brag—why, even your name.

**Starbuck.**

What's wrong with my name?

**Lizzie.**

It sounds fake! It sounds like you made it up!

**Starbuck.**

You're darn right! I did make it up.

**Lizzie.**

There! Of course!

**Starbuck.**

Why not? You know what name I was born with? Smith! Smith, for the love of Mike, *Smith!* Now what kind of a handle is that for a fella like me? I needed a name that had the whole sky in it! And the power of a man! Starbuck! Now there's a name—and it's mine.

**Lizzie.**

No, it's not. You were born Smith—and that's your name.

**Starbuck.**

You're wrong, Lizzie. The name you choose for yourself is more your own than the name you were born with. And if I was you I'd choose another name than Lizzie.

**Lizzie.**

Thank you—I'm very pleased with it.

**Starbuck.**

Oh, no you ain't. You ain't pleased with anything about yourself. And I'm sure you ain't pleased with "Lizzie."

**Lizzie.**

I don't ask *you* to be pleased with it, Starbuck. *I* am.

**Starbuck.**

Lizzie? Why, it don't *stand* for anything.

**Lizzie.**

It stands for me! *Me!* I'm not the Queen of Sheba—I'm not Lady Godiva—I'm not Cinderella at the Ball.

**Starbuck.**

Would you like to be?

**Lizzie.**

Starbuck, you're ridiculous!

**Starbuck.**

What's ridiculous about it? Dream you're somebody—*be* somebody! But Lizzie? That's nobody! So many millions of wonderful women with wonderful names! (*In an orgy of delight*) Leonora, Desdemona, Carolina, Paulina! Annabella, Florinda, Natasha, Diane! (*Then, with a pathetic little lift of his shoulders*) Lizzie.

**Lizzie.**

Good night, Starbuck!

**Starbuck.**

(*With a sudden inspiration*) Just a minute, Lizzie—just one little half of a minute. I got the greatest name for you—the greatest name—just listen. (*Then, like a love lyric*) Melisande.

**Lizzie.**

(*Flatly*) I don't like it.

**Starbuck.**

That's because you don't know anything about her. But when I tell you who she was—lady, when I tell you who she was!

**Lizzie.**

Who?

**Starbuck.**

(*Improvising*) She was the most beautiful . . .! She was the beautiful wife of King Hamlet! Ever hear of him?

**Lizzie.**

(*Giving him the rope*) Go on! Go on!

**Starbuck.**

He was the fella who sailed across the ocean and brought back the Golden Fleece! And you know why he did that? Because Melisande begged him for it! I tell you, that Melisande—she was so beautiful and her hair was so long and curly—every time he looked at her he just fell right down and died. And this King Hamlet, he'd do anything for her—anything she wanted. So when she said: "Hamlet, I got a terrible hankerin' for a soft Golden Fleece," he just naturally sailed right off to find it. And when he came back—all bleedin' and torn—he went and laid that Fleece of Gold right down at her pretty white feet. And she took that fur piece and wrapped it around her pink naked shoulders and she said: "I got the Golden Fleece —and I'll never be cold no more." . . . Melisande! What a woman! What a *name!*

**Lizzie.**

(*Quietly*) Starbuck, you silly jackass. You take a lot of stories—that I've read in a hundred different places—and you roll them up into one big fat ridiculous lie!

**Starbuck.**

(*Angry, hurt*) I wasn't lyin'—I was dreamin'!

**Lizzie.**

It's the same thing!

**Starbuck.**

(*With growing anger*) If you think it's the same thing then I take it back about your name! Lizzie—it's just right for you. I'll tell you another name that would suit you—Noah! Because you and your brother—you've got no dream.

**Lizzie.**

(*With an outcry*) You think all dreams have to be your kind! Golden Fleece and thunder on the mountain! But there are other dreams, Starbuck! Little quiet ones that come to a woman when she's shining the silverware and putting moth flakes in the closet.

**Starbuck.**

Like what?

**Lizzie**

(*Crying*) Like a man's voice saying: "Lizzie, is my blue suit pressed?" And the same man saying: "Scratch between my shoulder blades." And kids laughing and teasing and setting up a racket. And how it feels to say the word

"Husband!" . . . There are all kinds of dreams, Mr. Starbuck. Mine are small ones—like my name—Lizzie. But they're *real* like my name—real! So you can have yours—and I'll have mine! (*Unable to control her tears, she starts to run away. This time he grabs her fully, holding her close.*)

**Starbuck.**

Lizzie . . .

**Lizzie.**

Please . . .

**Starbuck.**

I'm sorry, Lizzie! I'm sorry!

**Lizzie.**

It's all right—let me go!

**Starbuck.**

I hope your dreams come true, Lizzie—I hope they do!

**Lizzie.**

They won't—they never will!

**Starbuck.**

Believe in yourself and they will!

**Lizzie.**

I've got nothing to believe in.

**Starbuck.**

You're a woman! Believe in that!

**Lizzie.**

How can I when nobody else will?

**Starbuck.**

*You* gotta believe it first! (*Quickly*) Let me ask you, Lizzie—are you pretty?

**Lizzie.**

(*With a wail*) No—I'm plain!

**Starbuck.**

There! You see? You don't know you're a woman!

**Lizzie.**

I am a woman! A plain one!

**Starbuck.**

There's no such thing as a plain woman! Every real woman is pretty! They're all pretty in a different way— but they're all pretty!

**Lizzie.**

Not me! When I look in the looking glass . . .

**Starbuck.**

Don't let Noah be your lookin' glass!

**Lizzie.**

He's not. My looking glass is right on the wall.

**Starbuck.**

It's in the wrong place. It's gotta be inside you.

**Lizzie.**

No . . .

**Starbuck.**

Don't be afraid—*look!* You'll see a pretty woman, Lizzie. Lizzie, you gotta be your own lookin' glass. And then one day the lookin' glass will be the man who loves you. It'll be his eyes, maybe. And you'll look in that mirror and you'll be more than pretty—you'll be beautiful!

**Lizzie.**

(*Crying out*) It'll never happen!

**Starbuck.**

Make it happen! Lizzie, why don't you think "pretty" and take down your hair? (*He reaches for her hair.*)

**Lizzie.**

(*In panic*) No!

**Starbuck.**

Please, Lizzie! (*He is taking the pins out of her hair.*)

**Lizzie.**

No—no . . .

**Starbuck.**

Nobody sees you, Lizzie—nobody but me! (*Taking her in his arms*) Now close your eyes, Lizzie—close them! (*As she obeys*) Now—say: "I'm pretty!"

**Lizzie.**

(*Trying*) I'm—I'm—I can't!

**Starbuck.**

Say it! Say it, Lizzie!

**Lizzie.**

I'm . . . pretty.

**Starbuck.**

Say it again!

**Lizzie.**

(*With a little cry*) Pretty!

**Starbuck.**

Say it—mean it!

**Lizzie.**

(*Exalted*) I'm pretty! I'm pretty! I'm pretty. (*He kisses her. A long kiss and she clings to him, passionately, the bonds of her spinsterhood breaking away. The kiss over, she collapses on the cot, sobbing.*)

**Lizzie.**

(*Through the sobs*) Why did you do that?

**Starbuck.**

(*Going beside her on the cot*) Because when you said you were pretty, it was true! (*Her sobs are louder, more heartrending because, for the first time, she is happy.*)

**Starbuck.**

Lizzie—look at me!

**Lizzie.**

I can't!

**Starbuck.**

(*Turning her to him*) Stop cryin' and look at me! Look at my eyes! What do you see?

**Lizzie.**

(*Gazing through her tears*) I can't *believe* what I see!

**Starbuck.**

Tell me what you see!

**Lizzie.**

(*With a sob of happiness*) Oh, is it me? Is it really me? (*Now she goes to him with all her giving.*)

### THIRD SCENE

The tack room.

(*Starbuck and Lizzie are sitting on the floor, leaning against the back of the wagon-seat bench. They are quite intimately close, looking out through the open door at the bright expanse of sky. Lizzie has the shine of moonlight over her face and this glow, meeting her inner radiance, makes her almost beautiful.*)

**Starbuck.**

And I always walk so fast and ride so far I never have time to stop and ask myself no question.

**Lizzie.**

If you did stop, what question would you ask?

**Starbuck.**

Well . . . I guess I'd say: "Big Man, where you goin'?"

**Lizzie.**

(*Quietly*) Big Man, where *are* you going?

**Starbuck.**

(*After an indecisive moment*) I don't know.

**Lizzie.**

Where do you want to *get* to?

**Starbuck.**

(*Inarticulate for the first time*) I—I want to touch somethin'. Somethin' big—to send shivers down my spine!

**Lizzie.**

Yes . . . I get shivers just thinking about it.

**Starbuck.**

But every time I get near anything big like that, I blink my eyes and it's gone. (*With a little revolt*) Why *is* that? Why is it the things you want are only there for the blinkin' of an eye? Why don't nothin' *stay*?

**Lizzie.**

(*Quietly*) Some things stay forever.

**Starbuck.**

Like what?

**Lizzie.**

(*A little abashed*) Never mind.

**Starbuck.**

You gotta tell me! Please!

**Lizzie.**

You fall in love with somebody—not *me*, I don't expect it'll be me—just *somebody*. And get married and have kids. And if you do, you'll live forever.

**Starbuck.**

(*Yearning*) I'd sure like to live forever. (*As they look at each other intently*) I reckon I better kiss you again. (*He kisses her and they are close for a moment*) Didn't anybody ever kiss you before I did, Lizzie?

**Lizzie.**

(*With a wan smile*) Yes—once.

**Starbuck.**

When was that?

**Lizzie.**

I was about twelve, I guess. I didn't know then whether I was pretty or plain—I just didn't think about it. There was a boy with freckles and red hair—and I thought he was the beginning of the world. But he never paid me any mind. Then one day he was standing around with a lot of other boys and they were whispering and cutting up. And suddenly, he shot over to me and kissed me hard right on the mouth! And for a minute I was so stirred up and so happy . . . ! But then he ran back to the other kids and I heard him say: "I'll kiss anything on a dare, even your old man's pig!" So I ran home and up the back stairs and I locked my door and looked at myself in the mirror—and from that day on I knew I was plain.

**Starbuck.**

Are you plain, Lizzie?

**Lizzie.**

(*Looking at him, smiling*) No—I'm beautiful.

**Starbuck.**

You are—and don't you ever forget it!

**Lizzie.**

(*A little sadly; reconciled to his ultimate going*) I'll try to remember—everything—you ever said. (*Starbuck rises restively. Somehow, he is deeply disturbed, lonely. He walks to the door, his back to Lizzie, and looks out at the night. There is searching in his face, and yearning. At last it comes out in a little outcry:*)

**Starbuck.**

Lizzie, I want to live forever!

**Lizzie.**

(*Full of compassion*) I hope you do—wherever you are —I hope you do!

**Starbuck.**

You don't say that as if you think I'll ever get what I'm after.

**Lizzie.**

(*Gently*) I don't really *know* what you're after.

**Starbuck.**

I'm after a clap of lightnin'! I want things to be as pretty when I *get* them as they are when I'm *thinkin'* about them!

**Lizzie.**

(*Hurt. He seems to disparage the moment of realization they've had together*) I think they're prettier when you get them. I think when you get something you've been dreaming about—oh, it's so beautiful!

**Starbuck.**

I wasn't talkin' about us, Lizzie.

**Lizzie.**

Weren't you?

**Starbuck.**

No—I'm talkin' about everything. Nothin's as pretty in your hands as it was in your head. There ain't no world near as good as the world I got up here. (*Angrily tapping his forehead*) Why?

**Lizzie.**

I don't know. Maybe it's because you don't take time to see it. Always on the go—here, there, nowhere. Running away . . . keeping your own company. Maybe if you'd keep company with the *world* . . .

**Starbuck.**

(*Doubtfully*) I'd learn to love it?

**Lizzie.**

You might—if you saw it *real*. Some nights I'm in the kitchen washing the dishes. And Pop's playing poker with the boys. Well, I'll watch him real close. And at first I'll just see an ordinary middle-aged man—not very interesting to look at. And then, minute by minute, I'll see little things I never saw in him before. Good things and bad things—queer little habits I never noticed he had—and ways of talking I never paid any mind to. And suddenly I know who he is—and I love him so much I could cry! And I want to thank God I took the time to see him *real*.

**Starbuck.**

(*Breaking out*) Well, I ain't got the time.

**Lizzie.**

Then you ain't got no world—except the one you make up in your head. So you better just be satisfied with that.

**Starbuck.**

No!

**Lizzie.**

I'm sorry. I didn't mean to hurt you. (*A long moment. When at last he speaks, it is with painful difficulty.*)

**Starbuck.**

Lizzie . . . I got somethin' to tell you . . . You were right . . . I'm a liar and a con man and a fake. (*A moment. The words tear out of him*) I never made rain in my life! Not a single raindrop! Nowhere! Not anywhere at all!

**Lizzie.**

(*In a compassionate whisper*) I know. . . .

**Starbuck.**

All my life—wantin' to make a miracle! . . . Nothin'! . . . I'm a great big blowhard!

**Lizzie.**

(*Gently*) No . . . You're all dreams. And it's no good to live in your dreams.

**Starbuck.**

(*With desperation*) It's no good to live outside them either!

**Lizzie.**

Somewhere between the two . . . !

**Starbuck.**

Yes! (*After a moment*) The two of us maybe. . . .

**Lizzie.**

(*Forcing herself to believe it might work*) . . . Yes!

**Starbuck.**

Lizzie! Lizzie, would you like me to stick around for a while?

**Lizzie.**

(*Unable to stand the joy of it*) Did I hear you right?

**Starbuck.**

Not for good, understand—just for a few days!

**Lizzie.**

You're—you're not fooling me, are you, Starbuck?

**Starbuck.**

No—I mean it!

**Lizzie.**

(*Crying*) Would you stay? Would you?

**Starbuck.**

A few days—yes!

**Lizzie.**

(*Her happiness bursting*) Oh! Oh, my goodness! Oh!

**Starbuck.**

Lizzie . . .

**Lizzie.**

I can't stand it—I just can't stand it!

**Starbuck.**

(*Taking her in his arms*) Lizzie . . .

**Lizzie.**

You look up at the sky and you cry for a star. You know you'll never get it. And then one night you look down—and there it is—shining in your hand! (*Half laughing, half crying, she goes into his arms again as the lights fade.*)

from
ETHAN FROME
by Owen and Donald Davis

Two Scenes from Act I, scene 3, and Act III, scene 3
MATTIE, ETHAN

In *Ethan Frome* (see introductory comments on page 293), the paths of love and tragedy run parallel, are never far apart, and ultimately merge. Ethan and Mattie, drawn together, are also drawn inexorably—or so the novelist and playwrights make it seem—toward hopelessness and disaster. Two key scenes in this progression—a scene of beginning and a scene of ending—are given the same setting, the place where two paths cross at the top of a snow-covered hill, a crest above a sheer steep drop into the valley below. This setting can well be viewed symbolically. Though it does not change, its full meaning is not clear until the audience has seen it for a second time, when the ominous aspects, there from the first, are unavoidable.

It is a winter night. After a dance in the village, a young man offered to walk Mattie home to the Frome farm. Ethan, who planned to walk her home, was annoyed and said so. Mattie decided to walk, but when Ethan turned to one path she set out on the other. Each called the other stubborn and kept to his own path. Now they meet at the spot where the paths cross on the hillside.

At stage center, the snow has been packed down around a V-like indentation which is the starting place for the village bobsled slide. A small sled with wooden runners lies half-buried in the snow, left, and there is a log, down left center. Ethan enters along his path, up right. He advances slowly toward center.

**Mattie.**

(*calling from off down right*) Ethan, oh, Ethan! (*Ethan stops. She enters on path right.*)

**Ethan.**

(*over right, almost formally*) Hello, Matt.

**Mattie.**

(*she is quite embarrassed, crosses center, looks at him for a moment, then says:*) It's an awful nice night . . . don't let's be stubborn.

**Ethan.**

(*crosses center matter-of-factly*) I won't if you won't. (*Then generously.*) I guess you got a right to go home with him, if you want.

**Mattie.**

(*right center, irritably*) That's what makes me so mad!

**Ethan.**

(*center, blankly*) Well—you have.

**Mattie.**

You thinkin' I'd want to walk home with him! Don't you suppose I know that walkin' two miles in to Starkfield and back ain't much fun for you after a day's work around the farm . . . and you wouldn't walk it anyways, if Zeena didn't make you do it!

**Ethan.**

(*it's hard for him to give an inch*) I might.

**Mattie.**

(*eagerly*) Would you?

**Ethan.**

(*pauses, thinks, then speaks very honestly*) I don't mind the walk.

**Mattie.**

(*quickly*) Don't you, Ethan?

**Ethan.**

Nope . . . lately I been gettin' so I kind of like it.

**Mattie.**

So do I! I like it an awful lot!

**Ethan.**

It gets kind of lonesome out to the farm.

**Mattie.**

(*eagerly, grasping for his understanding*) Don't it, though!

**Ethan.**

(*hesitates, then says with unusual volubility*) Sometimes I kind of like getting away awhile.

**Mattie.**

It's real nice all right, ain't it?

**Ethan.**

(*impulsively*) Zeena ain't a whole lot of company when she's feelin' low.

**Mattie.**

(*honestly*) No, she ain't.

**Ethan.**

(*hastily*) Not that I blame her!

**Mattie.**

Oh, no, Ethan! (*He cannot think of anything at all to say and he looks at her helplessly—after a moment she helps him.*) I ain't a mite cold . . . are you, Ethan?

**Ethan.**

Me? No!

**Mattie.**

I was thinkin' . . . I don't know as there'd be any harm in settin' awhile!

**Ethan.**

(*sits on log*) Don't know as there would. (*She sits, eagerly, beside him on the log. There is a pause.*)

**Mattie.**

(*at last, eagerly*) It ain't often we get a chance to say much around the house, and you know when you get started talkin' sometimes, like take now, it's real interestin'.

**Ethan.**

(*warming up*) Yes—'tis! (*Pause.*) I ain't talked so much since before I was married! (*They laugh.*)

**Mattie.**

Well, you ain't bad's you was . . . and that's a fact, Ethan! (*She looks at him and smiles encouragingly.*) I was awful glad when I seen you waitin' outside the social hall there tonight. I thought maybe you couldn't come back for me.

**Ethan.**

Couldn't! Why, who'd ever stop me?

**Mattie.**

Oh, I don't know! (*Thoughtfully.*) I knew she wasn't feelin' any too good today. I figured maybe you might have to stay and do for her till I got back.

**Ethan.**

No, no, she's in bed long ago.

**Mattie.**

I had an awful funny dream last night. You know what I dreamed? I dreamed Zeena come downstairs sayin' she was feelin' better and for a while this mornin' I didn't know if it was a dream or not . . . till I heard her!

**Ethan.**

Feelin' better! (*Pause.*) Well, that's one thing I ain't never heard her complainin' about! (*They are silent, sitting side by side on the log, close to the sheer drop at back. After a moment, Mattie peers down over the edge of the crest of the hill.*)

**Mattie.**

(*they rise*) Awful steep down there, ain't it?

**Ethan.**

A-yeah. (*Mattie laughs nervously.*)

**Mattie.**

There was a lot of them out here coastin' tonight before the moon set. (*He crosses up to edge—she crosses up stage.*)

**Ethan.**

(*interestedly*) There was?

**Mattie.**

(*nods*) Oh, an awful lot of them. (*She glances down incline off right.*) I never been coastin' . . . even once in my life!

**Ethan.**

(*after a moment*) Would you like to go sometime?

**Mattie.**

Would I? You just ask me!

**Ethan.**

(*shortly*) We could go sometime.

**Mattie.**

Could we really?

**Ethan.**

(*with difficulty*) We could go tomorrow night maybe—if there's a moon.

**Mattie.**

I was watchin' them tonight—but my—I never thought I'd get a chance to go myself!

**Ethan.**

(*determinedly*) We'll go tomorrow night!

**Mattie.**

(*joyously*) Oh, Ethan . . . Say! (*She moves close to him and says excitedly:*) You know . . . Ned Hale . . . and Ruth Varnum . . . they went down together and we was all watchin' and all of sudden! . . . (*She stops abruptly, looks at him, frightenedly, then adds quickly:*) You should've seen . . . why, they come just as close to run-

nin' right plumb into a big tree . . . and gettin' theirselves
killed . . . (*Glances down over the hillside.*) I guess it
was that big black elm down there at the bend . . . see it?
(*She draws back from edge of the hillside.*) Wouldn't
it have been just too awful for anythin'!

**Ethan.**

(*close to her*) A-yeah—well, Ned ain't so much on
steerin', but . . . I guess't I could take you down all right.

**Mattie.**

Could you, Ethan? (*She peers down over the edge of the
hill.*) Right past the big elm? . . . It's awful dangerous-
lookin' . . .

**Ethan.**

(*positively*) I guess you wouldn't have to be afraid with
me.

**Mattie.**

No . . . I don't guess I would!

**Ethan.**

Say, Matt . . . that's Sam Colt's sled settin' over there
and he don't never use it, and you know there ain't no
reason in the world why we couldn't borrow it.

**Mattie.**

(*looking up at him, daring to hope for a second*) You
mean right now?

**Ethan.**

(*suddenly doubtful*) Well . . .

**Mattie.**

I guess maybe it is kind of late to go down tonight. . . .
(*Crosses down left.*) Maybe we could go tomorrow night.

**Ethan.**

Yeah. (*Mattie crosses down. After a moment he thinks
of something to say, looking up right.*) There's lots of
stars out tonight, though, ain't there?

**Mattie.**

(*coming down*) Ain't there just! (*She stands beside him,
looking up.*) Did you ever try to count 'em all? . . . Oh,
my! Don't it seem like there's most a million of them?

**Ethan.**

A-yeah. (*Authoritatively.*) There's more'n that.

**Mattie.**

(*amazed at his knowledge*) What do you know!

**Ethan.**

(*eagerly, as he points*) See that one, that big fellow there
—see? (*She nods.*) I think they call him Aldebaran—or
some such.

**Mattie.**

(*incredulously*) They do!

**Ethan.**

(*rapidly*) And that bright one . . . that's Orion. And that bunch of little ones . . . no, over there—see? Swarming about there?

**Mattie.**

(*crosses to right center*) I see! Ain't they though . . . just like a little flock of bees! (*She glances at him, and then up at the sky and murmurs.*) Oh, my! Don't it look like it was all just painted!

**Ethan.**

(*practically*) They call them the Pleiades.

**Mattie.**

They do! Well! Thk! (*Turns, looks at him admiringly.*) Gorry, you know an awful lot, don't you, Ethan? How'd you ever find it all out? (*Ethan looks at her.*)

**Ethan.**

(*with pardonable pride*) Had pretty near a year in Worcester . . . down there to the technological college.

**Mattie.**

You did!

**Ethan.**

A-yeah. But then the old man died and I had to come back and take care of the farm. So I didn't get to learn much to speak of, just enough to get me wonderin' about things once in a while.

**Mattie.**

You know, I get to wonderin' once in a while myself . . . about things, and places. Nice, warm places mostly, like take down South!

**Ethan.**

Ever seen any pictures of them palm trees they have down there? (*She nods eagerly.*) Mighty pretty.

**Mattie.**

I can just imagine!

**Ethan.**

(*dryly*) A-yeah. Well, for a good while there I could call up the sight of them pictures easy . . . but these last couple of winters the recollection's been gettin' kind of snowed under!

**Mattie.**

(*sighs*) Oh, my . . . it must be real nice to travel places. . . .

**Ethan.**

A-yeah.

**Mattie.**

I got's far down as Hartford once. . . . (*She sighs.*) Guess that's 'bout's far's I ever will get.

**Ethan.**

Hartford's quite a ways at that. . . .

**Mattie.**

Yes . . . 'tis.

**Ethan.**

Most to New York.

**Mattie.**

Can you picture it! And I didn't get tired travelin' at all. . . . I could've kept right on goin' an' goin' an' goin' . . . (*She sighs longingly.*) Oh, dear.

**Ethan.**

Glad you didn't.

**Mattie.**

It's awful interestin' to talk about things like that though, ain't it? I still ain't a mite cold . . . are you?

**Ethan.**

Me? No . . . 'course not!

**Mattie.**

I was thinkin' we might set awhile longer. (*She sits. He follows. She considers for a moment.*) Ain't it funny the way things go now when you just stop to think about 'em? Just supposin' my father hadn't of married Zeena's cousin . . . why, I most probably wouldn't've been born at all! (*Then thoughtfully.*) Still 'n' all . . . I don't know's I'd mind that!

**Ethan.**

Some people might!

**Mattie.**

Well . . . anyhow . . . bein' me, I'm glad he did.

**Ethan.**

A-yeah. . . . Well . . . I'm kind of glad myself . . . bein's that's why you're here.

**Mattie.**

Ain't it just the luckiest thing! Why, I'm just so glad to be here . . . 'stead of down there in them big towns! You know, I never did take to workin' in the mills . . . first off I ain't got the stren'th . . . and then them foremen used to get me so flustered . . . why, the harder I tried the more flustered I'd get and the sooner I'd get fired . . . and then first thing you know . . . I got fired so much

. . . there wasn't any more jobs. . . . (*She sighs contentedly.*) An' my health's better here an' everything, and I don't have to fuss about a place to sleep and somethin' to eat . . .! Oh, my, yes, bein' here's been real pleasant.

**Ethan.**

(*after a moment, reluctantly*) A-yeah . . . still . . . I presume what folks says is only natural. . . .

**Mattie.**

Why, what is folks sayin', Ethan?

**Ethan.**

(*very reluctantly*) They say—that sooner or later—you'll be leavin' us.

**Mattie.**

(*rises, worriedly*) Why, what do you mean, Ethan?

**Ethan.**

Well . . . I don't know.

**Mattie.**

Why—(*Looks at him and then is suddenly terrified.*) You mean it's Zeena, you mean she ain't suited? Oh, Ethan, has she said anything? (*She stares at him.*) I know I ain't near as smart as I ought to be, and Zeena says there's lots of things around the house want doin', that a regular hired girl . . . she c'd do them all right, but I ain't got the stren'th in my arms! (*Then sits.*) Oh, Ethan . . . if Zeena sends me away I don't know wherever I'd go or whatever I'd do . . . if she'd only tell me what I don't do right . . . but she don't hardly say a word for days . . . and sometimes I can see she ain't suited . . . yet, still 'n' all, I don't know why! (*With an impetuous gesture toward him she says indignantly:*) You'd ought to tell me what to do, Ethan Frome. You'd ought to tell me yourself. (*She stares at him for a second.*) Unless you want me to go too!

**Ethan.**

Now don't fret, Matt . . . don't fret . . . if you don't want to go of your own accord . . .

**Mattie.**

Where'd I go?

**Ethan.**

Well . . . all I was *tryin'* to say was . . . folks is sayin' that sooner or later . . . you might be wantin' to leave us to get married.

**Mattie.**

(*with great relief and amazement*) Married! (*She laughs nervously.*) Why, whoever'd want to go and marry me!

**Ethan.**

Well, now . . . folks do marry . . . no gettin' away from that. So if you was to marry some fellow . . . why, it'd be only natural you'd be leavin' us!

**Mattie.**

If! That's a mighty big "if," Ethan! (*Rises, faces right. Ethan rises.*)

**Ethan.**

Say, Matt, you ain't cryin'?

**Mattie.**

'Course I ain't! (*Turns to him.*)

**Ethan.**

Why, Matt, lots of folks'd want to marry you. . . .

**Mattie.**

I ain't noticed any great rush so far.

**Ethan.**

(*as she moves away*) Well . . . take now . . . I would . . . if I could.

**Mattie.**

(*stops abruptly, turns, and looks at him*) That's interestin', ain't it? (*She shrugs.*) Oh, well—Maybe you would, Ethan . . . but nobody else . . . anyhow you couldn't.

**Ethan.**

No, I don't guess I could . . . but I mean, if I could . . . I would. (*Crosses to right. She follows, taking his arm.*)

**Mattie.**

Oh, well, sayin' that don't mean anythin'! (*As they exit she looks up at him and smiles.*) Still 'n' all . . . it's real nice of you to say it!

## Second Scene

Zeena has demanded that Mattie be sent away, and Ethan has been forced to agree. Mattie's suitcase is packed, it is time for her to go, but Ethan has insisted that she walk with him to the hilltop one last time.

(*At the crest of the hill. It is dusk. The delicate blue shadows on the snow-covered hillside are rapidly turning black, and the reflection of the cold, red winter sun mingles with the rising blur of the night. The hillside is deserted . . . the tinkling sound of sleigh bells is heard ap-*

*proaching . . . the sound stops abruptly with a last jingle
as the sleigh stops off right.*

(*Ethan enters first . . . walking slowly . . . to the crest of
the hill at back . . . Mattie enters and stops at right. They
stand there for a moment . . . listening tensely to the stillness.*)

**Mattie.**

(*after a moment, in a low voice*) We'd ought to go.

**Ethan.**

(*doesn't answer her immediately . . . then suddenly he
says in a low voice, tense with tingling nervousness.*) I
feel dizzy . . . like I'd stopped in at the saloon down to
Starkfield for a drink.

**Mattie.**

(*after a time, nervously*) We mustn't stay here any longer,
Ethan!

**Ethan.**

(*turns to her. Almost impatiently*) I just wanted't we
sh'd stand here a minute, Mattie. (*She crosses center to
him . . . they stand looking out across the valley below
for a moment. Then he says dully:*) Remember bein' here
the other night . . . !

**Mattie.**

(*in a low, dull voice*) It seems like it was years ago . . .
don't it?

**Ethan.**

(*after a moment, pointing down over the slope at back to
right*) Over there's where we sat at the church picnic
last summer. (*She nods.*) I remember findin' your locket
for you when you'd went and lost it . . .

**Mattie.**

I never knowed anyone for such sharp eyes. . . .

**Ethan.**

(*thoughtfully*) You know . . . you was awful pretty in
that pink hat.

**Mattie.**

(*very gratefully*) Aw—I wouldn't go's far's that—I guess
it was just the hat. (*They are looking at each other intently . . . suddenly she crosses center a step.*)

**Ethan.**

(*vaguely as he watches her*) There's plenty of time. (*He
follows her, and says abruptly and tensely:*) Matt . . .
where'll you go . . . what'll you do!

**Mattie.**

(*looks up at him*) Oh well . . . maybe I'll get a place in the mills.

**Ethan.**

You know you can't . . . and if you did . . . the standin' and heavy liftin' . . . nearly done for you before!

**Mattie.**

Well . . . I'm a whole lot stronger'n I was though . . .

**Ethan.**

And now you're just goin' to go and throw away all the good bein' here's done you! (*There isn't any answer to this. After a moment he says hopefully:*) Ain't there any of your father's folks'd help you?

**Mattie.**

(*with a sudden fierceness and bitterness*) There ain't any of them I'd ask!

**Ethan.**

(*center, moves closer to her*) Matt . . . you know there's nothin' I wouldn't do for you . . . if I could! (*He is silent for a moment . . . then:*) Oh, Matt . . . if I only could'a gone with you now . . . I'd a done it!

**Mattie.**

(*quickly, center. Faces right*) I know!

**Ethan.**

Matt . . . if I coulda done it . . . gone somewheres with you . . . (*He hesitates*). Would you've gone with me?

**Mattie.**

(*with quick tears*) Oh Ethan . . . Ethan . . . what's the use!

**Ethan.**

Tell me, Matt! Tell me!

**Mattie.**

I used to think of it sometimes, summer nights when the moon was shinin' in my windows so bright't I couldn't sleep . . .

**Ethan.**

(*in amazement*) As long ago as that!

**Mattie.**

(*nods very honestly*) The first time was . . . at the picnic in the beginning of summer . . . (*She sees his look of strange wonder and smiles a little.*) Still 'n' all . . . I guess we didn't get to be what you might call friends for a long while after that . . . did we?

**Ethan.**

I guess I was thinkin' a lot about you . . . right from the first, Matt.

**Mattie.**

You was! My, you'd never've knowed it!

**Ethan.**

(*with great difficulty*) I guess I didn't get to know it myself . . . right up till we was here . . . the other night . . . (*He stands looking at her intently for a moment and then says abruptly and tensely:*) I'm tied hand and foot, Matt . . . there just ain't anythin' I c'n do!

**Mattie.**

You c'n write me sometimes . . .

**Ethan.**

What good'll writin' do! I want to do for you and care for you like you need! I want to put out my hand and touch you . . . I want to be there if you're sick and when you're lonesome!

**Mattie.**

(*urgently, trying hard to convince him*) Oh you mustn't think but what I'll be all right, Ethan! (*Then suddenly.*) Oh, I wish't I was dead! I wish't I was!

**Ethan.**

Matt! Don't you say it!

**Mattie.**

(*more frantically and frightenedly*) Why shouldn't I when it's true? I been thinkin' it all night and all day!

**Ethan.**

Matt!

**Mattie.**

It's so, it's so, and I want to be dead!

**Ethan.**

(*simultaneously*) You be quiet, Matt, and don't you even think of it!

**Mattie.**

There's nobody been good to me but you!

**Ethan.**

(*sharply*) Don't go and say that neither, 'cause I can't so much's lift my hand for you!

**Mattie.**

But it's true all the same! (*The cries of the children playing on the opposite slope of the hill reach them faintly*). Listen . . . the kids is coastin' . . . over on the other slope!

**Ethan.**

(*off up right. Stands watching for a moment, then says bitterly*) We was goin' coastin' tonight . . . remember? (*She nods quickly. The children's voices fade out.*) I ain't even took you coastin' . . . (*Looks at her for a moment and then says determinedly:*) You know what? We'll go now! (*Crosses up left*).

**Mattie.**

(*quickly and nervously, as he turns from her and crosses up left to the sled*) Oh no, Ethan, we can't . . . we can't! (*Follows up left.*)

**Ethan.**

(*almost angrily*) Yes we can too . . . I guess we can do that all right . . . you wait now! (*Gets sled put in place on runners.*)

**Mattie.**

(*crosses up to him. Really frightened now*). I don't want to go, Ethan! And anyhow, the new girl'll be waitin' at the station. Her train gets in more'n an hour before mine and she'll be waitin'!

**Ethan.**

Let her wait . . . you'd have to . . . if she didn't.

**Mattie.**

No, Ethan, it's away too dark. . . .

**Ethan.**

Come on, Matt—(*But she shakes her head and turns away from him*). It's the last chance we'll get! You ain't a-scared, are you?

**Mattie.**

(*turns on him fiercely*) I told you onc't I ain't the kind to be a-scared! (*She looks up at him as he comes toward her.*) Oh, Ethan . . . Ethan! (*He has drawn close to her and she moves closer to him . . . until their bodies are touching and her head is buried in his coat. He stands there looking down at her . . . she looks up at him and then suddenly throws her arms around his neck, draws his face down to hers, and kisses him. He holds her tightly to him, and kisses her with fierce passion. Mattie murmurs:*) Good-by . . . good-by, Ethan! (*She kisses him again and then releases herself from his hold.*)

**Ethan.**

I can't let you go now! I can't.

**Mattie.**

Oh, I can't go either! (*The clock strikes in the distant valley below—five chimes.*)

**Ethan.**

(*murmuring vaguely*) What'll we do . . . what'll we do!

**Mattie.**

Oh, Ethan, it's time!

**Ethan.**

I'm not goin' to leave you.

**Mattie.**

If I miss my train . . . where'll I go?

**Ethan.**

Where'll you go . . . if you catch it! (*They are silent for a moment.*) And what's the use of either of us goin' any place now without the other one.

**Mattie.**

(*breathlessly*) Ethan, Ethan, we're goin'!

**Ethan.**

(*bewilderedly*) But where . . . Matt?

**Mattie.**

I want you sh'd take me down with you!

**Ethan.**

Down where?

**Mattie.**

Down the coast right off. (*Without waiting for him, she whispers faster and more urgently and breathlessly.*) Down that coast so't we'll never, never come up again . . . never!

**Ethan.**

What do you mean?

**Mattie.**

Right into that big elm down there . . . you c'd do it . . . you c'd, Ethan . . . so't we'd never have to leave each other any more!

**Ethan.**

What're you sayin' . . . what're you sayin' . . . Oh Matt . . . Matt.

**Mattie.**

(*still more rapidly and breathlessly and sweeping him along with her*) Ethan, where'll I go if I leave you . . . I don't know however I'd get along alone . . . you said so yourself . . . you said I couldn't never do it . . . an' I don't want to.

**Ethan.**

(*in her breathless, hurried tone*) I can't go back there . . . I can't go back to that place never again!

**Mattie.**

(*is now drawing him with her to the sled*) Hurry, Ethan

. . . hurry . . . let's go now . . . (*She seats herself on the front of the sled quickly.*)

**Ethan.**

(*suddenly*) Get up!

**Mattie.**

No!

**Ethan.**

(*vehemently*) Get up! (*Picks her up.*) We're goin' down head first and together . . . holdin' each other tight! (*Without waiting for her to reply . . . he seizes her roughly.*) I want to feel you holdin' me!

**Mattie.**

(*a murmur*) Is it goin' to hurt, Ethan?

**Ethan.**

Don't be a-scared, Matt . . . it ain't goin' to hurt . . . it ain't goin' to hurt at all . . . we're goin' to fetch that elm so hard we won't feel anything at all . . . exceptin' only each other! (*Both on sled. He stretches out at her side and their arms go around each other. He murmurs:*) Matt . . . Matt . . .

**Mattie.**

Hold me . . . hold me tight, Ethan! (*The sled is heard in the darkness . . . bounding faster and faster down the slope.*)

from
# THE DEEP BLUE SEA
by Terence Rattigan

Three Scenes from Acts I, II, and III
HESTER, FREDDY

Rattigan's study of the end of an affair opens with an attempted suicide and closes with the would-be victim's first, tentative attempts to get on with life. In between, the playwright reveals in sharply pointed scenes the natures of the ill-matched lovers: Hester, who loves too well, and Freddy, who cannot love enough. They are viewed together and in contrast or complement to other characters: Freddy with Jackie, the golfing pal who can't make it clear to him why a woman might try to kill herself just because a man failed to turn up for a birthday dinner; Hester and the solid, reliable husband she deserted in order to live with Freddy, a ne'er-do-well who lives from his golf winnings; Hester and Dr. Miller, a doctor who has lost his license and his profession but not his ability to persuade a troubled patient that there is good merely in living and going on.

The first of the scenes between Hester and Freddy reprinted here occurs at the close of Act I. At the opening of the act, Hester has been found sprawled by a gas heater; she is alive only because she did not put a shilling in the heater coin-box and the gas shut off. Revived and more or less herself again, she waits now for Freddy to come home from his golf week end. Freddy, of course, knows nothing of the attempted suicide.

The setting is the sitting room of a furnished flat in London. "It is a big room for it is on the second floor of a large and gloomy Victorian mansion . . . but it has an air of dinginess, even of squalor. . . ." Hester stands at the window, peering between the curtains to keep an eye on the street below. She is "in the middle thirties with a thoughtful, remote face that has no pretensions to great beauty." She sighs, then goes to the sofa, lies down on it, her back to the door, and picks up a book. After a moment she puts the book down on her lap and stares sightlessly ahead.

(*The door opens and Freddy Page comes in. He is in his late twenties or early thirties, with a sort of boyish good looks that do not indicate age. He carries a suitcase and a bag of golf clubs. The latter he deposits in a corner with a rattle. It is plain that Hester has heard him come in, but she does not turn her head. During the ensuing scene she never looks at him at all, until the moment indicated later.*)

**Freddy.**

Hullo, Hes; how's tricks?

**Hester.**

(*At window*) I thought you were playing golf?

**Freddy.**

We gave up the idea. It started to rain.

**Hester.**

It's not raining here.

**Freddy.**

Pouring down in Sunningdale.

**Hester.**

Well, you're up to town early—it's not ten yet.

**Freddy.**

Jackie Jackson gave me a lift. He's got a Jaguar. Terrific job. We did ninety-three miles an hour down the Great West Road. By the way, there was a bloody great Rolls moving off from here just as I came in. Wonder whose it was. (*He kisses her on the back of her head*) Do you know? (*He takes his golf shoes into the kitchen*) You don't suppose old Pa Elton's lashed out and invested his life's savings, do you? I wouldn't be surprised, considering what he makes out of us.

**Hester.**

Did you have a good week end?

**Freddy.**

Not bad. Won both my matches. Took five pounds off Jackie. Won a bottle of Scotch. Match bye—and bye-bye. Jackie was livid. I wanted to double the stakes, but he wouldn't hear of it.

**Hester.**

You can't blame him, can you? How much did you win altogether?

**Freddy.**

Seven.

**Hester.**

Could you let Mrs. Elton have some of it?

**Freddy.**

I thought you were going to sell those pictures. Is there any coffee left?

**Hester.**

I'm not now.

**Freddy.**

Why not?

**Hester.**

I've given one away. (*She goes into the kitchen.*)

**Freddy.**

(*Mildly*) That was a bloody silly thing to go and do, wasn't it?

**Hester.**

Yes. I suppose it was.

**Freddy.**

Oh, hell! All right. She can have three. I need the rest for lunch. I'm taking a South American to the Ritz! Get me, giving lunch parties at the Ritz.

**Hester.**

What South American?

**Freddy.**

Bloke I met at golf yesterday. Aircraft business. I got myself given the old intro to him—you know—one of England's most famous test pilots, D.F.C. and bar, D.S.O., all the old ex-Spitfire bull. He seemed impressed.

**Hester.**

So he should.

**Freddy.**

Funny thing about gongs, when you think what a lottery they were. They don't mean a damn thing in war—except as a line-shoot, but in peacetime they're quite useful.

**Hester.**

That's what they're for, isn't it?

**Freddy.**

This bloke's worth bags of dough, Hes. He's got some sort of tie-up with Vickers over here, I think. He might fix something. Anyway he ought to be good for a touch.

I say, do you know you haven't looked at me once since I came in?

**Hester.**

Haven't I, Freddy?

**Freddy.**

Why's that?

**Hester.**

I can remember what you look like.

**Freddy.**

(*With a guilty look*) I haven't done anything, have I?

**Hester.**

(*Smiling*) No, Freddy. You haven't done anything.

**Freddy.**

You're not still peeved about last night, are you? You see, the blokes wanted to play again today, and if I'd let 'em down—

**Hester.**

That's all right.

**Freddy.**

You were funny on the phone, too, I remember. There wasn't any special reason you wanted me back to dinner last night, was there? (*Hester, still not looking at him, does not reply. She gets up from the sofa, her back to him. A sudden thought strikes Freddy. Explosively*) Oh, my God! (*After an embarrassed pause*) Many happy returns.

**Hester.**

Thank you, Freddy.

**Freddy.**

Blast! I remembered it on Saturday too. I was going past Barkers' and I thought, it's too late to get her a present now. I'll have to find a shop open on Sunday. Cigarettes, or something. Had you arranged anything special for dinner?

**Hester.**

No, nothing special. Just a steak and a bottle of claret.

**Freddy.**

We'll have it tonight.

**Hester.**

Yes.

**Freddy.**

Come on now, Hes. I've said I'm sorry. I can't say more?

**Hester.**

No, Freddy.

**Freddy.**

Give us a shot of those gorgeous blue orbs. I haven't seen 'em for two whole days—(*He goes to her and lifts her chin*) This is me, Freddy Page. Remember?

**Hester.**

I remember. (*He kisses her. Instantly she responds, with intensity of emotion that is almost ugly. After a moment he pushes her away and smacks her playfully.*)

**Freddy.**

Naughty to sulk with your Freddy. Go and get dressed. We'll have a quick one at the Belvedere to celebrate.

**Hester.**

That will be fun.

**Freddy.**

(*Putting his clubs away*) What have you been up to over the week end?

**Hester.**

Oh, nothing very much. I went to a picture.

**Freddy.**

Bet you didn't practice your golf.

**Hester.**

I did too. For all of an hour! You don't believe me, do you? (*Freddy shakes his head "no"*) It's true. At the end, I was swinging like a pro. Well, a little better, anyway. When are you going to take me with you?

**Freddy.**

Pretty soon!

**Hester.**

Are you?

**Freddy.**

Go and get dressed, you.

**Hester.**

(*At bedroom door*) Want me to lunch with your South American?

**Freddy.**

No, I think better not. I can shoot him a better line without your beady eyes on me.

**Hester.**

They were gorgeous orbs a moment ago.

**Freddy.**

They get beady in company. Go on, darling. Hurry.

**Hester.**

Yes.

**Freddy.**

Still love me?

**Hester.**

I still love you. (*She goes into bedroom leaving the door open. She is taking off her dressing gown as she speaks and hanging it up on a hook on the door*) Oh, darling, where are you going to be between five and six?

**Freddy.**

Nowhere special, why?

**Hester.**

Do you mind being out? I've got someone coming in I want to see alone.

**Freddy.**

A customer?

**Hester.**

Yes.

**Freddy.**

All right. I'll go to that new club down the road.

**Hester.**

(*Smiling*) And don't get sozzled, either. Remember our dinner.

**Freddy.**

Shut up, you. Go on, darling, hurry. (*She disappears, leaving the door open. Freddy goes to the bedroom door and looks in the dressing gown for cigarettes. He finds a pack and a letter in Hester's pocket. He is about to replace the letter when he glances at the envelope. He raises his eyebrows, and brings the letter into the room. He lights a smoke, and opens the envelope, then begins to read.*)

**Hester.**

(*Off stage*) Oh, darling, don't forget your coffee.

**Freddy.**

(*As he sits*) What? Ahh, no—I won't forget.

## SECOND SCENE

Freddy knows now about the suicide attempt and he has read the letter Hester meant him to find after her death. You could never, she wrote, feel about me as I do about you—though it's not your fault. Freddy is puzzled and angry. "How I hate getting tangled up in other people's emotions," he tells his friend Jackie. "It's the one thing I've tried to avoid all my life, and yet it always seems to be happening to me. Always." Later, in a talk with Dr.

Miller, Freddy begins to comprehend what Hester meant in saying that they did not love in the same way. He goes to the local pub to think it over. When he returns, he hurries into the bedroom to change his clothes; apparently he is going out again.

**Hester.**

(*goes quickly to the bedroom door. She knocks. Calling*) Freddy, let me in, darling. (*There is no answer. She knocks again*) Freddy, don't be childish. Let me in. (*There is no answer. Hester walks away from the door and goes to get a cigarette. As she is lighting it Freddy emerges from the bedroom. He has changed into a blue suit*) You're looking very smart. Going out somewhere?

**Freddy.**

Yes.

**Hester.**

Where?

**Freddy.**

To see Lopez about a job.

**Hester.**

Lopez?

**Freddy.**

The South American I had lunch with.

**Hester.**

Oh, yes. Of course, I'd forgotten. How did it go off?

**Freddy.**

It went off all right.

**Hester.**

Oh, good. You think you'll get the job?

**Freddy.**

Yes, I think so. He made a fairly definite offer. Of course it's up to his boss.

**Hester.**

Let's have a look at you. (*She inspects him*) Oh, darling, you might have changed your shirt.

**Freddy.**

Well, I hadn't a clean one.

**Hester.**

No. The laundry's late again. I'll wash one out for you tomorrow.

**Freddy.**

Yes. Does it look too bad?

**Hester.**

No. It'll pass. Your shoes need a cleaning.

**Freddy.**

Yes. I'll give them a rub.

**Hester.**

No. Take them off. I'll do them. (*She goes toward the kitchen*) Somehow or other you always manage to get shoe polish over your face—Lord knows how. (*She disappears into the kitchen. Freddy takes his shoes off. Hester comes back with shoe brushes and a tin of polish. She takes the shoes from him and begins to clean them. There is a fairly long silence*) Well, what's the job?

**Freddy.**

(*Muttering*) Yes. I suppose I must tell you. (*Hester gives him a quick glance.*)

**Hester.**

Yes, Freddy. I think I'd like to know.

**Freddy.**

Look, Hes. *I've* got to talk for a bit now. It's not going to be easy, so don't interrupt, do you mind? You always could argue the hind leg off a donkey—and just when I've got things clear in my mind I don't want them muddled up again.

**Hester.**

I'm sorry, Freddy. I must interrupt at once. The way you've been behaving this afternoon, how could you have things clear in your mind?

**Freddy.**

I'm all right now, Hes. I had a cup of black coffee, and after that a bit of a walk. I know what I'm doing.

**Hester.**

And what are you doing, Freddy?

**Freddy.**

Accepting a job in South America as a test pilot.

**Hester.**

Test pilot? But you've said a hundred times you could never go back to that. After that crash in Canada you told me you had no nerve or judgment left.

**Freddy.**

They'll come back. I had too many drinks that time in Canada. You know that.

**Hester.**

Yes, I know that. So did the Court of Inquiry know that. Does this man Lopez know that?

**Freddy.**

No, of course not. He won't hear either. Don't worry about my nerve and judgment, Hes. A month or two on the wagon and I'll be the old ace again—the old dicer with death.

**Hester.**

(*Sharply*) Don't use that idiotic RAF slang. (*More gently*) Do you mind? This is too important—

**Freddy.**

Yes. It is important.

**Hester.**

Whereabouts in South America?

**Freddy.**

Somewhere near Rio.

**Hester.**

I see. (*She continues to clean the shoes mechanically*) Well, when do we start?

**Freddy.**

We don't.

**Hester.**

We don't?

**Freddy.**

You and I don't, Hes. That's what I'm trying to tell you. I'm going alone.

**Hester.**

(*At length*) Why, Freddy?

**Freddy.**

If I'm to stay on the wagon, I've got to be alone.

**Hester.**

(*In a near whisper*) Have you?

**Freddy.**

Oh, hell—that's not the real reason. Listen, Hes, darling. (*There is a pause while he paces the room as if concentrating desperately on finding the words. Hester watches him*) You've always said, haven't you, that I don't really love you? Well, I suppose, in your sense I don't. But what I do feel for you is a good deal stronger than I've ever felt for anybody else in my life, or ever will feel, I should think. That's why I went away with you in the first place, that's why I've stayed with you all this time, and that's why I must go away from you now.

**Hester.**

(*At length*) That sounds rather like a prepared speech, Freddy.

**Freddy.**

Yes. I suppose it is a bit prepared. I worked it out on my walk. But it's still true, Hes. I'm too fond of you to let things slide. That letter was a hell of a shock. I knew often you were a bit unhappy—you often knew I was a bit down too. But I hadn't a clue how much the—difference in our feelings had been hurting you. It's asking too damn much of any bloke to go on as if nothing had happened when he knows now for a fact that he's driving the only girl he's ever loved to suicide.

**Hester.**

(*In a low voice*) Do you think your leaving me will drive me away from suicide?

**Freddy.**

(*Simply*) That's a risk I shall just have to take, isn't it? It's a risk both of us will have to face. (*Pauses.*)

**Hester.**

Freddy, you mustn't scare me like this.

**Freddy.**

No scare, Hes. Sorry, this is on the level.

**Hester.**

You know perfectly well you'll feel quite differently in the morning.

**Freddy.**

No, I won't, Hes. Not this time. (*Pause*) Besides, I don't think I'll be here in the morning.

**Hester.**

Where will you be?

**Freddy.**

I don't know. Somewhere. I think I'd better get out to-night.

**Hester.**

No, Freddy, no!

**Freddy.**

It's better that way. I'm scared of your arguing. (*Passionately*) I know this is right, you see. I know it, but with your gift of the gab, you'll muddle things up for me again, and I'll be lost.

**Hester.**

I won't Freddy. I won't. I promise I won't. But you must stay tonight. Just tonight.

**Freddy.**

(*Unhappily*) No, Hes.

**Hester.**

Just tonight, Freddy. Only one night.

**Freddy.**

No. Sorry, Hes.

**Hester.**

Don't be so cruel, Freddy. How can you be so cruel?

**Freddy.**

Hes, this is our last chance. If we miss it, we're done for. We're death to each other, you and I.

**Hester.**

That isn't true.

**Freddy.**

It is true, darling, and you've known it longer than I have. I'm such a damn fool and that's been the trouble, or I should have done this long ago. That's it, you know. It's written in great bloody letters of fire over our heads— "You and I are death to each other." (*Hester is unrestrainedly weeping. Freddy comes over to her and picks up his shoes.*)

**Hester.**

I haven't finished them.

**Freddy.**

They're all right. (*He begins to put them on*). Please don't cry. You know what it does to me. (*He rises*) I'm sorry, Hes. My God, I'm sorry.

**Hester.**

Not now. Not this minute. Not this minute, Freddy? (*Freddy finishes putting on his shoes, and then turns away from her, brushing his sleeve across his eyes. Going to him*) You've got all your things here. You've got to pack—

**Freddy.**

I'll send for them.

**Hester.**

You promised to come back for dinner.

**Freddy.**

I know. I'm sorry about that. (*He kisses her quickly and goes to the door.*)

**Hester.**

(*Frantically*) But you can't break a promise like that, Freddy. You can't. Come back just for our dinner, Freddy. I won't argue, I swear, and then if you want to go away afterward— (*Freddy goes out. Hester runs to the door after him*) Don't go. Freddy, come back. Don't leave me alone tonight. Not tonight. Freddy, don't leave me alone tonight. (*She follows him out.*)

## THIRD SCENE

Freddy has not come back. Again Hester has considered killing herself, but Dr. Miller has put her to a test: has she the same courage to live, he asks, that she has to condemn herself to death? When Freddy appears, Dr. Miller excuses himself and leaves.

**Hester.**
Come in, Freddy. Don't stand in the door. (*Freddy shuffles in*) How are you feeling now?

**Freddy.**
All right.

**Hester.**
Thank you for coming.

**Freddy.**
That's O.K. I shouldn't have sent the kid anyway, I suppose.

**Hester.**
Had any food?

**Freddy.**
Yes. I had a bite at the Belvedere. What about you?

**Hester.**
Oh, I'll get myself something later. (*There is a pause, while Freddy still watches her apprehensively*) When exactly are you off to Rio?

**Freddy.**
Thursday. I told you.

**Hester.**
Oh, yes, of course. By boat?

**Freddy.**
Oh, no. Flying.

**Hester.**
Oh, yes.

**Freddy.**
Oh, by the way—About the rent—those clubs'll fetch thirty or forty quid. They'll take care of old Ma Elton and the few odd bills.

**Hester.**
Won't you need them?

**Freddy.**
No. I can't fly them.

**Hester.**
I'll pack the rest of your things tonight and get them round to Charing Cross in the morning.

**Freddy.**

There's no hurry. (*Another pause*) I dropped a note in at Bill's house. He'll probably be round.

**Hester.**

He's been round.

**Freddy.**

Oh. Are you—?

**Hester.**

No.

**Freddy.**

I'm sorry.

**Hester.**

It's all right. It wouldn't have worked.

**Freddy.**

No, I suppose not. I didn't know. You'll go on with your painting, will you?

**Hester.**

Yes. I think so. As a matter of fact, I might even go to an art school, and start from the beginning again.

**Freddy.**

It's never too late to begin again. Isn't that what they say?

**Hester.**

Yes. They do. (*There is a long pause. Freddy seems to be waiting for Hester to say something, but she stands quite still, looking at him.*)

**Freddy.**

(*At length*) Well—

**Hester.**

(*In a clear calm voice*) Well, good-bye, Freddy.

**Freddy.**

Good-bye, Hes. (*He moves to the door. Hester still does not move. Freddy turns, waiting for her to say something. She does not. He suddenly walks up to her and embraces her*) I wish I knew what the hell I was going to do without you. (*He kisses her. She accepts the embrace without in any way returning it. After a moment, Freddy releases her, goes quickly to the door and turns around. He goes out, closing the door.*)

(*Hester stands quite still for a second. She looks around the room. Then she goes to the coat hooks and takes down Freddy's clothes. She brings them and piles them on the sofa. She reaches down a suitcase off a shelf. Then lights the gas fire. After lingering at the fire for a moment, she returns to Freddy's clothes and continues to pack.*)

from
FIVE-FINGER EXERCISE
by Peter Shaffer

Two Scenes from Act I, scene 2, and Act II, scene 1
LOUISE, WALTER
and
Two Scenes from Act I, scene 2
STANLEY, CLIVE

The play is appropriately named, for it is an "exercise"
for five characters: husband, wife, son, daughter, and
the daughter's young German tutor. The action begins
with the introduction of an outsider, the tutor, into the
family. He is the catalyst who makes active the long-
smoldering conflicts among the other four people; he becomes the ally whose friendship each of the others seeks
to win; and he serves as the mirror in which each of
them, first, sees himself as he would like to be seen and,
later, sees himself as he actually is. For the tutor, also,
there are envisioned ideals and discovered realities: he
longs to share the warmth and mutual love of a family,
but this family, he finds, is torn by antagonisms—it is
self-destroying, destructive of each of its members, and
ultimately destroys the outsider, shattering the dreams on
which he had hoped to build a new life in a new country. In a series of sharply drawn scenes, the playwright
"exercises" his five characters by twos and threes. The
tutor is wooed by mother, son, and daughter. The divi-
sions between husband and wife and between children
and parents are intensified. Individual conflicts are brought
to moments of personal crisis and revelation, character
relations shift, until the battles within the family are
stopped short by the tutor's attempted suicide. He lives
but he goes away, leaving the others once again alone
with themselves, the ugly and inadequate selves that they
have discovered in their relations with the outsider. And
there the play ends.

Two of the "exercises" for two characters are spotlighted
in the scenes below. The first pair of scenes presents two
views of Louise Harrington, the mother of the family, and

Walter, the tutor she has hired to teach her daughter. Louise is a "smart woman in her forties, dressed stylishly, even ostentatiously, for a country week end. Her whole manner bespeaks a constant preoccupation with style, though without apparent insincerity or affection. She is very good looking." Walter is "a slim German of twenty-two, handsome, secret, diffident." His intelligence, skill as a musician, and charming manners delight Louise—they are qualities so lacking, she feels, in her husband, the very successful manufacturer of furniture which will never win any awards for originality or excellence of design.

The setting is the Harringtons' week-end cottage in Suffolk, in England. The living room is well furnished—it "almost aggressively expresses Mrs. Harrington's personality. We are let to know by it that she is a Person of Taste; but also that she does not often let well enough alone. There is more here of the town, and of the expensive town, than is really acceptable in the country: the furnishings are sufficiently modish and chic to make her husband feel, and look, perpetually out of place."

The time is evening. Mr. Harrington has gone off to the local pub, the place in which he does feel comfortable and at home. To Louise's surprise, her son Clive has also gone out to a pub; he left when Louise suggested that Walter recite German poetry to them (she does not understand German).

Clive has just stalked out of the room. Walter stands stiffly, very uncomfortable.

### FIRST SCENE

**Louise.**
Poor boy. I'm afraid he gets rather upset down here. He's essentially a town person, really, like me. And I get it from my mother. Being French, of course. Like all Parisians she detested the country. She used to say: "Fields are for cows. Drawing-rooms are for ladies." Of course, it sounds better in French. If I had my way I'd never stir from London. I did all this (*indicating the cottage*) for Mr. Harrington. He's what we call here an open-air type, you know.

**Walter.**
(*smiling*) Yes. I know this word.

**Louise.**

And for Clive's sake, too. We'd all been a little restless in
town, and I thought it would be amusing if we could have
a little retreat . . . Calm ourselves with country air . . .
And really, it's been quite successful, I think . . . On the
whole . . . (*Walter sits on the sofa. She drinks some
coffee.*) A very clever boy I was recommended to did it
up for us. Bunny Baily—d'you know him?

**Walter.**

No, I'm afraid not.

**Louise.**

(*lightly and rapidly*) Well you will, I'm sure. He's very
up and coming. Not just chic; I mean really *original*. He
wanted to make us entirely early Medieval; stone flagging
and rushes strewn on the floor. But my husband didn't
quite see eye to eye with us on that. (*Drinks more coffee.*)
Mr. Harrington's very conservative, you know. Well, most
men are, aren't they, essentially? . . . Englishmen, anyway.
The French are different . . . And the Germans too. I'm
sure. (*She smiles at him and points to the cigarettes on
the coffee table.*) Would you like to smoke?

**Walter.**

(*reaching for the cigarette box*) Thank you.

**Louise.**

You look a little upset too, Hibou. What's the matter?

**Walter.**

Oh, it's nothing.

**Louise.**

It must be something. Has Clive been teasing you? He can
be very naughty sometimes.

**Walter.**

Oh, no. You know, Mrs. Harrington, I think he is not
very happy.

**Louise.**

(*putting cup on table next to armchair*) He gets that from
me too.

**Walter.**

(*impulsively*) Is there anything that I can do? Anything
at all?

**Louise.**

(*regardless*) I'm not a very happy person either, you
know. (*Rises. Crosses left to below armchair.*) Well, you
can see for yourself. Whatever you do, my dear boy,
marry a girl who's your equal. If you can find one. I'm
sure it'll be hard. When I married I was a very young girl.

Believe it or not (*puts cup on table left of armchair*) I'd
hardly met anyone outside Bournemouth. (*Sits in the armchair.*) My parents didn't consider it proper for me to
run about on my own. And when I met Stanley, they did
everything in their power to encourage the match. You
see they weren't very dependable people. My mother was
an aristocratic little lady from France who had never
learnt to do a thing for herself all her life. And helplessly
extravagant as well. Of course, highborn people so often
seem to have extravagance as a sort of inherited characteristic, don't they? My father was more stable, at least
he was conscious of money though he never made very
much. (*Drinks more coffee.*) And when he actually inherited something, he lost it all in speculation. Do you
understand that word, dear? Speculation?

**Walter.**

Oh yes . . . he was a stockbroker.

**Louise.**

Heavens, no—a lawyer. Both my parents came from
professional people, so naturally they had reservations
about marrying me into the furniture business. (*Gives her
cup to Walter, who puts it on the tray.*) Still, I was attracted to Stanley. I won't deny it. He had sort of rugged
charm, as they say. Obviously I was interested in all kinds
of things like art and music and poetry which he, poor
man, had never had time for. But when you're young,
those things don't seem to matter. It's only later when the
first excitement's gone, you start looking a little closer.
(*An audible sigh.*) Walter, these past few years have been
intolerable. (*Rises and goes toward Walter.*) There are
times when I listen to you playing when I go almost mad
with sheer pleasure. Year after year I've had to kill that
side of myself. Smother it. Stamp it out. Heaven knows
I've tried to be interested in his bridge and his golf and
his terrible business friends. I can't do it—I just can't do
it. I'm sorry. I didn't mean to talk like this. I'm embarrassing you.

**Walter.**

No.

**Louise.**

I'm being vulgar, aren't I?

**Walter.**

You could never be.

**Louise.**

Dear Hibou . . . you know, don't you? You of all people must know. You understand why I stayed. (*Sits in arm-chair.*) The children. At least I could see that they weren't stifled too . . . Do you condemn me?

**Walter.**

(*puts out cigarette*) How could I condemn—in your house?

**Louise.**

(*wryly*) I think we can leave hospitality to one side.

**Walter.**

(*pursuing his own thought*) No, no. In the house you have given me also to live in, so I can sit here and talk to you as if always I had the right.

**Louise.**

(*sympathetically*) Dear Walter . . .

**Walter.**

Where I worked before, I taught the children for two or three hours. I was paid by their mothers and back always to my small room— (*a faint smile*) —with my cooking which is not so good. You will never know how much I owe to you.

**Louise.**

My dear boy . . . Tell me about your family. Your people in Germany. (*Walter stiffens perceptibly into withdrawal.*)

**Walter.**

There is nothing to tell.

**Louise.**

There must be something.

**Walter.**

I was an orphan.

**Louise.**

Like Stanley.

**Walter.**

(*rises and goes right to dining table*) My parents died when I was too young to remember them. I was brought up by my uncle and his wife.

**Louise.**

Were they good to you?

**Walter.**

(*noncommittal*) Very good, yes.

**Louise.**

And—that's all you want to say?

**Walter.**

There is nothing else.

**Louise.**

Don't think I'm being inquisitive . . . It's only that you've
come to mean so much to us all in this past two months.

**Walter.**

I do not deserve it.

**Louise.**

(*warmly. Rises*) You deserve far more. Far, far more. I
knew as soon as I saw you at that terrible cocktail party in
London, standing all by yourself in the corner pretending
to study the pictures. Do you remember—before even I
spoke to you I knew you were something quite exceptional. I remember thinking: such delicate hands . . . and
that fair hair— (*touching it*) —it's the hair of a poet. And
when he speaks he'll have a soft voice that stammers a
little from nervousness, and a lovely Viennese accent . . .

**Walter.**

(*stiffly*) I am not Viennese, you know. I am German.

**Louise.**

Well, it's not so very different . . .

**Walter.**

(*dogged*) I am German. This is not so poetic. (*He crosses
below Louise to the left end of sofa.*)

**Louise.**

(*a little intimidated by the darkness in him*) But Hibou,
there's good and bad in all countries—surely?

**Walter.**

(*gently. Crosses below Louise and the armchair to the
left edge of the sofa*) You are too good to understand. I
know how they seem to you, the Germans: so kind and
quaint. Like your yourself said: miller's daughters and
woodcutters . . . But they can be monsters.

**Louise.**

(*prepared to mock him as she breaks downstage—left of
armchair*) Really now . . .

**Walter.**

Yes! . . . (*He is plainly distressed. Louise looks at him
curiously.*)

**Louise.**

Even in England we're not all angels.

**Walter.**

Angels to me! Because this to me is Paradise.

**Louise.**

How charming you are.

**Walter.**

(*with increasing heat*) No, I am sincere. You see . . . here in England most people want to do what's good. Where I come from this is not true. They want only power . . . They are a people that is enraged by equality. They need always to feel ashamed, to breathe in shame—like oxygen —to go on living. Because deeper than everything else they want to be hated. From this they can believe they are giants, even in chains . . . (*Recovering as he sits on the sofa.*) I'm sorry. It's difficult to talk about.

**Louise.**

Anything one feels deeply is hard to speak of, my dear.

**Walter.**

One thing I do know. I will never go back. Soon I'll be a British subject.

**Louise.**

(*crossing right a few steps*) You really want to stay here.

**Walter.**

If you had seen what I have, you would know why I call it Paradise.

**Louise.**

I can see for myself how you've suffered. It's in your face . . . (*Extending her hand to him.*) Walter . . . You musn't torment yourself like this. (*She takes Walter's hand.*) It's not good for you. You're among friends now. People who want to help you. People who love you . . . Doesn't that make a difference?

**Walter.**

You are so good to me! So good, good. . . . (*Impulsively he bends and kisses her hands.*)

**Louise.**

(*suddenly she takes his head in her hands and holds it close to her. Tenderly*) Oh, my dear . . . you make me feel ashamed. (*Clive comes in abruptly through the garden door. He stares at them fascinated.*) It's been so long since anyone has talked like this to me. (*Clive bangs the door.*) Jou-Jou . . . (*Trying to recover her composure.*) Did you have a nice talk? Did you see Pam?

## SECOND SCENE

It is the following morning. Walter has spoken to Clive of his hope to share the wonderful things of a family and Clive has warned him bitterly that this family is not the one he seeks. From upstairs comes the sound of Louise's voice calling Walter. "Answer her," Clive says, "it's your duty, isn't it?"

As Louise comes down the stairs, Clive goes abruptly out the front door.

**Louise.**

(*coming into the living room*) Ah, there you are, my dear boy, all alone . . . ? (*going to coffee table*) Come and talk to me, it's not good for you to be on your own too much.

**Walter.**

I was not alone. Clive was here. He's just gone out.

**Louise.**

(*takes cigarette and holder*) Where?

**Walter.**

I don't know—Mrs. Harrington, I'm most worried for him.

**Louise.**

(*smiling*) Poor Hibou, you worry about everybody, don't you? But you mustn't about Clive, really. It's just a tiny case of old-fashioned jealousy, that's all. (*Walter lights her cigarette.*) Well, it's only to be expected, isn't it? (*Crosses to armchair.*) We've always been so wonderfully close, he and I.

**Walter.**

(*courteously*) Of course.

**Louise.**

He'll get over it. One day he'll understand about women. At the moment, of course, he thinks there must only be room in my heart for one boy. So silly . . . (*She sits. Warmly.*) I don't believe you can ration love, do you?

**Walter.**

(*sits, sofa. Admiringly*) With someone like you it is not possible.

**Louise.**

Nor with you, my dear. You know, last night held the most beautiful moments I've known for many years. I felt—well, that you and I could have a really warm friendship. Even with the difference . . . I mean in— our ages.

**Walter.**

Between friends there are no ages, I think.

**Louise.**

(*tenderly*) I like to think that, too.

**Walter.**

Oh, it's true. Like in a family—you don't notice how old people are, because you keep growing together.

**Louise.**

Yes. Dear little owl . . . What's the matter? . . . Are you embarrassed? (*He shakes his head "No."*) It's the last thing you must ever be with me. (*Walter smiles.*) What are you thinking? Come on: tell me.

**Walter.**

Some things grow more when they are not talked about.

**Louise.**

Try, anyway, I want you to.

**Walter.**

(*looking away from her*) It is only that you have made me wonder—

**Louise.**

(*prompting eagerly*) Tell me.

**Walter.**

(*lowering his voice still more as he walks toward Louise*) Mrs. Harrington, forgive me for asking this, but do you think it's possible for someone to find a new mother? (*Louise sits very still. The expression of eagerness fades, and its remnant hardens on her face. She stares at him.*) Have I offended you?

**Louise.**

(*smiles, without joy*) Of course not. I am . . . very touched.

**Walter.**

(*moved. Kneels*) I'm so glad. (*Eagerly.*) That is why I feel I can talk to you about Clive, for example. I am most worried for him. He is not happy now. And I do not think it is jealousy. It is something else—more deep in him— trying to explode. Like the beginning of an earthquake or so.

**Louise.**

(*with increasing coolness. Rises. Crosses to coffee table*) Really, my dear, don't you think you're being a little over-dramatic?

**Walter.**

(*dogged. Rises*) No. I mean exactly this. You see . . . that boy . . . It is very difficult for me to explain.

**Louise.**

(*wryly*) I appreciate your attempt. . . . (*Crosses to center table.*) But really, I'm sure I know my children a little better than you.

**Walter.**

(*persisting*) Of course. But just in this case—with Clive —I feel something which frightens me—I don't know why—

**Louise.**

(*her temper breaking*) Oh, for heaven's sake! (*Walter recoils. Recovering quickly, Louise crosses to dining table with dirty ash tray.*) I mean . . . after all, as you admit yourself, you *are* only a newcomer to the family, remember. (*Sweetly.*) Now why don't you go and play me some of your nice music? (*Walter looks confused, and lowers his eyes before her strained smile. He exits into kitchen. Louise starts to pick up dishes and silverware, but puts them down with a big crash.*)

## THIRD SCENE

Stanley Harrington is "a forceful man in middle age, well built and self-possessed, though there is something deeply insecure about his assertiveness." His son Clive is "nineteen, quick, nervous, taut, and likable. There is something about him oddly and disturbingly young for his age, the nakedness of someone in whom intellectual development has outstripped the emotional." Clive is much more the son of his mother than of his father. With Louise, he is very much the little boy; with Stanley, he is ill at ease or petulant. Clive has been away at Cambridge—his first year in the university—and now, his first week end at home, the gap which always has separated him from his father has grown wider than ever.

The time is evening, Stanley and Clive have had one of their arguments—this one concerned a conversation in which Clive told the manager of Stanley's factory that the furniture turned out there was "shoddy and vulgar." Louise has tried to be the peacemaker; after all, she says, this is Clive's first visit home from Cambridge. She has gone to the kitchen to make more coffee, a gesture toward "a quiet evening with the family."

**Clive.**

I'm sorry I said that about the furniture, Father. I suppose it was tactless of me.

**Stanley.**

Never mind. How are you settling down at Cambridge? What about the other boys, do you get on with them?

**Clive.**

It's not exactly like prep school, you know. You rather pick your own friends.

**Stanley.**

Yes, I suppose you do. Well, what do they do there? I mean apart from lessons.

**Clive.**

Anything you like. There are all sorts of clubs and societies.

**Stanley.**

Do you belong to any?

**Clive.**

Yes, I joined a Dramatic Society as a matter of fact.

**Stanley.**

You mean for acting?

**Clive.**

It's quite professional, you know. They have their own theater and get reviews in *The Times*.

**Stanley.**

Don't any of your friends play games?

**Clive.**

Yes, but—the cricket and football are sort of professional standards. I thought of taking up fencing, it's not as odd as it sounds. It's meant to be very good for co-ordination—

**Stanley.**

What's that?

**Clive.**

Muscles, I think.

**Stanley.**

Clive, as you know your mother and I didn't see eye-to-eye about sending you to University. But that's past history now. The point is what use are you going to make of it? Well?

**Clive.**

That's rather as it turns out, I should have thought. I mean you can't judge things in advance, can you?

**Stanley.**

Ah now, that's just what I mean. If you don't know where you're going you might just as well pack up.

**Clive.**

Why?

**Stanley.**

It's quite simple, I should have thought.

**Clive.**

It isn't. It just isn't like that. I mean if I knew where I was going I wouldn't have to go there would I? I'd be there already.

**Stanley.**

What kind of silly quibble is that?

**Clive.**

It's not a quibble. Look, education—being educated—you just can't talk about it in that way. It's something quite different—like setting off on an expedition into the jungle. Gradually all the things you know disappear. The old birds fly out of the sky, new ones fly in you've never seen before, and everything surprises you too. Trees you expected to be a few feet high grow right up overhead, like the nave of Wells Cathedral. Anyway if you had seen all this before, you wouldn't have to go looking. I think education is simply the process of being taken by surprise, do you see?

**Stanley.**

Be that as it may.

**Clive.**

You don't see.

**Stanley.**

(*rises—crosses to above dining table*) Clive, I'm not talking about education. By all means, take advantage of your lessons. Look here boy, let's not pretend. Everyone doesn't get to Cambridge, you know it and I know it. You're in a privileged position and you must make the most of it. What you do now will influence the rest of your life. You know that, don't you?

**Clive.**

Yes, I suppose it will.

**Stanley.**

Take your friends for example. What kind of friends do you have?

**Clive.**

Do you want a list?

**Stanley.**

Now don't start getting on any high-horse. I'm simply saying this . . . (*Sits above the dining table. Leans toward Clive.*) People still judge a man by the company he keeps. You go around with a lot of drifters and arty boys, and you'll be judged as one of them.

**Clive.**

I don't . . .

**Stanley.**

(*cuts him off immediately and closes his book*) I don't say
you do, and you're old enough to decide for yourself anyway. Right? (*Clive nods.*) Number two is this. Now's the
time for you to be making contacts with the right people,
I mean people who will be useful to you later on. I don't
mean the smart people or the fancy la-de-da people your
mother's always on about. I mean the people that matter.
The people who will have influence. Get in with them
now and you won't go far wrong. I never had your opportunities, the contacts I made I had to work up myself.
So I know what I'm talking about. Do you understand?

**Clive.**

Yes, I do.

**Stanley.**

Good. Now you've got a good brain and I'll see to it
you've got enough money. There's no harm in having a
few pounds in your pocket, you know. (*Louise enters.
Closes kitchen door.*) Never be so foolish as to look down
on money. It's the one thing that counts in the end.

**Louise.**

(*at the commode putting on her jewelry*) Money! Is that
all you ever think about? Money!

**Stanley.**

You don't have any difficulty spending it, I notice. (*To
Clive.*) Now let's see, how long have you been at Cambridge? Is this your half-term holiday?

**Louise.**

(*crossing to the sofa above the armchair*) Half-term! You
talk about it as if it were a grammar school instead of our
leading University. Really, Stanley, I don't know how one
can even begin to talk to you.

**Stanley.**

(*rises, crosses right a few steps as if to answer Louise.
Then turns to Clive*) Would you like to walk with me
over to Benton's?

**Clive.**

I—I've got some reading to do actually.

**Stanley.**

We can stop in at the Red Lion for a quick one.

**Clive.**

No. I don't think so really.

**Stanley.**

Very well.

**Clive.**

It's important, or I would. (*Stanley nods and goes out of the front door.*)


## FOURTH SCENE


It is later the same evening. Clive and Stanley have been out, separately. Clive, rather drunk, has come home to find his mother in a cozy chat with Walter (the second of their scenes above). Now Clive and Walter have talked; Clive has spoken of his loneliness and asked Walter to take a trip with him during Christmas vacation. Walter has refused and gone to his room, leaving Clive angry and hurt. Clive pours himself a drink, then, as Stanley comes in through the front door, he puts down the glass guiltily and leaves it on the sideboard.


**Stanley.**

What are you doing?

**Clive.**

(*breaks downstage*) Stealing your drink.

**Stanley.**

(*crossing center*) Stealing? You don't have to steal from me, Clive. You're old enough to take a drink if you want one. I don't keep it locked up. (*At commode.*) Where's your mother?

**Clive.**

(*crosses to sofa and sits*) I don't know—upstairs . . .

**Stanley.**

You ought to have come with me to Benton's. We went over to the Golf Club. Jolly nice crowd there. (*Crosses to Clive.*) The sort of fellows *you* ought to be mixing with. There was a chap there in publishing. You'd have been interested . . . Clive, I've told you before, in this world you want to get in with the people that matter. But you've got to make an effort, my boy. Make yourself a bit popular. And you're not going to do that sitting here drinking by yourself. Are you?

**Clive.**

(*still low*) No, I suppose not.

**Stanley.**

What d'you want to do it for anyway?

**Clive.**

(*shrugging*) I don't know.

**Stanley.**

(*crosses to armchair*) Well, it's damn silly and it's not normal. (*Sits.*) If you want to drink—drink with others. Everyone likes a drink. You come over to the Golf Club with me, you'll soon find that out. I'll make you a member. You'll get in with them in a jiffy if you'll only try.

**Clive.**

(*rises and goes to stairs*) Yes. Well . . . I think I'll go to bed now.

**Stanley.**

Just a minute. What's the matter? Aren't they good enough for you? Is that it?

**Clive.**

No, of course it isn't.

**Stanley.**

Then what?

**Clive.**

(*gaining courage and coming back into the room*) Well, all this stuff—right people, wrong people—people who matter. It's all so meaningless.

**Stanley.**

It's not a bit meaningless.

**Clive.**

Well, all right, they matter! But what can I say to them if they don't matter to me? Look, you just can't talk about people in that way. It's idiotic. As far as I'm concerned one of the few people who really matters to me in Cambridge is an Indian.

**Stanley.**

Well, there's nothing wrong in that. What's his father? A rajah or something?

**Clive.**

His father runs a pastry shop in Bombay. (*He sits on sofa.*)

**Stanley.**

Well, what about him?

**Clive.**

He's completely still. I don't mean he doesn't move—I mean that deep down inside him there's this happy stillness, that makes all our family rows and raised voices here like a kind of—blasphemy almost. That's why he matters

—because he loves living so much. Because he understands birds and makes shadow puppets out of cardboard, and loves Ella Fitzgerald and Vivaldi, and Lewis Carroll; and because he plays chess like a devil and makes the best prawn curry in the world. And this is him.

**Stanley.**

Do you want to be a cook?

**Clive.**

No. I don't want to be a cook.

**Stanley.**

(*bewildered and impatient*) Well, Clive, I'm glad to know you've got some nice friends.

**Clive.**

(*sharp*) Don't. Don't do that.

**Stanley.**

What?

**Clive.**

(*rises and crosses left a few steps*) Patronize. It's just too much.

**Stanley.**

I'm not patronizing you, Clive.

**Clive.**

Oh yes, you are. That's precisely what you're doing.

**Stanley.**

That's very unfair.

**Clive.**

(*working himself into a deep rage*) Precisely. Precisely! (*Goes to the commode.*) "I'm glad you have some nice chums, Clive. I had too at your age." . . . These aren't my play-pals; they're important people. Important to me. (*He breaks downstage, left of the armchair with the glass of whisky he poured earlier.*)

**Stanley.**

Did I say they weren't?

§ (*Pamela returns from the bathroom. She listens for a brief moment at the top of the stairs, then goes into the schoolroom, closes door, and on into her bedroom.*) §

**Clive.**

(*frantic*) Important! It's important they should be alive. Every person they meet should be altered by them, or at least remember them with terrific—terrific excitement. That's an important person. Can't you understand?

**Stanley.**

(*rises, crosses to the commode. Crushingly*) No, Clive. I told you: I don't understand you at all. Not at all. (*A slight pause. Clive subsides. When he speaks again it is to renew the attack in a colder and more accusing voice.*)

**Clive.**

You're proud of it too.

**Stanley.**

(*getting angry*) What now?

**Clive.**

That you don't understand me at all. Almost as if it defined you. "I'm the Man Who Doesn't Understand." (*Directly, his voice shaking with resentment.*) Has it ever occurred to you that *I* don't understand *you*? No. Of course not. Because you're the one who does the understanding around here—or rather fails to. (*Furiously.*) What work did you put in to being able to understand anybody?

**Stanley.**

I think you'd better go to bed.

**Clive.**

(*he puts his glass on the commode*) I'll go to bed when I'm good and ready! . . . (*Breaks downstage to Stanley.*) D'you think it falls into your lap—some sort of a grace that enters you when you become a father?

**Stanley.**

You're drunk.

**Clive.**

Yes, you think you can treat me like a child—but you don't even know the right way to treat a child. Because a child is private and important and itself. Not an extension of you. Any more than I am. (*He falls quiet, dead quiet— as if explaining something very difficult. His speech slows and his face betrays an almost obsessed sincerity as he sits in the chair right of the dining table.*) I am myself. Myself. Myself. You think of me only as what I might become. What I might make of myself. But I am myself now—with every breath I take, every blink of the eyelash. The taste of a chestnut or a strawberry on my tongue is me. The smell of my skin is me, the trees and tables that I see with my own eyes are me. You should want to become me and see them as I see them, but we can never exchange. Feelings don't unite us, don't you see? They keep us apart. (*Rises and goes to sofa.*) And words are no good because they're unreal. We live away in our skins from minute to minute, feeling everything quite differently, and any one minute's just as true about us as any other. That's why a question like "What are you going to be?" just doesn't mean anything at all— (*Sits during pause.*) Yes, I'm drunk. You make me drunk.

**Stanley.**

I do?

**Clive.**

(*losing heart*) You and everything . . .

**Stanley.**

(*a little afraid now*) . . . You've given me something to think about, old boy. It's getting a bit late. Don't you think you'd better go upstairs . . . we'll talk about it in the morning. Well, I'll say good night. (*He steps upstage.*) Clive . . . I said good night. (*Still Clive takes no notice. Stanley shrugs and goes up the stairs.*)

from
## THE CORN IS GREEN
by Emlyn Williams

3 scenes from Act I, scene 2, Act II, scene 1, and Act III
MISS MOFFAT, MORGAN EVANS

Emlyn Williams' popular play concerns a schoolteacher and the Welsh miner's child whom she determinedly educates and sends to Oxford. It is a sentimental play, yet strong, and in the characters of Morgan Evans and Miss Moffat it offers two richly developed, rewarding parts, the kind that actors search for. Ethel Barrymore chose to play Miss Moffat when she made her farewell tour of the United States.

The scene of the play is Wales at the end of the nineteenth century. The setting is Miss Moffat's house in Glansarno, a small village in a remote Welsh countryside. Miss Moffat has tried to establish a school in this place, to bring education and hope to children whom custom and necessity have condemned to lives spent as laborers in the mines. She has tried and she has, she feels, failed. This afternoon she has told her assistant that she is ready to close the school. However, she continues to correct the essay papers that are piled on her desk. One of these papers catches her attention and she begins to read it aloud. Miss Moffat is "about forty, a healthy Englishwoman with an honest face, clear, beautiful eyes, a humorous mouth, a direct friendly manner, and unbounded vitality. Her most prominent characteristic is her complete unsentimentality. She wears . . . a collar and tie, and a dark, unexaggerated skirt."

### FIRST SCENE

Miss M.

(*She begins to read, slowly, with difficulty*.) "The mine is dark. . . . If a light come in the mine . . . the rivers in the mine will run fast with the voice of many women; the walls will fall in, and it will be the end of the world."

(*Morgan enters brusquely from the front door. He has made no attempt to wash, but now that he is alone he half-emerges as a truculent arresting boy, with, latent in him, a very strong personality which his immaturity and natural inclination make him shy to display. * * * Miss Moffat, who has not looked up from the paper, begins to read again.*)

**Miss M.**

(*reading*) ". . . So the mine is dark . . ." (*Morgan stops, turns, sees what she is holding, and stops abruptly. She continues without having noticed him. Reading.*) ". . . But when I walk through the Tan—something—shaft, in the dark, I can touch with my hands the leaves on the trees, and underneath . . . (*turning over a page*) . . . where the corn is green." (*A pause.*)

**Morgan.**

Go on readin'. (*Miss Moffat looks up at him, then back at the paper.*)

**Miss M.**

(*reading*) ". . . There is a wind in the shaft, not carbon monoxide they talk about, it smell like the sea, only like as if the sea had fresh flowers lying about . . . and that is my holiday." (*A pause. She looks at the front of the book.*) Are you Morgan Evans?

**Morgan.**

Yes, Miss.

**Miss M.**

Did you write this?

**Morgan.**

(*after hesitation, sullenly*) No, Miss.

**Miss M.**

But it's in your book.

**Morgan.**

Yes, Miss.

**Miss M.**

Then who wrote it?

**Morgan.**

I dunno, Miss. (*Miss Moffat nods to Miss Ronberry, who patters discreetly into the study. Morgan makes for the garden.*)

**Miss M.**

Did you write this? (*It is difficult to tell from the crisp severity of her manner that she is expressing a growing inward excitement. Morgan stops and looks at her, distrustfully.*)

**Morgan.**

I dunno, Miss. . . . (*After hesitating, bursting out.*) What is the matter with it?

**Miss M.**

Sit down. (*He stares at her, looks uncertainly toward the garden door, and moves towards the bench.*) And take your cap off. (*He stares at her again, on the brink of revolt, then doffs his cap and sits on the bench.*) Spelling's deplorable, of course. "Mine" with two "n's," and "leaves" l, e, f, s.

**Morgan.**

(*interested, against his will*) What wass it by rights?

**Miss M.**

A "v," to start with.

**Morgan.**

I never 'eard o' no "v's," Miss.

**Miss M.**

Don't call me Miss.

**Morgan.**

Are you not a Miss?

**Miss M.**

Yes I am, but it is not polite.

**Morgan.**

(*uninterested*) Oh.

**Miss M.**

You say "Yes, Miss Moffat," or "No, Miss Moffat." M, o, double f, a, t.

**Morgan.**

(*after a pause*) No "v's"?

**Miss M.**

No "v's." Where do you live?

**Morgan.**

Under the ground, Miss.

**Miss M.**

I mean your home.

**Morgan.**

Llyn-y-Mwyn, Miss . . . Moffat. Four miles from 'ere.

**Miss M.**

How big is it?

**Morgan.**

Four 'ouses and a beer-'ouse.

**Miss M.**

Have you any hobbies?

**Morgan.**
Oh yes.

**Miss M.**
What?

**Morgan.**
Rum.

**Miss M.**
Rum? (*He takes his bottle from his pocket, holds it up, and puts it back.*) Do you live with your parents?

**Morgan.**
No, by me own self. Me mother iss dead, and me father and me four big brothers wass in the Big Shaft Accident when I wass ten.

**Miss M.**
Killed?

**Morgan.**
Oh yes, everybody wass.

**Miss M.**
What sort of man was your father?

**Morgan.**
'E was a mongrel.

**Miss M.**
A what?

**Morgan.**
'E had a dash of English. He learned it to me.

**Miss M.**
D'you go to chapel?

**Morgan.**
No thank you.

**Miss M.**
Who taught you to read and write?

**Morgan.**
Tott?

**Miss M.**
Taught. The verb "to teach."

**Morgan.**
Oh, teached.

**Miss M.**
Who taught you?

**Morgan.**
I did.

**Miss M.**
Why?

**Morgan.**
I dunno.

**Miss M.**
What books have you read?

**Morgan.**
Books? A bit of the Bible and a book that a feller from the Plas kitchen nab for me.

**Miss M.**
What was it?

**Morgan.**
*The Ladies' Companion.* (*A pause. She rises, and walks thoughtfully up toward her desk, studying him. He sits uncomfortably, twirling his cap between grimy fingers. Rising, at last, making to don his cap.*) Can I go now, pliss——

**Miss M.**
(*suddenly, decisively*) No. (*He sits, taken aback. She walks round the bench and stands near the garden door, facing him.*) Do you want to learn any more?

**Morgan.**
No thank you.

**Miss M.**
Why not?

**Morgan.**
The other men would have a good laugh.

**Miss M.**
I see. (*A pause. She crosses slowly to the sofa, turns, and faces him again.*) Have you ever written anything before this exercise?

**Morgan.**
No.

**Miss M.**
Why not?

**Morgan.**
Nobody never ask me to. (*After a pause, truculently, feeling her eyes on him.*) What iss the matter with it?

**Miss M.**
(*sitting, looking thoughtfully at the book*) Nothing's the matter with it. Whether it means anything is too early for me to say, but it shows exceptional talent for a boy in your circumstances.

**Morgan.**
(*after blinking and hesitating*) Terrible long words, Miss Moffat.

**Miss M.**
This shows that you are very clever. (*A pause. He looks up slowly, not sure if he has heard aright, looks at her*

*searchingly, then away again. His mind is working, uncertainly, but swiftly.*)

**Morgan.**

Oh.

**Miss M.**

Have you ever been told that before?

**Morgan.**

It iss news to me.

**Miss M.**

What effect does the news have on you?

**Morgan.**

It iss a bit sudden. (*After a pause.*) It makes me that I—(*Hesitating, then plunging.*) I want to get more clever still. (*Looking slowly, wonderingly round the room.*) I want to know what iss—behind of all them books. . . .

**Miss M.**

(*after studying him a moment, calling suddenly*) Miss Ronberry! . . . (*To him.*) Can you come tomorrow?

**Morgan.**

(*taken by surprise*) Tomorrow—no—I am workin' on the six till four shift—

**Miss M.**

Then can you be here at five?

**Morgan.**

Five—no, not before seven, Miss—six miles to walk—

**Miss M.**

Oh yes, of course—seven then. In the meantime I'll correct this for spelling and grammar.

**Morgan.**

(*staring at her, fascinated, after a pause*) Yes, Miss Moffat. (*She walks briskly toward the study. He has not moved. She turns and looks at him.*)

**Miss M.**

That will be all. Good night.

**Morgan.**

(*after a pause*) Good night, Miss Moffat. (*He goes toward the front door, putting on his cap.*)

**Miss M.**

Are you the one I spanked? (*He turns at the door, looks at her, blinks, and goes. Calling, excitedly.*) Miss Ronberry! Mr. Jones! * * * I have been a deuce of a fool. It doesn't matter about the barn; we are going to start the school, in a small way at first, in this room. . . . And I am going to get those youngsters out of that mine if I have to black my face and go down and fetch them my-self! Get Jonesy before he posts those letters, and tell those others I'll be ready for them in five minutes. We are going on with the school! \* \* \* (*She looks down at the exercise-book she is still carrying. Reading.*) ". . . and when I walk—in the dark . . . I can touch with my hands . . . where the corn is green . . ." (*The fitful joyous clang of the school bell above. She looks up, excited, listening.*)

## SECOND SCENE

It is an evening in early August, two years later. The room is now a complete jumble of living room and school-room. There are desks, a table heaped with books, a black-board and maps, and every sign of cheerful overcrowding. Miss Moffat has been pleased with Morgan Evans' work and she is thinking now of sending him to try for a scholar-ship at Oxford. Indeed, she has just persuaded the local squire to write a letter to his brother who teaches in the university. As the squire leaves, she looks around the room with a sigh of pleasure, then calls—

**Miss M.**
Evans! (*She pulls the table round the sofa to the center of the room, takes the milk jug and cup from the table to the desk, pulls the desk chair up to the table, and sits at it, studying the exercise-book she has been correcting earlier. She holds her eyes a moment; it is obvious that she could be tired if she allowed herself to be.*

(*Morgan comes in from the study, carrying a pen, books and papers; his mantle of reserve has descended on him again; his inward rebellion is only to be guessed at from his eyes, which she does not see. He pulls the table chair up to the table and sits opposite her, half behind the sofa; it is apparent that this is a daily procedure at this hour. He makes fitful notes of her ensuing comments. The day-light begins to wane.*) Is this your essay on the Wealth of Nations?
**Morgan.**
Yes.

**Miss M.**

(*reading briskly*) Say so and underline it. Nothing irritates examiners more than that sort of vagueness. (*She crosses out three lines with a flourish, reads further, then hands him the exercise book.*) I couldn't work this sentence out.

**Morgan.**

(*reading*) "The eighteenth century was a cauldron. Vice and elegance boiled to a simmer until the kitchen of society reeked fulminously, and the smell percolated to the marble halls above."

**Miss M.**

(*as he hands the book back to her*) D'ye know what that means?

**Morgan.**

Yes, Miss Moffatt.

**Miss M.**

Because I don't. Clarify, my boy, clarify, and leave the rest to Mrs. Henry Wood. . . . "Water" with two "t's" . . . (*scoring heavily*) . . . that's a bad lapse. . . . (*After reading quickly to herself while he broods.*) The Adam Smith sentence was good. Original, and clear as well. (*Writing.*) Seven out of ten, not bad but not good—you *must* avoid long words until you know exactly what they mean. Otherwise domino. . . . (*Handing the essay back to him.*) Your reading?

**Morgan.**

(*concentrating with an effort*) Burke "Cause of the Present Discontents."

**Miss M.**

Style?

**Morgan.**

His style appears to me . . . as if there was too much of it.

**Miss M.**

(*mechanically*) His style struck me as florid.

**Morgan.**

(*repeating*) "His style struck me as florid."

**Miss M.**

Again.

**Morgan.**

(*mumbling*) "His style struck me as florid."

**Miss M.**

Subject matter?

**Morgan.**

A sound argument, falsified by—by the high color of the sentiments.

**Miss M.**

Mmmm. "The high color of the sentiments" . . . odd but not too odd, good and stylish. . . . For next time. (*Dictating, as Morgan writes.*) Walpole and Sheridan as representatives of their age; and no smelly cauldrons. (*Opening another book.*) By the way, next Tuesday I'm starting you on Greek.

**Morgan.**

(*looking up, feigning interest*) Oh yes? (*He writes again.*)

**Miss M.**

(*subduing her excitement*) I am going to put you in for a scholarship to Oxford. (*A pause. He looks up at her, arrested.*)

**Morgan.**

Oxford? Where the lords go?

**Miss M.**

(*amused*) The same. (*Rising happily, and crossing to the desk with the two books with which she wooed the Squire.*) I've made a simplified alphabet to begin with. It's jolly interesting after Latin. . . . (*She searches among her papers. The matter-of-factness with which she is—typically—controlling her excitement over the scholarship seems to gall him more and more; he watches her, bitterly.*) Have a look at it by Tuesday, so we can make a good start—oh, and before we go on with the lesson, I've found the nail file I mentioned—(*In his mood, this is the last straw. He flings his pen savagely down on the table. Without noticing, rummaging briskly.*) I'll show you how to use it. I had them both here somewhere—

**Morgan.**

(*quietly*) I shall not need a nail file in the coal mine.

**Miss M.**

(*mechanically, still intent at the desk*) In the what?

**Morgan.**

I am going back to the coal mine. (*She turns and looks at him. He rises, breathing fast. They look at each other. A pause.*)

**Miss M.**

(*perplexed*) I don't understand you. Explain yourself.

**Morgan.**

I do not want to learn Greek, nor to pronounce any long English words, nor to keep my hands clean.

**Miss M.**

(*staggered*) What's the matter with you? Why not?

**Morgan.**

Because . . . (*plunging*) . . . because I was born in a Welsh hayfield when my mother was helpin' with the harvest—and I always lived in a little house with no stairs only a ladder—and no water—and until my brothers was killed I never sleep except three in a bed. I know that is terrible grammar but it is true.

**Miss M.**

What on earth has three in a bed got to do with learning Greek?

**Morgan.**

It has—a lot! The last two years I have not had no proper talk with English chaps in the mine because I was so busy keepin' this old grammar in its place. Tryin' to better myself . . . (*his voice rising*) . . . tryin' to better myself, the day and the night! . . . You cannot take a nail file into the "Gwesmor Arms" public bar!

**Miss M.**

My dear boy, file your nails at home! I never heard anything so ridiculous. Besides, you don't go to the Gwesmor Arms!

**Morgan.**

Yes, I do, I have been there every afternoon for a week, spendin' your pocket-money, and I have been there now, and that is why I can speak my mind! (*She looks at him, alarmed and puzzled.*)

**Miss M.**

I had no idea that you felt like this.

**Morgan.**

Because you are not interested in me.

**Miss M.**

(*incredulously*) Not interested in you?

**Morgan.**

(*losing control*) How can you be interested in a machine that you put a penny in and if nothing comes out you give it a good shake? "Evans, write me an essay, Evans, get up and bow, Evans, what is a subjunctive!" My name is Morgan Evans, and all my friends call me Morgan, and if there is anything gets on the wrong side of me it is callin' me Evans! . . . And do you know what they call me in the village? Ci bach yr ysgol! The schoolmistress's little dog. What has it got to do with you if my nails are dirty? Mind your own business! (*He bursts into sobs and buries his head in his hands on the end of the sofa. She turns away from him, instinctively shying from the spectacle of his grief. A pause. She is extremely upset, but tries hard not to show it. She waits for him to recover, and takes a step towards him.*)

**Miss M.**

I never meant you to know this. I have spent money on you— (*as he winces quickly*) —I don't mind that, money ought to be spent. But time is different. Your life has not yet begun, mine is half over. And when you're a middle-aged spinster, some folk say it's pretty near finished. Two years is valuable currency. I have spent two years on you. (*As he raises his head and stares before him, trying not to listen to her.*) Ever since that first day, the mainspring of this school has been your career. Sometimes, in the middle of the night, when I have been desperately tired, I have lain awake, making plans. Large and small. Sensible and silly. Plans for you. And you tell me I have no interest in you. If I say any more I shall start to cry; and I haven't cried since I was younger than you are, and I'd never forgive you for that. (*Walking brusquely to the front door and throwing on her cloak.*) I am going for a walk. I don't like this sort of conversation, please never mention it again. If you want to go on, be at school tomorrow. (*Going.*) If not, don't.

**Morgan.**

(*muttering, fiercely*) I don't want your money, and I don't want your time! . . . I don't want to be thankful to no strange woman—for anything! (*A pause.*)

**Miss M.**

(*shaking her head, helplessly*) I don't understand you. I don't understand you at all. (*She goes out by the front door.*)

### THIRD SCENE

Nearly a year has passed. It is July now, the school has been moved next door, and the room is much less crowded. Morgan Evans has not given up his education. After his outburst at Miss Moffat, he had a nip of rum and a fling with a girl, and he came back to study for the Oxford examinations. He does not yet know that the girl has borne his child, for, when she came to tell him that she was pregnant, Miss Moffat headed her off, promising to care for her and to adopt the baby if she would stay away from Morgan at least until after he knows whether or not he will be able to go to the university.

Today Morgan Evans is to come home from the interviews at Oxford. Miss Moffat paces the room, on edge and apprehensive. She starts to leave, but the garden door opens suddenly and Morgan appears. "He wears a new dark suit, carries a traveling bag and his cap, and looks dusty and tired. His manner is excited and unstable; he is alternately eager and intensely depressed." Miss Moffat stares at him, not daring to speak.

**Morgan.**
I caught the early train. I knew they would all be watching for me, so I got out at Llanmorfedd and got a lift to Gwaenygam.

**Miss M.**
(*fearfully*) Does that mean——

**Morgan.**
Oh, no news. (*He puts down his bag and cap next to the armchair; she relaxes, comes down, and sits on the lower end of the sofa.*) Except that I am not hopeful.

**Miss M.**
Why not?

**Morgan.**
(*sitting in the armchair*) They talked to me for one hour at the Viva——

**Miss M.**
That doesn't mean anything. Go on.

**Morgan.**
They jumped down hard on the New Testament question. As you said they would—you are very pale.

**Miss M.**
Better than a raging fever. Go on.

**Morgan.**
I spent five minutes explaining why Saint Paul sailed from a town three hundred miles inland.

**Miss M.**
Oh dear. (*Their manner together has changed since we last saw them together; they are hardly at all teacher and pupil, superior and inferior, adult and child; they are more like two friends held solidly by a bond unsentimental and unself-conscious. Morgan's English has immensely improved, and he expresses himself with ease.*) Parnell?

**Morgan.**

Parnell. . . . Oh yes—I was going to stick up for the old
chap, but when they started off with "that fellow Parnell,"
I told the tale against him for half an hour, I wasn't born
a Welshman for nothing.

**Miss M.**

Ha . . . And the French?

**Morgan.**

Not good. I said "naturellement" to everything, but it
didn't fit every time.

**Miss M.**

And the Greek verbs?

**Morgan.**

They were sarcastic.

**Miss M.**

Did the President send for you?

**Morgan.**

I had half an hour with him—

**Miss M.**

You did?

**Morgan.**

Yes, but so did the other nine candidates! He was a very
kind and grand old gentleman sitting in a drawing-room
the size of Penlan Town Hall. I talked about religion, the
same as you said—

**Miss M.**

(*correcting him, mechanically*) Just as you advised—

**Morgan.**

Just as you advised. He asked me if I had ever had strong
drink, and I looked him straight in the eye and said "No."

**Miss M.**

Oh.

**Morgan.**

I was terrible—terribly nervous. My collar stud flew off
and I had to hold on to my collar with one hand, and he
did not seem impressed with me at all. . . . He was very
curious about you. Did you know there was an article
in the *Morning Post* about the school?

**Miss M.**

(*waving aside the news*) Was there? . . . But what else
makes you despondent?

**Morgan.**

The other candidates. They appeared to me brilliant—I
had never thought they would be, somehow! Two from
Eton and one from Harrow, one of them very rich. I had

never thought a scholarship man might be rich. He had his own servant.

**Miss M.**

Gosh!

**Morgan.**

And the servant looked so like my father I thought it was at first. . . . And as I was leaving the examiners appeared to be sorry for me in some way, and I received the impression that I had failed. I—(*He is suddenly depressed, rises and wanders toward the stairs. She catches his mood.*)

**Miss M.**

When shall we know?

**Morgan.**

The day after tomorrow. They are writing to you.

**Miss M.**

(*rising and pacing toward the desk*) The villagers are all in their best, and talking about a holiday tomorrow. It is very stupid of them, because if you have failed it will make you still more sick at heart—

**Morgan.**

If I have failed? (*In sudden desperation.*) Don't speak about it!

**Miss M.**

(*turning to him, surprised*) But we must! You faced the idea the day you left for Oxford—

**Morgan.**

I know, but I have *been* to Oxford, and come back, since then! (*Sitting on the lower end of the sofa, facing her.*) I have come back—from the world! Since the day I was born, I have been a prisoner behind a stone wall and now somebody has given me a leg-up to have a look at the other side . . . (*vehement*) . . . they cannot drag me back again, they cannot, they *must* give me a push and send me over!

**Miss M.**

(*sitting beside him, half-touched, half-amused*) I've never heard you talk so much since I've known you.

**Morgan.**

That is just it! I *can* talk, now! The three days I have been there, I have been talking my head off!

**Miss M.**

Ha! If three days at Oxford can do that to you, what would you be like at the end of three years?

**Morgan.**

That's just it again—it would be everything I need, everything! Starling and I spent three hours one night discussin' the law—Starling, you know, the brilliant one. . . . The words came pouring out of me—all the words that I had learnt and written down and never spoken—I suppose I was talking nonsense, but I was at least holding a conversation! I suddenly realized that I had never done it before—I had never been *able* to do it. (*With a strong Welsh accent.*) "How are you Morgan? Nice day, Mr. Jones! Not bad for the harvest!"—a vocabulary of twenty words; all the thoughts that you have given to me were being stored away as if they were always going to be useless—locked up and rotting away—a lot of questions with nobody to answer them, a lot of statements with nobody to contradict them . . . and there I was with Starling, nineteen to the dozen. (*Suddenly quieter.*) I came out of his rooms that night, and I walked down the High. That's their High Street, you know.

**Miss M.**

(*nodding, drinking in the torrent with the most intense pleasure*) Yes, yes. . . .

**Morgan.**

(*looking before him*) I looked up, and there was a moon behind Magd—Maudlin. Not the same moon I have seen over the Nant, a different face altogether. Everybody seemed to be walking very fast, with their gowns on, in the moonlight; the bells were ringing, and I was walking faster than anybody and I felt—well, the same as on the rum in the old days!

**Miss M.**

Go on.

**Morgan.**

All of a sudden, with one big rush, against that moon, and against that High Street . . . I saw this room; you and me sitting here studying, and all those books—and everything I have ever learnt from those books, and from you, were lighted up—like a magic lantern—ancient Rome, Greece, Shakespeare, Carlyle, Milton . . . everything had a meaning, because I was in a new world—my world! And so it came to me why you worked like a slave to make me ready for this scholarship. . . . (*Lamely.*) I've finished.

**Miss. M.**
  (*smiling, dreamily*) I didn't want you to stop.
**Morgan.**
  I had not been drinking.
**Miss. M.**
  I know.
**Morgan.**
  I can talk to you too, now.
**Miss. M.**
  Yes. I'm glad.

# CHAPTER V

## 'ADVANCED SCENES

. . . The purpose of Playing, whose end, both at first and now, was and is, to hold, as 'twere, the mirror up to nature; to show virtue her own feature, scorn her own image, and the very age and body of the time his form and pressure.

William Shakespeare, *Hamlet*

from
# DEATH OF A SALESMAN
by Arthur Miller

## Act I
## BIFF, HAPPY

In *Death of a Salesman* (see comments on page 135),
Arthur Miller presents the tragedy of Willy Loman's sons
as well as of Willy himself. They are lost, Miller says. Biff,
the older son, was a high-school football hero, a university had offered him an athletic scholarship, and his
father dreamed of the great career that would naturally
follow his triumphs at college. But Biff flunked a math
course, never entered the university, and became a wanderer. At thirty-four, he is a dreamer, like Willy, but his
dreams are of open spaces and farmland. His younger
brother, Happy, has never left home, rarely dreamed, and
he counts his successes by the number of girls he has won.

The scene below, which follows the scene on page 135,
takes place in the brothers' bedroom. Biff has come home
for a visit, as he does from time to time. He has had his
usual argument with his father and now has the chance
to talk things over with Happy. Downstairs, Willy roams
about the house, lost in his world of memories and dreams.
He talks to himself, and once in a while the sound of his
voice interrupts the conversation in the bedroom.

(*Biff gets out of bed, comes downstage a bit, and stands
attentively. Biff is two years older than his brother Happy,
well built, but in these days bears a worn air and seems
less self-assured. He has succeeded less, and his dreams
are stronger and less acceptable than Happy's. Happy is
tall, powerfully made. Sexuality is like a visible color on
him, or a scent that many women have discovered. He,
like his brother, is lost, but in a different way, for he has
never allowed himself to turn his face toward defeat and
is thus more confused and hard-skinned, although seemingly more content.*)

**Happy.**

(*getting out of bed*) He's going to get his license taken away if he keeps that up. I'm getting nervous about him, y'know, Biff?

**Biff.**

His eyes are going.

**Happy.**

No, I've driven with him. He sees all right. He just doesn't keep his mind on it. I drove into the city with him last week. He stops at a green light and then it turns red and he goes. (*He laughs*)

**Biff.**

Maybe he's color-blind.

**Happy.**

Pop? Why he's got the finest eye for color in the business. You know that.

**Biff.**

(*sitting down on his bed*) I'm going to sleep.

**Happy.**

You're not still sour on Dad, are you, Biff?

**Biff.**

He's all right, I guess.

§ **Willy.**

(*underneath them, in the living room*) Yes, sir, eighty thousand miles—eighty-two thousand! §

**Biff.**

You smoking?

**Happy.**

(*holding out a pack of cigarettes*) Want one?

**Biff.**

(*taking a cigarette*) I can never sleep when I smell it.

§ **Willy.**

What a simonizing job, heh! §

**Happy.**

(*with deep sentiment*) Funny, Biff, y'know? Us sleeping in here again? The old beds. (*He pats his bed affectionately*) All the talk that went across those two beds, huh? Our whole lives.

**Biff.**

Yeah. Lotta dreams and plans.

**Happy.**

(*with a deep and masculine laugh*) About five hundred women would like to know what was said in this room. (*They share a short laugh*)

**Biff.**

Remember that big Betsy something—what the hell was her name—over on Bushwick Avenue?

**Happy.**

(*combing his hair*) With the collie dog!

**Biff.**

That's the one. I got you in there, remember?

**Happy.**

Yeah, that was my first time—I think. Boy, there was a pig! (*They laugh, almost crudely*) You taught me everything I know about women. Don't forget that.

**Biff.**

I bet you forgot how bashful you used to be. Especially with girls.

**Happy.**

Oh, I still am, Biff.

**Biff.**

Oh, go on.

**Happy.**

I just control it, that's all. I think I got less bashful and you got more so. What happened, Biff? Where's the old humor, the old confidence? (*He shakes Biff's knee. Biff gets up and moves restlessly about the room*) What's the matter?

**Biff.**

Why does Dad mock me all the time?

**Happy.**

He's not mocking you, he—

**Biff.**

Everything I say there's a twist of mockery on his face. I can't get near him.

**Happy.**

He just wants you to make good, that's all. I wanted to talk to you about Dad for a long time, Biff. Something's—happening to him. He—talks to himself.

**Biff.**

I noticed that this morning. But he always mumbled.

**Happy.**

But not so noticeable. It got so embarrassing I sent him to Florida. And you know something? Most of the time he's talking to you.

**Biff.**

What's he say about me?

**Happy.**

I can't make it out.

**Biff.**

What's he say about me?

**Happy.**

I think the fact that you're not settled, that you're still kind of up in the air . . .

**Biff.**

There's one or two other things depressing him, Happy.

**Happy.**

What do you mean?

**Biff.**

Never mind. Just don't lay it all to me.

**Happy.**

But I think if you just got started—I mean—is there any future for you out there?

**Biff.**

I tell ya, Hap, I don't know what the future is. I don't know—what I'm supposed to want.

**Happy.**

What do you mean?

**Biff.**

Well, I spent six or seven years after high school trying to work myself up. Shipping clerk, salesman, business of one kind or another. And it's a measly manner of existence. To get on that subway on the hot mornings in summer. To devote your whole life to keeping stock, or making phone calls, or selling or buying. To suffer fifty weeks of the year for the sake of a two-week vacation, when all you really desire is to be outdoors, with your shirt off. And always to have to get ahead of the next fella. And still—that's how you build a future.

**Happy.**

Well, you really enjoy it on a farm? Are you content out there?

**Biff.**

(*with rising agitation*) Hap, I've had twenty or thirty different kinds of jobs since I left home before the war, and it always turns out the same. I just realized it lately. In Nebraska where I herded cattle, and the Dakotas, and Arizona, and now in Texas. It's why I came home now, I guess, because I realized it. This farm I work on, it's spring there now, see? And they've got about fifteen new colts. There's nothing more inspiring or—beautiful than the sight of a mare and a new colt. And it's cool there now, see? Texas is cool now, and it's spring. And whenever spring comes to where I am, I suddenly get the feeling, my God, I'm not gettin' anywhere! What the hell am I doing, playing around with horses, twenty-eight dollars a week! I'm thirty-four years old, I oughta be makin' my future. That's when I come running home. And now, I get here, and I don't know what to do with myself. (*After a pause*) I've always made a point of not wasting my life, and every time I come back here I know that all I've done is to waste my life.

**Happy.**

You're a poet, you know that, Biff? You're a—you're an idealist!

**Biff.**

No, I'm mixed up very bad. Maybe I oughta get married. Maybe I oughta get stuck into something. Maybe that's my trouble. I'm like a boy. I'm not married, I'm not in business, I just—I'm like a boy. Are you content, Hap? You're a success, aren't you? Are you content?

**Happy.**

Hell, no!

**Biff.**

Why? You're making money, aren't you?

**Happy.**

(*moving about with energy, expressiveness*) All I can do now is wait for the merchandise manager to die. And suppose I get to be merchandise manager? He's a good friend of mine, and he just built a terrific estate on Long Island. And he lived there about two months and sold it, and now he's building another one. He can't enjoy it once it's finished. And I know that's just what I would do. I don't know what the hell I'm workin' for. Sometimes I sit in my apartment—all alone. And I think of the rent I'm paying. And it's crazy. But then, it's what I always wanted. My own apartment, a car, and plenty of women. And still, goddammit, I'm lonely.

**Biff.**

(*with enthusiasm*) Listen, why don't you come out West with me?

**Happy.**

You and I, heh?

**Biff.**

Sure, maybe we could buy a ranch. Raise cattle, use our muscles. Men built like we are should be working out in the open.

**Happy.**

(*avidly*) The Loman Brothers, heh?

**Biff.**

(*with vast affection*) Sure, we'd be known all over the counties!

**Happy.**

(*enthralled*) That's what I dream about, Biff. Sometimes I want to just rip my clothes off in the middle of the store and outbox that goddam merchandise manager. I mean I can outbox, outrun, and outlift anybody in that store, and I have to take orders from those common, petty sons-of-bitches till I can't stand it any more.

**Biff.**

I'm tellin' you, kid, if you were with me I'd be happy out there.

**Happy.**

(*enthused*) See, Biff, everybody around me is so false that I'm constantly lowering my ideals . . .

**Biff.**

Baby, together we'd stand up for one another, we'd have someone to trust.

**Happy.**

If I were around you—

**Biff.**

Hap, the trouble is we weren't brought up to grub for money. I don't know how to do it.

**Happy.**

Neither can I!

**Biff.**

Then let's go!

**Happy.**

The only thing is—what can you make out there?

**Biff.**

But look at your friend. Builds an estate and then hasn't the peace of mind to live in it.

**Happy.**

Yeah, but when he walks into the store the waves part in front of him. That's fifty-two thousand dollars a year coming through the revolving door, and I got more in my pinky finger than he's got in his head.

**Biff.**

Yeah, but you just said—

**Happy.**

I gotta show some of those pompous, self-important executives over there that Hap Loman can make the grade. I want to walk into the store the way he walks in. Then I'll go with you, Biff. We'll be together yet, I swear. But take those two we had tonight. Now weren't they gorgeous creatures?

Biff.

Yeah, yeah, most gorgeous I've had in years.

Happy.

I get that any time I want, Biff. Whenever I feel disgusted. The only trouble is, it gets like bowling or something. I just keep knockin' them over and it doesn't mean anything. You still run around a lot?

Biff.

Naa. I'd like to find a girl—steady, somebody with substance.

Happy.

That's what I long for.

Biff.

Go on! You'd never come home.

Happy.

I would! Somebody with character, with resistance! Like Mom, y'know? You're gonna call me a bastard when I tell you this. That girl Charlotte I was with tonight is engaged to be married in five weeks. (*He tries on his new hat*)

Biff.

No kiddin'!

Happy.

Sure, the guy's in line for the vice-presidency of the store. I don't know what gets into me, maybe I just have an overdeveloped sense of competition or something, but I went and ruined her, and furthermore I can't get rid of her. And he's the third executive I've done that to. Isn't that a crummy characteristic? And to top it all, I go to their weddings! (*Indignantly, but laughing*) Like I'm not supposed to take bribes. Manufacturers offer me a hundred-dollar bill now and then to throw an order their way. You know how honest I am, but it's like this girl, see. I hate myself for it. Because I don't want the girl, and, still, I take it and—I love it!

Biff.

Let's go to sleep.

Happy.

I guess we didn't settle anything, heh?

Biff.

I just got one idea that I think I'm going to try.

Happy.

What's that?

**Biff.**
Remember Bill Oliver?

**Happy.**
Sure, Oliver is very big now. You want to work for him again?

**Biff.**
No, but when I quit he said something to me. He put his arm on my shoulder and he said, "Biff, if you ever need anything, come to me."

**Happy.**
I remember that. That sounds good.

**Biff.**
I think I'll go to see him. If I could get ten thousand or even seven or eight thousand dollars I could buy a beautiful ranch.

**Happy.**
I bet he'd back you. 'Cause he thought highly of you, Biff. I mean, they all do. You're well liked, Biff. That's why I say to come back here, and we both have the apartment. And I'm tellin' you, Biff, any babe you want . . .

**Biff.**
No, with a ranch I could do the work I like and still be something. I just wonder though. I wonder if Oliver still thinks I stole that carton of basketballs.

**Happy.**
Oh, he probably forgot that long ago. It's almost ten years. You're too sensitive. Anyway, he didn't really fire you.

**Biff.**
Well, I think he was going to. I think that's why I quit. I was never sure whether he knew or not. I know he thought the world of me, though. I was the only one he'd let lock up the place.

**Happy.**
Shh! (*Biff looks at Happy, who is gazing down, listening. Willy is mumbling in the parlor*)

§ **Willy.**
(*below*) You gonna wash the engine, Biff? §

**Happy.**
You hear that? [He's talking to himself!] (*They listen. Willy laughs warmly.*)

**Biff.**
(*growing angry*) Doesn't he know Mom can hear that?

**§ Willy.**

Don't get your sweater dirty, Biff! (*A look of pain crosses Biff's face*) §

**Happy.**

Isn't that terrible? Don't leave again, will you? You'll find a job here. You gotta stick around. I don't know what to do about him, it's getting embarrassing.

**§ Willy.**

What a simonizing job! §

**Biff.**

Mom's hearing that!

**§ Willy.**

No kidding, Biff, you got a date? Wonderful! §

**Happy.**

Go on to sleep. But talk to him in the morning, will you?

**Biff.**

(*reluctantly getting into bed*) With her in the house. Brother!

**Happy.**

(*getting into bed*) I wish you'd have a good talk with him.

**Biff.**

(*to himself in bed*) That selfish, stupid . . .

**Happy.**

Sh . . . Sleep, Biff.

from
MARY OF SCOTLAND
by Maxwell Anderson

Act III
MARY, ELIZABETH

In Maxwell Anderson's retelling of the downfall of Mary
of Scotland, the political rivalry of the two queens—a
competition between two political parties—is made a
desperate and personal contest between two strong-willed,
very human women. Elizabeth is Mary's evil genius, who
secretly plots to weaken and destroy her. For two acts the
scene shifts from Scotland to London and back again as
Elizabeth sets her traps and Mary struggles to escape them,
knowing and not knowing who is her enemy. In Act III
the queens meet face to face. The playwright, who in an
earlier play (see page 216) painted a sympathetic portrait
of the English queen, has this time taught his audience to
stand on the side of her opponent and, he suggests,
victim. In the confrontation which ends the play he sees
to it that Mary wins a kind of victory. More than that, he
creates a brilliant, sustained scene of argument, intriguing
thematically and exciting theatrically—a lesson to playwrights in scene-construction, the controlled build-up of
tension, and the interplay of characters in conflict.

The scene is a room in Carlisle Castle, in England. Here
Mary is held prisoner, by whom and for what crimes she
does not know. "There are two windows at right, both
barred, a door at the rear and another, the hall-door, at
the left. It is a prison room, but furnished scantily now
for the queen's habitation. It is evening, but still light."
Mary has been visited by two lords who have demanded
that she sign her abdication. Refusing, she demands to be
told what charges are made against her, who is her
accuser, and who has ordered her imprisonment in England to which she fled for safety. The answers, the lords
reply, must come from a judge higher than they. They
leave Mary and she "stands unmoving, watching the door.

After a pause the Guard pushes back the door and with-
draws. Elizabeth comes to the doorway. Mary looks at
her questioningly."

**Mary.**

I have seen but a poor likeness, and yet I believe
This is Elizabeth.

**Eliz.**

I am Elizabeth.
May we be alone together?
(*At a sign from Mary the Maids go out the rear door.
Elizabeth enters and the hall-door swings to behind her*)

**Mary.**

I had hoped to see you.
When last you wrote you were not sure.

**Eliz.**

If I've come
So doubtfully and tardigrade, my dear,
And break thus in upon you, it's not for lack
Of thinking of you. Rather because I've thought
Too long, perhaps, and carefully. Then at last
It seemed if I saw you near, and we talked as sisters
Over these poor realms of ours, some light might break
That we'd never see apart.

**Mary.**

Have I been so much
A problem?

**Eliz.**

Have you not? When the winds blow down
The houses, and there's a running and arming of men,
And a great cry of praise and blame, and the center
Of all this storm's a queen, she beautiful—
As I see you are—

**Mary.**

Nay—

**Eliz.**

Aye, with the Stuart mouth
And the high forehead and French ways and thoughts—
Well, we must look to it.—Not since that Helen
We read of in dead Troy, has a woman's face
Stirred such a confluence of air and waters
To beat against the bastions. I'd thought you taller,
But truly, since that Helen, I think there's been
No queen so fair to look on.

**Mary.**

You flatter me.

**Eliz.**

It's more likely envy. You see this line
Drawn down between my brows? No wash or ointments
Nor wearing of straight plasters in the night
Will take that line away. Yet I'm not much older
Than you, and had looks, too, once.

**Mary.**

I had wished myself
For a more regal beauty such as yours,
More fitting for a queen.

**Eliz.**

Were there not two verses
In a play I remember:
  Brightness falls from the air;
  Queens have died young and fair—?
They must die young if they'd die fair, my cousin,
Brightness falls from them, but not from you yet; be-
  lieve me,
It's envy, not flattery.

**Mary.**

Can it be—as I've hoped—
Can it be that you come to me as a friend—
Meaning me well?

**Eliz.**

Would you have me an enemy?

**Mary.**

I have plenty to choose among as enemies—
And sometimes, as your word reached out to me
Through embassies, entangled with men's tongues,
It has seemed you judged me harshly, even denying
My right to a place beside you. But now you are here,
And a woman like myself, fearing as I do,
With the little dark fears of a woman, the creeping of age
On a young face, I see truer—I think I see truer,
And that this may be someone to whom I can reach a
  hand
And feel a clasp, and trust it. A woman's hand,
Stronger than mine in this hour, willing to help.
If that were so—

**Eliz.**

Aye.

**Mary.**

Oh, if that were so,
I have great power to love! Let them buzz forever
Between us, these men with messages and lies,
You'll find me still there, and smiling, and open-hearted,
Unchanging while the cusped hills wear down!

**Eliz.**

(*Smiling*)

Nay, pledge
Not too much, my dear, for in these uncertain times
It's slippery going for all of us. I, who seem now
So firm in my footing, well I know one mis-step
Could make me a most unchancy friend. If you'd keep
Your place on this rolling ball, let the mountains slide
And slip to the valleys. Put no hand to them
Or they'll pull you after.

**Mary.**

But does this mean you can lend
No hand to me, or I'll pull you down?

**Eliz.**

I say it
Recalling how I came to my throne as you did,
Some five or six years before, beset as you were
With angry factions—and came there young, loving
    truth,
As you did. This was many centuries since,
Or seems so to me, I'm so old by now
In shuffling tricks and the huckstering of souls
For lands and pensions. I learned to play it young,
Must learn it or die.—It's thus if you would rule;
Give up good faith, the word that goes with the heart,
The heart that clings where it loves. Give these up, and
    love
Where your interest lies, and should your interest change
Let your love follow it quickly. This is queen's porridge,
And however little stomach she has for it
A queen must eat it.

**Mary.**

I, too, Elizabeth,
Have read my Machiavelli. His is a text-book
Much studied in the French court. Are you serious
To rede me this lesson?

**Eliz.**

You have too loving a heart,
I fear, and too bright a face to be a queen.

**Mary.**

That's not what's charged against me. When I've
lost
So far it's been because my people believed
I was more crafty than I am. I've been
Traduced as a murderess and adulteress
And nothing I could have said, and nothing done
Would have warded the blow. What I seek now is only
My freedom, so that I may return and prove
In open court, and before my witnesses,
That I am guiltless. You are the queen of England,
And I am held prisoner in England. Why am I held,
And who is it holds me?

**Eliz.**

It was to my interest, child,
To protect you, lest violence be offered to a princess
And set a precedent. Is there anyone in England
Who could hold you against my will?

**Mary.**

Then I ask as a sovereign,
Speaking to you as an equal, that I be allowed
To go, and fight my own battles.

**Eliz.**

It would be madness.

**Mary.**

May I not judge of that?

**Eliz.**

See, here is our love!

**Mary.**

If you wish my love and good-will you shall have it
freely
When I am free.

**Eliz.**

You will never govern, Mary. If I let you go
There will be long broils again in Scotland, dangers,
And ripe ones, to my peace at home. To be fair
To my own people, this must not be.

**Mary.**

Now speak once
What your will is, and what behind it! You wish me here,
You wish me in prison—have we come to that?

**Eliz.**

It's safer.

**Mary.**

Who do you wish to rule in Scotland,
If not my Stuart line?

**Eliz.**

Have I said, my dear,
That I'd bar the Stuarts from Scotland, or bar your reign
If you were there, and reigned there? I say only
You went the left way about it, and since it's so
And has fallen out so, it were better for both our king-
doms
If you remained my guest.

**Mary.**

For how long?

**Eliz.**

Until
The world is quieter.

**Mary.**

And who will rule in my place?

**Eliz.**

Why, who rules now? Your brother.

**Mary.**

He rules by stealth—

**Eliz.**

But all this could be arranged,
Or so I'm told, if your son were to be crowned king,
And Moray made regent.

**Mary.**

My son in Moray's hands—
Moray in power—

**Eliz.**

Is there any other way?

(*A pause*)

**Mary.**

Elizabeth—I have been here a long while
Already—it seems so. If it's your policy
To keep me—shut me up— I can argue no more—
No—I beg now. There's one I love in the north,
You know that—and my life's there, my throne's there,
my name
To be defended—and I must lie here darkened
From news and from the sun—lie here impaled
On a brain's agony—wondering even sometimes
If I were what they said me—a carrion-thing

In my desires—can you understand this?—I speak it
Too brokenly to be understood, but I beg you
As you are a woman and I am—and our brightness falls
Soon enough at best—let me go, let me have my life
Once more—and my dear health of mind again—
For I rot away here in my mind—in what
I think of myself—some death-tinge falls over one
In prisons—

**Eliz.**

It will grow worse, not better. I've known
Strong men shut up alone for years—it's not
Their hair turns white only; they sicken within
And scourge themselves. If you would think like a queen
This is no place for you. The brain taints here
Till all desires are alike. Be advised and sign
The abdication.

**Mary.**

Stay now a moment. I begin to glimpse
Behind this basilisk mask of yours. It was this
You've wanted from the first.

**Eliz.**

This that I wanted?

**Mary.**

It was you sent Lord Throgmorton long ago
When first I'd have married Bothwell. All this while
Some evil's touched my life at every turn.
To cripple what I'd do. And now—why now—
Looking on you—I see it incarnate before me—
It was your hand that touched me. Reaching out
In little ways—here a word, there an action—this
Was what you wanted. I thought perhaps a star—
Wildly I thought it—perhaps a star might ride
Astray—or a crone that burned an image down
In wax—filling the air with curses on me
And slander; the murder of Rizzio, Moray in that
And you behind Moray—the murder of Darnley, Throg-
morton
Behind that too, you with them—and that winged
scandal
You threw at us when we were married. Proof I have
none
But I've felt it—would know it anywhere—in your
eyes—
There—before me.

**Eliz.**

What may become a queen
Is to rule her kingdom. Had you ruled yours I'd say
She has her ways, I mine. Live and let live
And a merry world for those who have it. But now
I must think this over—sadness has touched your brain.
I'm no witch to charm you, make no incantations;
You came here by your own road.

**Mary.**

I see how I came.
Back, back, each step the wrong way, and each sign
      followed
As you'd have me go, till the skein picks up and we stand
Face to face here. It was you forced Bothwell from me—
You there, and always. Oh, I'm to blame in this, too!
I should have seen your hand!

**Eliz.**

It has not been my use
To speak much or spend my time—

**Mary.**

How could I have been
Mistaken in you for an instant?

**Eliz.**

You were not mistaken.
I am all women I must be. One's a young girl,
Young and harrowed as you are—one who could weep
To see you here—and one's a bitterness
At what I have lost and can never have, and one's
The basilisk you saw. This last stands guard
And I obey it. Lady, you came to Scotland
A fixed and subtle enemy, more dangerous
To me than you've ever known. This could not be borne,
And I set myself to cull you out and down,
And down you are.

**Mary.**

When was I your enemy?

**Eliz.**

Your life was a threat to mine, your throne to my
      throne,
Your policy a threat.

**Mary.**

How? Why?

**Eliz.**

It was you
Or I. Do you know that? The one of us must win

And I must always win. Suppose one lad
With a knife in his hand, a Romish lad who planted
That knife between my shoulders—my kingdom was
    yours.
It was too easy. You might not have wished it.
But you'd take it if it came.

**Mary.**
And you'd take my life
And love to avoid this threat?

**Eliz.**
Nay, keep your life.
And your love, too. The lords have brought a parchment
For you to sign. Sign it and live.

**Mary.**
If I sign it
Do I live where I please? Go free?

**Eliz.**
Nay, I would you might,
But you'd go to Bothwell, and between you two
You might be too much for Moray. You'll live with me
In London. There are other loves, my dear.
You'll find amusement there in the court. I assure you
It's better than a cell.

**Mary.**
And if I will not sign
This abdication?

**Eliz.**
You've tasted prison. Try
A diet of it.

**Mary.**
And so I will.

**Eliz.**
I can wait.

**Mary.**
And I can wait. I can better wait than you.
Bothwell will fight free again. Kirkaldy
Will fight beside him, and others will spring up
From these dragon's teeth you've sown. Each week that
    passes
I'll be stronger, and Moray weaker.

**Eliz.**
And do you fancy
They'll rescue you from an English prison? Why,
Let them try it.

**Mary.**

Even that they may do. I wait for Bothwell—
And wait for him here.

**Eliz.**

Where you will wait, bear in mind,
Is for me to say. Give up Bothwell, give up your throne
If you'd have a life worth living.

**Mary.**

I will not.

**Eliz.**

I can wait.

**Mary.**

And will not because you play to lose. This trespass
Against God's right will be known. The nations will
    know it,
Mine and yours. They will see you as I see you
And pull you down.

**Eliz.**

Child, child, I've studied this gambit
Before I play it. I will send each year
This paper to you. Not signing, you will step
From one cell to another, step lower always,
Till you reach the last, forgotten, forgotten of men,
Forgotten among causes, a wraith that cries
To fallen gods in another generation
That's lost your name. Wait then for Bothwell's rescue.
It will never come.

**Mary.**

I may never see him?

**Eliz.**

Never.

It woud not be wise.

**Mary.**

And suppose indeed you won
Within our life-time, still looking down from the heavens
And up from men around us, God's spies that watch
The fall of great and little, they will find you out—
I will wait for that, wait longer than a life,
Till men and the times unscroll you, study the tricks
You play, and laugh, as I shall laugh, being known
Your better, haunted by your demon, driven
To death, or exile by you, unjustly. Why,
When all's done, it's my name I care for, my name and
    heart,
To keep them clean. Win now, take your triumph now,

For I'll win men's hearts in the end—though the sifting takes
This hundred years—or a thousand.

**Eliz.**
Child, child, are you gulled
By what men write in histories, this or that,
And never true? I am careful of my name
As you are, for this day and longer. It's not what happens
That matters, no, not even what happens that's true,
But what men believe to have happened. They will believe
The worst of you, the best of me, and that
Will be true of you and me. I have seen to this.
What will be said about us in after-years
By men to come, I control that, being who I am.
It will be said of me that I governed well,
And wisely, but of you, cousin, that your life,
Shot through with ill-loves, battened on lechery, made you
An ensign of evil, that men tore down and trampled.
Shall I call for the lord's parchment?

**Mary.**
This will be said—?
But who will say it? It's a lie—will be known as a lie.

**Eliz.**
You lived with Bothwell before Darnley died,
You and Bothwell murdered Darnley.

**Mary.**
And that's a lie!

**Eliz.**
Your letters, my dear. Your letters to Bothwell prove it.
We have those letters.

**Mary.**
Then they're forged and false!
For I never wrote them!

**Eliz.**
It may be they were forged.
But will that matter, Mary, if they're believed?
All history is forged.

**Mary.**
You would do this?

**Eliz.**
It is already done.

**Mary.**

And still I win.

A demon has no children, and you have none,

Will have none, can have none, perhaps. This crooked track

You've drawn me on, cover it, let it not be believed

That a woman was a fiend. Yes, cover it deep,

And heap my infamy over it, lest men peer

And catch sight of you as you were and are. In myself

I know you to be an eater of dust. Leave me here

And set me lower this year by year, as you promise,

Till the last is an oubliette, and my name inscribed

On the four winds. Still, STILL I win! I have been

A woman, and I have loved as a woman loves,

Lost as a woman loses. I have borne a son,

And he will rule Scotland—and England. You have no heir!

A devil has no children.

**Eliz.**

By God, you shall suffer

For this, but slowly.

**Mary.**

And that I can do. A woman

Can do that. Come, turn the key. I have a hell

For you in mind, where you will burn and feel it,

Live where you like, and softly.

**Eliz.**

Once more I ask you,

And patiently. Give up your throne.

**Mary.**

No, devil.

My pride is stronger than yours, and my heart beats blood

Such as yours has never known. And in this dungeon,

I win here, alone.

**Eliz.**

(*Turning*)

Goodnight, then.

**Mary.**

Aye, goodnight.

(*Elizabeth goes to the door, which opens before her. She goes out slowly. As the door begins to close upon her Mary calls*)

Beaton.

**Eliz.**

(*Turning*)

You will not see your maids again,
I think. It's said they bring you news from the north.

**Mary.**

I thank you for all kindness.

(*Elizabeth goes out. Mary stands for a moment in thought, then walks to the wall and lays her hand against the stone, pushing outward. The stone is cold, and she shudders. Going to the window she sits again in her old place and looks out into the darkness*)

from
TOYS IN THE ATTIC
by Lillian Hellman

Act I
CARRIE, ANNA

The place is New Orleans, "the Berniers' living room, the entrance porch to the house, and a small city garden off the porch. The house is solid, middle-class of another generation. The furniture is heavy and old. Everything inside and outside is neat, but in need of repairs. The porch has two rocking chairs and is crowded with plants. . . . It is a house lived in by poor, clean, orderly people who don't like where they live."

The people are Carrie and Anna Berniers—Anna is the sensible one, Carrie the soft one. They have a brother, Julian, who was married a while back and moved to Chicago to take over a business. The sisters, especially Carrie, have great hopes for Julian; they always have had. One day he will be the success he has wanted so to be, he'll come home with money, and the Berniers will go off to see Europe. When Julian does come home, however, he is nearly broke, for Julian is one of those eager gamblers who always lose, at life as at cards. The play concerns Julian's realization of his failure and its effect on his sisters and his childlike wife, who is certain that he does not love her but married her only in return for a gift of money from her mother. At the end, it is Carrie, the soft one, whose strength prevails—a selfish, dominating kind of strength that comforts Julian at the same time that it enfolds him, binding him to the house, its people, and the old ways forever.

The scene below (three excerpts) opens the play.

(*Anna Berniers, carrying her gloves and purse and still wearing her hat, pushes open the blinds of the windows that give on the garden. She lifts a large camellia pot and puts it outside. She pours a glass of water on the plant and*

501

*moves back into the room to take off her hat. Anna is a nice-looking woman, calm and quiet. She is about forty-two. Carrie Berniers appears from the street, climbs the porch steps, and sits down in a porch chair. She is about thirty-eight, still pretty, but the prettiness is wearing thin and tired. She fans herself, rocks back and forth, the chair creaks and sways, and, wearily, she rises and moves to the other chair.)*

**Carrie.**

*(As she hears Anna moving about in the kitchen)* That you, Anna?

**Anna.**

*(Her voice)* Just got home.

**Carrie.**

Hot.

**Anna.**

Paper says a storm.

**Carrie.**

I know. I'll take the plants in.

**Anna.**

I just put them out. Let them have a little storm air.

**Carrie.**

I don't like them out in a storm. Worries me. I don't like storms. I don't believe plants do, either.

**Anna.**

*(Appears in the living room with a broom and a dust rag; speaks out toward the porch)* Did you have a hard day?

**Carrie.**

He let me leave the office after lunch. "You're looking a little peaked, Miss Berniers, from the heat." I said I've been looking a little peaked for years in heat, in cold, in rain, when I was young, and now. You mean *you're* hot and want to go home, you faker, I said. Only I said it to myself.

**Anna.**

We had a private sale at the store. Coats. Coats on a day like this. There was a very good bargain, red with black braid. I had my eye on it for you all last winter. But—

**Carrie.**

Oh, I don't need a coat.

**Anna.**

Yes, you do. Did you go to the park? I wanted to, but the sale went so late. Old lady Senlis and old lady Condelet just sat there, looking at everything, even small coats. How can rich people go to a sale on a day like this?

**Carrie.**

I feel sorry for them. For all old ladies. Even rich ones. Money makes them lonely.

**Anna.**

(*Laughs*) Why would that be?

**Carrie.**

Don't you feel sorry for old ladies? You used to.

**Anna.**

When my feet don't hurt and I don't have to sell them coats at a sale. Was it nice in the park?

**Carrie.**

I didn't go to the park. I went to the cemetery.

**Anna.**

(*Stops dusting, sighs*) Everybody still there?

**Carrie.**

I took flowers. It's cool there. Cooler. I was the only person there. Nobody goes to see anybody in summer. Yet those who have passed away must be just as lonely in summer as they are in winter. Sometimes I think we shouldn't have put Mama and Papa at Mount Olive cemetery. Maybe it would have been nicer for them at Mount Great Hope with the new, rich people. What would you think if we don't get buried at Mount Olive with Mama and Papa?

**Anna.**

Any place that's cool.

**Carrie.**

I bought you a small bottle of Eau d'haut Alpine. Cologne water of the high Alps, I guess. (*Holds up a package*) Your weekly present. What did you buy me, may I ask, who shouldn't?

**Anna.**

Jar of candied oranges.

**Carrie.**

Oh, how nice. We'll have them for a savory. Do you know I read in our travel book on England that *they* think a proper savory is an anchovy. Anchovy after dinner. They won't make me eat it. What are you doing?

**Anna.**

Nothing. I'm going to clean.

**Carrie.**

Oh, don't. Sunday's cleaning day. Was this house always so big?

**Anna.**
It grew as people left it.

**Carrie.**
I want to tell you something I've never told you before. I never, ever, liked this house. Not even when we were children. I know *you* did, but I didn't.

**Anna.**
You know I liked it?

**Carrie.**
I don't think Julian ever liked it, either. That's why we used to have our supper out here on the steps. Did you ever know that's why I used to bring Julian out here, even when he was a baby, and we'd have our supper on the steps? I didn't want him to find out about the house. Julian and I. Nice of Mama and Papa to let us, wasn't it? Must have been a great deal of trouble carrying the dishes out here. Mama had an agreeable nature.

**Anna.**
I carried the dishes out.

**Carrie.**
Did you? Yes, so you did. Thank you, Anna. Thank you very much. Did you mind eating with Mama and Papa (*Points off*)—in that awful oak tomb?

**Anna.**
Yes, I minded.

**Carrie.**
Well, it sure was a nice thing to do. I never knew you minded. Funny how you can live so close and long and not know things, isn't it?

**Anna.**
Yes, indeed. I called Mr. Shine today. He said he hadn't had an inquiry in months. He said we should reduce the price of the house. I said we would, but there wasn't anything to reduce it to.

**Carrie.**
(*Gets up, goes into the living room*) Oh, somebody'll come along will like it, you'll see.

**Anna.**
Nobody's ever liked this house, nobody's ever going to.

**Carrie.**
You always get mean to the house when something worries you. What's the matter?

**Anna.**
And you always go to the cemetery.

**Carrie.**

(*Opens the waist of her dress*) Just cooler. I so much like the French on the graves. *Un homme brave, mort pour la cité pendant la guerre*—Sounds better in French. A man gallant is so much more than just a gallant man. Nobody in our family's ever been killed in a war. Not Grandpapa, not Papa—Why, don't you think?

**Anna.**

Some people get killed, some people don't.

**Carrie.**

(*Laughs*) Papa always said he was scared to death and ran whenever he could. But Papa said just anything. Julian didn't like it when he said things like that. No little boy would. Papa shouldn't have talked that way.

**Anna.**

Papa's been dead twenty-two years, Carrie. You should have taken it up with him before this.

**Carrie.**

No letter for two weeks. I went to the main post office today, and said I was sure there'd been some confusion. Would they please call the other Berniers and see if a letter was there. And Alfie said, "Carrie, there are no other Berniers in New Orleans. There are some live in Biloxi, Mississippi, with a hardware store, but the central government of the United States does not give money to Louisiana to make calls to Mississippi, although maybe you could change that if you said it was Julian who had written the letter he didn't write." I was angry, but I didn't show it. How do you know it's Julian I am talking about, I said. We're expecting letters from Paris and Rome in reply to inquiries about our forthcoming tour. (*She stops, suddenly, run down*)

**Anna.**

Julian's busy. That's all. * * *

**Carrie.**

(*Goes toward the piano*) I bought a book called *French Lessons in Songs.* I don't believe it. Never been two weeks before in his whole life. (*Softly, slowly*) I telephoned to Chicago and the hotel manager said Julian and Lily had moved months ago. Why didn't Julian tell us that?

**Anna.**

(*Quietly*) I knew. I knew last week. Two letters came back here with address unknown. Carrie, Julian's married, he's moved away, he's got a business to take care of, he's busy. That's all.

**Carrie.**

He's never been too busy to write or phone to us. You know that.

**Anna.**

I know things have changed. That's as it should be.

**Carrie.**

Yes, of course. Yes. * * *

Let's get out our travel books this evening and write out all our plans.

**Anna.**

No. Don't let's ever speak about it, until we're ready to go, or think about it, or listen to each other, or tell Gus —I don't want to write things down again.

**Carrie.**

It was you who wanted to wait last time. After the wedding.

**Anna.**

It was you, Carrie.

**Carrie.**

For a very good reason. Could we give them a smaller wedding present? Lily is a very rich girl and the one thing a very rich girl knows about is sterling silver. Her mother gave them ten thousand dollars. What would Lily have thought of us?

**Anna.**

I don't know. I don't think she cares about things like that. Lily was so in love with Julian—

**Carrie.**

Oh, I imagine even in love you take time off to count your silver.

**Carrie.**

(*Softly*) We could still go to Europe this year. Do you want to? How much money have we got? Did you make the deposit this week?

**Anna.**

Twenty-eight hundred and forty-three dollars. No, I didn't have time.

**Carrie.**

(*Quickly*) Oh, it's too hot tonight. Should we treat our-selves and go out for supper? It's been so long since we ate in a restaurant. Let's start doing our French lessons again because we'll need them now for the trip—(*She moves to the piano and plays and sings the next speech*)

*"Une chambre pour deux dames."* Have you one room for two ladies? *"Ah non! Trop chère!"* Oh no! Too expensive! *"Merci, M'sieur. Trop chère."* We'll stay in Paris, of course, for just as long as we want. Then we'll go to Strasbourg, have the famous pâté, and put flowers on the graves of Mama's relatives.

**Anna.**

I'll have the pâté. You put flowers on the graves of Mama's relatives.

**Carrie.**

Remember the night Julian told us about the marriage? He said that night we would all go to Europe together, the way we always planned. Mama would want us to put flowers on the graves in Strasbourg. She would, Anna, and so we must.

**Anna.**

I don't know what the dead would like. Maybe Mama's changed.

**Carrie.**

As soon as we do set a date for departure, I'll have my evening dress fixed. No, I won't. Pink's no good for me now. I've kind of changed color as I got older. You, too. Funny. To change color. *"C'est trop chère, M'sieur."* I don't want to go if we have to say that all the time.

**Anna.**

We've always said it, we always will say it. And why not?

**Carrie.**

I just think it would be better not to go to Europe right now.

**Anna.**

(*Laughs*) We weren't going.

**Carrie.**

Save enough until we can go real right. That won't take long. Maybe just another year.

**Anna.**

A year is a long time—now.

**Carrie.**

If you want to go, just let's get up and go. (*In sudden, false excitement*) Come on. Let's do. I can't tell you how much I want to go— (*Points to the piano*) That and a good piano. Every time there's a wishbone I say I want a good life for Julian, a piano, a trip to Europe. That's all. You know, even if we can't go to Europe we could afford a little trip to Chicago. The coach fares are very cheap—

**Anna.**

I don't think we should run after Julian and Lily and intrude on their lives.

**Carrie.**

Who's doing that? What an unpleasant idea. (*As Anna starts toward the kitchen*) We haven't got twenty-eight hundred and forty-three dollars. I took out a thousand dollars yesterday and sent it to Chicago. I didn't know then that Julian had moved from the hotel. But I am sure they'll forward the money—I signed the wire with love from Anna and Carrie, so he knows it comes from you, too.

**Anna.**

(*Slowly*) I don't think you should have done that.

**Carrie.**

But I knew you would want to send it—

**Anna.**

How do you know what I would want?

**Carrie.**

(*Slowly, hurt*) Shouldn't I know what you want for Julian? (*When Anna does not answer*) I'm sorry our trip will have to wait a little longer, but—

**Anna.**

I'm sorry, too. But it's not the trip. Nor the money. We are interfering, and we told ourselves we wouldn't.

**Carrie.**

But if he needs money—

**Anna.**

Needs it? Julian has a good business. Why do you think he needs it?

**Carrie.**

He's always needed it. (*Quickly*) I mean I don't mean that. I mean it's because the letter didn't come. Anyway, even people with a good business can use a little money— You think I did wrong?

**Anna.**

Yes, I do. (*She exits*)

**Carrie.**

(*Calling after Anna*) Julian won't be angry with me. He never has been. I'll just telephone to him and say— (*She makes a half move to the phone*) But there's no place to phone to. Anna, what do you think? (*There is no answer*)

from
ANGEL STREET
by Patrick Hamilton

Act I
BELLA, MANNINGHAM, (NANCY)

The play, which the author has labeled "a Victorian Thriller," is among the most successful suspense dramas in the modern theater. It opened on Broadway in 1942, ran for 1,291 performances, was made into a film, has twice been presented "live" on television, and still turns up regularly in summer stock and community theaters. *Angel Street* also established Vincent Price as the most suave of theatrical villains. Mr. Price played Jack Manningham, a handsome bounder who sets out to torture his wife into madness. He accuses her of little thefts and deceptions, which he has arranged himself, and half convinces her that she has inherited the insanity of which her mother died. Mrs. Manningham—Bella—is saved by a benign police inspector who drops in late one afternoon while Mr. Manningham is out of the house. The inspector suspects, and ultimately proves, that Jack Manningham is the maniacal murderer who fifteen years earlier, in this same house on Angel Street, killed a rich old woman but failed in his efforts to steal her jewels (he could not find them and he is still searching the house for them). Before the proof of Manningham's guilt is obtained, there are two and a half hours of melodrama and near escapes, tightly written, neatly worked out, and thoroughly spine-tingling.

The scene below (two excerpts) is from Act I, before the inspector's first visit to Mrs. Manningham. The setting is the living room of the house on Angel Street in a gloomy, unfashionable section of London in the latter part of the last century. "The room is furnished in all the heavily draped and dingy profusion of the period, and yet, amidst this abundance of paraphernalia, an air is breathed of poverty, wretchedness, and age."

It is late afternoon and the Manninghams are about to

509

have tea. He is tall, good-looking, about forty-five. "She
has been good-looking, almost a beauty—but now she has
a haggard, wan, frightened air, with rings under her eyes,
which tell of sleepless nights and worse." At the moment,
her face is flushed with excitement, for Mr. Manningham
has promised to take her to the theater. As she hurries about
the room, getting things ready for tea, her manner is almost
lighthearted.

**Mrs. Manningham.**
  (*Arranging chairs by the tea table.*) Come along, my dear.
You sit one side, and I the other—like two children in
the nursery.

**Mr. Manningham.**
  (*Stands with back to fire.*) You seem wonderfully pleased
with yourself, Bella. I must take you to the theater more
often, if this is the result.

**Mrs. Manningham.**
  (*Sitting left of the table.*) Oh, Jack—I wish you could.

**Mr. Manningham.**
  I don't really know why we shouldn't. I used to like
nothing so much when I was a boy. In fact, you may
hardly believe it, but I even had an ambition to be an
actor myself at one time.

**Mrs. Manningham.**
  (*Lifting tea pot.*) I can well believe it, dear. Come along
to your tea now.

**Mr. Manningham.**
  (*As he moves up back of the settee.*) You know, Bella,
that must be a very superb sensation. To take a part and
lose yourself entirely in the character of someone else. I
flatter myself I could have made an actor.

**Mrs. Manningham.**
  (*Pouring tea.*) Why, of course, my dear. You were cut
out for it. Anyone can see that.

**Mr. Manningham.**
  (*Crosses slowly left behind settee*) No—do you think so
—seriously? I always felt a faint tinge of regret. Of
course, one would have required training, but I believe
I should have made out—and might have reached the top
of the tree for all I know.
      "To be or not to be. That is the question.
      Whether 'tis nobler in the mind to suffer
      The slings and arrows of outrageous fortune,

Or to take arms—against a sea of troubles,
And, by opposing, end them." * * *

**Mrs. Manningham.**

You see how fine your voice is? Oh—you've made a great mistake.

**Mr. Manningham.**

(*Crosses to right of table. Lightly.*) I wonder.

**Mrs. Manningham.**

Then if you had been a famous actor, I should have had a free seat to come and watch you every night of my life. And then called for you at the stage door afterwards. Wouldn't that have been paradise?

**Mr. Manningham.**

(*As he sits right of table.*) A paradise of which you would soon tire, my dear. I have no doubt that after a few nights you would be staying at home again, just as you do now.

**Mrs. Manningham.**

Oh, no, I wouldn't. I should have to keep my eye on you for all the hussies that would be after you.

**Mr. Manningham.**

There would be hussies after me, would there? That is an added inducement, then.

**Mrs. Manningham.**

Yes—I know it, you wretch. But you wouldn't escape me. (*Lifting cover of muffin dish.*) They look delicious. Aren't you glad I thought of them? (*Passes the salt.*) Here's some salt. You want heaps of it. Oh, Jack dear, you must forgive me chattering on like this, but I'm feeling so happy.

**Mr. Manningham.**

I can see that, my dear.

**Mrs. Manningham.**

I'm being taken to the play, you see. Here you are. I used to adore these as a child, didn't you? (*Offers muffin to Mr. Manningham.*) I wonder how long it is since we had them? (*Mr. Manningham looks up center at wall.*) We haven't had them since we've been married anyway. Or have we? Have we?

**Mr. Manningham.**

I don't know, I'm sure. (*Suddenly rising, looking at the wall upstage and speaking in a calm, yet menacing way.*) I don't know—Bella—

**Mrs. Manningham.**

(*After pause, dropping her voice almost to a whisper.*) What is it? What's the matter? What is it now?

**Mr. Manningham.**

(*Walking over to fireplace in front of settee, and speaking with his back to her.*) I have no desire to upset you, Bella, but I have just observed something very much amiss. Will you please rectify it at once, while I am not looking, and we will assume that it has not happened.

**Mrs. Manningham.**

Amiss? What's amiss? For God's sake don't turn your back on me. What has happened?

**Mr. Manningham.**

You know perfectly well what has happened, Bella, and if you will rectify it at once I will say no more about it.

**Mrs. Manningham.**

I don't know. I don't know. You have left your tea. Tell me what it is. Tell me.

**Mr. Manningham.**

Are you trying to make a fool of me, Bella? What I refer to is on the wall behind you. If you will put it back, I will say no more about it.

**Mrs. Manningham.**

The wall behind me? What? (*Turns.*) Oh—yes— The picture has been taken down—Yes— The picture— Who has taken it down? Why has it been taken down?

**Mr. Manningham.**

Yes. Why has it been taken down? Why, indeed. You alone can answer that, Bella. Why was it taken down before? Will you please take it from wherever you have hidden it, and put it back on the wall again?

**Mrs. Manningham.**

But I haven't hidden it, Jack. (*Rises.*) I didn't do it. Oh, for God's sake look at me. I didn't do it. I don't know where it is. Someone else must have done it.

**Mr. Manningham.**

Someone else? (*Turning to her.*) Are you suggesting perhaps that I should play such a fantastic and wicked trick?

**Mrs. Manningham.**

No, dear, no! But someone else. (*Going to him.*) Before God, I didn't do it! Someone else, dear, someone else.

**Mr. Manningham.**

(*Shaking her off.*) Will you please leave go of me. (*Walking over to bell.*) We will see about "someone else."

**Mrs. Manningham.**

(*Crossing to front of settee.*) Oh, Jack—don't ring the
bell. Don't ring it. Don't call the servants to witness my
shame. It's not my shame for I haven't done it—but
*don't* call the servants! Tell them not to come. (*He has
rung the bell. She goes to him.*) Let's talk of this between ourselves! Don't call that girl in. Please!

**Mr. Manningham.**

(*Shaking her off violently.*) Will you please leave go of
me and sit down there! (*She sits in chair above the desk.
He goes to fireplace.*) Someone else, eh? Well—we shall
see. (*Mrs. Manningham in chair, sobs.*) You had better
pull yourself together, hadn't you? * * *

**Mrs. Manningham.**

(*Going to him.*) Jack—spare me that girl. Don't call her
in. I'll say anything. I'll say that I did it. I did it, Jack, I
did it. Don't have that girl in. Don't!

**Mr. Manningham.**

Will you have the goodness to contain yourself? (*There is
a knock at the left center door. Mrs. Manningham sits
in chair below fireplace.*) Come in.

**Nancy.**

(*Opens doors, enters and leaves doors open. Crossing to
settee.*) Yes, sir. Did you want me?

**Mr. Manningham.**

Yes, I do want you, Nancy.—If you will look at the wall
behind you, you will see that the picture has gone.

**Nancy.**

(*Going upstage.*) Why. My word. So it has. (*Turns.*)
What a rum go! (*Turns to Manningham.*)

**Mr. Manningham.**

I did not ask for any comment on your part, Nancy.
Kindly be less insolent and answer what I ask you. Did
*you* take that picture down, or did you not?

**Nancy.**

Me? Of course I didn't. (*Comes to him slyly.*) What
should I want to move it for, sir?

**Mr. Manningham.**

Very good. Now will you kiss that Bible lying there,
please, as a solemn oath that you did not—and you may
go.

**Nancy.**

Willingly, sir. (*She does so, and places Bible on center
table again with a little smile.*) If I'd done it I'd've—

**Mr. Manningham.**

That is all, Nancy. You may go. (*Nancy goes out and closes doors. Going to Bible as if to replace it on the desk.*) There! (*As he crosses down left and faces Mrs. Manningham.*) I think we may now be said to have demonstrated conclusively—

**Mrs. Manningham.**

(*Rises; crossing left to him.*) Give me that Bible! Give it to me! Let me kiss it, too! (*Snatches it from him.*) There! (*Kisses it.*) There! Do you see? (*Kisses it.*) There! Do you see that I kiss it?

**Mr. Manningham.**

(*As he puts out his hand for the Bible.*) For God's sake be careful what you do. Do you desire to commit sacrilege above all else?

**Mrs. Manningham.**

It is no sacrilege, Jack. Someone else has committed sacrilege. Now see—I swear before God Almighty that I never touched that picture. (*Kisses it.*) There! (*She comes close to him.*)

**Mr. Manningham.**

(*He grabs Bible.*) Then, by God, you are mad, and you don't know what you do. You unhappy wretch—you're stark gibbering mad—like your wretched mother before you.

**Mrs. Manningham.**

Jack—you promised you would never say that again.

**Mr. Manningham.**

(*Crosses right. Pause.*) The time has come to face facts, Bella. (*Half turns to her.*) If this progresses you will not be much longer under *my* protection.

**Mrs. Manningham.**

(*Crossing to him.*) Jack—I'm going to make a last appeal to you. I'm going to make a last appeal. I'm desperate, Jack. Can't you see that I'm desperate? If you can't, you must have a heart of stone.

**Mr. Manningham.**

(*Turns to her.*) Go on. What do you wish to say?

**Mrs. Manningham.**

Jack, (*Crosses to front of settee.*) I may be going mad, like my poor mother—but if I am mad, you have got to treat me gently. Jack—before God—I never lie to you knowingly. If I have taken down that picture from its place I have not known it. *I have not known it.* If I took it down on those other occasions I did not know it, either.

(*Turns and crosses to center.*) Jack, if I steal your things —your rings—your keys—your pencils and your handkerchiefs, and you find them later at the bottom of my box, as indeed you do, then I do not know that I have done it— Jack, if I commit these fantastic, meaningless mischiefs—so meaningless— (*A step toward him.*) why should I take a picture down from its place? (*Pause.*) If I do all these things, then I am certainly going off my head, and must be treated kindly and gently so that I may get well. (*Crosses to him.*) You must *bear* with me, Jack, *bear* with me—not storm and rage. God knows I'm trying, Jack, I'm trying! Oh, for God's sake believe me that I'm trying and be kind to me!

**Mr. Manningham.**

Bella, my dear—have you any idea where that picture is now?

**Mrs. Manningham.**

Yes, yes, I suppose it's behind the cupboard.

**Mr. Manningham.**

Will you please go and see?

**Mrs. Manningham.**

(*Vaguely.*) Yes—yes— (*Crosses below him, goes right to upper end of secretary and produces it.*) Yes, it's here.

**Mr. Manningham.**

(*Reproachfully. As he crosses to the desk, places the Bible on it and crosses up left.*) Then you did know where it was, Bella. (*Turns to her.*) You did know where it was.

**Mrs. Manningham.**

(*As she starts toward him.*) No! No! I only *supposed* it was! I only supposed it was because it was found there before! It was found there twice before. Don't you see? I *didn't* know—I didn't!

**Mr. Manningham.**

There is no sense in walking about the room with a picture in your hands, Bella. Go and put it back in its proper place.

**Mrs. Manningham.**

(*Pause as she hangs the picture on wall- she comes to the back of the chair right of table.*) Oh, l ok at our tea. We were having our tea with muffins—

**Mr. Manningham.**

Now, Bella, I said a moment ago that we have got to face facts. And that is what we have got to do. I am not going to say anything at the moment, for my feelings are running too high. In fact, I am going out immediately, and I suggest that you go to your room and lie down for a little in the dark.

**Mrs. Manningham.**

No, no—not my room. For God's sake don't send me to my room! (*Grabbing chair.*)

**Mr. Manningham.**

There is no question of sending you to your room, Bella. (*Crosses to her.*) You know perfectly well that you may do exactly as you please.

**Mrs. Manningham.**

I feel faint, Jack— (*He goes quickly to her and supports her.*) I feel faint—

**Mr. Manningham.**

Very well— (*Leading her to settee and she sinks down with her head to left end.*) Now, take things quietly and come and lie down, here. Where are your salts? (*Crosses to secretary, gets salts and returns to her back of settee.*) Here they are— (*Pause.*) Now, my dear, I am going to leave you in peace—

**Mrs. Manningham.**

(*Eyes closed, reclining.*) Have you got to go? Must you go? Must you always leave me alone after these dreadful scenes?

**Mr. Manningham.**

Now, no argument, please. I had to go in any case after tea, and I'm merely leaving you a little earlier, that's all. (*Pause. Going into wardrobe and returning with undercoat on.*) Now is there anything I can get for you?

**Mrs. Manningham.**

No, Jack dear, nothing. You go.

**Mr. Manningham.**

Very good—(*Goes toward his hat and overcoat which are on the chair above desk, and stops.*) Oh, by the way, I shall be passing the grocer and I might as well pay that bill of his and get it done with. Where is it, my dear? I gave it to you, didn't I?

**Mrs. Manningham.**

Yes, dear. It's on the secretary. (*Half rising.*) I'll—

**Mr. Manningham.**

(*Crossing to secretary.*) No, dear—don't move—don't move. I can find it. (*At secretary and begins to rummage.*) I shall be glad to get the thing off my chest. Where is it, dear? Is it in one of these drawers?

**Mrs. Manningham.**

No—it's on top. I put it there this afternoon.

**Mr. Manningham.**

All right. We'll find it— We'll find it— Are you sure it's here, dear? There's nothing here except some writing paper.

**Mrs. Manningham.**

(*Half rising and speaking suspiciously.*) Jack, I'm quite sure it *is* there. Will you look carefully?

**Mr. Manningham.**

(*Soothingly.*) All right, dear. Don't worry. I'll find it. Lie down. It's of no importance, I'll find it— No, it's not here— It must be in one of the drawers—

**Mrs. Manningham.**

(*She has rushed to the secretary.*) It is not in one of the drawers! I put it out here on top! You're not going to tell me *this* has gone, are you?

*(Together)*

**Mr. Manningham.**

(*Speaking at the same time*) My dear. Calm yourself. Calm yourself.

**Mrs. Manningham.**

(*Searching frantically.*) I laid it out here myself! Where is it? (*Opening and shutting drawers.*) Where is it? Now you're going to say I've hidden this!

**Mr. Manningham.**

(*Walking away to left end of settee.*) My God!—What new trick is this you're playing upon me?

**Mrs. Manningham.**

(*At right lower end of settee.*) It was there this afternoon! I put it there! This is a plot! This is a filthy plot! You're all against me! It's a plot! (*She screams hysterically.*)

**Mr. Manningham.**

(*Coming to her and shaking her violently.*) Will you control yourself! Will you control yourself! (*Pause until she calms down.*) Listen to me, Madam, if you utter another sound I'll knock you down and take you to your room and lock you in darkness for a week. I have been too lenient with you, and I mean to alter my tactics.

**Mrs. Manningham.**

(*Sinks to her knees.*) Oh, God help me! God help me!

**Mr. Manningham.**

May God help you, indeed.

from
# A STREETCAR NAMED DESIRE
by Tennessee Williams

Act I, scene 1
BLANCHE, STELLA

The setting is the battered New Orleans house on the
street called Elysian Fields (for introductory notes to the
play, see page 328). Blanche du Bois has just arrived and
been shown into her sister's apartment, a dingy, cramped
place which shocks her deeply. Now, as she waits for
Stella herself to appear, Blanche is eager and afraid. She
has left the world she has always known (more accurately,
she has been run out of town), she has come to New
Orleans seeking a sanctuary and found instead this squalor,
and she wonders whether her sister, too, will be less than
she has expected.

*(Blanche sits in a chair very stiffly with her shoulders
slightly hunched and her legs pressed close together and
her hands tightly clutching her purse as if she were quite
cold. After a while the blind look goes out of her eyes
and she begins to look slowly around. A cat screeches.
She catches her breath with a startled gesture. Suddenly
she notices something in a half opened closet. She springs
up and crosses to it, and removes a whiskey bottle. She
pours a half tumbler of whiskey and tosses it down. She
carefully replaces the bottle and washes out the tumbler
at the sink. Then she resumes her seat in front of the
table)*

**Blanche.**
*(Faintly to herself)* I've got to keep hold of myself!
*(Stella comes quickly around the corner of the building
and runs to the door of the downstairs flat)*

**Stella.**
*(Calling out joyfully)* Blanche! *(For a moment they stare
at each other. Then Blanche springs up and runs to her
with a wild cry)*

**Blanche.**

Stella, oh, Stella, Stella! Stella for Star! (*She begins to speak with feverish vivacity as if she feared for either of them to stop and think. They catch each other in a spasmodic embrace*) Now, then, let me look at you. But don't you look at me, Stella, no, no, no, not till later, not till I've bathed and rested! And turn that over-light off! Turn that off! I won't be looked at in this merciless glare! (*Stella laughs and complies*) Come back here now! Oh, my baby! Stella! Stella for Star! (*She embraces her again*) I thought you would never come back to this horrible place! What am I saying? I didn't mean to say that. I meant to be nice about it and say—Oh, what a convenient location and such—Ha-a-ha! Precious lamb! You haven't said a *word* to me.

**Stella.**

You haven't given me a chance to, honey! (*She laughs, but her glance at Blanche is a little anxious*)

**Blanche.**

Well, now you talk. Open your pretty mouth and talk while I look around for some liquor! I know you must have some liquor on the place! Where could it be, I wonder? Oh, I spy, I spy! (*She rushes to the closet and removes the bottle; she is shaking all over and panting for breath as she tries to laugh. The bottle nearly slips from her grasp*)

**Stella.**

(*Noticing*) Blanche, you sit down and let me pour the drinks. I don't know what we've got to mix with. Maybe a coke's in the icebox. Look'n see, honey, while I'm—

**Blanche.**

No coke, honey, not with my nerves tonight! Where—where—where is—?

**Stella.**

Stanley? Bowling! He loves it. They're having a—found some soda!—tournament . . .

**Blanche.**

Just water, baby, to chase it! Now don't get worried, your sister hasn't turned into a drunkard, she's just all shaken up and hot and tired and dirty! You sit down, now, and explain this place to me! What are you doing in a place like this?

**Stella.**

Now, Blanche—

**Blanche.**

Oh, I'm not going to be hypocritical, I'm going to be honestly critical about it! Never, never, never in my worst dreams could I picture— Only Poe! Only Mr. Edgar Allan Poe!—could do it justice! Out there I suppose is the ghoul-haunted woodland of Weir! (*She laughs*)

**Stella.**

No, honey, those are the L & N tracks.

**Blanche.**

No, now seriously, putting joking aside. Why didn't you tell me, why didn't you write me, honey, why didn't you let me know?

**Stella.**

(*Carefully, pouring herself a drink*) Tell you what, Blanche?

**Blanche.**

Why, that you had to live in these conditions!

**Stella.**

Aren't you being a little intense about it? It's not that bad at all! New Orleans isn't like other cities.

**Blanche.**

This has got nothing to do with New Orleans. You might as well say—forgive me, blessed baby! (*She suddenly stops short*) The subject is closed!

**Stella.**

(*A little drily*) Thanks. (*During the pause, Blanche stares at her. She smiles at Blanche*)

**Blanche.**

(*Looking down at her glass, which shakes in her hand*) You're all I've got in the world, and you're not glad to see me!

**Stella.**

(*Sincerely*) Why, Blanche, you know that's not true.

**Blanche.**

No?—I'd forgotten how quiet you were.

**Stella.**

You never did give me a chance to say much, Blanche. So I just got in the habit of being quiet around you.

**Blanche.**

(*Vaguely*) A good habit to get into . . . (*Then, abruptly*) You haven't asked me how I happened to get away from the school before the spring term ended.

**Stella.**

Well, I thought you'd volunteer that information—if you wanted to tell me.

**Blanche.**

You thought I'd been fired?

**Stella.**

No, I—thought you might have—resigned . . .

**Blanche.**

I was so exhausted by all I'd been through my—nerves broke. (*Nervously tamping cigarette*) I was on the verge of—lunacy, almost! So Mr. Graves—Mr. Graves is the high school superintendent—he suggested I take a leave of absence. I couldn't put all of those details into the wire . . . (*She drinks quickly*) Oh, this buzzes right through me and feels so *good!*

**Stella.**

Won't you have another?

**Blanche.**

No, one's my limit.

**Stella.**

Sure?

**Blanche.**

You haven't said a word about my appearance.

**Stella.**

You look just fine.

**Blanche.**

God love you for a liar! Daylight never exposed so total a ruin! But you—you've put on some weight, yes, you're just as plump as a little partridge! And it's so becoming to you!

**Stella.**

Now, Blanche—

**Blanche.**

Yes, it is, it is or I wouldn't say it! You just have to watch around the hips a little. Stand up.

**Stella.**

Not now.

**Blanche.**

You hear me? I said stand up! (*Stella complies reluctantly*) You messy child, you, you've spilt something on that pretty white lace collar! About your hair—you ought to have it cut in a feather bob with your dainty features. Stella, you have a maid, don't you?

**Stella.**

No. With only two rooms it's—

**Blanche.**
What? *Two* rooms, did you say?

**Stella.**
This one and— (*She is embarrassed*)

**Blanche.**
The other one? (*She laughs sharply. There is an embarrassed silence*) I am going to take just one little tiny nip more, sort of to put the stopper on, so to speak. . . . Then put the bottle away so I won't be tempted. (*She rises*) I want you to look at *my* figure! (*She turns around*) You know I haven't put on one ounce in ten years, Stella? I weigh what I weighed the summer you left Belle Reve. The summer Dad died and you left us . . .

**Stella.**
(*a little wearily*) It's just incredible, Blanche, how well you're looking.

**Blanche.**
You see I still have that awful vanity about my looks even now that my looks are slipping! (*She laughs nervously and glances at Stella for reassurance.*)

**Stella.**
(*dutifully*) They haven't slipped one particle.

**Blanche.**
After all I've been through? You think I believe that story? Blessed child! (*She touches her forehead shakily.*) Stella, there's—only two rooms?

**Stella.**
And a bathroom.

**Blanche.**
Oh, you do have a bathroom! First door to the right at the top of the stairs? (*They both laugh uncomfortably.*) But, Stella, I don't see where you're going to put me!

**Stella.**
We're going to put you in here.

**Blanche.**
What kind of bed's this—one of those collapsible things? (*She sits on it.*)

**Stella.**
Does it feel all right?

**Blanche.**
(*dubiously*) Wonderful, honey. I don't like a bed that gives much. But there's no door between the two rooms, and Stanley—will it be decent?

**Stella.**
Stanley is Polish, you know.

**Blanche.**

Oh, yes. They're something like Irish, aren't they?

**Stella.**

Well—

**Blanche.**

Only not so—highbrow? (*They both laugh in the same way.*) I brought some nice clothes to meet all your lovely friends in.

**Stella.**

I'm afraid you won't think they are lovely.

**Blanche.**

What are they like?

**Stella.**

They're Stanley's friends.

**Blanche.**

Polacks?

**Stella.**

They're a mixed lot, Blanche.

**Blanche.**

Heterogeneous—types?

**Stella.**

Oh, yes. Yes, types is right!

**Blanche.**

Well—anyhow—I brought nice clothes and I'll wear them. I guess you're hoping I'll say I'll put up at a hotel, but I'm not going to put up at a hotel. I want to be *near* you, got to be *with* somebody, I *can't* be *alone*! Because —as you must have noticed—I'm—*not* very *well* . . . (*Her voice drops and her look is frightened.*)

**Stella.**

You seem a little bit nervous or overwrought or something.

**Blanche.**

Will Stanley like me, or will I be just a visiting in-law, Stella? I couldn't stand that.

**Stella.**

You'll get along fine together, if you'll just try not to— well—compare him with men that we went out with at home.

**Blanche.**

Is he so—different?

**Stella.**

Yes. A different species.

**Blanche.**

In what way; what's he like?

**Stella.**

Oh, you can't describe someone you're in love with! Here's a picture of him! (*She hands a photograph to Blanche*)

**Blanche.**

An officer?

**Stella.**

A Master Sergeant in the Engineers' Corps. Those are decorations!

**Blanche.**

He had those on when you met him?

**Stella.**

I assure you I wasn't just blinded by all the brass.

**Blanche.**

That's not what I—

**Stella.**

But of course there were things to adjust myself to later on.

**Blanche.**

Such as his civilian background! (*Stella laughs uncertainly*) How did he take it when you said I was coming?

**Stella.**

Oh, Stanley doesn't know yet.

**Blanche.**

(*Frightened*) You—haven't told him?

**Stella.**

He's on the road a good deal.

**Blanche.**

Oh. Travels?

**Stella.**

Yes.

**Blanche.**

Good. I mean—isn't it?

**Stella.**

(*Half to herself*) I can hardly stand it when he is away for a night . . .

**Blanche.**

Why, Stella!

**Stella.**

When he's away for a week I nearly go wild!

**Blanche.**

Gracious!

**Stella.**

And when he comes back I cry on his lap like a baby . . . (*She smiles to herself*)

**Blanche.**

I guess that is what is meant by being in love . . . (*Stella looks up with a radiant smile*) Stella—

**Stella.**

What?

**Blanche.**

(*In an uneasy rush*) I haven't asked you the things you probably thought I was going to ask. And so I'll expect you to be understanding about what *I* have to tell *you*.

**Stella.**

What, Blanche? (*Her face turns anxious*)

**Blanche.**

Well, Stella—you're going to reproach me, I know that you're bound to reproach me—but before you do—take into consideration—you left! I stayed and struggled! You came to New Orleans and looked out for yourself! *I* stayed at *Belle Reve* and tried to hold it together! I'm not meaning this in any reproachful way, but *all* the burden descended on my shoulders.

**Stella.**

The best I could do was make my own living, Blanche. (*Blanche begins to shake again with intensity*)

**Blanche.**

I know, I know. But you are the one that abandoned Belle Reve, not I! I stayed and fought for it, bled for and almost died for it!

**Stella.**

Stop this hysterical outburst and tell me what's happened? What do you mean fought and bled? What kind of—

**Blanche.**

I knew you would, Stella. I knew you would take this attitude about it!

**Stella.**

About—what?—please!

**Blanche.**

(*Slowly*) The loss—the loss . . .

**Stella.**

Belle Reve? Lost, is it? No!

**Blanche.**

Yes, Stella. (*They stare at each other across the yellow-checked linoleum of the table. Blanche slowly nods her head and Stella looks slowly down at her hands folded on the table. * * * Blanche touches her handkerchief to her forehead*)

**Stella.**

But how did it go? What happened?

**Blanche.**

(*Springing up*) You're a fine one to ask me how it went!

**Stella.**

Blanche!

**Blanche.**

You're a fine one to sit there *accusing me* of it!

**Stella.**

*Blanche!*

**Blanche.**

I, I, *I* took the blows in my face and my body! All of those deaths! The long parade to the graveyard! Father, mother! Margaret, that dreadful way! So big with it, it couldn't be put in a coffin! But had to be burned like rubbish! You just came home in time for the funerals, Stella. And funerals are pretty compared to deaths. Funerals are quiet, but deaths—not always. Sometimes their breathing is hoarse, and sometimes it rattles, and sometimes they even cry out to you, "Don't let me go!" Even the old, sometimes, say, "Don't let me go." As if you were able to stop them! But funerals are quiet, with pretty flowers. And, oh, what gorgeous boxes they pack them away in! Unless you were there at the bed when they cried out, "Hold me!" you'd never suspect there was the struggle for breath and bleeding. You didn't dream, but I saw! *Saw! Saw!* And now you sit there telling me with your eyes that I let the place go! How in hell do you think all that sickness and dying was paid for? Death is expensive, Miss Stella! And old Cousin Jessie's right after Margaret's, hers! Why, the Grim Reaper had put up his tent on our doorstep! . . . Stella. Belle Reve was his headquarters! Honey—that's how it slipped through my fingers! Which of them left us a fortune? Which of them left a cent of insurance even? Only poor Jessie—one hundred to pay for her coffin. That was all, Stella! And I with my pitiful salary at the school. Yes, accuse me! Sit there and stare at me, thinking I let the place go! *I* let the place go? Where were *you!* In bed with your—Polack!

**Stella.**

(*Springing*) Blanche! You be still! That's enough! (*She starts out*)

**Blanche.**

Where are you going?

**Stella.**

I'm going into the bathroom to wash my face.

**Blanche.**

Oh, Stella, Stella, you're crying!

**Stella.**

Does that surprise you?

**Blanche.**

Forgive me—I didn't mean to—

from
# A CLEARING IN THE WOODS
by Arthur Laurents

Act II
VIRGINIA, ANDY

The acting-out of a marriage day that does not end with
a wedding is a central and climactic scene in Arthur
Laurents' play (for introductory comments, see page 100).
Here, in the confrontation of a woman and a man she
has loved deeply, the emotions, which the playwright says
*are* the play, burst out. And here the actor in search of
"units and objectives," exercises in emotional memory,
shifting motivations, conflict, and intense communication
between characters is all but overwhelmed with opportunities.

By the time this scene occurs, the woman, Virginia, has
grown used to the fantastic real world of the clearing in
the woods—and the audience has accepted Laurents' nonrealistic approach. Virginia—and the audience—establish
the convention of a "magic circle," a safe place from which
the bad and wrong of the past are shut out and in which
the time is this moment, not the past. "I have changed,"
Virginia says, "I have changed so that I can change things
as they were—into things as they will be! No more alone-
ness! I can even have—Andy." As she speaks his name, he
steps out of the trees. "He is older than she, he is
personable, dressed casually. He has a quiet assurance and
an ease—and a strength not to be tested." She invites him
to step into the magic circle, to find a day that happened
two years before yesterday, and he does.

The scene (two excerpts) is interrupted from time to
time by the laughs and comments of three young girls,
Ginna, Nora, and Jigee.

**Andy.**

I'm bewitched. That day never happened, the words were never said. I remember only up to that day. That's where we are, isn't it?

**Virginia.**

No! We're here, it's now! We've just dropped that day out of the world.

**Andy.**

It had better be a very strong magic circle.

**Virginia.**

Oh, it is!

**Andy.**

Then we must hurry. We're late.

**Virginia.**

For what?

**Andy.**

Our wedding. Two years late.

**Virginia.**

(*Happily*) But not too late, are we?

**Andy.**

No. Right on time!

**Virginia.**

Better than before!

**Andy.**

Much! Come on, get your coat.

**Virginia.**

Coat?

**Andy.**

Hurry. I have to get back to the lab.

**Virginia.**

Last time we hurried; not now. It's not raining. It's a clean new day and I'm a new girl. That's quite apparent, isn't it?

**Andy.**

Some change is apparent, but you'd better tell me just where.

**Virginia.**

Inside. I've driven them out.

**Andy.**

Who?

**Virginia.**

The phantoms who have been driving me. I've been cleaning out memories: they're banished! Moved out, so we can move—Yes! We're moving. I have lovely news!

**Andy.**
You found us an apartment.

**Virginia.**
It's enormous. Well, big.

**Andy.**
How big?

**Virginia.**
I signed the lease. I had to, Andy, the man said—

**Andy.**
(*Laughs*) All right.

**Virginia.**
I'm going to give away all that spindly French furniture of mine—we'll use yours and get more like it—and, oh, there is one whole room for you!

**Andy.**
One whole small room.

**Virginia.**
It has a view of the river and the city—

**Andy.**
Still small—

**Virginia.**
There's more than enough space for your books and your records—

**Andy.**
And those paintings you don't like—

**Virginia.**
Don't understand—

**Andy.**
Same thing.

**Virginia.**
Well—yes.

**Andy.**
(*Laughs*) You were so surprised the first time you saw my place.

**Virginia.**
Well, it's so handsome.

**Andy.**
What did you expect? Antiseptic modern.

**Virginia.**
No. Filing cabinets with an unpainted door across them for a desk, and lots of test tubes and microscopes and burners. And the missing back seat of your car for the bed.

**Andy.**
(*They laugh and kiss*) I really have to get back to the store.

**Virginia.**
Why does kissing me always remind you of work?
**Andy.**
It reminded me of that license. Come on.
**Virginia.**
Shall we take my car?
**Andy.**
No.
**Virginia.**
But—
**Andy.**
No.
**Virginia.**
All right, we're off!
**Andy.**
What about your coat?
**Virginia.**
Do you feel one drop of rain?
**Andy.**
No.
**Virginia.**
You see? It's not that other day.
**Andy.**
O.K. It's a new day, you're a new girl, but I'm the same old workhorse—
**Virginia.**
No.
**Andy.**
And I still have to get back to the hospital.
**Virginia.**
They can wait.
**Andy.**
For me?
**Virginia.**
You're a new man. Yes, that's it. You're a very important man now! You got the new appointment! (*A tremor of music.*)
**Andy.**
Virginia—
**Virginia.**
You did!
**Andy.**
I didn't and you know it. I told you—* * *
**Virginia.**
I can't keep us in the circle!

**Andy.**
Must we stay there?

**Virginia.**
Yes. Please.

**Andy.**
All right. Lead me back. (*She takes his hand and they again step up and over into the circle, to music*) Here I am again.

**Virginia.**
(*Lightly*) And you're late. I've been calling you.

**Andy.**
Your father came by the hospital just as I was leaving. No, purely a social call.

**Virginia.**
On you?!

**Andy.**
Yes. That one lunch the three of us had years ago wasn't much of an opportunity to talk, so I dropped him a note last fall and asked him—

**Virginia.**
(*Sharply*) Why didn't he tell me?

**Andy.**
Perhaps he did and you forgot.

**Virginia.**
Anyway, I'm glad you saw him. Barney's fun, isn't he? And much deeper than he seems at first. He's so busy raking leaves over what he feels that—well, for one thing, you'd never guess how deeply he loves me.

**Andy.**
Virginia, don't let him hurt you.

**Virginia.**
He doesn't. And he wouldn't!

**Andy.**
Your father is amusing, and easy to get on with so long as—

**Virginia.**
I almost forgot to tell you; I have wonderful news!

**Andy.**
Virginia—

**Virginia.**
I found us an apartment! Finally! And it's enormous!

**Andy.**
Not too enormous, I hope.

**Virginia.**
Why? You said—

**Andy.**
I didn't get the appointment.

**Virginia.**
Oh . . . (*A tremor of music*) It really isn't such a big apartment. You know how I exaggerate. We can certainly manage if I keep my job—

**Andy.**
But you wanted to give it up.

**Virginia.**
I'll give it up next year—or the year after.

**Andy.**
I'm sorry. I know it's disappointing to—

**Virginia.**
If we're going to get that license—

**Andy.**
Virginia—

**Virginia.**
It's late and you have to be back, don't you?

**Andy.**
Yes.

**Virginia.**
Your car or mine?

**Andy.**
Mine's outside.

**Virginia.**
Then let's be on our way—

**Andy.**
Downtown. (*Music begins to build.*)

**Virginia.**
Andy!

**Andy.**
That's where the license bureau is.

**Virginia.**
Yes . . . (*She turns toward cottage.*)

**Andy.**
It looks like rain.

**Virginia.**
(*Going to the cottage*) Yes.

**Andy.**
You'd better take a coat.

**Virginia.**
Yes. § (*Ginna laughs in the trees, then Nora.*) §

**Andy.**
What is it?

**Virginia.**
(*Walking slowly, without turning*) Nothing.

§ **Ginna.**
(*Voice*) Liar. §

**Andy.**
The appointment meant a good deal to you, didn't it?

**Virginia.**
No.

§ **Nora.**
(*Voice*) Liar. §

**Andy.**
You're very disappointed.

**Virginia.**
No.

§ **Jigee.**
(*Voice*) Liar. §

**Virginia.**
(*Whirling around*) I'm not lying! I'm not disappointed!
(*Music stops.*)

**Andy.**
No, you're angry!

**Virginia.**
Yes, I'm angry. I'm angry because—

§ **Ginna.**
(*Voice*) He's a failure! §

**Virginia.**
Because politics are always involved in these appointments. It's not fair, and I'm angry for you!

**Andy.**
It was perfectly fair and there were no politics.

**Virginia.**
Then—why didn't you get it?

**Andy.**
The other man was better.

§ **Ginna.**
(*Voice*) How noble! §

**Virginia.**
Stop it!

**Andy.**
I don't take pleasure in admitting that.

**Virginia.**
Then why do you?

**Andy.**
Because he is better.

**Virginia.**
He isn't! He couldn't be!

**Andy.**
Look—

**Virginia.**

I know you: you're brilliant, you've a wonderful mind and a wonderful talent, and you work so hard—you are the best!

**Andy.**

Virginia, I am not the best . . . I'm good; I'm working hard to be better. And I think I will be. But that fantasy of yours of a near-genius—Virginia, that I am not, nor will I ever be.

**§ Ginna.**

(*Voice*) Translation: mediocre.

**Nora.**

(*Voice*) Everyday.

**Jigee.**

(*Voice*) Ordinary. §

**Virginia.**

No . . .

**Andy.**

I'll never be the best, either. But there are other appointments—

**§ Ginna.**

(*Voice*) He'll never get them.

**Nora.**

(*Voice*) He's given up.

**Jigee.**

(*Voice*) Settled—

**Nora.**

(*Voice*) Quit!

**Ginna.**

(*Voice*) He should: he's ordinary! §

**Andy.**

Virginia—

**Virginia.**

I won't let you be ordinary! I mean—you're not, and you haven't given up, have you?

**Andy.**

Given up what?

**Virginia.**

You haven't settled for being less than you can be and should be? You haven't stopped trying?

**Andy.**

No.

**§ Ginna.**

(*Voice*) No, he's just no good. §

**Virginia.**

You *are* good! You didn't try!

**Andy.**
Now, wait—

**Virginia.**
I know there's a comfort in settling—

§ **Nora.**
(*Voice*) You settled for him— §

**Virginia.**
A relief in sitting with the spectators—

§ **Ginna.**
(*Voice*) How do you like your seat? §

**Virginia.**
A safeness in saying, All right, I'm ordinary—

**Andy.**
*That's about enough! . . .* Now I am not ordinary. Nor
have I settled for anything but the knowledge of what
my limitations are. I'm old enough to accept them and
that makes life a helluva lot happier. People who don't,
Virginia, those people draw and quarter themselves. And
if they keep at it too long, there is no thread strong
enough to stitch them back together . . . I tried for that
appointment—hard. I always try—and you know that,
don't you?

**Virginia.**
Yes.

**Andy.**
Then you can't be angry with me for not trying.

**Virginia.**
No.

**Andy.**
But you are angry.

**Virginia.**
I—

**Andy.**
Why?

**Virginia.**
I don't know.

**Andy.**
There can only be one other reason. You're angry at me
because I failed. § (*From each side come the voices of the
three girls, in turn: "True! True! True!"*) § Well?

**Virginia.**
The circle—!

**Andy.**
There is no magic.

**Virginia.**

Help me back—!

**Andy.**

We are back.

**Virginia.**

Andy—

**Andy.**

Say it: you're angry because I failed!

**Virginia.**

Yes! I am! It's true! (*A pause.*)

**Andy.**

Why didn't you tell me how important it is to you that I succeed?

**Virginia.**

I was afraid. I was afraid if you knew, you'd stop loving me.

**Andy.**

Why?!

**Virginia.**

It doesn't mat—

**Andy.**

*Why?*

**Virginia.**

Because you'd know me. I'd give myself away and you'd realize I was not what you thought. And I'm not! To care so much about—well, success. And your car—I *am* ashamed being seen in it. I've lied to my friends about your real position—I invent awards and prizes—

**Andy.**

You're talking like a child, like a bad little girl who—

**Virginia.**

Don't say that to me! *Don't you ever say that to me!*

**Andy.**

But you are talking like a child! No, you listen! I am obviously less, much less than you thought. That's clear now. You thought I was so brilliant, I'd walk away with that appointment and probably the whole laboratory *and* the hospital. All right. You know otherwise now, Virginia, but that hasn't made you stop— (*He stops. A pause.*)

**Virginia.**

It hasn't. I swear it hasn't.

**Andy.**

The idiots we can be, the arrogant idiots. I love you as

you are, so of course you love me as I am. We take others for granted when we ourselves can be taken for granted.

**Virginia.**

I do love you!

**Andy.**

But you know me now. And you said if I knew you, I couldn't love you. No, look at me. LOOK AT ME! . . . Don't you know that *loving is knowing someone and still loving?*

**Virginia.**

*No!*

**Andy.**

No, for you, it's the opposite, isn't it? For you, the man who knows you and still loves you can only be ordinary. And an ordinary human being isn't worth your love, so you're protected! You're safe from the pain of ever loving! How neat and—clean—and—disgusting! . . . You know how long you loved me? Exactly as long as you loved that ex-husband I was fool enough to be jealous of: NOT ONE MINUTE! You loved a dream he never was, and a dream I never was! But a real person—that you've *never* loved, have you? A real, live human being with four heads and black thoughts and weaknesses and flaws and *failures*—have you? Can you? There's a point: *can* you love? Can you even feel? Right now, right this instant, standing right here—*do you feel anything?*

**Virginia.**

(*Savagely*) Yes! *Hatred—of me! I am the enemy!* I hate that I demand you be extraordinary, and yet I demand it! I hate that I demand *I* be, and yet I demand it! I hate that because you are not, I don't love you. But I don't, I can't! And if I cannot love you—*You*—The riddle is unriddled! The joker is pulled out and the card house falls in! I cannot love you because I—*cannot—love—anyone!* The truth came out of your anger; how do you like the sound of it? *I cannot love!*

**Andy.**

Virginia—

**Virginia.**

§ They are Virginia, not I! § I am no one! How can you *be* when you don't have even the hope of loving!

**Andy.**

Wait. You're in trouble now, but it's nothing that can't be—

**Virginia.**
Then, even my trouble is ordinary, and I hate that! It's as common as a cold, but how do you cure it? How do you end it? How do I end it? How do I stop me from doing what I am doing right this minute? I—*destroy!* (*Pause*) Loving is knowing someone and still loving? Very well, you know me now. Now *you* look at *me*. (*For a brief instant, she looks up at his pained face. There is scarcely any light except that on them. She turns away just as he speaks, but at the same moment there is music and she does not hear him.*)

**Andy.**
I love you.

**Virginia.**
(*Bitterly*) How very clear is the answer.

from
# THE DEATH OF BESSIE SMITH
by Edward Albee

Scene 6
NURSE, INTERN

Near Memphis, in the late afternoon of September 26, 1937, Bessie Smith, the Negro blues singer, was injured in an automobile accident. She died the same day, after two "For Whites Only" hospitals had refused to treat her. These circumstances, Edward Albee wrote, "provided the initial stimulus for the play; . . . but while I was getting the thing to mind, while the incident, itself, was brawling at me, and while the characters I had elected to carry the tale were wresting it from me, I discovered that I was, in fact, writing about something at the same time slightly removed from and more pertinent to what I had imagined."

In the finished play, Bessie Smith does not appear. Most of the action takes place in one of the two hospitals, and the characters who captured the playwright's attention are a nurse, a colored orderly, and an intern. From the conflicting attitudes of these three different sorts of Southerners evolves the drama for which the death of Bessie Smith provides a resolution and final, sharp comment. When Bessie's friend comes to the hospital seeking help, the orderly tells him to take her to a colored hospital, the nurse says the same thing less politely, and the intern hurries out to the car to look at the injured woman.

The relationship between the nurse and the intern, a tense relationship of oddly mingled hate, comradeship and desire, is exposed in the scene below. She is twenty-six, "full-blown, dark or red-haired, pretty, with a wild laugh." He is thirty, "well put-together, with an amiable face." The setting is the hospital admissions room, with the admissions desk and a chair stage center, facing the audience.

**Nurse.**

Well, how is the Great White Doctor this evening?

**Intern.**

(*Irritable*) Oh . . . drop it.

**Nurse.**

Oh, my . . . where is your cheerful demeanor this evening, Doctor?

**Intern.**

(*Smiling in spite of himself*) How do you do it? How do you manage to just dismiss things from your mind? How can you say a . . . cheerful hello to someone . . . dismissing from your mind . . . excusing yourself for the vile things you have said the evening before?

**Nurse.**

(*Lightly*) I said nothing vile. I put you in your place . . . that's all. I . . . I merely put you in your place . . . as I have done before . . . and as I shall do again.

**Intern.**

(*Is about to say something; thinks better of it; sighs*) Never mind . . . forget about it . . . Did you *see* the sunset?

**Nurse.**

(*Mimicking*) No, I didn't *see* the sunset. *What* is it doing?

**Intern.**

(*Amused. Puts it on heavily*) The west is burning . . . fire has enveloped fully half of the continent . . . the . . . the fingers of the flame stretch upward to the stars . . . and . . . and there is a monstrous burning circumference hanging on the edge of the world.

**Nurse.**

(*Laughs*) Oh, my . . . oh, my.

**Intern.**

(*Serious*) It's a truly beautiful sight. Go out and have a look.

**Nurse.**

(*Coquettish*) Oh, Doctor, I am chained to my desk of pain, so I must rely on you. . . . Talk the sunset to me, you . . . you monstrous burning intern hanging on the edge of my circumference . . . ha, ha, *ha*.

**Intern.**

(*Leans toward her*) When?

**Nurse.**

When?

**Intern.**

(*Lightly*) When . . . when are you going to let me nearer, woman?

**Nurse.**

Oh, my!

**Intern.**

Here am I . . . here am I tangential, while all the while I would serve more nobly as a radiant, not outward from, but reversed, plunging straight to your lovely vortex.

**Nurse.**

(*Laughs*) Oh, la! You must keep your mind off my lovely vortex . . . you just remain . . . uh . . . tangential.

**Intern.**

(*Mock despair*) *How* is a man to fulfill himself? Here I offer you love . . . consider the word . . . love. . . . Here I offer you my love, my self . . . my bored bed . . .

**Nurse.**

I note your offer . . . your offer is noted. (*Holds out a clip board*) Here . . . do you want your reports?

**Intern.**

No . . . I don't want my reports. Give them here. (*Takes the clip board*)

**Nurse.**

And while you're here with your hot breath on me, hand me a cigarette. I sent the nigger down for a pack. I ran out. (*He gives her a cigarette*) Match?

**Intern.**

Go light it on the sunset. (*Tosses match to her*) He says you owe him for three packs.

**Nurse.**

(*Lights her cigarette*) Your bored bed . . . indeed.

**Intern.**

Ma'am . . . the heart yearns, the body burns . . .

**Nurse.**

And *I* haven't time for *in*terns.

**Intern.**

. . . the heart yearns, the body burns . . . and I haven't time . . . Oh, I don't know . . . the things you women can do to art. (*More intimate, but still light*) Have you told your father, yet? Have you told your father that I am hopelessly in love with you? Have you told him that at night the sheets of my bed are like a tent, poled center-upward in my love for you?

**Nurse.**

(*Wry*) I'll tell him . . . I'll tell my father just that . . .

just what you said . . . and he'll be down here after you for talking to a young lady like that! Really!

**Intern.**

My God! I forgot myself! A cloistered maiden in whose house trousers are never mentioned . . . in which flies, I am sure, are referred to only as winged bugs. Here I thought I was talking to someone, to a certain young nurse, whose collection of anatomical jokes for all occasions . . .

**Nurse.**

(*Giggles*) Oh, you be still, now. (*Lofty*) Besides, just because I play coarse and flip around here . . . to keep my place with the rest of you . . . don't you think for a minute that I relish this turn to the particular from the general. . . . If you don't mind, we'll just cease this talk.

**Intern.**

(*Half sung*) I'm always in tumescence for you. You'd never guess the things I . . .

**Nurse.**

(*Blush-giggle*) Now stop that! Really, I mean it!

**Intern.**

Then marry me, woman. If nothing else, marry me.

**Nurse.**

Don't, now.

**Intern.**

(*Joking and serious at the same time*) Marry me.

**Nurse.**

(*Matter-of-fact, but not unkindly*) I am sick of this talk. My poor father may have some funny ideas; he may be having a pretty hard time reconciling himself to things as they are. But not me! Forty-six dollars a month! Isn't that right? Isn't that what you make? Forty-six dollars a month! Boy, you can't afford even to think about marrying. You can't afford marriage. . . . Best you can afford is lust. That's the best you can afford.

**Intern.**

(*Scathing*) Oh . . . gentle woman . . . nineteenth-century lady out of place in this vulgar time . . . maiden versed in petit point and murmured talk of the weather . . .

**Nurse.**

Now I mean it . . . you can cut that talk right out.

**Intern.**

. . . type my great-grandfather fought and died for . . .

forty-six dollars a month and the best I can afford is lust!
Jesus, woman!

**Nurse.**

All right . . . you can quit making fun of me. You can
quit it right this minute.

**Intern.**

*I!* Making fun of *you* . . . !

**Nurse.**

I am tired of being toyed with; I am tired of your im-
practical propositions. Must you dwell on what is not
going to happen? Must you ask me, constantly, over and
over again, the same question to which you are already
aware you will get the same answer? Do you get pleasure
from it? What unreasonable form of contentment do you
derive from persisting in this?

**Intern.**

(*Lightly*) Because I love you?

**Nurse.**

Oh, that would help matters along; it really would . . .
even if it were *true.* The economic realities would pick up
their skirts, whoop, and depart before the lance-high,
love-smit knight. My knight, whose real and true interest,
if we come right down to it, as indicated in the order of
your propositions, is, and always has been, a convenient
and uncomplicated bedding down.

**Intern.**

(*Smiling, and with great gallantry*) I have offered to
marry you.

**Nurse.**

Yeah . . . sure . . . you have offered to marry me. The
United States is chuck-full of girls who have heard that
great promise—I will marry you . . . I will marry you
. . . IF! If! The great promise with its great conditional
attached to it. . . .

**Intern.**

(*Amused*) Who are you pretending to be?

**Nurse.**

(*Abrupt*) What do you mean?

**Intern.**

(*Laughing*) Oh, *nothing.*

**Nurse.**

(*Regards him silently for a moment; then*) Marry me!
Do you know . . . do you know that nigger I sent to fetch
me a pack of butts . . . do you know he is in a far better
position . . . realistically, economically . . . to ask to

marry me than you are? Hunh? Do you know that? That nigger! Do you know that nigger outearns you . . . and by a *lot*?

**Intern.**

(*Bows to her*) I know he does . . . and I know what value you, you and your famous family, put on such things. So, I have an idea for you . . . why don't you just *ask* that nigger to marry you? 'Cause, boy, he'd never ask you! I'm sure if you told your father about it, it would give him some pause at first, because we know what type of man your father is . . . don't we? . . . But then he would think about it . . . and realize the advantages of the match . . . realistically . . . economically . . . and he would find some way to adjust his values, in consideration of your happiness, and security. . . .

**Nurse.**

(*Flicks her still-lit cigarette at him, hard; hits him with it*) You are disgusting!

**Intern.**

Damn you, bitch!

**Nurse.**

Disgusting!

**Intern.**

Realistic . . . practical . . . (*A little softer, now*) Your family is a famous *name*, but those thousand acres are *gone*, and the pillars of your house are blistered and flaking . . . (*Harder*) Not that your family ever *had*, within human memory, a thousand acres to *go* . . . *or* a house with pillars in the first place. . . .

**Nurse.**

(*Angry*) I am fully aware of what is true and what is not true. (*Soberly*) Go about your work and leave me be.

**Intern.**

(*Sweetly*) Aw.

**Nurse.**

I said . . . leave me be.

**Intern.**

(*Brushing himself*) It is a criminal offense to set fire to interns . . . orderlies you may burn at will, unless you have other plans for them . . . but interns . . .

**Nurse.**

. . . are a dime a dozen. (*Giggles*) Did I burn you?

**Intern.**

No, you did not burn me.

**Nurse.**
That's too bad . . . would have served you right if I had.
(*Pauses; then smiles*) I'm sorry, honey.

**Intern.**
(*Mock formal*) I accept your apology . . . and I await
your surrender.

**Nurse.**
(*Laughs*) Well, you just await it. (*A pause*) Hey, what
are you going to do about the mayor being here now?

**Intern.**
What am I supposed to do about it? I am on emergencies,
and he is not an emergency case.

**Nurse.**
I told you . . . I told you what you should do.

**Intern.**
I know . . . I should go upstairs to his room . . . I should
pull up a chair, and I should sit down and I should say,
How's tricks, Your Honor?

**Nurse.**
Well, you make fun if you want to . . . but if you listen
to me, you'll know you need some people *behind* you.

**Intern.**
Strangers!

**Nurse.**
Strangers don't stay strangers . . . not if you don't let
them. He could do something for you if he had a mind to.

**Intern.**
Yes he could . . . indeed, he *could* do something for me.
. . . He could give me his car . . . he could make me a
present of his Cord automobile. . . . That would be the
finest thing any mayor ever did for a private citizen. Have
you seen that car?

**Nurse.**
Have I seen that car? Have I seen this . . . have I seen
that? Cord automobiles and . . . and sunsets . . . those
are . . . fine preoccupations. Is that what you think
about? Huh? Driving a fine car into a fine sunset?

**Intern.**
(*Quietly*) Lord knows, I'd like to get away from here.

**Nurse.**
(*Nodding*) I know . . . I know. Well, maybe you're going
to *have* to get away from here. People are aware how
dissatisfied you are . . . people have heard a lot about
your . . . dissatisfactions. . . . My father has heard . . .
people got wind of the way you feel about things. People

here aren't good enough for your attentions. . . . Foreigners . . . a bunch of foreigners who are cutting each
other up in their own business . . . that's where you'd like
to be, isn't it?

**Intern.**

(*Quietly; intensely*) There are over half a million people
killed in that war! Do you know that? By airplanes. . . .
Civilians! You misunderstand me so! I am . . . all right
. . . this way. . . . My dissatisfactions . . . you call them
that . . . my dissatisfactions have nothing to do with
loyalties. . . . I am not concerned with politics . . . but I
have a sense of urgency . . . a dislike of waste . . . stagna-
tion . . . I am *stranded* . . . *here*. . . . My talents are not
large . . . but the emergencies of the emergency ward of
this second-rate hospital in this second-rate state . . .
No! . . . it isn't enough. Oh, you listen to me. If I could
. . . if I could bandage the arm of one person . . . if I
could be over there right this minute . . . you could take
the city of Memphis . . . you could take the whole state
. . . and don't you forget I was born here . . . you could
take the whole goddam state. . . .

**Nurse.**

(*Hard*) Well, I have a very good idea of how we could
arrange that. I have a dandy idea. . . . We could just tell
the mayor about the way you feel, and he'd be delighted
to help you on your way . . . out of this hospital at the
very least, and maybe out of the state! And I don't think
he'd be giving you any Cord automobile as a going-away
present, either. He'd set you out, all right . . . he'd set
you right out on your *butt!* That's what he'd do.

**Intern.**

(*With a rueful half-smile*) Yes . . . yes . . . I imagine he
would. I feel lucky . . . I feel doubly fortunate, now . . .
having you . . . feeling the way we do about each other.

**Nurse.**

You are so sarcastic!

**Intern.**

Well, how the hell do you expect me to behave?

**Nurse.**

Just . . . (*Laughs*) . . . oh, boy, this is good . . . just
like I told the nigger . . . you walk a straight line, and
you do your job . . . (*Turns coy, here*) . . . and . . .
and unless you are kept late by some emergency more
pressing than your . . . (*Smiles wryly*) . . . "love" . . .

for me . . . I may let you drive me home tonight . . . in your beat-up Chevy.

**Intern.**

Woman, as always I anticipate with enormous pleasure the prospect of driving you home . . . a stop along the way . . . fifteen minutes or so of . . . of tantalizing preliminary love play ending in an infuriating and inconclusive wrestling match, during which you hiss of the . . . the liberties I should not take, and I sound the horn once or twice accidentally with my elbow . . . (*She giggles at this*) . . . and, finally, in my beat-up car, in front of your father's beat-up house . . . a kiss of searing intensity . . . a hand in the right place . . . briefly . . . and your hasty departure within. I am looking forward to this ritual . . . as I always do.

**Nurse.**

(*Pleased*) Why, thank you.

**Intern.**

I look forward to this ritual because of how it sets me apart from other men . . .

**Nurse.**

Aw . . .

**Intern.**

. . . because I am probably the only white man under sixty in two counties who has *not* had the pleasure of . . .

**Nurse.**

LIAR! You no-account mother-grabbing son of a nigger!

**Intern.**

(*Laughs*) Boy! Watch you go!

**Nurse.**

FILTH! You are filth!

**Intern.**

I am honest . . . an honest man. Let me make you an honest woman.

**Nurse.**

(*Steaming . . . her rage between her teeth*) You have done it, boy . . . you have played around with me and you have done it. I am going to get you . . . I am going to fix you . . . I am going to see to it that you are *through* here . . . do you understand what I'm telling you?

**Intern.**

There is no ambiguity in your talk now, honey.

**Nurse.**

You're damn right there isn't. (*The orderly re-enters*

*from stage-rear. The Nurse sees him*) Get out of here!
(*But he stands there*) Do you hear me? You get the hell
out of here! GO! (*He retreats, exits, to silence*)
**Intern.**
(*Chuckling*) King of the castle. My, you *are* something.
**Nurse.**
Did you get what I was telling you?
**Intern.**
Why, I heard every word . . . every sweet syllable. . . .
**Nurse.**
You have overstepped yourself . . . and you are going to
wish you hadn't. I'll get my father . . . I'll have you done
with *myself*.
**Intern.**
(*Cautious*) Aw, come on, now.
**Nurse.**
I mean it.
**Intern.**
(*Lying badly*) Now look . . . you don't think I meant . . .
**Nurse.**
(*Mimicking*) Now you don't think I meant . . . (*Laughs
broadly*) Oh, my . . . you are the funny one. (*Her threat,
now, has no fury, but is filled with quiet conviction*) I
said I'll fix you . . . and I will. You just go along with
your work . . . you do your job . . . but what I said . . .
you keep that burning in the back of your brain. We'll
go right along, you and I, and we'll be civil . . . and it'll
be as though nothing had happened . . . nothing at all.
(*Laughs again*) Honey, your neck is in the *noose* . . .
and I have a whip . . . and I'll set the horse from under
you . . . when it pleases me.
**Intern.**
(*Wryly*) It's going to be nice around here.
**Nurse.**
Oh, yes it is. I'm going to enjoy it . . . I really am.
**Intern.**
Well . . . I'll forget about driving you home tonight. . . .
**Nurse.**
Oh, no . . . you will *not* forget about driving me home
tonight. You will drive me home *tonight* . . . you will
drive me home *tonight* . . . and *tomorrow* night . . . you
will see me to my *door* . . . you will be my gallant. We
will have things between us a little bit the way I am told
things *used* to be. You will *court* me, boy, and you will
do it *right!*

**Intern.**
(*Stares at her for a moment*) You impress me. No matter
what else, I've got to admit that.
(*The Nurse laughs wildly at this.*)

from
# THE PLAYBOY OF THE WESTERN WORLD
by J. M. Synge

## Act II
## PEGEEN MIKE, CHRISTY MAHON

To a public house in Ireland—a rough and untidy local
pub—comes a slight young man, Christy Mahon, very
tired and frightened and dirty. He is running from the
police (which means that he receives an extra welcome
from the men in the pub) and his crime is a great one
(which makes him a figure of some glamor). He has,
Christy says, killed his father: "He was a dirty man, God
forgive him, and he getting old and crusty, the way I
couldn't put up with him at all." The owner of the pub
agrees to give Christy a place to stay or hide; he does so
at the urging of his daughter, Pegeen Mike, "a wild-looking
but fine girl of about twenty." By the following morning,
Pegeen has given Christy a job sweeping up and polishing
the beer pots, and she has grown greatly annoyed at the
interest taken in him by the local girls and the Widow
Quin, who keep coming around to see and cluck over this
"wonder of the western world." By that afternoon, Christy
and Pegeen are engaged and Christy, the village hero, has
collected all the prizes at the athletic contests. At nightfall,
however, it is all over and done; Christy's father appears
(the tap on his head was not hard enough), Pegeen's affection fades, and, when Christy gives the old man another
crack on the skull, everyone is shocked instead of thrilled.
"There's a great gap," Pegeen says, "between a gallous
story and a dirty deed." But Christy has the last laugh.
Once again his father returns from the dead, though this
time he is submissive to his son, and they go off together,
joking about the fools they've seen in this place. Pegeen
is left to mourn the loss of "the only playboy of the western
world."

"On the stage," John M. Synge wrote, "one must have
reality, and one must have joy. . . . In a good play every

speech should be as fully flavored as a nut or apple, and such speeches cannot be written by anyone who works among people who have shut their lips on poetry. In Ireland, for a few years more, we have a popular imagination that is fiery and magnificent and tender."

In his own plays, Synge caught the flavor and the poetry, and the fire, magnificence, and imagination. For young actors—and for actors who are not Irish—they are not easy plays to act. But they are "grand, good plays" and "worth having a go at." The scene here is from Act II. The local girls have been about, admiring Christy, and Pegeen is angry. As they leave, she turns on Christy.

**Pegeen.**
(*imperiously*) Fling out that rubbish and put them cups away. (*Christy tidies away in great haste.*) Shove in the bench by the wall. (*He does so.*) And hang that glass on the nail. What disturbed it at all?

**Christy.**
(*very meekly*) I was making myself decent only, and this a fine country for young lovely girls.

**Pegeen.**
(*sharply*) Whisht your talking of girls. (*Goes to counter on right.*)

**Christy.**
Wouldn't any wish to be decent in a place . . .

**Pegeen.**
Whisht, I'm saying.

**Christy.**
(*looks at her face for a moment with great misgivings, then as a last effort takes up a loy, and goes towards her, with feigned assurance*) It was with a loy the like of that I killed my father.

**Pegeen.**
(*still sharply*) You've told me that story six times since the dawn of day.

**Christy.**
(*reproachfully*) It's a queer thing you wouldn't care to be hearing it and them girls after walking four miles to be listening to me now.

**Pegeen.**
(*turning round astonished*) Four miles?

**Christy.**

(*apologetically*) Didn't himself say there were only bona fides living in the place?

**Pegeen.**

It's bona fides by the road they are, but that lot came over the river lepping the stones. It's not three perches when you go like that, and I was down this morning looking on the papers the postboy does have in his bag. (*With meaning and emphasis.*) For there was great news this day, Christopher Mahon. (*She goes into room on left.*)

**Christy.**

(*suspiciously*) Is it news of my murder?

**Pegeen.**

(*inside*) Murder, indeed.

**Christy.**

(*loudly*) A murdered da?

**Pegeen.**

(*coming in again and crossing right*) There was not, but a story filled half a page of the hanging of a man. Ah, that should be a fearful end, young fellow, and it worst of all for a man destroyed his da; for the like of him would get small mercies, and when it's dead he is they'd put him in a narrow grave, with cheap sacking wrapping him round, and pour down quicklime on his head, the way you'd see a woman pouring any frish-frash from a cup.

**Christy.**

(*very miserably*) Oh, God help me. Are you thinking I'm safe? You were saying at the fall of night I was shut of jeopardy and I here with yourselves.

**Pegeen.**

(*severely*) You'll be shut of jeopardy no place if you go talking with a pack of wild girls the like of them do be walking abroad with the peelers, talking whispers at the fall of night.

**Christy.**

(*with terror*) And you're thinking they'd tell?

**Pegeen.**

(*with mock sympathy*) Who knows, God help you?

**Christy.**

(*loudly*) What joy would they have to bring hanging to the likes of me?

**Pegeen.**

It's queer joys they have, and who knows the thing they'd do, if it'd make the green stones cry itself to think of you swaying and swiggling at the butt of a rope, and you with a fine, stout neck, God bless you! the way you'd be a half an hour, in great anguish, getting your death.

**Christy.**

(*getting his boots and putting them on*) If there's that terror of them, it'd be best, maybe, I went on wandering like Esau or Cain and Abel on the sides of Neifin or the Erris plain.

**Pegeen.**

(*beginning to play with him*) It would, maybe, for I've heard the Circuit Judges this place is a heartless crew.

**Christy.**

(*bitterly*) It's more than Judges this place is a heartless crew. (*Looking up at her.*) And isn't it a poor thing to be starting again, and I a lonesome fellow will be looking out on women and girls the way the needy fallen spirits do be looking on the Lord?

**Pegeen.**

What call have you to be that lonesome when there's poor girls walking Mayo in their thousands now?

**Christy.**

(*grimly*) It's well you know what call I have. It's well you know it's a lonesome thing to be passing small towns with the lights shining sideways when the night is down, or going in strange places with a dog noising before you and a dog noising behind, or drawn to the cities where you'd hear a voice kissing and talking deep love in every shadow of the ditch, and you passing on with an empty, hungry stomach failing from your heart.

**Pegeen.**

I'm thinking you're an odd man, Christy Mahon. The oddest walking fellow I ever set my eyes on to this hour today.

**Christy.**

What would any be but odd men and they living lonesome in the world?

**Pegeen.**

I'm not odd, and I'm my whole life with my father only.

**Christy.**

(*with infinite admiration*) How would a lovely, handsome woman the like of you be lonesome when all men should be thronging around to hear the sweetness of your voice, and the little infant children should be pestering your steps, I'm thinking, and you walking the roads.

**Pegeen.**

I'm hard set to know what way a coaxing fellow the like of yourself should be lonesome either.

**Christy.**

Coaxing.

**Pegeen.**

Would you have me think a man never talked with the girls would have the words you've spoken today? It's only letting on you are to be lonesome, the way you'd get around me now.

**Christy.**

I wish to God I was letting on; but I was lonesome all times, and born lonesome, I'm thinking, as the moon of dawn. (*Going to door.*)

**Pegeen.**

(*puzzled by his talk*) Well, it's a story I'm not understanding at all why you'd be worse than another, Christy Mahon, and you a fine lad with the great savagery to destroy your da.

**Christy.**

It's little I'm understanding myself, saving only that my heart's scalded this day, and I going off stretching out the earth between us, the way I'll not be waking near you another dawn of the year till the two of us do arise to hope or judgment with the saints of God, and now I'd best be going with my wattle in my hand, for hanging is a poor thing (*turning to go*) and it's little welcome only is left me in this house today.

**Pegeen.**

(*sharply*) Christy. (*He turns round.*) Come here to me. (*He goes towards her.*) Lay down that switch and throw some sods on the fire. You're pot-boy in this place, and I'll not have you mitch off from us now.

**Christy.**

You were saying I'd be hanged if I stay.

**Pegeen.**

(*quite kindly at last*) I'm after going down and reading the fearful crimes of Ireland for two weeks or three, and there wasn't a word of your murder. (*Getting up and going over to the counter.*) They've likely not found the body. You're safe so with ourselves.

**Christy.**

(*astonished, slowly*) It's making game of me you were (*following her with fearful joy*), and I can stay so, working at your side, and I not lonesome from this mortal day.

**Pegeen.**

What's to hinder you staying, except the widow woman or the young girls would inveigle you off?

**Christy.**

(*with rapture*) And I'll have your words from this day filling my ears, and that look is come upon you meeting my two eyes, and I watching you loafing around in the warm sun, or rinsing your ankles when the night is come.

**Pegeen.**

(*kindly, but a little embarrassed*) I'm thinking you'll be a loyal young lad to have working around, and if you vexed me a while since with your leaguing with the girls, I wouldn't give a thraneen for a lad hadn't a mighty spirit in him and a gamey heart.

from

THE ENCHANTED

by Jean Giraudoux (adapted by Maurice Valency).

Act III
ISABEL, THE SUPERVISOR, THE GHOST

The play, like Giraudoux's *The Madwoman of Chaillot*, is
a fantasy that proclaims the wonderful mundane things of
the world that men call real. It is a ghost story, and it is a
tale of the conflict between imagined, longed-for perfection
and the experience of things as they are. Giraudoux por-
trays the conflict as a contest between life and death, a
contest which centers about the wooing of a young girl,
Isabel. To the adaptor, Maurice Valency, Isabel and the
other young girls who appear in Giraudoux's plays represent the playwright's "supreme achievement as a dramatist."
Each of these girls is made "a point of incandescence in the
darkness, a being through whom the two worlds [of the
real and the fantastic, the perfect and the common, and
life and death] communicate, in whom everything is possible and nothing ever happens. . . . We see in them the
love that moves the sun and the other stars, but they have
excellent appetites and are accustomed to put away a hearty
breakfast." To them belongs the mystery of the girl "in
whose eyes one sees the ineffable, and in whose arms one
finds the cook."

In *The Enchanted*, the young girl is a schoolteacher in
a provincial town in France. The town has suddenly become haunted by a handsome ghost. Things have begun
to go wrong—or, rather, they have begun to go right, un-
predictably and most irregularly: the Mother Superior does
not win the bicycle in the raffle, the richest man in the city
fails to win the money prize, and even the dogs have begun to act strangely. It is to Isabel, however, that the
presence of the ghost has the greatest meaning. The idea
of his ghostliness—that he has seen the other side of death
—fascinates her. She is drawn to him, or to the idea of him.
In fact, it is the ghost who has chosen Isabel; he would

woo her. But Isabel has another suitor, the Supervisor, a minor functionary in the civil service, who represents all the plainness, the seeming dullness, the unadventurousness of day-to-day life on earth.

In the scene below, each of the suitors proposes to Isabel. Each tries to paint in words the wonders of the world he asks Isabel to share. She is torn between them, for in herself she has something of both worlds. At the end of the scene, she seems to turn to the ghost, she faints, and seems about to die. At the play's end, however, she is revived by the noises of gossiping old ladies, chattering schoolchildren, the inflated oratory of a town official, and the supervisor's repeating of "I love you"—a symphony of life, says the doctor who conducts it, the life that Isabel chooses for herself.

The setting is Isabel's room, which has a balcony with French windows that look out across the city square. It is late afternoon. Isabel has been talking with her friend the doctor, who has come to warn her that the ghost is likely to visit her and ask her to join him in death. Isabel asks the doctor to stay with her, but he tells her that she must meet the ghost alone. As the doctor leaves, the supervisor enters. "He looks pale and very formal. He stands silent a moment, dressed in his Sunday best—black jacket, striped trousers, chamois gloves. He has a bowler hat in his right hand, a gold-headed stick in his left. Isabel gazes at him in astonishment."

**Supervisor.**

Not a word, if you please.

**Isabel.**

I don't know what to say.

**Supervisor.**

Don't say anything. Just listen.

**Isabel.**

Do you mind if I look?

**Supervisor.**

That is permitted. In fact, please do.

**Isabel.**

You look so grand.

**Supervisor.**

Don't poke fun at my finery. It is all that sustains me at

the moment. Except the thought of those who should be
wearing it. They would certainly be here with me, if they
were alive. As it is, let me present—my grandfather: his
cane. My great-uncle: his watch and chain. My father: his
hat. My Uncle Albert: his gloves. The rest is myself.

**Isabel.**

I am delighted to meet you all. Please sit down.

**Supervisor.**

May I stow my relatives in this chair? There's quite a lot
of them. (*He puts down his hat, stick and gloves.*)

**Isabel.**

And to what am I indebted for the pleasure of receiving
your family on this occasion?

**Supervisor.**

You haven't guessed? (*He bows ceremonially.*) We have
come for the purpose of asking your hand in marriage,
Mademoiselle.

**Isabel.**

But, really . . . !

**Supervisor.**

Not a word, if you please. We ask you for your hand,
not for your answer. We ask you, by withholding your
answer until tomorrow, to give me the happiest day of
my life—a day during which I can say to myself that at
last I have asked you, and as yet you have not refused.
A day in which I am permitted to think that you may be
a little touched, perhaps, by the thought that there is
someone, however unworthy, who lives only for you.
Someone, incidentally, called Robert—my father (*He
takes up the hat.*) will have told you my name by now.
Someone who is brave, honest, conscientious, reliable—
and even modest. For my grandfather (*He takes up the
cane.*) can hardly be expected to spare you even the least
of my virtues. Someone who—come, Uncle Albert— (*He
takes his gloves.*) has the honor to wish you good day,
Mademoiselle. Until tomorrow.

**Isabel.**

No, no. Don't go. Only—you come at such a moment!

**Supervisor.**

I chose the moment deliberately. It is his moment. And
therefore, the logical time for me to offer you another
road to the other world.

**Isabel.**

What road is that? Are there more than one?

**Supervisor.**

There is a road which leads slowly, easily, but very surely, to death.

**Isabel.**

What road?

**Supervisor.**

Life.

**Isabel.**

Life with you?

**Supervisor.**

That's not the important thing. I, as an individual, don't count for much in this affair. What I offer you is not so much life with me, as life with a government employee. I offer you a career which ends quite pleasantly in the other world. I suppose I go with it. But perhaps you don't understand me?

**Isabel.**

I think perhaps I do.

**Supervisor.**

In the civil service, we move from post to post, from year to year, with the smoothness of time. We are borne as on a gentle stream from increment to increment, from youth to age, from age to death, without break and without transition.

**Isabel.**

It doesn't sound so terribly exciting.

**Supervisor.**

It is immensely exciting. It is all sheer poetry.

**Isabel.**

Really? I wish you'd explain that to me. You find it all sheer poetry in the Bureau of Weights and Measures?

**Supervisor.**

Say, I am checking the volume of the barrels in a distillery. So many liters, so many liters, so many liters. The moment I am bored—I transform these liters into gallons, and in a twinkling, I am in America. On the way home, I have ten kilometers to travel. If I put it into versts, I am in Russia; in parasangs, in Persia; in fathoms, I am under the sea.

**Isabel.**

Oh.

**Supervisor.**

I check a load of grain in hins—the owner becomes an ancient Hebrew; in talents—a Roman; in drachmae—a

Greek. I take a height in cubits—I am with Cleopatra; in ells, with Alfred the Great.

**Isabel.**

You *are* a poet, aren't you?

**Supervisor.**

The poetry of a life like mine is surpassed only by its continual surprises . . . !

**Isabel.**

Its surprises? Do you have surprises in the Weights and Measures? I should like to understand that. Because, frankly, surprises are what I love best of all in life.

**Supervisor.**

We have the most delightful, the most exquisite surprises. You know, of course, Miss Isabel, that in my bureau we have to change posts every three years. . . .

**Isabel.**

It seems rather long to be in one place.

**Supervisor.**

But at the very beginning of each assignment, we are given the names of the two towns from which our next assignment will be drawn.

**Isabel.**

So you always know where you are going next.

**Supervisor.**

That's just it. I know and I don't know. I know that it will be either Nice or Tours. But I won't know which until the very week I leave. Can you possibly appreciate the delicious torment of this continual uncertainty?

**Isabel.**

So that every day of the three years you have spent with us, your thoughts have been vibrating between Nice . . .

**Supervisor.**

The beach, the casino, the boardwalk, the sea . . .

**Isabel.**

And Tours?

**Supervisor.**

The castles, the churches, the plain and the river. Now do you see what life can be? Tell me frankly—between the riddle of life with me, and the riddle of death—with him—which seems the more interesting?

**Isabel.**

I didn't know about this. It sounds marvelous. So that when you are in Nice . . .

**Supervisor.**

Or will it be Tours . . . ?

**Isabel.**
You will have three whole years in which to wonder about the next possibility?

**Supervisor.**
Chartres and Grenoble.

**Isabel.**
The valley and the mountain . . .

**Supervisor.**
And so by a series of pendulum swings involving every earthly possibility—we come at last to . . .

**Isabel.**
Paris.

**Supervisor.**
Yes.

**Isabel.**
What a beautiful cruise your life must be! One can see its wake in your eyes!

**Supervisor.**
People talk of sailors' eyes. It's because when they pay their taxes, they never look into the eyes of the collector. It's because when they pass the customs, they never look at the eyes of the official. It's because in a courtroom, it never occurs to a litigant to take the judge's head in his hands, and turn it gently to the light and gaze into his pupils. In the eyes of a government official, believe me, they would see the reflection of an ocean no sailor ever saw. It is the ocean of life, Miss Isabel.

**Isabel.**
It's true. It's strange. I see it now in yours. It is blue.

**Supervisor.**
And do you like it, Miss Isabel?

**Isabel.**
I think—I like it very much.

**Supervisor.**
Ah! In that case . . . (*He goes to the door with a decisive air.*)

**Isabel.**
What are you doing?

**Supervisor.**
Bolting the doors. Locking the windows. (*He goes to the fireplace.*) Shutting the damper. So. The room is now sealed off from the universe. I serve formal notice upon all intruders to keep out. Sit down, Miss Isabel. We have only to wait quietly a few minutes, and we shall be safe.

**Isabel.**

Oh, but . . .

**Supervisor.**

But be careful, Miss Isabel. No regrets. No reservations. In all likelihood, he is listening. The slightest word may be construed as an invitation.

**Isabel.**

My poor ghost! (*The bolted door flies open. The Ghost appears. He is paler and more transparent than before, and rather more appealing.*)

**Ghost.**

I may come in?

**Supervisor.**

You may not come in. The door is locked and bolted.

**Ghost.**

I have the key to the enigma, Isabel! I can tell you everything, Isabel. Isabel—ask this man to leave us.

**Supervisor.**

I regret. That is out of the question.

**Ghost.**

I am speaking to Isabel.

**Supervisor.**

You will notice that Isabel is not speaking to you.

**Ghost.**

Do you fancy that you are protecting her? (*The Supervisor bows.*) From what?

**Supervisor.**

I don't know. Therefore I must be doubly careful.

**Ghost.**

Don't be afraid. I am not in the least dangerous.

**Supervisor.**

Perhaps not. But what you represent is dangerous.

**Ghost.**

You mean—Death?

**Supervisor.**

It's your word.

**Ghost.**

You think you can save her from that?

**Supervisor.**

I am quite sure.

**Ghost.**

And suppose I am not alone? Suppose that Death is here with me? Suppose that Isabel sees something that you do not see?

**Supervisor.**

A girl sees all sorts of things that her husband doesn't see. It makes no difference—so long as he's there.

**Ghost.**

Oh. So you are married, Isabel?

**Supervisor.**

Not yet.

**Ghost.**

You are engaged?

**Supervisor.**

The word is a little strong. I have asked Isabel to be my wife and she has not refused. I don't know exactly what you call this relationship. . . .

**Ghost.**

I call it vague.

**Supervisor.**

Then obviously I cannot leave her with you for a moment.

**Ghost.**

And suppose *I* leave, and come back when you're gone?

**Supervisor.**

You won't. You haven't the stamina. You haven't the time. The fact is, you, too, seem a little vague, my friend —you are fading. You grow more transparent by the moment. I don't think that in coming back like this, you are making use of any new-found power. I think you have merely some little residue of human energy—and by the looks of you, it will hardly last you an hour. I warn you, unless you go pretty soon, you are likely to suffer the ultimate indignity of disintegrating before her very eyes. If I were you, I'd make a good exit while I still had the wherewithal.

**Ghost.**

Isabel . . .

**Supervisor.**

If you can pass only through closed doors, I'll be glad to close this one for you.

**Ghost.**

Isabel . . .

**Isabel.**

Dear Supervisor . . . Tomorrow I will listen to you, I promise. But let me have this moment—this last little moment—with him.

**Supervisor.**

If I should desert you in the face of my enemy, tomorrow you would despise me.

**Isabel.**

But he has come to give me the answer to the riddle that has troubled me all my life!

**Supervisor.**

I'm not in favor of the answers to riddles. A riddle is amusing only while it is a riddle. An answered riddle has no dignity whatever—it becomes an absurdity. What riddle?

**Isabel.**

The riddle of death.

**Supervisor.**

The death of a star, of an ideal, of a flower?

**Isabel.**

The death of a man.

**Supervisor.**

That's not even a riddle. Do these trifles interest you? Everyone in the Weights and Measures knows the answer to that. Death is the next step after the pension—it's perpetual retirement without pay. And even if that were a riddle—which it isn't—what makes you think the dead would know the answer? If the dead know any more about death than the living know about life, I congratulate them on their insight. And that's all I have to say.

**Isabel.**

Well, if you won't go, let him speak in your presence. Perhaps he will?

**Ghost.**

He will not.

**Isabel.**

You could stop your ears a moment.

**Supervisor.**

I'm sorry, but that is just what I can't do. I am provided with eyelids. But not with ear-lids.

**Ghost.**

Such is the lump of concrete out of which destiny is forced to make spirits!

**Supervisor.**

Don't worry about me, my friend. If there's one thing I'm sure of, it's that when my turn comes I will make a perfectly adequate spirit.

**Ghost.**

Oh, you think so?

**Supervisor.**

When I come to my final assignment, my colleagues will know that I was always dependable as a man and that

I can be relied upon as a ghost. They will know that I lived my life fully to the extent of my capacity—that I never flagged in my duty to those I served nor in my devotion to those I loved. They will know that in the years I spent in Isabel's town, I never let a day pass without assuring myself that Isabel was well and happy. They may remember the hour I spent one night scratching out with my penknife the word that someone had painted on her door, the morning when I replaced the broken milk bottles on her doorstep, the afternoon when I saved her mail from being soaked by the rain. They will realize that in my modest way, I did my best always to soften the blows that fortune aimed at her.

**Isabel.**
Dear Robert . . . !

**Ghost.**
I beg pardon?

**Isabel.**
Nothing.

**Ghost.**
Why do you say, "Dear Robert"?

**Isabel.**
Because . . . Why? Do you mind my saying it?

**Ghost.**
Not at all. I thank you for saying it. It shows me where I stand with relation to dear Robert. Thanks very much. You have saved me from committing a great folly, the greatest possible folly. I was about to betray an inviolable secret for the sake of a girl. Luckily she betrayed me first.

**Isabel.**
But how have I betrayed you?

**Ghost.**
And that's how it always is and how it always will be. And there you have the whole story of young girls.

**Supervisor.**
Now what is he talking about?

**Ghost.**
I am speaking of young girls. Sitting in the park, staring at the passer-by without looking at him; lounging with their bicycles at a railroad crossing, in order to welcome the traveler with a gesture of parting; seated at their windows with a book in the lamplight, a pool of radiance between shadow and shadow; like flowers in summer, in winter, like thoughts of flowers, they dispose themselves so gracefully in the world of men that we are convinced

we see in them not the childhood of humanity, but its supreme expression. Between the world of a young girl and the world of the spirit, the wall seems no more than a gossamer; one would say that at any moment, through the soul of a girl, the infinite could flow into the finite and possess it utterly. But all at once . . .

**Supervisor.**

Now, please . . . !

**Ghost.**

The man appears. They watch him intently. He has found some tricks with which to enhance his worth in their eyes. He stands on his hind legs in order to shed the rain better and to hang medals on his chest. He swells his biceps. They quail before him with hypocritical admiration, trembling with such fear as not even a tiger inspires, not realizing that of all the carnivorous animals, this biped alone has ineffective teeth. And as they gaze at him, the windows of the soul, through which once they saw the myriad colors of the outer world, cloud over, grow opaque, and in that moment, the story is over.

**Supervisor.**

And life begins . . .

**Ghost.**

Yes. The pleasure of the bed begins. And the pleasure of the table. And the habit of pleasure. And the pleasure of jealousy—and the pleasure of cruelty.

**Supervisor.**

It's a lie. Don't listen to him, Isabel.

**Ghost.**

And the pleasure of suffering. And last of all, the pleasure of indifference. So, little by little the pearl loses its luster and long before it dies, it is dead.

**Isabel.**

Oh, Ghost—Ghost . . . ! If this is what life is, save me from it!

**Ghost.**

No, Isabel. Your Supervisor is right. You belong not to us, but to him. You are as false and as shallow as the others. What you really love is not the truth, but the pleasure of vibrating endlessly between two falsehoods, between Nice and Tours. Well, you are welcome to your little game. It is not through you that the riddle will be solved and the miracle accomplished.

**Isabel.**

Oh, please—tell me.

**Ghost.**
I will tell you nothing. I will tell you not even the name of the little flower which carpets the fields of death, whose petals I shall bring one day to someone more fortunate than you. Take her in your arms now, Supervisor. Spring that wolf-trap of yours about her—and may she never again escape while she lives!

**Isabel.**
Oh, please—please! (*She runs into the arms of the Ghost, who kisses her tenderly, then pushes her away.*)

**Ghost.**
Farewell, Isabel. (*He goes. Isabel stands still a moment, then she falls. The Supervisor runs to her.*)

**Supervisor.**
Doctor! Doctor! Help! Quickly!

# Scenes Classified by Number of Characters

(Letters in brackets indicate general classifications of types of plays: Drama [D], Comedy [C], Comedy-Drama [C-D], Melodrama [M].)

*The Editor's Suggestions for Values to be Emphasized in Scenes in Chapter III*

## FOR COMMUNICATION BETWEEN CHARACTERS:

## FOR COMMUNICATION BETWEEN CHARACTERS IN CONFLICT:

## FOR UNITS AND OBJECTIVES:

PLAYWRIGHTS AND PLAYS—a listing of the major plays by writers included in *Great Scenes from the World Theater*. (Note: The dates which follow the titles of the plays indicate the years of first performances.)

Edward Albee (1928–    )—The Zoo Story (1959), The Death of Bessie Smith (1959), The Sandbox (1960), The American Dream (1961), Who's Afraid of Virginia Woolf? (1962), The Ballad of the Sad Cafe (adaptation of Carson McCuller's novel, 1963), Tiny Alice (1964).

Maxwell Anderson (1888–1959)—What Price Glory? (with Robert Stallings, 1924), Saturday's Children (1927), Elizabeth the Queen (1930), Mary of Scotland (1933), Both Your Houses (Pulitzer Prize, 1933), Winterset (N. Y. Critics Circle Award, 1935), High Tor (N. Y. Critics Circle Award, 1936), Knickerbocker Holiday (1938), Key Largo (1939), Eve of St. Mark (1942), Joan of Lorraine (1946), Lost in the Stars (1949), The Bad Seed (1954).

Jean Anouilh (1910–    )—The Traveler Without Baggage (1937), Thieves' Carnival (Bal de Voleurs, 1938), Antigone (1944), Eurydice (Legend for Lovers), Ring Round the Moon (L'Invitation au Château, 1947), Mlle. Colombe (1950), Time Remembered (Léocadia, 1950), The Lark (1952), The Waltz of the Toreadors (1953).

Philip Barry (1896–1949)—In a Garden (1925), Paris Bound (1927), Cock Robin (with Elmer Rice, 1928), Holiday (1928), Hotel Universe (1930), The Animal Kingdom (1932), The Joyous Season (1934), Bright Star (1935), Here Come the Clowns (1938), The Philadelphia Story (1939), Foolish Notion (1939), Second Threshold (1951, with revisions by Robert E. Sherwood).

S. N. Behrman (1893–    )—The Second Man (1927), Serena Blandish (1929), Brief Moment (1931), Biography (1932), Rain from Heaven (1936), End of Summer (1936), Amphitryon 38 (adapted from Jean Giraudoux's play, 1937), Wine of Choice (1938), No Time for Comedy (1939), The Pirate (1941), Jacobowsky and the Colonel (adapted from Franz Werfel's play, 1944), Jane (adapted from Somerset Maugham's story, 1952), Fanny (with Joshua Logan, based on Pagnol's *Marius* cycle, with music by Harold Rome, 1954), Lord Pengo (1962), But for Whom Charlie (1963).

Guy Bolton (1884–    )—The Fallen Idol (1914), Ninety in the Shade (1915), Have a Heart (with P. G. Wodehouse, 1917), Leave It to Jane (with P. G. Wodehouse, 1917), Sally (1920), Lady Be Good (with Fred Thompson, 1924), The Dark Angel (1925), Oh, Kay! (with P. G. Wodehouse, 1926), Rio Rita (with Fred Thompson, 1927), Girl Crazy (with John McGowan, 1931), Anything Goes (with P. G. Wodehouse, 1934), Three Blind Mice (with Virginia de Lanty, 1938), Theatre (with Somerset Maugham, 1940), Follow the Girls (with Eddie Davis, 1944), Humoresque (1948), Anastasia (adapted from Marcelle Maurette's play, 1954), Come on Jeaves (with P. G. Wodehouse, 1955).

Mary Chase (1907–    )—Harvey (Pulitzer Prize, 1944), Mrs. McThing (1952), Bernardine (1952), Midgie Purvis (1961).

Owen Davis (1874–1956)—Alibi (1919), Detour (1921), Icebound (Pulitzer Prize, 1923), The Great Gatsby (adaptation of F. Scott Fitzgerald's novel, 1926), Ethan Frome (with Donald Davis, adaptation of Edith Wharton's novel, 1936).

Jean Giraudoux (1882–1944)—Amphitryon 38 (1929), The Enchanted (Intermezzo, 1933), Tiger at the Gates (La Guerre de Troie n'aura pas lieu, 1935), Electra (1937), Ondine (1939), Sodom and Gomorrah (1943), The Madwoman of Chaillot (1945), Duel of Angels (Pour Lucrece, 1953).

Lillian Hellman (1904–    )—The Children's Hour (1934), The Little Foxes (1939), Watch on the Rhine (N. Y. Critics Circle Award, 1941), The Searching Wind (1944), Another Part of the Forest (1946), The Autumn Garden (1951), Candide (book for the musical adaptation of Voltaire's satire, with music by Leonard Bernstein and lyrics by Richard Wilbur, Dorothy Parker,

571

John La Touche, 1956), Toys in the Attic (1960).

James Leo Herlihy (1927–    )—Blue Denim (with William Noble, 1958), Crazy October (1959).

Sidney Howard (1891–1939)—Swords (1921), They Knew What They Wanted (Pulitzer Prize, 1925), The Late Christopher Bean (1932), Alien Corn (1933), Yellow Jack (1934), Paths to Glory (1935), Idiot's Delight (Pulitzer Prize, 1935), Lute Song (with Will Irwin, 1946).

William Inge (1913–    )—Come Back Little Sheba (1950), Picnic (Pulitzer Prize, N. Y. Critics Circle Award, 1953), Dark at the Top of the Stairs (1957), A Loss of Roses (1959), Natural Affection (1962).

Jean Kerr (1924–    )—King of Hearts (with Eleanor Brooke, 1954), Goldilocks (book for the musical, with Walter Kerr), Mary, Mary (1960), Poor Richard (1964).

Arthur Kopit (1937–    )—The Questioning of Nick (1957), On the Runway of Life You Never Know What's Coming Off (1958), Duet ( two plays with music by Victor Ziskin and Thomas Beveridge, 1959), Oh Dad, Poor Dad, Mama's Hung You in the Closet and I'm Feelin' So Sad (1960).

Arthur Laurents (1918–    )—Home of the Brave (1947), Clearing in the Woods (1957), West Side Story (book for the musical with lyrics by Stephen Sondheim and music by Leonard Bernstein, 1958), Gypsy (book for the musical with music by Jule Styne, 1960), Invitation to a March (1960), Anyone Can Whistle (book for the musical with music and lyrics by Stephen Sondheim, 1963).

Richard Leslie (1930–    )—The Summer with Elaina (1959).

Carson McCullers (1917–    )—The Member of the Wedding (N. Y. Critics Circle Award, 1950), The Ballad of the Sad Cafe (novel dramatized by Edward Albee, 1963).

Arthur Miller (1915–    )—All My Sons (N. Y. Critics Circle Award, 1946), Death of a Salesman (Pulitzer Prize, N. Y. Critics Circle Award, 1948), The Crucible (1953), A View from the Bridge (1955), After the Fall (1963).

N. Richard Nash (1913–    )—See the Jaguar (1952), The Rainmaker (1954), Handful of Fire (1960).

Eugene O'Neill (1888–1953)—Beyond the Horizon (Pulitzer Prize, 1920), The Emperor Jones (1920), Anna Christie (Pulitzer Prize, 1920), Gold (1921), The Hairy Ape (1922), All God's Chillun Got Wings (1924), Desire Under the Elms (1924), The Great God Brown (1926), Lazarus Laughed (1926), Marco Millions (1928), Strange Interlude (Pulitzer Prize, 1928), Mourning Becomes Electra (1936), Ah, Wilderness! (1933), The Iceman Cometh (1946), Long Day's Journey into Night (Pulitzer Prize, N. Y. Critics Circle Award, 1956), Touch of the Poet (1958).

Paul Osborn (1901–    )—Hotbed (1928), The Vinegar Tree (1930), On Borrowed Time (1937), Mornings at Seven (1939).

Terence Rattigan (1911–    )—French Without Tears (1936), While the Sun Shines (1943), Love in Idleness (O Mistress Mine, 1944), The Winslow Boy (1946), The Browning Version (1949), The Deep Blue Sea (1952), The Sleeping Prince (1954), Separate Tables (1954), Ross (1961), Man and Boy (1963).

Elmer Rice (1892–    )—On Trial (1914), The Iron Cross (1917), It is the Law (1922), The Adding Machine (1923), Cock Robin (with Philip Barry, 1928), See Naples and Die (1929), Street Scene (Pulitzer Prize, 1929), Counsellor at Law (1931), We the People (1933), Between Two Worlds (1934), American Landscape (1938), Two on an Island (1940), A New Life (1943), Dream Girl (1945), The Winner (1954).

Dore Schary (1905–    )—Sunrise at Campobello (1958).

Peter Shaffer (1931–    )—Five-Finger Exercise (1958), The Private Ear and The Public Eye (1962).

William Shakespeare (1564–1616)*—Comedy of Errors (1590), Two Gentlemen of Verona (1591), Henry VI, parts 1, 2, and 3 (1592), Titus Andronicus (1593), Love's Labour's Lost (1593), Richard III (probably 1594), Midsummer Night's Dream (1595), Richard III (1595), Romeo and Juliet (1596), The Merchant of Venice (1596), King John (1596), Henry IV, parts 1 and 2 (1597), The

* The dating of first productions of Shakespeare's plays, a matter about which scholars sometimes differ, is here based on the chronology established by E. K. Chambers and amended by later editors.

Taming of the Shrew (1598), Much Ado About Nothing (1598), Henry V (1599), The Merry Wives of Windsor (1599), Julius Caesar (1599), As You Like It (1600), Twelfth Night (1600), Hamlet (1600), All's Well That Ends Well (1602), Troilus and Cressida (1602), Measure for Measure (1604), Othello (1604), King Lear (1605), Timon of Athens (1606), Macbeth (1606), Antony and Cleopatra (1607), Pericles, Prince of Tyre (1607), Coriolanus (1608), Cymbeline (1609), The Winter's Tale (1611), The Tempest (1611), Henry VIII (possibly not entirely Shakespeare's, 1611).

John Millington Synge (1871–1909)—The Shadow of the Glen (1903), Riders to the Sea (1904), The Well of the Saints (1905), Playboy of the Western World (1907), The Tinker's Wedding (1909), Deidre of the Sorrows (1910).

John van Druten (1901–1957) Young Woodley (1928), After All (1929), There's Always Juliet (1931), The Distaff Side (1933), The Voice of the Turtle (1943), I Remember Mama (1944), Bell, Book and Candle (1950), I've Got Sixpence (1952), I am a Camera (N. Y. Critics Circle Award, 1952).

Emlyn Williams (1905–    )—And So to Bed (1927), Night Must Fall (1935), He Was Born Gay (1937), The Corn is Green (1938), The Light of Heart (1940), Someone Waiting (1953).

Tennessee Williams (1914–    )—The Glass Menagerie (N. Y. Critics Circle Award, 1945), A Streetcar Named Desire (Pulitzer Prize, N. Y. Critics Circle Award, 1947, Summer and Smoke (1947), The Rose Tattoo (1950), Camino Real (1952), Cat on a Hot Tin Roof (Pulitzer Prize, N. Y. Critics Circle Award, 1955), Garden District (1957), Sweet Bird of Youth (1959), Night of the Iguana (1961), The Milk Train Doesn't Stop Here Any More (1962).

# INDEX